MAINE

THE WILDER HALF OF NEW ENGLAND

"The question, whether the sovereigns of Europe had a right to grant the lands in America, can never be answered in the affirmative, with any pretensions to justice and reason."
—*The History of the District of Maine* by James Sullivan (Boston, 1795)

Engraving of James Sullivan (1744–1808) after Gilbert Stuart (1755–1828). Born in Berwick, Maine, son of an immigrant Irishman and an English indentured servant, Sullivan embodied the American dream, becoming an attorney, revolutionary leader and thinker, author of the first history of Maine, and governor of Massachusetts. His study of Maine in the context of America is substantive, lawyerly, and challenging. COLLECTION OF THE MAINE HISTORICAL SOCIETY, PORTLAND, MAINE

MAINE

THE WILDER HALF OF NEW ENGLAND

❖

William David Barry

TILBURY HOUSE, PUBLISHERS
Gardiner, Maine

TILBURY HOUSE, PUBLISHERS
103 Brunswick Avenue
Gardiner, Maine 04345
800-582-1899 • www.tilburyhouse.com

First edition: July 2012

Text copyright © 2012 by William David Barry

All Rights Reserved. No part of this publication may be reproduced or transmitted in any form or by any means, electronic or mechanical, including photocopy, recording, or any information storage or retrieval system, without permission in writing from the publisher.

Portions of this book were previously published in *Maine: The Pine Tree State from Prehistory to the Present*, University of Maine Press, Orono, Maine, 1995.

Cataloging-in-Publication Data
Barry, William David.
  Maine : the wilder half of New England / William David Barry. -- 1st ed.
      p. cm.
  Includes bibliographical references and index.
  ISBN 978-0-88448-333-5 (pbk. : alk. paper)
  1. Maine--History. 2. Maine--History--Pictorial works. I. Title.
  F19.B37 2012
  974.1--dc23
                                       2012003308

Copyediting: Genie Dailey, Fine Points Editorial Services, Jefferson, Maine
Printing and Binding: Versa Press, East Peoria, Illinois

Front Cover Image:
Size and inaccessibility left Maine's northeast boundary uncertain even after statehood. Frictions with American settlers and New Brunswick timber harvesters led to a near war in the 1830s and instigated surveys. The federal Talcott Survey, completed in 1842, used a camera lucida—a prism that reflected an image onto paper where it was traced and later colored—to produce sixteen watercolor views. P. Harry made this view of relaxing surveyors labeled "Co-cum-go-muc-sis Lake—bearing from S. 15 E. to South 30 E.—and in the distance Katahdin bearing about S. 35 E.—and Spencer Mount S. 5 W—the small lake at right is on the stream connecting Hompona." COLLECTION OF THE NATIONAL ARCHIVES, WASHINGTON, D.C.

Back Cover Image:
On the evening of July 6, 1854, a nativist mob burned Bath's Old South Meeting House, which was being used by Irish Catholic citizens. This was one of several outrages, including the tarring of Father John Bapst at Ellsworth, which swept Maine during the height of the nativist "Know-Nothing" movement. With the arrival of the Irish in the 1830s, immigrants began to change the ethnic texture of Maine. Firefighter John Hilling (1826–1894) accurately depicted the attack on Old South in several paintings. COLLECTION OF THE MAINE HISTORICAL SOCIETY

This book is dedicated with continuing love and admiration to
❖
DEBRA VERRIER BARRY
❖
Friend, spouse of thirty-one years, and co-worker in the trenches of historical research.
You said you knew what you were signing on for. I'm not so sure,
but through all our successes and losses, we have shared the adventure
and the most remarkable friends a couple could ever deserve.

COLLECTION OF THE MAINE HISTORICAL SOCIETY

CONTENTS

	Foreword by Earle G. Shettleworth, Jr.	*viii*
	Acknowledgments	*x*
1	Europeans, Native Americans, and the Age of Exploration (Before 1623)	*1*
2	New England and New France (1623–1763)	*16*
3	The Revolutionary Era (1763–1783)	*38*
4	The Struggle for Statehood (1783–1820)	*56*
5	The Achievement of Identity (1820–1861)	*78*
6	Maine and the Civil War (1861–1865)	*108*
7	Diminishing Expectations (1865–1920)	*126*
8	The Early Twentieth Century (1914–1941)	*160*
9	World War II in Maine (1941–1945)	*186*
10	Changing Visions from "Dignified Work for All" to Unkind Cuts and Whoopie Pies (1945–2012)	*204*
	Bibliography	*242*
	Index	*256*

FOREWORD

William David Barry's engaging state history, *Maine: The Wilder Half of New England*, is the latest in a long line of books to chronicle the story of the Pine Tree State. Tracing Maine's development from Native American habitation to the present, Barry gives us a skillfully written and handsomely illustrated narrative that reflects the seasoned researcher and writer that he is. Each of his ten chapters is an insightful overview of the period it covers, drawing upon the author's rich understanding of the state's political, economic, social, and cultural history.

William Barry follows in the footsteps of a distinguished company of historians. More than two centuries ago, in 1795, James Sullivan, a native of Berwick, wrote *The History of the District of Maine*. Stating as his purpose to arrange "facts and events . . . into a distinct history of an extensive and important part of the country," Sullivan sought to define a distinctive identity for Maine, which helped lead to statehood in 1820. Sullivan did not live to see this achieved, dying in office as governor of Massachusetts in 1808.

Maine's next historian was William D. Williamson, a Bangor attorney, who served in 1821 as the second governor of the state. In 1832 Williamson published his two-volume *History of the State of Maine*, in which he covered events from seventeenth-century settlement to separation from Massachusetts in 1820. Like Sullivan, Williamson strove to establish Maine as a special place, declaring it "a corner-pillar in the American Republic. Its territory equals one half of New England,—its natural resources are great and various—its climate is good—its population now considerably exceeds 400,000."

In 1859 A. J. Coolidge and J. B. Mansfield compiled *A History and Description of New England*, of which the first and only volume contained alphabetically arranged accounts of the towns and cities of Maine, New Hampshire, and Vermont. While not technically a state history, the Coolidge and Mansfield gazetteer provides an invaluable snapshot of Maine on the eve of the Civil War, and remains an important reference book to this day.

A similar view of the post–Civil War period is provided by George J. Varney's *A Gazetteer of Maine*, which appeared in 1882. Building on Coolidge and Mansfield's work, Varney believed that "a Gazetteer of the State, in which every town, plantation, mountain, lake and bay should receive due mention would be welcomed by the intelligent people of Maine." He was encouraged to compile his gazetteer on the strength of the popularity of his 1873 *The Young People's History of Maine*, long a fixture in classrooms across the state.

Another widely read book of the era was *The History of Maine* by John S. C. Abbott, a Congregational minister whose literary efforts were exceeded by the extensive output of his brother Jacob Abbott, a prolific children's author. Issued in

1875, John Abbott's history is flawed by moralizing and romanticizing in his text at the expense of the facts. After Abbott's death, an updated edition was released in 1892, which benefited from revisions and additions by Edward H. Elwell, the longtime editor of the *Portland Transcript*.

In 1918 Maine newspapers carried an announcement that "Dr. Louis C. Hatch of Bangor has under consideration the writing of a new history of the State of Maine, to be published in connection with the 1920 centennial celebration." A Bowdoin- and Harvard-educated historian, Hatch produced his impressive three-volume *Maine: A History* the next year with the assistance of several contributors. Reprinted in 1974, Hatch's book has stood the test of time for its accurate and comprehensive treatment of Maine's first century of statehood, especially in the area of political history.

Twentieth-century writers of Maine history proved to be as prodigious in their output as their nineteenth-century counterparts, but much of their production was focused on either local or specific topics or biography. One notable exception is Elizabeth Ring's 1996 *Maine in the Making of the Nation, 1783–1870*, which complements Hatch's account of the state's political development from the Revolution to the Civil War. Also successfully building on Hatch is *Maine: The Pine Tree State from Prehistory to the Present*, a 1995 compilation of chronologically arranged essays by twenty-seven scholars, edited by Richard W. Judd, Edwin A. Churchill, and Joel W. Eastman. Of a more popular nature are Neil Rolde's two fine pictorial histories of the state, *An Illustrated History of Maine* (1995) and *Maine, Downeast and Different* (2006).

To this bookshelf of Maine histories that go back in time to 1795 we now add William David Barry's *Maine: The Wilder Half of New England*, a worthy successor to the volumes that have preceded it—an accurate, articulate, informative, insightful, and visually attractive account of Maine for the twenty-first century.

Earle G. Shettleworth, Jr.
Maine State Historian

ACKNOWLEDGMENTS

I used to say that "There is no such thing as an historical emergency." It seemed obvious that everything "historical" was in the past, over with, kaput. The deeds were accomplished, the participants had done what they had done, and boundaries were fixed, wars won, and people gone to their rewards. But the older I became, the more students, scholars, genealogists, and family researchers I assisted from behind the desks of the Portland Public Library and Maine Historical Society, the more I came to realize that people, in great numbers, wanted to know "right now" what happened, or what became of Uncle Zack, "back then." It was no joke. It concerned adopted children and people whose "official records" were lost or poorly kept, and institutions and businesses whose records were destroyed or never well maintained. There is usually a back channel.

This overview history of the State of Maine has its genesis in 1990 and could not have been finished without the sustained encouragement, support, and humor of my surprisingly numerous friends and local historical and writing community. The original plan once included business histories by my colleague and sometimes co-author, the late Patricia McGraw Anderson, but failed for reasons beyond our control. With the assistance of the late Frances W. Peabody, I secured legal rights to my part of the manuscripts and the illustrations. Stanley R. Howe, then director, now curator of the Bethel Historical Society, and Earle G. Shettleworth, Jr, director of the Maine Historic Preservation Commission and now State Historian, read the original manuscript, now heavily revised and brought up to 2012. In the interim, Debra Verrier Barry—my muse, my love, my amanuensis and wife of thirty-one years—kept the faith and encouraged the thought that someday we would publish it. So we kept the correspondence, new changes, loan agreements, and through hard times and fair made additions and changes when appropriate.

Keeping our ship afloat were our longtime extraordinary friends Randolph and Sheryl Dominic, Stephen Booth, and new friends Edward and Fidelma McCarron. Keeping our spirits flying were Bill and Nancy Frost, Harriet and George Price, Philip Grime, Gael May McKibben, Linda and Benjamin Blue, and Susan Cummings-Lawrence, who took time from her own project on the Jewish communities in Maine to assist. At my place of work, the Maine Historical Society, my colleagues all encouraged the project, from Richard D'Abate to Nicholas Noyes, Dani Fazio, Candace Kanes, Jamie Kingman Rice, Nancy Noble, and John Mayer.

Our "historical emergency" occurred when Deb and I were approached by publisher-editor Jennifer Bunting of Tilbury House, Publishers, about reviving and publishing the manuscript. It was a surprise and delight, though it entailed updating or rewriting two decades of work. Most of the new information appears in the last chapter, though the writer has corrected errors and old notions in earlier sections. There have been major historical discoveries, which, when possible, I have referred to, but in cases such as Carol B. Smith-Fisher's theory on the naming of Maine (*Bangor Daily News*, 2002), Sir Ferdinando Gorges's ancestral towns of "Broadmayne" and "Parva Maen" (not the mainland or the Province of Maine in France), I have let things stand, not wanting to deconstruct my text any more than needed. The Smith-Fisher theory, which makes sense, is complicated and would have broken the narrative.

Likewise, I have tried to avoid polemics and my own political opinions in a time that both right and left describe as dysfunctional, accusing each other of not providing leadership. In the interest of full disclosure on my views, one of the few practical heroes I find is Cape Elizabeth's Robert A. G. Monks, capitalist visionary and perennial corporate critic. Monks has written: "Only a few years after the fall of the Berlin Wall, it would be supreme irony if Karl Marx's ultimate prophecy comes true and capitalism fails because of its inner contradictions—the inability of flesh and blood human beings to threaten their own comfort by effective confrontation of a system of power." I am an historian, not a political scientist; for those interested in current arguments and their root causes, turn to Monks's writings and those of his adversaries, or the excellent Hilary Rosenberg's *A Traitor to His Class: Robert A. G. Monks and the Battle to Change Corporate America* (New York: John Wiley & Sons, Inc., 1999).

I am also personally grateful to John O'Brien of O'Brien Design, who designed the first edition of this planned book, preserved the original disks, and remained faithful; I wish it could have gone full circle.

Special thanks go to Neil Rolde, Bill Bunting, Earle G. Shettleworth, Jr., Candace Kanes, and Richard D'Abate for reading the new manuscript. Because of their knowledge and expertise, the author now looks far less fallible than he normally would have.

Richard D'Abate, the most successful executive director the Maine Historical Society has ever had, immediately supported the new publishing effort and was very generous with society images. Earle G. Shettleworth, Jr., has been a supporter since the very beginning and a generous sharer of images and ideas. This would have been impossible without his advice and knowledge. Dr. Emerson "Tad" Baker, then director of the Dyer/York Institute (Dyer Library Saco Museum), gave generously of his time in helping to shape Chapters 1 and 2. Professor William B. Jordan, Jr., late of Westbrook College (now University of New England), proved similarly helpful on the Civil War, and the late Professor Neal W. Allen, Jr., gave assistance relating to legal history. Professor Joel W. Eastman, late of the University of Southern Maine, and historian Kenneth E. Thompson shared material on the Second World War. Don King, the dean of Maine book-review editors, kindly opened his scrapbooks to the project, and the late Don MacWilliams gave me a timeline of the state's athletic history. Gary Libby took over from Don concerning sports discussions.

John J. McAuliffe II of St. Joseph's College, Windham, served as an expert consultant and reader. That superb librarian Sally Regan provided excellent translations of French correspondence. Dear friend and old employer Dr. Thomas L. Gaffney lent his unique knowledge of pre–WW II Maine politics and other topics. Geraldine Tidd Scott, who wrote the book on the Northeast Boundary "War," *Ties of Common Blood* (Bowie, MD, 1992), took Deb and me, along with Wilbur and Joan Tidd, on a 997-mile working journey of Aroostook that proved as indispensable as it was fun. Gladys Hager and Paul D'Alessandro provided early editing skills. Old friends F. M.

O'Brien, Elizabeth Ring, Dorothy Healy, Franny Peabody, Jim Vickery (who assisted mightily with images), Paul H. Robeson, John Holverson, Tom Renner, and Janet Riker were integral.

We appreciate the participation, patience, and goodwill of all image donors, past and present, including Ann Roy of the Acadian Village; Anna McGrath of the Library of the University of Maine at Presque Isle; Archbishop Pio Laghi at the Vatican Library; Marie Baboyant of the Library of the City of Montreal; Donald P. Lemon of the New Brunswick Museum; S. Kay Young of the Detroit Institute of Art; Kathryn Lattanzi and Craig B. Palmer of the Museum of Art–Olin Art Center at Bates College; Diane Vatne and Abigail Ewing Zelz of the Bangor Historical Society (now the Bangor Museum and Center for History); Susan Y. Elter of the Franklin D. Roosevelt Library; John Rexine of the Everson Museum of Art; Sylvia Lahvis and Brenda J. Wetzel of the State Museum of Pennsylvania; Hugh J. Gourley III of the Colby College Museum of Art; J. Fraser Cox III of the Colby College Special Collections; Judy Franke of Central Maine Power; Melvin Johnson at the Special Collections Library at the University of Maine at Orono; Cally Gurley of the Maine Women Writers Collection at the University of New England; Abraham Schecter, Special Collections librarian and archivist at the Portland Public Library; Edith McCauley; Mary Peverada of the Portland Public Library; Dr. Katharine J. Watson and Hetty Tye at the Bowdoin College Museum of Art; Jane Batzell of the Freeport Historical Society; Nathan Lipfert of the Maine Maritime Museum; Martha Severens and Michele Butterfield of the Portland Museum of Art; Paul Poirier of the National Archives of Canada; Bill and Virginia Weston of Rumford Area Historical Society; James Dolph of the Portsmouth Naval Shipyard; Joseph A. LoSchiavo of the Fordham University Library; Barbara O'Donnell of the Aroostook Historical Society and Art Museum; W. Thomas Shoener of the Maine Department of Inland Fisheries and Wildlife; S. Mendoza and Edna Rodriguez of the National Archives of Canada; Nancy Haywood of the Essex Institute; John LaBranche of the Old York Historical Society; Ludia DuFore of the Frick Art Reference Library, American Heritage Art Resources; Paul Rivard, Katherine McBrien, Steven Miller, and Shelia McDonald of the Maine State Museum; Kathy Flynn of the Peabody Museum; Rita F. Conant, Jane Porter, Richard Candee, and Joe Frost of the Portsmouth Athenaeum; Louis L. Tucker of the Massachusetts Historical Society; Susan Danforth of the John Carter Brown Library; Hugh Keller of *National Fisherman;* Dale Kuhnert and Ellen Ward of Down East Enterprises; John Murphy of Gannett Newspapers; Mark Sanducky of the *Kennebec Journal*, Jane G. Smith and Carol Verville of the Metropolitan Opera; Joyce Butler of the Brick Store Museum; Kerry O'Brien and Audrey Milne of the York Institute (now Saco Museum); Diane Gutscher of Special Collections at the Bowdoin College Library; Glen Uminowicz of the Victoria Society of Maine; and Robert Bohanan of the National Archives.

Also our thanks go to a veritable brigade of assistants in this project over the years, including Edie Fitzpatrick, Diane Hudson, Betsy Sheehan, Herb Adams, Judy Wentzel, Bob Greene, Jim Sappier, Tom Hardiman, Carol L. Weeks, Arthur F. Loux, Betty Berdan, Margaret Lovely McAtee, Miriam Barndt-Webb, Bruce Kennett, Terry Geaghan, Ron Johnson, Robert P. Fuller, Guy F. DuBay, Jim Swanson, Pat Davidson Reef, Tom Verde, Patrick Grace, Frank Peltier, Richard Rubenstein, Austin Wilkins, Karen Bowdin Cooper, Martin Dibner, Esta and Dave Astor, Peter E. Randall, Janet Cyr Verrier, Gerald Talbot, Elizabeth Hamill, Michael Connolly, Bruce Hazelton, Sophia West, Matthew J. Barker, Joseph Sawtelle, Mary Ann Forgit, Gordon Strubble, David and Brenda Cheney, John Wilson, Linda

Babcock, Reza Jalali, Daniel J. Barry, Kay Wilson, Edwin A. Churchill, Laura Sprague, Katherine Cassling, Susie Bock, Neal W. Allen, Jr., Dr. Charles P. M. Outwin, Josephine Detmer, Dr. Howard M. Solomon, Kim Clifford, Pious Ali, Michelle Souliere, Aubin Thomas, and the late Arthur Douglas Stover (historian, confidant, and eminent Mainer).

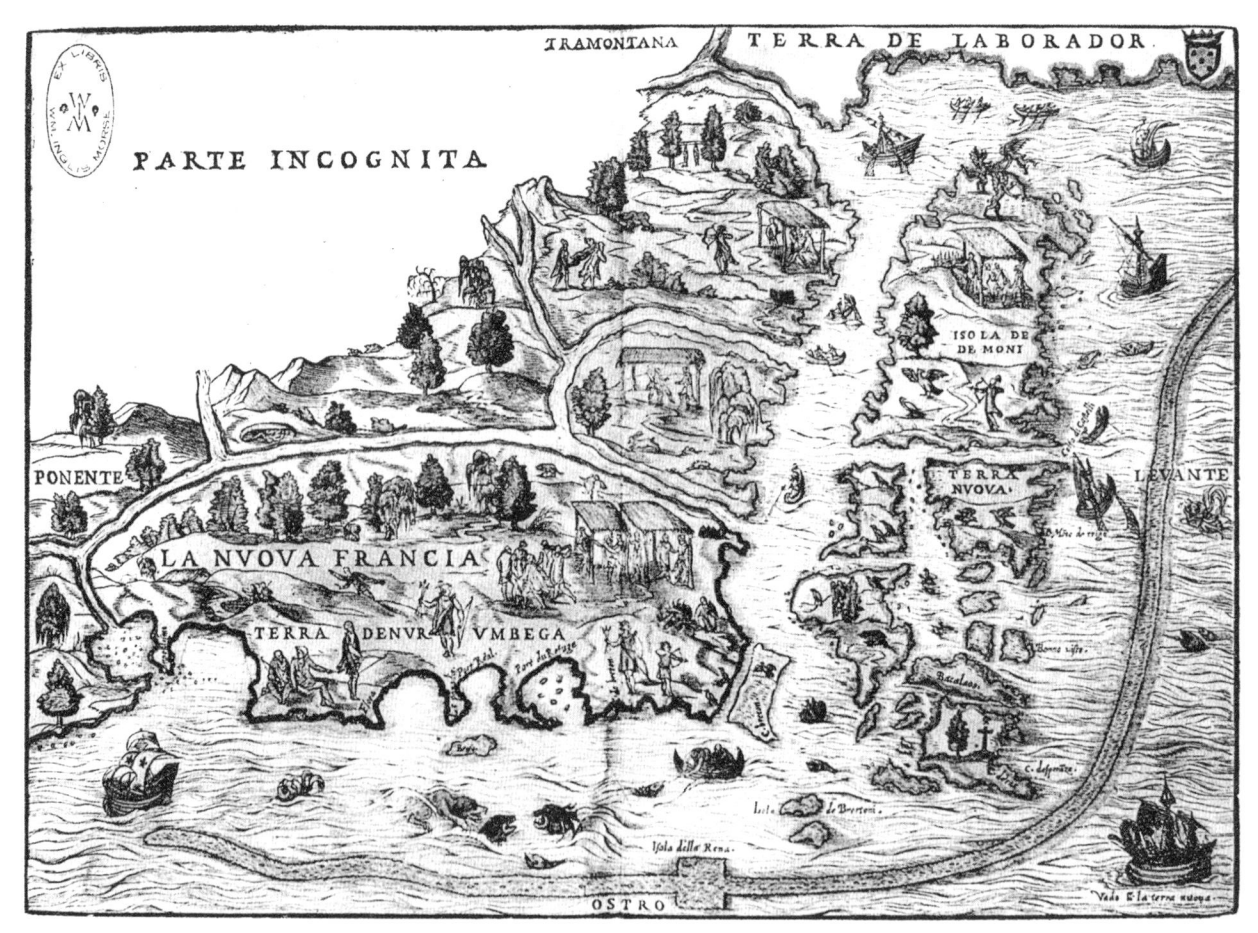

The thickly illustrated map entitled *La Nuova Francia* is the work of Giacomo Gastaldi and appeared in Giovanni Battista Ramusio's *Terzo Volume della Navigationi et Viaggi* of 1556. A mix of imagination and new information, it shows Verrazzano's Norumbega on the Atlantic shore, with New France and the St. Lawrence behind. To the right is Newfoundland. The offshore ribbon represents the fishing banks, and views of Europeans hand-lining and netting fish are accurate, while the Indians are more conjectural. The map is one of the true treasures of the Maine Historical Society Library. COLLECTION OF THE MAINE HISTORICAL SOCIETY, PORTLAND, MAINE

I

EUROPEANS, NATIVE AMERICANS, AND THE AGE OF EXPLORATION (BEFORE 1623)

Early in May of 1524, a French naval vessel, *La Dauphine*, under the command of the Italian navigator Giovanni da Verrazzano, made landfall off an unexplored coast. There, at a point possibly in eastern Casco Bay, the first recorded contact between Europeans and Native Americans occurred in what was to become Maine. While other European voyagers may have preceded Verrazzano, and while humans had flourished on shore for 11,000 years or more, it fell to him to write the first known reports, do the first rough charting, and provide Europe with the earliest tantalizing glimpse of the region.

The initial meeting between members of the two cultures appears almost vaudevillian in nature, until one considers the near-fatal impact it eventually had on Native societies. Indeed, Verrazzano had previously been warmly welcomed at stops in the Carolinas, New York, and Rhode Island. But on the rocky shore of Maine, he and his crew were greeted by blood-curdling shouts, derisive laughter, bared bottoms, and leisurely volleys of arrows.

That the well-born Verrazzano was not amused is made clear by the name he bestowed on the place: "The Land of Bad People" (Terra Onde di Mala Gente). Earlier, he had delighted in the disposition of other Indians, going so far as to dub the Carolina Coast "Arcadia," after the Virgilian land of virtuous people. Happily, the Land of Bad People label did not stick and, as *La Dauphine* scudded east, the explorer mellowed, naming Monhegan Island, Isle Au Haut, and Mount Desert the "Three Daughters of Navarre" and the mainland "Oranbega." Scholars are divided on the origin of the word Oranbega (Norumbega), which may be Native American, European, or a blend of both. It appears on the World Map of 1529, which was prepared by Verrazzano's brother Girolamo. Altered to "Norumbega," it was used with great promiscuity by decorative mapmakers and became the standard name for the place throughout the century. Gradually, the romantic sounding label, combined with a tincture of truth and a lot of imagination, came to be seen as an exotic country comparable with El Dorado and the Seven Cities of Cibola.

Ironically, Verrazzano and his sponsor, King Francis I, were not seeking treasure but something that was not there: the elusive Northwest Passage to Asia. This quest had begun with Christopher Columbus and his discovery of what would prove to be the West Indies. Sparked by rumors of Spanish discoveries, other European monarchs and syndicates of merchants began to take interest. In 1497 another Italian adventurer, John Cabot (Cabotto), left Bristol, England, in the *Mathew*. Flying the banner of King Henry VII, he discovered the island of Newfoundland and reported on the rich fisheries of the Grand Banks. In the following year, he led five vessels, one of which returned early. The others, along with

The first recorded visit to the Maine coast was made by Giovanni da Verrazzano (c. 1485–1528), a courtly, educated Italian navigator employed by the king of France. Arriving in the spring of 1524, he bestowed two names on the region: "Oranbega," which remained for three-quarters of a century as Norumbega; and "The Land of Bad People," which did not endure and might have been better applied elsewhere. On a subsequent voyage to the West Indies, Verrazzano was set upon, butchered, and eaten by members of the Carib nation. This portrait is a late-sixteenth-century copy of an earlier work. COURTESY OF THE SIG. SINDACO, MUNICIPIO DI PRATO

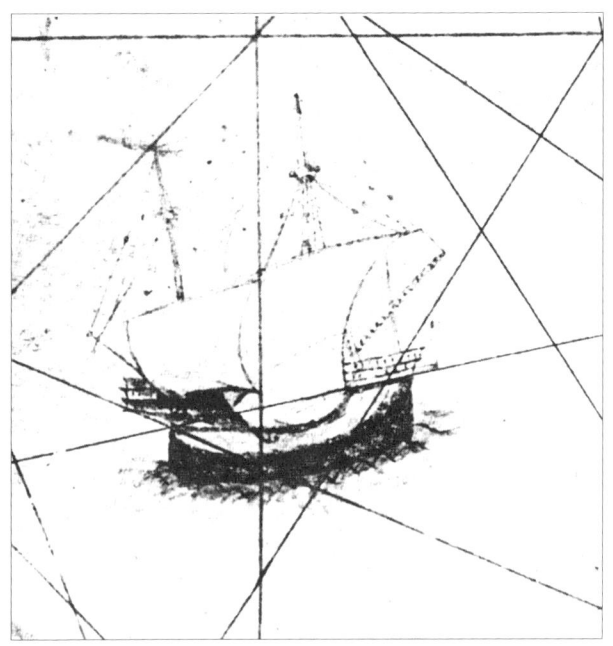

The detail drawing of a ship on Girolamo Verrazzano's *World Map of 1529* may represent his brother's ship, *La Dauphine*, and is certainly similar in construction. Built at Le Havre in 1519, the sturdy vessel belonged to the royal navy of France and was lent by King Francis I for the voyages of exploration. COURTESY OF THE VATICAN LIBRARY

Cabot, were never heard from again.

The English discovery of North America was, we now know, actually a rediscovery. The Norse had visited around 1000 A.D. and even settled for a time at L'Anse aux Meadows on the northern peninsula of Newfoundland. It is often speculated that they sailed further, but hard proof is lacking. An eleventh-century Norse coin found in Brooklin, Maine, is now in the collection of the Maine State Museum, but the coin was probably passed along the coast through what is believed to have been a well-defined Native American trade system. In fact, some scholars believe that the Norse coin was a hoax.

Cabot's disappearance slackened interest on the part of English authorities, but within a few years, commercial fishermen were harvesting the bounty of the Grand Banks. French fishermen were active by 1504, and the Portuguese joined in around the same time. Basques, Azoreans, and, more gradually, English joined the lucrative summer expeditions. For several decades the Portuguese dominated the offshore venture. They used the "green" process, which meant that the fish were cured wet by cleaning and salting on

2   MAINE: THE WILDER HALF OF NEW ENGLAND

board. This approach continued to be favored by southern Europeans, but after mid-century at least, French and English fishermen turned to the "dry" process, which required shore facilities including flakes (drying racks), stagings, storage buildings, and huts. This was done along protected areas of the Newfoundland coast while, after 1540, Basque whalers were summering at Red Bay on the Labrador shore. The English involvement in the dry fishery was stimulated in 1563 by an act of parliament that declared Wednesday and Saturday to be fish days. This official effort to "mayneteine fisshermen" created a great demand for stockfish in Protestant England. Catholic realms already had Friday set aside.

On the rim of North America, fishermen usually stuck to fishing, though some trade with the Indians certainly occurred. In particular, a trade in fur grew with the Souriquois (Micmac) and Montagnais of the Gulf of St. Lawrence region. In stark contrast to explorers, fishermen rarely left accounts of their voyages and observations. Some may have debarked in Maine. Indeed, the Native Americans' negative reaction to Verrazzano suggests some previous contact. Evidence points to Portuguese ship owner Joao Alvares Fagundes, who sailed to the Gulf of St. Lawrence in about 1520. Still, even after Verrazzano's voyage four years later, Maine remained "terra incognita" to European eyes. Curiously, it would take another three and a quarter centuries for the political boundaries of Maine to be fixed and for some sections to be mapped and explored.

The territory that would later be termed "the main" or "mainland" consisted of stark headlands, sweeping beaches, wooded isles, great rivers, and vast forests. The first Europeans looked for safe anchorages, found them in startling abundance, and, though their immediate quest was a passage to Asia, they could not help commenting on the potential richness of the country. They didn't know the particulars yet, but here was a place with a land area of 33,215 square miles, boasting some 2,000 islands, 5,000 streams and rivers, 2,500 lakes and ponds, and a bountiful, undulating 3,500-mile coastline. The rivers abounded with salmon, and game was readily observed in sporadic clearings. Offshore was the untapped Georges Bank. Then, stretching away toward the distant White Mountains, was the great forest of spruce, fir, hemlock, maple, birch, oak, and ash. Towering above the other species and sometimes reaching a height over 200 feet was the great white pine. To both fisherman and navigator the forest seemed daunting: a gloomy, impenetrable barrier.

The forest was no barrier to the Native American tribes, who lived in relative harmony with the environment. But even they had burned away small sections to make way for villages and subsistence farming, so the forest seen in the 1500s was hardly primeval. However, the various tribes were dependent on the continuation of wilderness. Their sleek birch-bark canoes slipped quickly along streams that tied them to places as distant as the St. Lawrence. They plied the coastal waters as well, connecting group to group, and in winter moved across snow on ingeniously designed snowshoes. They delighted in games of both chance and physical skill, and according to seventeenth-century observers, celebrated with feasts, songs, dances, and long speeches. They developed a rich, sustaining cosmology in which all aspects of daily life—eating, fishing, farming, construction of housing, music, and religion—were all bound together. In particular they shared tales of Gluskap, the trickster hero, stories that have survived and flourished into the present.

There is much disagreement about the names and composition of the Native American groups in Maine at the time of contact, in spite of accelerated interest and investigation in recent years. One current interpretation focuses on four large groups described to Samuel de Champlain by his guides. This view puts the Souriquois (the present-day

Micmac) in New Brunswick and Nova Scotia, but occasionally ranging along the coast of Maine. The Etchemin inhabited the region between the Kennebec and St. John Rivers. West of the Kennebec were the Almouchiquois. While the Etchemin and Souriquois relied entirely on hunting, fishing, and gathering for survival, the Armouchiquois farmed as well as hunted. Because of the somewhat milder climate in southern Maine, they were able to grow the traditional Native crops: corn, beans, and squash. In the interior, between the Chaudière River and the Kennebec headwaters, was a fourth group called the Abenaki. Present-day tribal names are quite different from those employed by Champlain. In part, this is due to changing terminology, but it also reflects several hundred years of unrest and change among Maine's first peoples.

In 1524 these groups, with the possible exception of the Souriquois (Micmac), probably had little direct contact with explorers or fishermen. Still, through their enviable trade network, Maine Indians had probably heard about the white men and their strange vessels. Gradually, too, European manufactured trade goods began to appear, which ultimately led to a decline in traditional technologies including weapons, tools, and clothing.

The reality of changes on the distant coast of Maine was little appreciated or understood by Europeans, be they fishermen on station, explorers moving rapidly from landfall to landfall, or scholars in their universities. This was one small region in a world that was just being measured and beginning to draw together in unheard-of and unexpected ways. Just emergent from the Middle Ages, the nation states were in their formative stages; in the British Isles clan chiefs ruled large portions of Scotland, Ireland, and even Northumbria. Conversely, it was an age of printed information and expanded educational opportunities, of artistic accomplishment, and religious ferment. By 1524 Magellan's expedition had circumnavigated the earth, Cortez held Mexico, Michelangelo was in mid-career, Luther had begun the Reformation, King Henry VIII ruled England, and the Ottoman Empire was nearing its heights of military might. Both the Spanish and Portuguese were building world commercial and political empires stretching from South America to East Asia and were having an impact on the cultures of Africa, Arabia, India, South East Asia, China, and Japan.

The dimly perceived coastline of Maine seemed of little interest unless, of course, it concealed the Northwest Passage. That possibility bothered the emperor Charles V, who believed that such a strait in the hands of one of Spain's rivals would menace his far-flung holdings. Upon hearing that Verrazzano was about to sail, the emperor prepared his own reconnaissance party. In the autumn of 1524, Estevan Gomez left Spain in the caravel *La Anunciada* and, after a winter near Newfoundland, moved south.

In June he was off Mount Desert and was soon sailing up the Penobscot River to the present site of Bangor. There he watched Indians catching salmon, named the stream "the River of Deer" (Rio de las Gamas), and noted the presence of iron pyrite. This, he wrote clearly, was not gold. In spite of, and perhaps because of, this warning, people would persist in equating the site with treasure.

The growth of the Norumbega myth can be tracked in brief. As early as 1545 the French writer Pierre Crignon's *Discourse of a Great French Sea Captain of Dieppe* proclaimed: "The land overflows with every kind of fruit; there grows the wholesome orange and the almond, and many sorts of sweet-smelling trees. The country is called by its people Norumbega." None of this description was true, and no mention is made of Verrazzano's uncomplimentary comments, let alone blackflies or winter snow. Indeed, Crignon and those who followed were producing perfect real-estate copy.

❖

The most notorious—and influential—of the tall tales focused on Maine as Norumbega came from a man who had most probably been there in the late 1560s. Abandoned on the Gulf Coast of Florida, David Ingram and two companions worked their way along the east coast to the St. John River in what is now New Brunswick, apparently staying for a time on the Penobscot. At the St. John they chanced on a French vessel. Once home in London, Ingram, a colorful storyteller, kept himself liquid by describing to fellow drinkers the fabulous City of Norumbega, "which hath many streets far broader than London," "pyllors of Cristoll," and citizens adorned in gold, silver, and pearls.

Ingram's tales, supported by decades of maps bearing the same name, caught the attention of the dashing Sir Humphrey Gilbert, who was planning a New World colony based on the Anglo-Irish plantations. In 1579 and 1580 he dispatched two probes to the Penobscot. The first was led by Simon Fernando in the *Squirrel*, the second by John Walker in an unnamed craft. Neither found a city, but Walker made off with a number of hides from an Indian encampment and was sure that he had located a silver mine. More tangibly, he termed the region "most excellent both for the soyle, diversity of sweete woode and other trees."

The brevity of reports, coupled with the embellishment of sailors, led to open-ended interpretations by cartographers. They generally abhorred blank spaces, as did their patrons, so they felt free to fill in the empty areas with all sorts of wonderful images from classical sources and the imagination. Aside from surviving Native American objects—most notably the petroglyphs at Birch Point in Machiasport and Embden—maps are the most available art form documenting the time and place.

Though the voyages of Jacques Cartier, beginning in 1534, did not include Maine, they did define the St. Lawrence and its environs. It was becoming clear that Norumbega was located on a great peninsula. On one side were the Atlantic Ocean and the Bay of Fundy, on the other the St. Lawrence River and the Gulf of St. Lawrence. In 1546 a settlement was started near the future site of Quebec City in what cartographers now called New France, but it failed as did another on the remote Atlantic outrider, Sable Island, in 1598.

Giacomo Gastaldi's much-consulted map, *La Nuova Francia*, of 1555, shows Norumbega as a region with a large imaginary river connecting to the St. Lawrence. It also boasts fanciful Natives and accurate depictions of French fishermen hand-lining for cod, netting fish, and drying them on shore stations. Still, the industry seems to have been largely confined to Newfoundland and the Grand Banks. Other publications, including *Mercator's World Map of 1569*, started the Ingram-inspired motif picturing Norumbega as a city near what became Bangor.

Late in the 1500s European activity in the Gulf of St. Lawrence and beyond began to heat up a bit, due to the Hakluyts and other interests. A particular benchmark was achieved in 1583 when Sir Humfrey Gilbert took formal possession of Newfoundland, or at least the Avalon Peninsula, in the name of England and Queen Elizabeth I. There, amid thirty-six multinational fishing craft, the new captain-general established the primacy of the Church of England and the laws of his nation. Though Gilbert and the *Squirrel* soon plunged to the bottom in a storm, the English overseas empire had begun. His effort was followed in 1585 by Sir Walter Raleigh and others who attempted a settlement at Roanoke in the newly named Virginia. Though the settlement vanished a few years later, the name Virginia continued to grace the land.

The defeat of the Spanish Armada in 1588 gave impetus to the English colonization plans. Still, it was not until the turn of the century that visits to Maine became frequent. In 1602 a group

This image in Nicholas Denys's *Description of North America* (1672) depicts Europeans on the shore fishery in the 1600. Flakes and staging of this type stretched raggedly from Newfoundland to the Gulf of St. Lawrence to Monhegan, Damariscove, and the Isles of Shoals on the Maine Coast. COLLECTION OF THE MAINE HISTORICAL SOCIETY

of Bristol merchants dispatched the bark *Concord* to North America to collect sassafras and spy out a Northwest Passage. Headed by Captains Bartholomew Gosnold and Bartholomew Gilbert (no relation to Sir Humfrey), the thirty-two-man team carried Verrazzano's account, helpfully provided by Hakluyt. On their return, Sir Walter Raleigh informed them that they had infringed on his rights to Virginia, but he forgave them. They did collect some sassafras, much sought-after as a cure for venereal disease, and also touched the shore, possibly near Cape Neddick. There, at a place called Savage Rock, they met an unusual group of Native Americans. John Brereton, a voyager, gave this account:

> . . . sixe Indians, in a Baske-shallope [coastal vessel] with mast and saile, an iron grapple,

and a kettle of copper, came boldly aboard us, one of them apparelled with a waistcoast and breeches of blacke serdge, made after our sea-fashion, hose and shoes on his feet; all the rest (saving one that had a paire of breeches of blue cloth) were all naked. These people were of tall stature, broad and grim vissage, of a blacke swart complection, their eie-browes painted white; their weapons are bowes and arrows. . . .

Brereton also observed copper ornaments, arrow points, and cups, suggesting additional contact

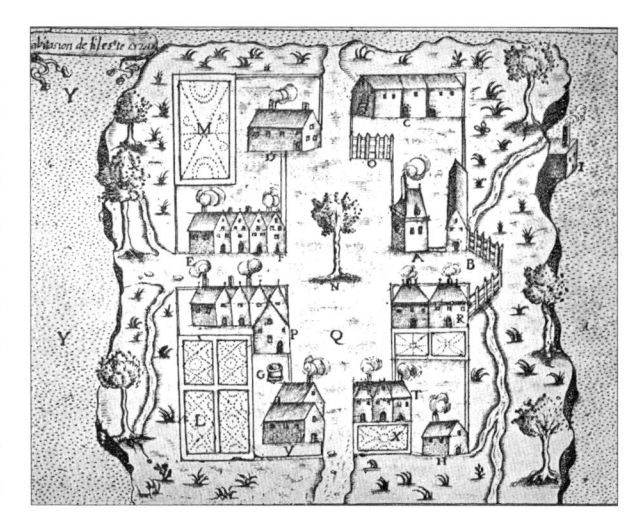

Samuel de Champlain (c. 1567–1635), the Father of New France, began as the right-hand man of Sieur de Monts in the founding of the St. Croix settlement in 1604. This was the first known European settlement tried in what is now Maine. Champlain left enjoyable narratives of his travels, along with sketches that mark him as the first European artist as well. Though his depictions of the St. Croix outpost may be embellished, they reflect the basic plan and what the French hoped to make it. After one cruel winter on the windswept rock, the colonists moved to Port Royal. COLLECTION OF THE MAINE HISTORICAL SOCIETY

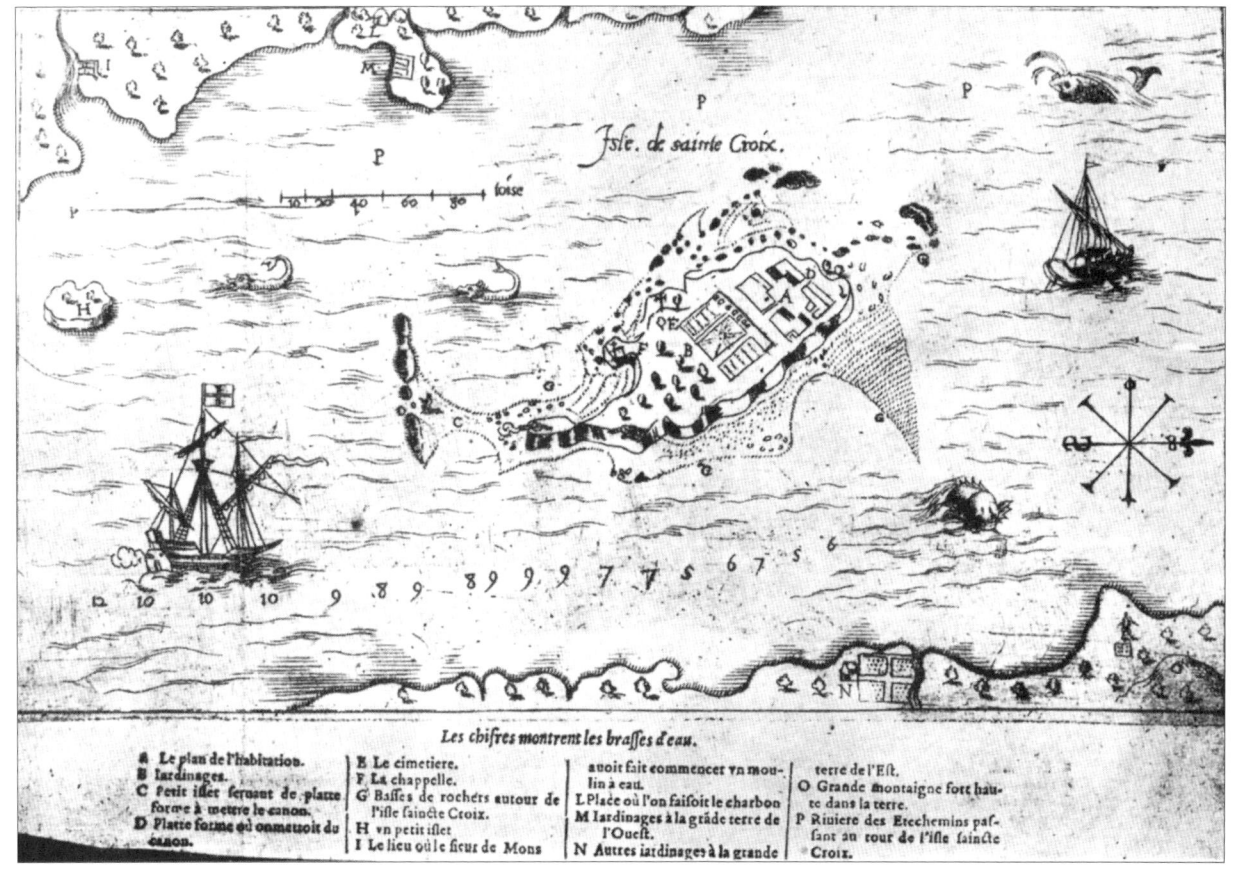

EUROPEANS, NATIVE AMERICANS, AND THE AGE OF EXPLORATION   7

with Basque or French traders. Still, these Europeans were probably stationed in the Gulf of St. Lawrence or Newfoundland. These seagoing tribesmen were most likely Micmac, a tribe whose members later raided Massachusetts and became middlemen in the fur trade.

In 1603 Captain Martin Pring, also of Bristol, fetched up off Plymouth, Massachusetts, in the ship *Speedwell* and the bark *Discoverer*. In the continuing search for sassafras and knowledge, he surveyed the Maine coast, which he termed "the Mayne" or the "maine land," from Saco to the Piscataqua. Back at Plymouth, the crew built a stockade and, as a grim harbinger of future policy, loosed their dogs on the local Indians.

The first known European attempt to plant a town in Maine began under the able direction of Pierre du Guast, Sieur de Monts, the newly confirmed first lieutenant-governor of La Cadie (Acadia). King Henry IV of France had granted his subject seignorial rights to a province that extended from Newfoundland to New Jersey. Oddly, de Monts chose the unpromising Dochet Island in the St. Croix River. The reason for this location, on the present border of New Brunswick and Maine, was probably their fear of the Spanish, who had slaughtered French settlers on the St. John's River in Florida in 1565. We know a considerable amount about the St. Croix Colony through the writings of Samuel de Champlain, de Monts's right-hand man and one of the great figures of the age. In the midst of the religious wars of Europe, his complement of 120 men in two ships contained both Protestants and Catholics. The king only granted the charter; it was the leading Huguenot businessmen who put up the cash. Champlain observed blandly:

> I have seen the minister and our priest come to blows over their religious differences. I do not know who was the stronger and gave the harder blow, but I well know that the minister sometimes complained to the Sieur de Monts that he had been beaten, and in this manner they settled their points of controversy.

This sorry attempt at ecumenism foreshadowed in microcosm the problems integral to long-term European settlement.

At St. Croix the French constructed a compound that was a transplant of their homeland and did little to meet the requirements of local climate and geography. The town included frame houses, a communal kitchen and workshop, and formal-looking gardens. It is not known whether these habitations were built from scratch or, as is more likely, prefabricated and shipped over. Given the short time of construction, it is almost certain that they lacked the old-world charm of Champlain's sketches and may have looked nothing like the plan. But then he was an artist, the first European one to work in Maine, and these illustrations were meant to promote the effort. Champlain was also a fine geographer and explorer. In 1604 he visited the Penobscot River, where he met the Etchemin leader Bessabez (Bashabes) and forever scrapped the Norumbega legend:

> I think this river is that which several pilots and historians call Norumbegue, which most described as large and extensive. . . . It is related also that there is a large, thickly settled town of savages, who are adroit and skillful, and who have cotton yarn. I am confident that most of those who mention it have not seen it, and speak of it because they have heard persons say so, who knew no more about it than they themselves.

Back at St. Croix, the colonists hunkered down for a nasty autumn and winter filled with brutally cold nights and days and topped off by an outbreak of scurvy. Of the seventy-nine who had elected to stay, thirty-five perished. In the spring of

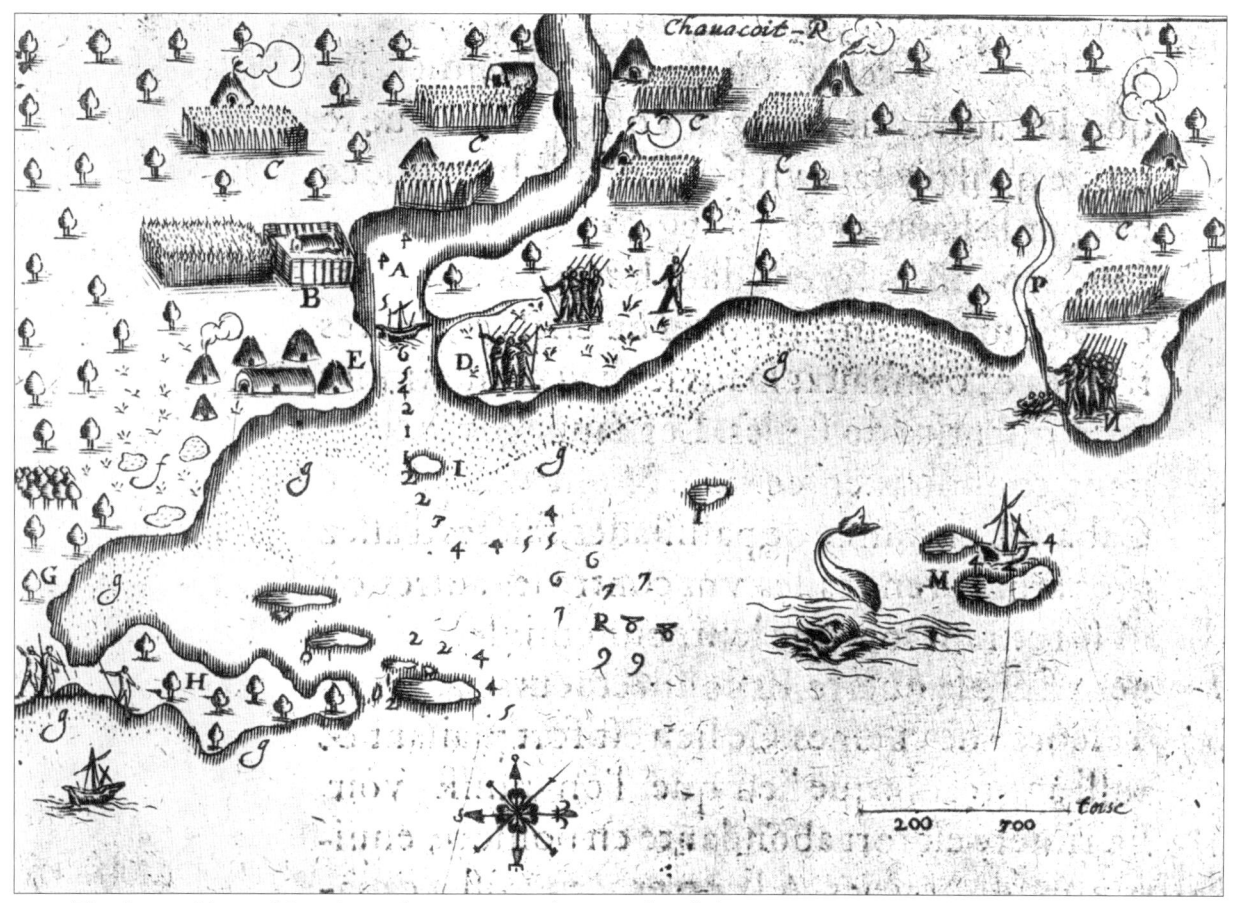

The large Almouchiquois settlement near the mouth of the Saco River was drawn by Samuel de Champlain and is one of the few surviving images of Indian habitation at the time of contact with the Europeans. The explorer described them as "an agile people with well-formed bodies," armed with pikes, clubs, and bows, and living in homes constructed of tree branches covered with bark. Their fort was "a large cabin surrounded by palisades" and they grew corn, beans, and squash in the surrounding cleared land. An important archeological dig at the site, now occupied by the University of New England, is ongoing. COLLECTION OF THE MAINE HISTORICAL SOCIETY

1605, de Monts ferried the survivors across the Bay of Fundy and, using some of the St. Croix structures, founded Port Royal on the Nova Scotia side. Several buildings and the garden remained as a staging area, and indeed Champlain used it to survey the coast. That year he cruised Maine and visited a large Indian settlement near the mouth of the Saco.

If the French had abandoned St. Croix, they had not given up on colonizing North America. In fact, the effort marks the foundation of both Acadia and New France. In 1607 de Monts lost his monopoly, but the effort was taken up again and new settlers dispatched to Port Royal. The major thrust of French settlement shifted to the St. Lawrence, where Champlain built the foundations of Quebec in 1608 and won the title "Father of New France."

The English had already pushed plans of their own for the settlement of Maine. In 1605 the ship

EUROPEANS, NATIVE AMERICANS, AND THE AGE OF EXPLORATION 9

Archangell under Captain George Waymouth was directed to the coast on a reconnaissance mission. The journey was underwritten by the English Catholic nobleman Thomas Arundell and others. Waymouth explored Monhegan, Thomaston, Pemaquid, and the St. George River. Carved on a rock near Cushing is "Abr King 1605," probably our first example of mariner's graffiti. Waymouth's men set up at least one cross to mark their visits. More insightful is James Rosier's account of the voyage, which he printed in the same year. That observant gentleman, who had earlier sailed with Gosnold, wrote of the geography, flora, and fauna, and provided first-rate views of the Indians, whom he liked and admired:

> Their clothing is beaver skins, or Deares skins, cast over them like a mantle, and hanging downe to their knees, made fast together upon their shoulder with leather; some of them had sleeves, most had none; some had buskins of such leather tewed. . . .

Rosier was most impressed by the Indians' "excellent ingenious art" of canoe construction and design.

Then, near Pemaquid, Weymouth kidnapped five "Salvages." The intent was not to make slaves of them but to take them to England, give them the grand tour, and after they were thoroughly impressed by the superiority of Western civilization, release them as goodwill ambassadors. The action did the opposite. It poisoned relations and made the Indians wary of contact.

Like the cast of characters in an Elizabethan revenge tragedy, the captives were listed as "Tahanedo, a Sagamo or Commander," "Amoret/Skidowaros/Maneddo, Gentlemen," and "Saffacomoit, a servant." Quite clearly, Waymouth and Rosier imposed their own social overlay on the group. For years the English were looking for an Indian king, a person and office that did not exist in tribal society.

Lord Chief Justice, Sir John Popham, K.B., (c. 1531–1607), etching by Charles E. Banks (1854–1931). Popham was a "stout and skillful man at sword and buckler," who went to Balliol College, Oxford, and was later admitted to the middle temple. Recent sources suggest he supported himself while at college as a highwayman. A powerful national figure, he owned land in England and Ireland and gave his name and backing to the short-lived Popham Colony, established near the mouth of the Kennebec River in 1607. He was among the first in a long line of absentee owners and speculators in Maine land. COLLECTION OF THE MAINE HISTORICAL SOCIETY

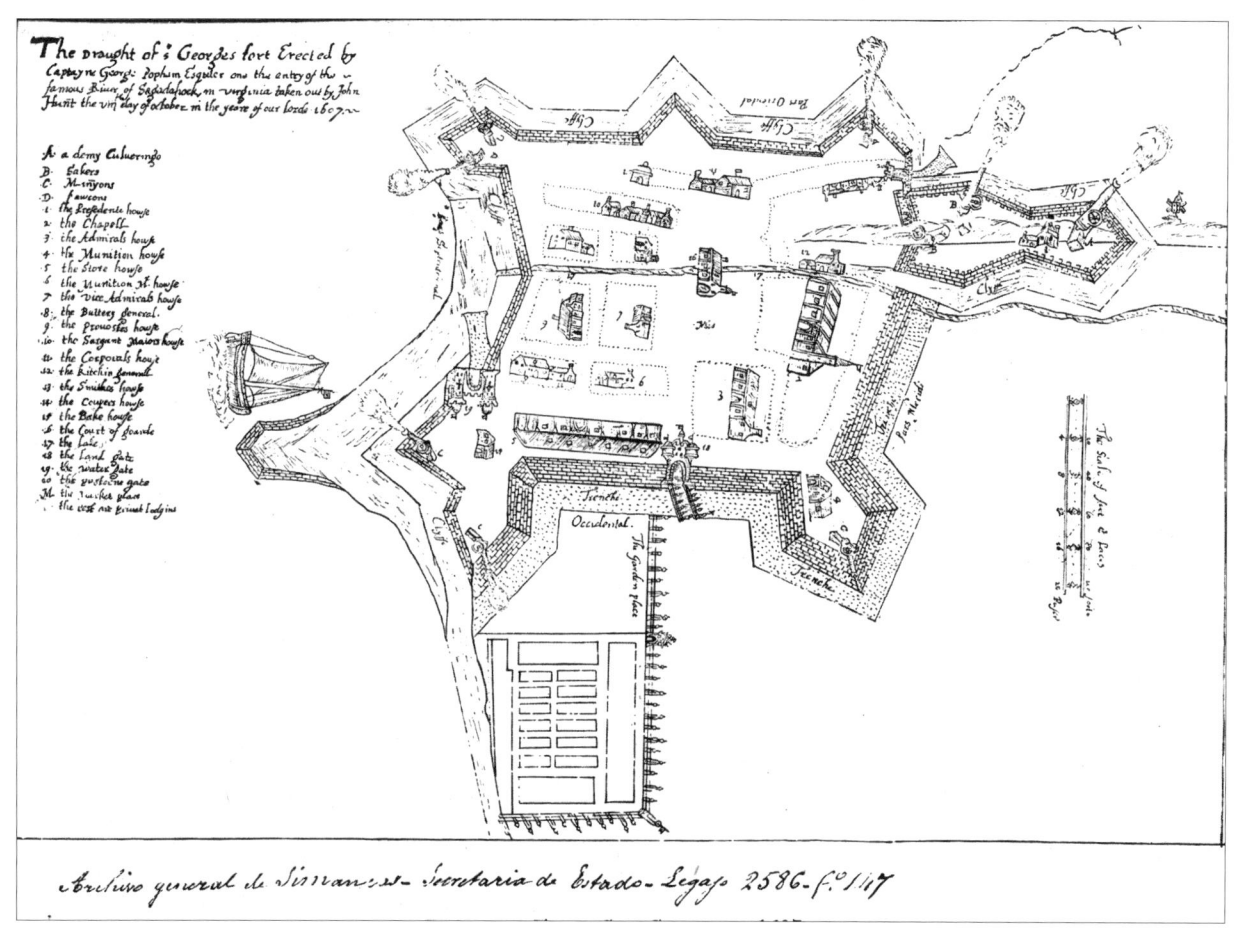

The initial English attempt to settle Maine, then called part of Northern Virginia, occurred in 1607, near the mouth of the Kennebec. The Popham or Sagadahoc colonists constructed Fort St. George, the first in a long series of defensive works built along the shore. Though the fort was well made, John Hunt certainly exaggerated its strength in his drawing; since it ended up in the hands of the Spanish government, its intent may have been to give the enemy second thoughts about attacking. It was, however, the death of the colony's leader, George Popham, and Raleigh Gilbert's return to England upon his brother's death that broke up the settlement. The English did build the *Virginia*, a vessel similar to the one in Hunt's sketch. COURTESY OF THE MAINE HISTORIC PRESERVATION COMMISSION

The backers in England were also hard at work planning a New World society based on the English model. Upon Waymouth's return, they petitioned King James I to establish a joint stock company for the colonization of North America. Instead, James granted two incongruously overlapping charters: to the London Company went all rights to the territory between latitudes 34 and 41, and to the Plymouth Company possession between 30 and 45. This was in 1606, the same year in which Captain Pring returned to the region, now called Sagadahoc, to release the sagamore Tahanedo. English settlement was to commence.

❖

In April of 1607, the London Company went into action establishing Jamestown in "Southern Virginia," which was to become the first permanent English settlement on the continent. In May the

EUROPEANS, NATIVE AMERICANS, AND THE AGE OF EXPLORATION 11

Plymouth Company, which included Thomas Arundell, Sir John Popham, and Sir Ferdinando Gorges, sent the vessels *Gift of God* and *Mary and John* on a similar mission to the mouth of the Kennebec River in "Northern Virginia." With them came Skidowaros (Skidwares), and at Camden they met another Indian who had been released on an earlier visit. In August they arrived at the Kennebec and the Sagadahoc or Popham Colony began.

The English set to work immediately building Fort St. George, a walled town guarded by twelve cannon. John Hunt's plan shows a medieval-looking city with stone walls and towers, something that certainly could not have been thrown up by October and would have remained for all to see. Since the drawing ended up in the Spanish Archives in Simancas, one wonders if it was planted to ward off potential attackers. Still, the town included houses, a storehouse, and a church with the Reverend Richard Seymour in attendance. Hunt's drawing also shows a trading vessel very similar to the *Virginia*, which the colonists constructed under the direction of a shipwright named Digby. This "pretty pinnace" of 30 tons was the first vessel built by the English on this side of the Atlantic. George Popham, a nephew of the chief backer, served as the colony's "president." In October the *Mary and John* sailed, followed by the *Gift of God* in December. Forty-five men chose to winter at Sagadahoc and remarkably, only two died. But one was George Popham, and word soon came that in England Sir John Popham and the brother of the new leader, Raleigh Gilbert (son of Sir Humphrey), had died. In order to secure his brother's estate, Gilbert left in the *Virginia* with the remaining men.

In 1609 Captain Henry Hudson arrived on the coast aboard the Dutch East India Company ship *Half Moon*. A crew member wrote of Indians in possession of two French shallops noting, "The French trade with them for red cassocks, knives, hatchets, copper, kettles, trivets, beads, and other trifles." Later, without any provocation it seems, the Dutch marched into an Indian village, fired their guns, and "took spoil of them. . . ."

The Dutch interlude was fleeting, but both English and French powers continued to make plans for settlement. In 1610 the French began yet another resettlement of Port Royal, and the Popham family dispatched summer fishermen to Monhegan. In the course of the next few years, two Jesuit priests arrived at Port Royal. With Charles de Biencourt, they explored coastal Maine. Father Pierre Biard, an alert observer, left an account of finding English boats on Monhegan and at the abandoned Popham Colony. He also met the Etchemin leader Bashabes, of whom he approved. Back at Port Royal, however, friction developed between the clergymen and the authorities. In 1613 a pious Frenchwoman, Madame de Guercheville, secured permission to found a new colony for the priests and sent a vessel under a Captain La Saussaye. With him the Jesuits sailed to Bar Harbor, where they met friendly Indians who settled them at Fernald's Point in Somes Sound.

The promising French mission was quickly discovered by a Virginia privateer-fishing vessel under Captain Samuel Argall. The Englishman had a commission to expel all foreign intruders and came in firing. In spite of the heroics of gunner Gilbert du Thet, the resistance was feeble. Du Thet was killed and four others wounded before the French gave in. The English then plundered the mission, took the French prisoners to Jamestown, and kept their vessel as a prize. Then the energetic Argall returned to Maine and burned what was left of St. Croix and Port Royal, which he found deserted.

The battle at Somes Sound left the region open to the English interests where, in 1615, six vessels were fishing. The next year there were eight. It was the now famous Captain John Smith who really called attention to the area and fixed the name of

Portrait of Antoinette de Pons-Ribérac, marquise de Guercheville, "souveraine du Canada" (1560–1632), one of the first powerful female figures in Acadian history. She was a pious aristocrat to whom King Louis XIII of France granted a vast chunk of Acadia. In 1613 she funded the Jesuit mission at Saint Sauveur (Somes Sound), which was destroyed by the Virginians soon after. COLLECTION OF THE MAINE HISTORICAL SOCIETY

New England to the map. With his historic work in Virginia done, Smith had sailed from England with two ships in 1614. He returned with a valuable cargo of furs and fish and in 1616 published *A Description of New England,* which included the famous map. As historian J. B. Harley noted, Smith and other mapmakers tended to ignore Indian settlements and place-names as if they were empty lands. By substituting familiar English names, Native cultural identities were erased. In point of fact, Smith invited the Prince of Wales (later King Charles I) and his favorites to fill in the blanks of New England, thus giving us Cape Ann, Cape Elizabeth, and the like. Some though, like Smith's Isles (Isles of Shoals) were subsequently changed again.

Ever the promoter, Smith sought out Sir Ferdinando Gorges and the Plymouth Company and sold them his vision of development. He emerged with the grandiose title "Admiral of New England" and funds for a two-ship expedition in 1615. His ship was damaged in a storm and forced to turn about. On a second try, his vessel was captured by a French pirate or privateer, and while he was aboard the other ship, his crew mutinied and sailed off. Gorges tired of Smith who, as a pamphleteer, continued to tout the limitless possibilities of New England. But Gorges had not lost interest in Maine and continued to plan.

❖

On the shores of Maine, terrible things had happened. In 1614 Captain Thomas Hunt, the master of Smith's second vessel, *Long-Robert,* kidnapped more than a score of Indians at Monhegan and points in southern New England. He then made for Spain to sell them as slaves. There the authorities forced Hunt to release some of the captives. One, named Squanto, was freed by friars. He then escaped to England and found his way to Newfoundland. In 1619 Captain Thomas Dermer saw Squanto as a perfect ambassador and took him on a voyage down the New England coast. Much had changed, due to plague and war, since the Indian had been kidnapped.

Even before the Europeans established permanent stations and villages, their proximity was generating social, political, and economic dislocation. Since prehistoric times, Native inhabitants in Maine had engaged in wars. Yet the availability of more lethal European weapons and the desire for manufactured goods apparently increased the level of hostility, and the casualties rose. Champlain's 1605 map of the Saco clearly depicts a palisaded

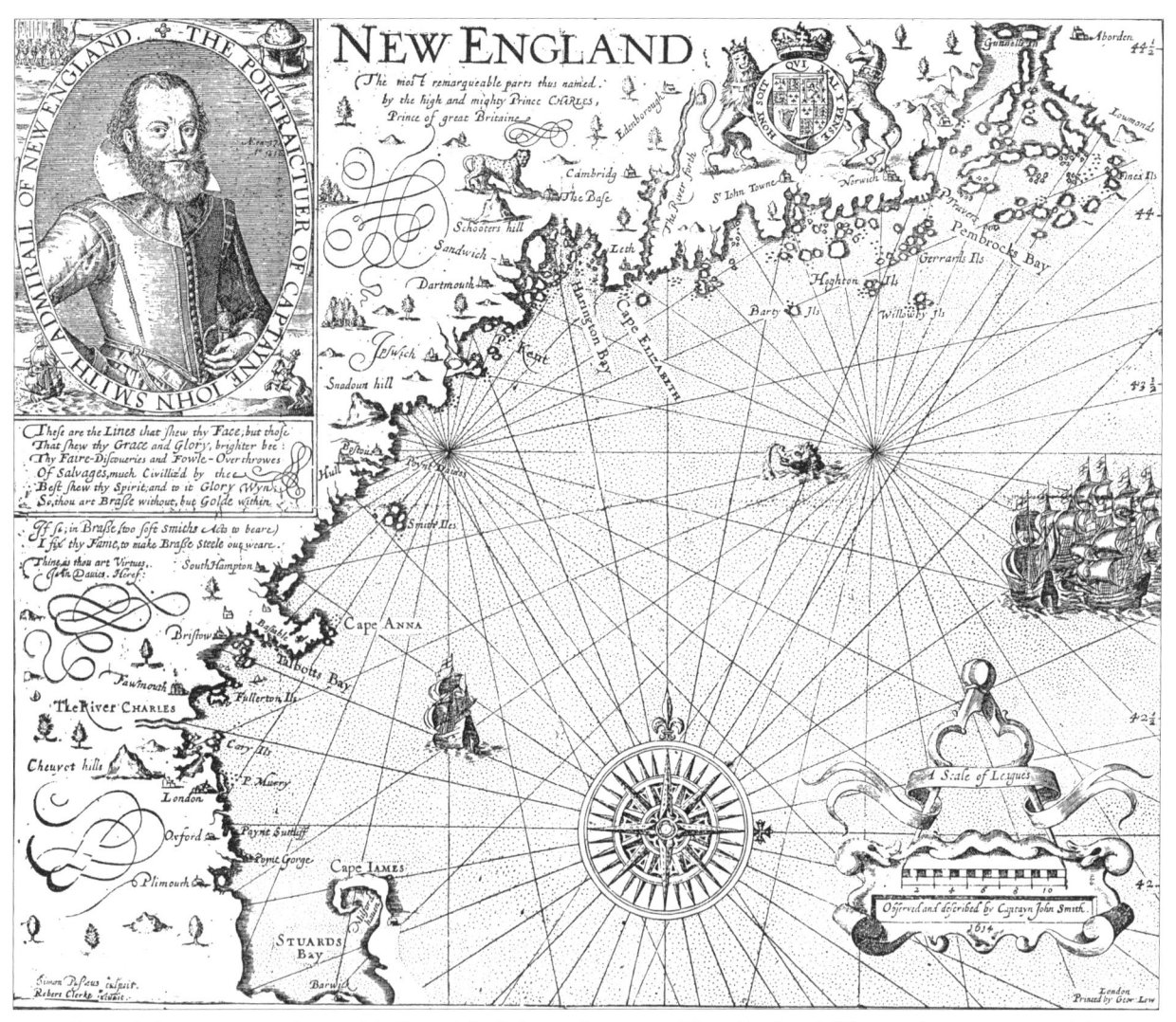

One of the most popular and influential of the early maps, *New England Observed*.... appeared in Captain John Smith's book *The Generall Historie of Virginia, New England, and the Summer Isles*, London, 1624. With this map, Smith (c. 1579–1631) fixed the term "New England" to the region long known as Norumbega or a part of Northern Virginia. He also included a bristling image of himself with his newly granted title, admiral of New England. In subsequent geographies, New France and New England now shared a common but indistinct border. As settlements began, hostility between Europeans grew with Native American tribes caught between them. The Native American name for the area, Wabanaki, meaning Dawn Land (where the sun rises), was apparently lost on mapmakers. COLLECTION OF THE MAINE HISTORICAL SOCIETY

fort, which was intended to protect the nearby Armouchiquois hamlets. In 1607, however, the far-traveling Souriquois devastated the settlement. The Indians of Maine would suffer many losses in this intertribal war, which did not end until 1615. In that year the Souriquois raided the Penobscot Valley and killed the powerful Etchemin leader Bashabes, an ally of the Armouchiquois. This conflict was apparently waged largely for control of the fur trade with the French.

What followed next was even more grim. Between 1617 and 1619, Maine and the Maritimes were swept by what has been called the New England Pandemic. The specific disease has not been identified, but it came from Europeans, who apparently had an immunity. Historians estimate that there were roughly 21,000 Native Americans living in Maine around 1600. By 1650, they probably numbered around 5,500. As a result of this shocking population collapse, there was a great deal of realignment among families and groups. Villages were abandoned, and, particularly in south coastal Maine, the English visitors found themselves in a position to extend their sovereignty with little or no immediate opposition.

In the early years of the century, seasonal fishing stations were in operation at Monhegan, Damariscove Island, and the Isles of Shoals, and in 1616–1617, the Gorges employee Richard Vines spent a pleasant winter at Winter Harbor (Biddeford Pool). In Plymouth, the Pilgrims were struggling to subsist in order to follow their religious beliefs. Much to their surprise an Indian appeared to assist them. This was Squanto's friend Samoset, a native of Pemaquid and certainly the most famous of all Native Americans in Maine. In 1622 the first year-round fishing settlement in Maine was founded on Damariscove Island by Gorges's men. There were thirty vessels in or near the narrow harbor and thirteen permanent inhabitants surrounded by a spruce palisade and protected by a cannon and "ten good dogs."

❖

Across the sea, an English political structure was about to be put in place. Soon after the Pilgrims departed in 1620, the Plymouth Company was dissolved and replaced by the Council for New England. Among the forty-eight worthies were Gorges and John Mason. In 1621 the council granted the Pilgrims the land on which they were settled. In the following year, on August 10, 1622, the council gave Sir Ferdinando Gorges and Captain John Mason the land between the Sagadahoc and Merrimac Rivers, which, "with the consent of the President and Council, [they] intend to name the Province of Maine." The name may have referred to the mainland, to the French Province of Maine, or to a river in Ireland where Gorges and Popham and others had plantations. No matter—the region had been given an enduring label, and a new epoch had begun.

This illustration from *Histoire de l'Amérique Septentrionale*, Paris, 1722, shows a well-equipped Canadian soldier, apparently one of Pierre Le Moyne, Sieur d'Iberville's, men. Such troops were among the first Europeans to live with the Indians and learn their methods of movement and warfare. Indian snowshoes had been effectively employed in the frontier conflict, notably in the raid on York, Maine, in February 1692. COURTESY OF THE NATIONAL ARCHIVES OF CANADA, OTTAWA, CANADA

2

NEW ENGLAND AND NEW FRANCE (1623–1763)

"And thus after many dangers, much labor, and charge, I have obtained a place of habitation in New England, where I have built a house, and fortified it in good fashion, strong enough against such enemies as are the savage people," boasted Christopher Levett of his arrival on a Casco Bay island in 1623. Though Levett's plantation only survived a few seasons, it marked the beginning of a regular English presence on the coast. His book, *A Voyage into New England* (1628), offers a unique glimpse of Maine at the outset of a century and a half of high adventure. Caught between the overlapping borders of New England and New France, English, Acadians, and Indians would face the daily struggle for survival between forest and shore, endless litigation over land titles, and guerrilla warfare at its most brutal. By 1763 it appeared that the English-speaking settlers, now called Yankees, had emerged triumphant, with Acadians dispersed and Indians reduced to a shocking remnant.

1623 was also the year when Sir Ferdinando Gorges and Captain John Mason, the respective fathers of Maine and New Hampshire, were partners in a grant referred to as Maine or Laconia. Though able and energetic, both men became bogged down in a confusion of plans, names, and administrative overlays. In French Acadia, internal quarrels and lack of support from abroad made for an equally confused situation. Indeed, for the next thirty years or so, government in both colonies remained weak and ineffective. Because of this, the area became a convenient buffer zone between the larger, more viable colonies in Massachusetts and Quebec.

Levett's arrival at the Isles of Shoals and the Piscataqua coincided with a number of firsts. Just after Levett debarked with deeds from the Council for New England, Sir Ferdinando's nephew, Robert Gorges, came in person replete with the title governor and lieutenant-governor of New England. With him came an admiral of New England and a representative of the Church of England, which was to be the official creed. Civil officers were appointed (Levett was made a member of the council) and land grants were made. Levett sailed east to plant his settlement and found early fears of Indians groundless. In fact, they granted him land near their own, and, after visiting beyond the Kennebec, he returned "with the king, queen, and prince, bow and arrows, dog and kettle in my boat, his noble attendance rowing by us in their canoes." With such pageantry Levett built on what probably became Cushing's or House Island in Casco Bay. Relations with the Indians were good; his clash occurred with fellow Englishmen who refused to recognize the authority of the council or Levett as its agent. When unlicensed ships trading for furs were observed, Levett complained that he found himself powerless in the face of fifty tough men and seventeen guns. Titles and regulations did not interest or influence such

nizer who never made it to Maine, he had great difficulty changing things. Gorges was very much a king's man, influential in the Stuart court. He dreamed of a late-feudal colony with himself in charge, but failed to attract many settlers.

Gorges saw the big picture, including potential border trouble with New France. Since the French had withdrawn from Acadia after Argall's raid, Gorges angled for a Scottish colony in Acadia. In 1628 a contingent of Scots occupied the area and proclaimed it Nova Scotia. The next year the British evicted the French from Quebec, and Claude de La Tour, the leading French operative in Acadia, joined the British and was made a baronet of Nova Scotia. For a short time, Maine enjoyed a buffer zone on its eastern border.

English settlers gradually appeared along the coast, and, increasingly, seasonal fishing stations took on a more permanent look. Outposts including the Isles of Shoals, Damariscove Island, Richmond's Island, and mainland Pemaquid became bustling, year-round establishments. Legends of a lawless fishing frontier live on, though the extent of the disorder remains unclear. Gorges complained of fishermen "behaving worse than savages," and decades later the Puritan divine, Cotton Mather, waxed poetic over the doings of these "Wild English." At Richmond's Island, a large well-run operation off Cape Elizabeth begun in the early 1630s, there was a minister influencing tight control over the distribution of wine and rum. The men worked six long days a week and spent most of the Sabbath sleeping. So in spite of complaints, there was scant time to be rowdy. Still, at the end of the fishing season, when payday arrived, entrepreneurs sailed in to lighten purses. One observer described "a walking tavern, a Bark laden with the Legitimate blood of the rich grape. . . ." At such times, the earthy, independent spirits cut loose and caused more than a bit of anarchy.

This was disturbing to more traditional settlers, who were hunkered down in clusters from

Christopher Levett (1586–1630) attempted to settle the Casco Bay area in 1623 and remained active in the development and promotion of the region until his death at sea. Levett's short, colorful, and informative volume, *A Voyage Into New England*, 1628, marks the change from the literature of exploration to the literature of settlement in Maine. It was recently reprinted with a solid introduction and critical remarks. COLLECTION OF THE MAINE HISTORICAL SOCIETY

interlopers, nor, for that matter, the scattering of fishermen. The new governor sailed within a year, leaving his agents to do their best.

Sir Ferdinando understood the reality of the situation on the coast, but as an armchair colo-

Kittery to the present Boothbay. Though they, too, disliked taxes and regulations, they craved protection so they could farm, cut timber, or fish. Drunken fishermen were not the only source of violence and disorder. In 1631 an English trader named Dixie Bull turned pirate after having been robbed by a French privateer (an armed vessel licensed to capture enemy ships). Bull raised a new crew, sailed into the harbor at English Pemaquid, sent the villagers flying into the woods, and proceeded to take everything of value. Though his second mate was shot while raising anchor, Bull cruised the Gulf of Maine spreading fear and prompting a naval action on the part of Gorges's authorities. The flotilla failed to catch the man, who escaped to England and died of natural causes.

Governor Winslow and the Puritans, who had settled on council territory around Boston, watched events to their eastward with great interest. In fact, they considered tracking Bull themselves. Having fled persecution in Britain, the Puritans, well-organized and numerous, arrived sure of their mission. Within a decade, 20,000 souls immigrated to New England with the majority going to Massachusetts Bay, and by century's end the Bible Commonwealth had absorbed Plymouth, Maine, and parts of Acadia. Their interest in Maine centered on the potentially lucrative fur, timber, and fish businesses.

In 1630 a series of large grants from crown and council further divided Maine in the region between the Kennebec and Penobscot. These included the Lygonia (Plow Patent) Grant; the Muscongus (Waldo) Patent; the Pemaquid Grant; and the huge tract given the Plymouth Colony on the Kennebec. A scattering of truck houses or trading posts near Indian villages characterized this region. The Plymouth men built fur-trading posts at Cushnoc (now Augusta) and Penobscot (now Castine) to raise revenue in hopes of paying off their sponsors. In 1634 a Piscataqua merchant

One of the Maine Historical Society's most intriguing little treasurers is just that, twenty gold and silver coins dating from 1563 to 1625. Uncovered by a Richmond Island farmer while plowing his field in 1855, the coins, a gold ring, and other objects may have belonged to Walter "Great Walt" Bagnall, a Cape Elizabeth trader killed in 1631 by Indians he cheated. Hard money was rare throughout the colonial era, with Iberian coins serving as the principal specie through the 1780s.
COLLECTION OF THE MAINE HISTORICAL SOCIETY

sailed up the Kennebec to challenge their monopoly and, in the shootout that followed, was killed with one of the Pilgrims. In a bizarre foretaste of shifting power, the newly established Puritans detained John Alden, who was a witness. After a protest from Plymouth Colony, Alden was released.

In 1632 Acadia was returned to France by treaty, and a strong leader, Isaac de Razilly, arrived with three ships and 300 settlers determined to fish, farm, and trade. In 1635 Razilly sent his lieutenant, Charles de Menou d'Aulnay, to capture the Pilgrim post at Penobscot and build Fort Pentagoet as Acadia's southwestern outpost. Pentagoet was a small, elegant, self-contained piece of France complete with chapel, smithy, twelve cannon, six mortars, and twenty-five soldiers. As Canadian archaeologist Christopher J. Turnbull wrote in *The French at Pentagoet*, "I was never so impressed as by the cramped quarters and narrow streets; it was a small enclave where Europeans

Charles de Menou d'Aulnay, Sieur de Charnisay (about 1604–1650), captured the Plymouth Colony outpost at Penobscot and built Fort Pentagoet as the southern outpost of French Acadia in 1635. A longtime governor of the colony, he settled some families but spent much precious time battering a rival Frenchman, Charles Saint-Etienne de La Tour. Ironically, d'Aulnay's widow wed La Tour just before the British captured the entire colony. Courtesy of the New Brunswick Museum/Le Musée du Nouveau-Brunswick, St. John, New Brunswick, Canada

huddled together behind their stone walls in the vastness of their new territory."

Razilly's death in the same year signaled fifteen years of lilliputian-scale civil war between d'Aulnay and another lieutenant, Charles de la Tour. During the Scottish occupation, La Tour remained loyal to France and even fought his father when he joined the enemy. Acadia was soon split into two rival camps. La Tour hired Massachusetts mercenaries and captured Port Royal, but d'Aulnay made a treaty with the Puritans, captured La Tour's fort on the St. John, and executed most of the garrison. When d'Aulnay died in 1650, La Tour married his rival's widow. In a weird finale, the Puritans captured Acadia the next year and, when La Tour promised to pay his debts, recognized him as baronet of Nova Scotia. Ironically, the king of France approved this shift of allegiance. In spite of bad government, the Acadian people had a foothold in Nova Scotia and would pursue a destiny distinct from the French in Quebec, thus playing an important role in the history of Maine. But their position bordering on New England made them a perceived threat. The British governed until 1670, and one official urged in 1662 that it was imperative to "drive away all the French people from America and even from Canada by beginning now in Acadia." It was some time before his words were considered.

❖

Gorges, too, was having trouble forming a workable administration in Maine. In 1634 he urged King Charles I to revoke Massachusetts' charter and create a royal government. The next year Gorges was appointed lord governor of New England, but his ship was wrecked in launching and shifts in politics scrapped the plan, much to Boston's relief.

In 1636 he sent a nephew to Maine as governor of New Somersetshire, another failed colony, and in 1639 Gorges was made lord of a new Province of Maine. He sent his cousin, Thomas Gorges, as deputy from 1639 to 1643. Thomas, probably the first trained lawyer in Maine, founded the "city" of Gorgeana (later York) and appointed a baroque set of officials (including a slot for lord bishop). The deputy reported in 1641 but wrote a year later: "As for slaves out of Ginney, if theyr bodyes can agree with the coldness of our Country, they would be excellent, but I believe I could frame an argument against the lawfulness of taking them from theyr own country and soe have them and them and theyrs." He also organized the first English expedition to the interior, reaching the White Mountains.

Trouble between Royalists and Puritans, which had been brewing for years in England, broke into civil war in 1642. Sir Ferdinando, though elderly, took the field for his king and Thomas left Gorgeana, ironically, to join the parliamentary cause. Out of contact with their leaders, the settlers of Kittery, Gorgeana, and Wells feared absorption by Massachusetts and so elected Edward Godfrey as governor of the Province of Maine. Functioning as a tiny republic, Maine extended religious liberty, perhaps in hopes of forestalling Puritan expansion. But even the capable Godfrey could not halt the tide of history. When Sir Ferdinando died in 1647, Kittery followed the New Hampshire towns in submitting to Massachusetts rule. Gorgeana, now York, submitted in 1652, and by 1658 Puritan domination extended to Casco Bay. Except for the years 1665–1668, when Charles II briefly restored a Maine government, the Bay Colony ruled. Internally they were opposed by such determined foes as Godfrey and Robert Jordan of Cape Elizabeth, and some evidence suggests that the easternmost English settlers even considered Acadian rule. In 1671 Massachusetts claimed all land east of the Kennebec, and in 1677 settled the Maine matter by buying all rights to the province from Gorges's heirs. From 1677 to 1691 Maine was a colony of a colony with a "president" to oversee affairs.

The best insights into the period include Levett's *A Voyage Into New England: Begun in 1623 and Ended in 1624*, which provides inquiring minds with the sometimes seamy details of everyday life; and John Josselyn's two books, *New-England Rareties Discovered* (1672) and *An Account of Two Voyages to New-England* (1674). Josselyn's works have the first real claim on local literature and describe his visits to a brother at Black Point (now Scarborough) in 1638–1639 and 1663–1671. He offers scenes of life among Indians and whites, lists and describes more than a hundred plants, and considers Indian medicine as well. He also recorded stories of mermen and sea serpents and has been called "Maine's first folklorist."

It is comforting to learn that "Cats and Dogs are as common as in England," but Josselyn accused "droanish" farmers of not working hard enough, so that they suffered "want of bread" in the winter.

In spite of such publications, all of which have been reprinted, the Bible remained the basic book. Probably half the settlers could not read, and those who could write were usually not very good at it. Life was a hardscrabble affair and even successful people had virtually no time for leisure.

There was a hierarchy in the settlements, but even community leaders were obliged to work alongside employees or neighbors. One might own a house, barn, cattle, boat, and many acres of land and yet be unable to produce hard money. Barter was the mainstay of the economy with Spanish and Portuguese gold and silver coins remaining the principal specie through the 1780s.

The planting of families, in place of single traders and adventurers, ensured the success and continuation of settlement. Families were the basic unit of production, and each member had a clearly defined role. As *Children and Youth in America* (Cambridge, 1970) put it, "The labor of children was social fact, not a social problem." The more children, the more successful the operation, be it farming, fishing, hunting, or winter cutting in the surrounding forest. In the absence of professionals—including medical doctors, teachers, and, on occasion, ministers—the family, connected to other families by blood or business, supplied the major social support system.

There was no retirement, and generations tended to live together under one roof. As time went on, the size and style of houses grew, but the first temporary colonial structures were crude affairs, probably sod houses. An observer of early settlement in Massachusetts wrote: "They burrow themselves into the Earth for their first shelter under some Hill-side, casting the Earth aloft upon Timber. . . ." Such shelters, meant for short duration, persisted among immigrants to Maine until outlawed by twentieth-century building codes. However, a map of the river between York and Kittery, executed around 1660, shows mostly one- and one-and-a-half-story frame buildings.

By the 1670s English Maine included "scatterings" of farms stretched out along the coast and near the mouths of rivers, as well as truck houses in the Kennebec region. Towns usually had a tavern in someone's home, but few could afford a regular meetinghouse and none could afford a school. There were courts and trial by jury, and Mainers were constantly dragging one another into court over deeds or disputes. Deviant individuals faced whips, stocks, or irons, but there were no true prisons in all of colonial America. Major criminals were tried and executed. There were no real holidays, though weddings, ship launchings, and co-operative house raisings provided a certain amount of social contact, especially when spiced by rum. If life was difficult, progress was slow.

All this was to collapse as Maine became the killing ground in a series of brutal, debilitating wars between the English and the combined forces of France and the Indians.

❖

Young John Gyles of Pemaquid described the terror of a sudden attack that took place in 1689:

> . . . looking over my shoulder I saw a stout fellow, painted, pursuing me with a gun and cutlass glittering in his hand which I expected every moment in my brains. I soon fell down, and the Indian seized me by the left hand. He offered me no abuse, but tied my arms, then lifted me up and pointed where the people were at work about the hay and led me that way. As we went, we crossed where my father was, who looked very pale and bloody, and walked very slowly. Then when we came to the place I saw two men shot down on the flats, and one or two more knocked on their heads with hatchets, crying out, "O Lord," &c.

The attack on Pemaquid might stand for any of the hundreds of attacks and ambushes that occurred between 1675 and the Treaty of Paris in 1763. It was a war of no quarter in which raiders on both sides killed old and young alike in a fury of racial hatred and struggle for land. All of this was set against the backdrop of Anglo-French rivalry on a worldwide scale.

Acadia, including Fort Pentagoet, had been returned to France in 1670. Four years later, idle Dutch privateers captured the outpost, turned the fort's cannon on the walls, and tortured Lieutenant Jean Vincent d'Abbadie de Saint-Castin. Initial English delight soured as the place became a pirate base, so a party from Boston arrested the Dutch. They were tried in Boston with some being acquitted and others banished. Young Baron Castin was left in charge on the Penobscot River.

Castin built a new trading post across from the ruins of the fort. In effect, Castin went native, marrying the daughter of the leading area chief, Madockawando, and maintaining French interests on the border of New England for some thirty years. Up the Kennebec, Jesuit missionaries had converted the majority of Indians to Catholicism and constructed a chapel around 1646. (From the 1640s through the 1660s war had raged between the Maine tribes and the Iroquois.) The slight presence of the French masked the powerful hold they exercised over the tribes. The English were confined largely to the coast and rivers and had scant knowledge of the interior forest. They had yet to consider crossing Maine to the St. Lawrence; it was as if a magic barrier existed across the map.

In 1675 King Philip's War broke out in Massachusetts and sparked a separate conflict in Maine. The Indians had been pressured for years, and the killing of a chief's son helped push them into combat. Attacks were made on unprotected farms in Saco, Casco (later Falmouth), Wells, South Berwick, and, in the next year, on Cape Neddick, Black Point, Pemaquid, and the Kennebec trading stations. It was in this time that settlers at Wiscasset, including Mary Davie, were driven out. Some English families were taken captive or cut down in their dooryards; others fled to islands or safer settlements. Some, like the aged Robert Jordan of Cape Elizabeth, never returned from exile. However, despite of continual threats, members of his family did. The pattern of loss and dispersal colored the eastern frontier for the next eighty years.

The first war, which ended in 1678, was largely an Anglo-Indian affair, though evidence suggests the limited unofficial involvement by Frenchmen. The conflict initiated great changes, with Madockawando leading his people east. The names Canibas and Maliseet apparently came to describe the former Etchemins. The name Micmac replaced Souriquois. Slowly the tribes in Maine were becoming loosely allied in what might be called the Abenaki (Wabanaki) Alliance. Distant events were also having an impact on English settlers. In 1680 a royal commission restored New Hampshire as a colony, free of Massachusetts, and abrogated the Bay Colony charter, creating instead a Dominion of New England. This lasted from 1685 to 1688, when England's Glorious Revolution brought William and Mary to the throne.

In 1689 a new round of conflict began in New England's woods. King William's War lasted until 1697 and partially mirrored the War of the League of Augsburg in Europe. It began when Indians fell on North Yarmouth and John Gyles's Pemaquid. In the autumn the General Court sent out 200 militiamen under the noted Indian fighter Major Benjamin Church. Sailing to Casco (later Fal-

This portrait of Mary Mirick Davie (1635–1752), attributed to Nathaniel Smibert, depicts a woman who, with her husband Captain George Davie, first settled Wiscasset. In 1675 they were driven out in the first of the Indian wars. By the end of King William's War, the English population in Maine had fallen to a thousand or less, with only four towns still populated. In Massachusetts the refugee problem was so severe that a law made it illegal for inhabitants to abandon the frontier. In 1711 the thrice-married Mary was on relief, but still spinning and shelling corn. Her remarkable longevity caused Governor Belcher to commission her likeness, a rare depiction of a humble inhabitant. COURTESY OF THE MASSACHUSETTS HISTORICAL SOCIETY, BOSTON

NEW ENGLAND AND NEW FRANCE

24 MAINE: THE WILDER HALF OF NEW ENGLAND

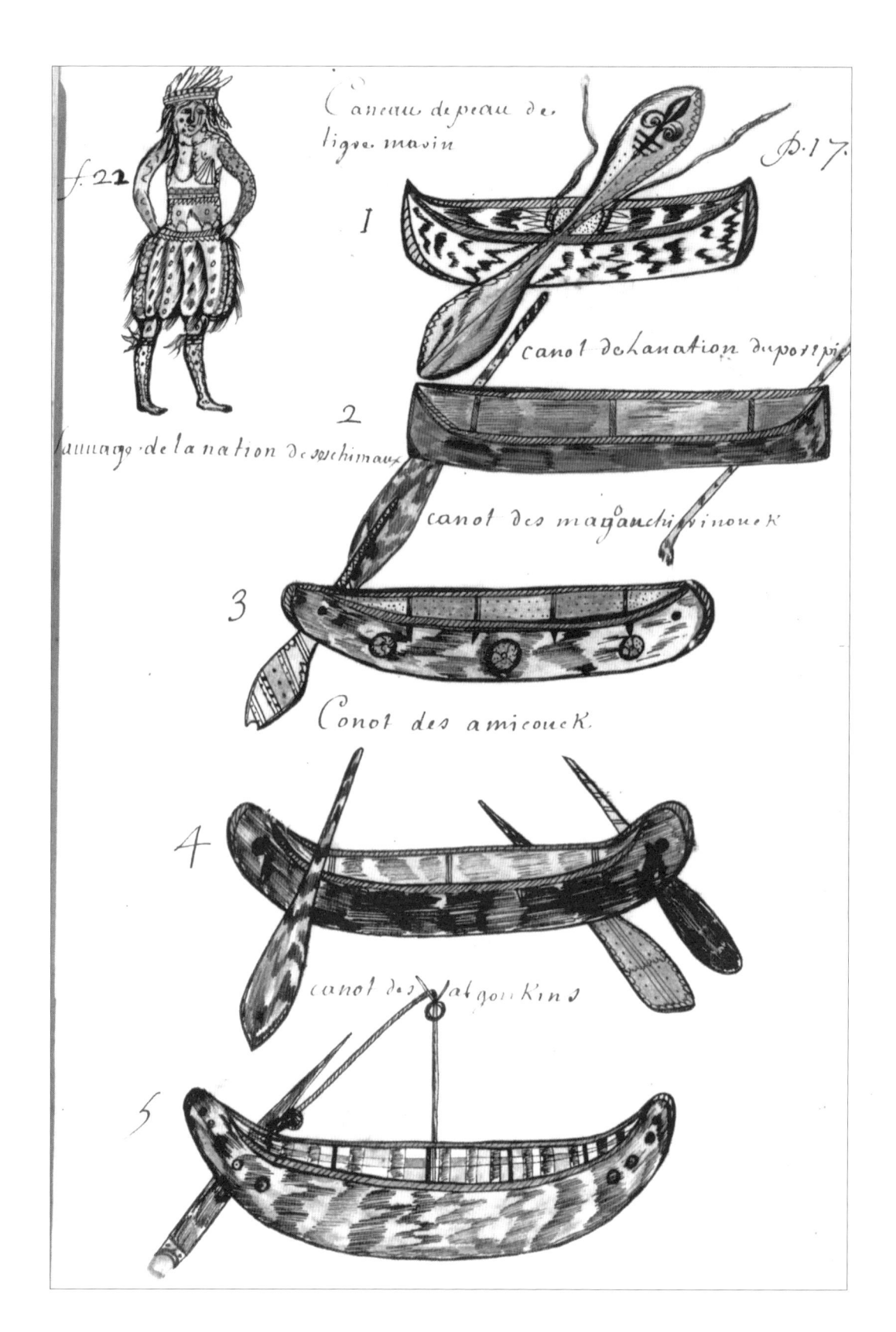

Saco Fort was built in 1693 on the falls of the Saco River (now Biddeford). It sheltered settlers fleeing from the "scatterings" of English farms during the horrors of King William's War and was replaced by a fort at Biddeford Pool in 1708. This detail drawing was executed in 1699, at a time when the engineer Colonel Wolfgang Romer found the fort ill designed and well situated, only as "a place for defence of salmon fishing." COURTESY OF THE SACO MUSEUM, SACO, MAINE

mouth), they fought an exhausting pitched battle between today's Deering Oaks and Union Plaza.

Church won the battle, but the next year the tide turned and the lightly protected Casco fell to 500 Indians in a flotilla of war canoes. This was in reaction to a Boston expedition against Port Royal commanded by the Maine-born adventurer Sir William Phips. Acadia fell, but so did Maine. By 1691 her villages lay in ash, deserted by the inhabitants. Sir William failed to take Quebec, and meanwhile only Kittery, York, Wells, and the Isles of Shoals remained. In 1692 York survived a punishing attack by a large party of Indians on snowshoes, even though half the town's population was captured or killed.

With the English in Maine all but driven into the sea, the local powers in Massachusetts were able to have Sir William Phips appointed by the king as their first royal governor. A native of Woolwich, Phips had been knighted after recovering a sunken treasure and enriching himself and his king. As governor, he ended the witchcraft trials, continued taxation in support of the Standing Order (Congregational) Church, and so favored unrestricted trade that he publicly caned a British customs collector. This so-called free trade (the British called it smuggling) continued as a major theme. Phips took a genuine interest in Maine, which became a district instead of a province in 1691. The loss of life appalled him, and in 1692 he lavished £20,000 on building Fort William Henry at Pemaquid. This fort, now partially recon-

Opposite: Roads were nonexistent or extremely poor throughout the colonial period so the sea and rivers provided the only reliable transportation network. The Indians had developed the canoe and dugout to points of perfection, and though European settlers built their own boats, nothing improved on the canoe design. An early dugout was recently discovered and preserved at Biddeford Pool, and the oldest surviving birch-bark canoe from Maine is at the Peabody Museum of Salem. These drawings, from the *Codex Canadensis* of about 1700, apparently include Micmac (1) and Maliseet (2) designs. COURTESY OF THE THOMAS GILCREASE INSTITUTE, TULSA, OKLAHOMA

NEW ENGLAND AND NEW FRANCE 25

Sir William Phips (1650/51–1694/95) was the area's first rags-to-riches commercial success story. Born into poverty in what became Woolwich, Phips began as a shepherd, became a ship's carpenter, contractor, and captain before discovering and raising a sunken treasure in the West Indies. Having enriched himself and Charles II, Sir William became the first American native knighted by a king of England. He subsequently led two invasions of New France and in 1691 became the first royal governor of Massachusetts. COURTESY OF THE GARDINER FAMILY, PHOTOGRAPH BY NICHOLAS DEAN

These objects belonged to Father Sébastian Râle (Rales) (1657–1724) of the mission at the Indian Village of Norridgewock. The brilliant priest designed and built the chapel, painted the interior panels, composed music for his parishioners, and began a dictionary of the Abenaki language. The English settlers raided the village on several occasions, and in 1724 destroyed the place, taking Râle's scalp and twenty-six others back to Boston. COLLECTION OF THE MAINE HISTORICAL SOCIETY

structed, was, in his opinion, "strong enough to resist all the Indians in America." Phips died suddenly in 1694/95 and did not witness the fall of Pemaquid.

In the autumn of 1696, three French warships, 100 soldiers, and 500 Indians surrounded the fort. Led by Baron Castin and the great Canadian swashbuckler Pierre Le Moyne, Sieur d'Iberville, they received the post's surrender the next day. Iberville had already led his troops to Hudson's Bay, would soon take Newfoundland, and would urge the capture of New York. One of the great figures of his day, he later founded Louisiana.

The decade of the 1690s proved the high-water mark for French and Indian success on the borderlands. In 1694 their position was strengthened by the arrival of Father Sébastian Râle (Rales or Rasle) at Norridgewock. With Castin, and Castin's son, the Jesuit served as the major French influence in Maine. Râle designed and built a new mission chapel, painted the interior paneling, and composed music for his parishioners. His mastery of languages led him to begin an Abenaki dictionary. On the surface, the Indians looked like victors, but their numbers were soon depleted in the epidemics that struck in 1695 and 1698.

The war seemed to put the English in Maine on the edge of extinction. Most settlements were totally destroyed, and thousands of refugees streamed into the Bay Colony. In 1694–1695 the General Court was so alarmed by the loss of its frontier buffer zone that it passed "An Act to Prevent the Deserting of the Frontiers." While they might weep patriotic tears over conditions in Maine, they were not about to spend much to protect the inhabitants, and expected them to remain loyal defenders. In 1697 a European peace treaty was signed, but it failed to establish an eastern border for Maine, and it was not until 1699 that the local English and Indians came to peace terms. By then fewer than 1,000 English were left in the district.

The turn of the century saw efforts to resettle the district. At first these were sporadic, but, for various reasons, soon won governmental and business assistance as eighteenth-century Mainers gained a better understanding of their relationship with Boston.

The first area to gain a level of mature power was Kittery and environs, which shared the Piscataqua with New Hampshire. Here, merchant families including the Frosts and Pepperrells came to dominate social, economic, and political life. In 1680 the first William Pepperrell moved in from the Isles of Shoals to Kittery Point, where he constructed a fine house, built ships, bought land, and engaged in the timber and fish trade. His merchant fleet traded with the West Indies and Europe. This also made it possible for his son to rise as a power in both Portsmouth and Boston. Relatively safe from Indian depredations, the Piscataqua leaders flourished, built great homes, and owned slaves.

The first Puritans frowned on the institution of African slavery, but it entered into the social system through custom rather than law. Blacks, though small in number, were an element of colonization from before the Indian wars. There were also a number of captive Scots sent in irons to New England as indentured servants.

The powers at Boston had become less theologically exacting as they shifted from Puritanism to Congregationalism. The new pragmatism excluded other religions but was willing to assimilate other views under the Standing Order banner.

This portrait of the wealthy Mary Pepperrell Frost (1685–1766) is one of several paintings attributed to the so-called Pepperrell-Frost Limner of about 1710. Though little is known about the artist, his presence in the Piscataqua area makes him the earliest working in the region. Aside from practical mechanics or craftsmen, including potters and blacksmiths, there were virtually no specialized artisans in colonial Maine.
COURTESY OF THE PORTSMOUTH ATHENAEUM, PORTSMOUTH, NEW HAMPSHIRE

In particular, Presbyterian immigrants were, during the uncertainty of frontier war, generally willing to worship in the Congregational fold. The pulpit became the central focus of each of the new or rebuilt towns. Supplying them were dedicated Harvard-educated ministers such as the Reverend Samuel Moody at York and later the Reverend Thomas Smith at Falmouth (formerly Casco). Ignoring theological fine points, they were more involved with building a successful community.

The Old Gaol in York was authorized in 1719, and the massive stone section was built soon after. Additions followed after 1729, when the gambrel roof and wooden walls were constructed. In its final state, it served as jail and jailor's residence. The earliest surviving public building in Maine, it is one of six structures run by the Old York Historical Society. COURTESY OF THE OLD YORK HISTORICAL SOCIETY, YORK, MAINE

Not only did such parsons stand as town spokesmen, but in the absence of professionals, they served as teachers and doctors.

Queen Anne's War lasted from 1703 to 1713 and demonstrated again the atrocities of which men are capable. Attacks were made on a variety of towns and settlements from Wells east, but this time no town was entirely destroyed. Fort New Casco, erected in 1700, now offered secure protection to Falmouth and allowed militia companies to take the offensive to the interior. Even before the outbreak of war, many Indians in Maine had evacuated to the refugee villages of St. Francis and Becancour in Quebec. In this period of movement and confusion, the term Abenaki (Wabanaki) came to refer to an overall alliance. In 1713 the French gave up claim to Acadia but continued to supply and use the Indians, especially at Norridgwock, as a guard blocking the Kennebec-Chaudière access to Quebec.

The same peace treaty allowed New England fishermen onto the Grand Banks, and Yankees, as they became known, were beginning to control much of the trade with the French West Indies. Fish and timber for sugar and molasses (later converted to rum) were the backbone of a lucrative trade system.

The mast trade, though it had a less direct impact on the local economy, played a major role in the resettling and development of Maine. As early as 1691, white pines measuring more than twenty-four inches at the butt were reserved for the Royal Navy. With decreasing supplies of mast pine in Europe, the Royal Navy had come to depend on the forests of New England. England had remained invasion-free since the time of

28   MAINE: THE WILDER HALF OF NEW ENGLAND

By law all Massachusetts towns were supposed to support a schoolmaster, but poverty ruled that out until 1701, when the town of York voted to pay Nathaniel Freeman "for one year Eight pounds in or as money and three pence per week for teaching readeing; and four pence per week for writing and sifering and no more." Other towns followed slowly. The Old Schoolhouse at York dates from around 1750 and is the site of first-rate living history programs. COURTESY OF THE OLD YORK HISTORICAL SOCIETY

The McIntire Garrison House was built in the Scotland neighborhood of York around 1707. It should, more properly, be called a "log building," for it was a home rather than a military structure. The walls of this wonderful survivor are constructed of thick, sawn logs dovetailed at the corners and sheathed in clapboards. The log house developed with the appearance of commercial lumbering in Maine. COURTESY OF THE MAINE HISTORIC PRESERVATION COMMISSION

NEW ENGLAND AND NEW FRANCE

By the outbreak of Queen Anne's War in 1702, most of the Kennebec area Indians had fled Maine for refugee villages at Becancour and Odanak in Quebec. This remarkable eighteenth-century watercolor shows an Abenaki man and woman at Becancour. The decorated cloth coats, leggings, and hoods remained typical formal garb for many Maine Indians well into the last century. COURTESY GAGNON COLLECTION, CITY OF MONTREAL LIBRARY, MONTREAL, CANADA

In 1751 Captain George Tate, Sr. (1700–1794), arrived in Falmouth (later Portland) as the mast agent for the British mast monopoly. He quickly became one of the vicinity's leading men, and in 1755 built his home above the mast landing in Stroudwater. While his predecessor had built a home nearby in 1728, it had been surrounded by a stockade and defended by cannon. Tate did not need to give thoughts to defense and built one of the region's most stylish homes. During Tate's tenure as agent, Falmouth replaced Portsmouth as the largest mast port in North America. The Tate House, now a museum, is the most tangible surviving monument to one of Maine's first great industries. COURTESY OF TATE HOUSE, NATIONAL SOCIETY OF COLONIAL DAMES OF AMERICA IN MAINE, PORTLAND, MAINE

Henry VII by virtue of the navy, and so assigned priority status to finding, cutting, and shipping the "great sticks." Surveyors-general of His Majesty's Woods and Forests marked trees, which were then cut and prepared under the eye of a mast agent. This person was not a crown official but an agent of the English mast monopoly. By the start of the Indian wars the center of the trade had moved from Massachusetts to the Piscataqua, which became a base for the Royal Navy. (In the 1690s several naval vessels were built on Badger's Island, Kittery.) By the 1720s the Boston press was demanding similar protection for Casco Bay because of its masting potential.

Protection was not the only change. Maine's English population would increase to 20,000. The number of incorporated towns also grew from eight to fifteen. Much of this increase had to do with the success of the Massachusetts government's resettlement policies following the peace of 1713 and the decimation of the Native Americans. Towns were to be resettled by at least twenty families, they were to hire a minister and a schoolmaster, and were to form a town government of elected volunteers. Everything was town-based, from the building of roads to the care of paupers. Occasionally Massachusetts sent out troops, provided a church subsidy, or sent food in time of

Sir William Pepperrell (1696–1759) was born at Kittery Point and became his father's clerk at an early age. Father and son made the family one of the greatest shipping firms in the colonies, and young William, one of Maine's great landholders, became a power in Massachusetts politics. In 1745 he led the New England forces in the capture of the French fortress at Louisbourg. The astonishing triumph of provincial arms led to his creation as a baronet, an honor never before granted to an American. COLLECTION OF THE MAINE HISTORICAL SOCIETY

The Reverend Samuel Moody (1675/76–1747) was born in Newbury, Massachusetts, and graduated from Harvard College in 1697. He came to York as a chaplain and became pastor of the church there in 1698. "Father" Moody's iron will helped turn a struggling frontier settlement into a Puritan town, and in 1745, as chaplain on the Louisbourg Expedition, he carried an axe called "the Sword of the Lord and Gideon." PHOTO BY PATRICK W. GRACE, YORK HARBOR, MAINE

famine. But such support was frowned on except in the most urgent situations.

In 1727 the General Court ordered a defensive line of townships laid out between Berwick on the New Hampshire line and Falmouth at Casco Bay. Some of these were granted to veterans of King Philip's War or their heirs (Narragansett Townships), and in 1735 a series of "Canada Townships" were deeded to survivors of the 1690 attack on Quebec.

For Falmouth (later Portland), 1727 was a year of destiny. The Reverend Thomas Smith was ordained pastor of First Parish Church, a position he would hold for sixty-eight years. Colonel Thomas Westbrook, the first business visionary, settled as an inhabitant and mast agent, and the mast trade began. Still there was quarreling as returning settlers (Old Proprietors) found their land taken by newcomers (New Proprietors). This situation remained until 1732, when the Reverend Smith wrote of their agreement: "This was the happiest meeting Falmouth ever had. Thanks to God."

32   MAINE: THE WILDER HALF OF NEW ENGLAND

John Greenwood (1727–1792) painted *Sea Captains Carousing in Surinam* around 1758. His Hogarthian, but not inaccurate, vision shows a number of New England mariners, some identifiable, in various states of drunkenness. Such acting out was difficult or impossible in the small ports of Maine, but not in the West Indies or South America. COURTESY OF THE SAINT LOUIS ART MUSEUM, ST. LOUIS, MISSOURI

As the towns took responsibility for their own destiny and grew in size, probes into the interior became more common. The village, fort, and mission at Norridgewock were raided in 1705 and 1722. In 1724 colonial troops caught Râle by surprise, destroyed the village, and sent his scalp to Boston with twenty-six others. Indeed, scalp bounties were offered by both sides and raiding parties sold shares like a stock company. In 1725 Captain John Lovewell attacked a large village near the present-day Fryeburg and was killed with fifteen of his men in an intense struggle. Generally called Dummer's or Lovewell's War, these actions were regional and not part of a larger conflict. They demonstrate a new self-confidence and aggressiveness—the mystery of the forest barrier was lessening.

War between the Indians and English was not the only violence on the frontier. In 1730 surveyor-general David Dunbar, briefly granted his own little province by the king, arrived at lumbering communities on the Sheepscot where, "with an armed force [he] turned them from their lands, seized their timber, [and] burned their settlements." Four years later his agents were driven off by an armed force when they attempted to enforce timber regulations in New Hampshire. Timber pirates cut and sold masts illegally, often with a wink from authorities. Settlers, who were supposed to leave mast-sized white pine standing, simply burned them to clear their land for farming. A number of these new Mainers were squatters on land assigned to absentees like the Kennebeck Proprietors (who bought the old Plymouth Grant in 1749) or veterans. Ownership of land remains a source of contention throughout Maine history.

In Falmouth, Colonel Thomas Westbrook became the economic center of gravity and

The Harpswell Meeting House, begun in 1757, is the oldest meetinghouse used for secular and religious purposes in Maine. Probably built by housewright Elisha Eaton, son of the first pastor, it served the sprawling community of Ancient North Yarmouth. Distinct in form from later churches, these rectangular, gable-roofed structures without steeples were common throughout the region. Generations of communicants lie in the adjacent graveyard. It is maintained by the Harpswell Historical Society. PHOTO BY GRACE TRAPPAN. COLLECTION OF WILLIAM AND DEBRA BARRY

changed the face of the town. Though functioning as mast agent for the monopoly, he served as commander of troops on the eastern frontier, speculated in land, and built mills. He founded the village of Stroudwater, where he built a fortified home and mast landings. From there he shipped the "great sticks" down the Fore River to the mast ships. These supercarriers were convoyed by the British Royal Navy to the mast ponds in England. In this respect Falmouth had become part of a true colonial system.

In order to expand, Westbrook took a partner, Samuel Waldo of Boston. They brought several craftsmen over from England and invested heavily in a papermaking operation. When the project failed, they sued each other, and in 1740, Waldo bankrupted the colonel and moved to Falmouth.

Taking over as mast agent, Waldo became the prime mover in the Muscongus (Waldo) Patent. This included part of the Dunbar Grant, and Waldo settled German immigrants at Waldoboro. His personal ambition led to the downfall of a governor and sent shockwaves throughout the region.

Waldo decided to make the most of King George's War (War of the Austrian Succession), for he had purchased the rights to the old Scottish Nova Scotia grant. In 1744 he petitioned the governor of Massachusetts to be appointed leader of an attack on the French fortress of Louisbourg at Cape Breton. Because of his personal unpopularity, Waldo had to settle for second in command under the younger William Pepperrell of Kittery. This was to be an all–New England effort led by Massachusetts, but a third of that colony's troops

34   MAINE: THE WILDER HALF OF NEW ENGLAND

Fort Western, on the banks of the Kennebec River in what is now Augusta, was built in 1754 by the Kennebeck Proprietors. Its mission was to protect the region from Indian raids that might threaten the newly planned settlements in the valley. The expensive outpost was designed by Gershom Flagg (1705–1771), who also planned Fort Shirley, Fort Pownal, and the Pownalborough Courthouse. Today, Fort Western's barracks stand as a remarkable survival of the late Indian wars. COURTESY OF THE MAINE HISTORIC PRESERVATION COMMISSION, PHOTOGRAPH BY RICHARD W. CHEEK

were Mainers. Commanding the flotilla was Edward Tyng of Falmouth, and backing him was a Royal Navy squadron. The unlikely expedition appeared off Louisbourg at the end of April 1745, and after a curiously inept siege, secured the French surrender in mid-June.

For New Englanders, the taking of the greatest fortress in North America was a tremendous exercise in confidence-building. They had done it almost single-handedly. For the chaplain, the Reverend Samuel Moody, it was the successful end of a religious crusade. For the leader there was a baronetcy, making him Sir William Pepperrell. He commissioned John Smibert to paint a full-length portrait of himself before the walls of Louisbourg. Brigadier General Waldo had an equally impressive likeness painted by Robert Feke. Mainers of all stripe, from volunteer soldiers to captains of supply vessels, gained a great sense of identity from the campaign and were much distressed when Louisbourg was returned to the French in 1748.

By the 1740s the few great merchants, including Pepperrell and Waldo, were being paralleled by smaller-scale entrepreneurs who built their own vessels, cut their own timber, and carried it to the West Indies. Family alliances were made through marriage and business, and for the first time a small measure of luxury became possible. Maine sea captains were known in a growing number of Atlantic ports, places where they were able to indulge such un-New England pastimes as drinking and gambling. (Back home, a religious revival within the Standing Order had swept through during the 1730s and 1740s.)

The Seven Years' War, which began in 1756 far from Maine, was to prove decisive in the Anglo-French contest for North America. In that year Massachusetts built Fort Halifax (now at Winslow), and the Kennebeck Proprietors erected Fort Western (now at Augusta). These were positioned for the defense of the Kennebec Valley and to stop any attack by way of the Kennebec-Chaudière corridor, and were very effective in checking advances into Maine. In 1758–1759 Governor Thomas Pownal constructed a fort (at present-day Stockton Springs) named for himself. This bastion guarded the Penobscot River from the French and helped bottle up the local Indians, now called the Penobscots. They had attempted to remain neutral, but the English insisted they take up arms against their fellow Indians. This pushed them into the French camp. It should be noted that during the building of Fort Pownal, Brigadier Waldo was seized by a fit of apoplexy, exclaimed, "Here is my bound," and died.

The English settlements suffered little damage during the war, though there were isolated attacks on places such as Windham and Meduncook (Friendship). Indeed, a number of settlements were actually made during the conflict.

In 1757 the British regulars and 500 colonials took Louisbourg again. This time they were led by Generals Amherst and Wolfe. It was Wolfe and the regular troops that began calling the Americans "Yankees" as a form of contempt. The word, cloudy in derivation, had been around for some time, but by the time of the Revolution, New Englanders embraced the term as a form of pride.

In 1755 the English authorities in Nova Scotia attempted to contain the Acadian French by making them swear an oath of allegiance. When the Acadians refused, some 6,000 men, women, and children were rounded up, put on ships, and deposited in ports from Falmouth to Boston to Louisiana. The former opened Maine's first almshouse to accommodate the eleven-member LeBlanc family. "Le Grand Derangement," as it became known, was ill planned, and many died on the voyage or in holding camps. Some managed to survive in the woods of New Brunswick, and some families walked back to Nova Scotia from Massachusetts after the Peace of Paris.

In 1759 the English made a series of decisive military moves. General Wolfe defeated General Montcalm on the Plains of Abraham, and Quebec City fell. In a bold and bloody move, Robert Rogers and his Rangers destroyed the great Abenaki village of Odanak on Quebec's St. Francis River. Over 200 men, women, and children were slain before the Rangers retreated. In 1760 the last French governor, the Marquis de Vaudreuil, surrendered. In 1763 the Treaty of Paris stripped France of all her North American possessions save the islands of St. Pierre and Miquelon and fishing rights around Newfoundland.

One of the first moves the British made after Canada was secured was to dispatch a skilled military engineer and surveyor, Lieutenant John Montresor, to explore the Kennebec-Chaudière region. In 1760 he led a party from Quebec to the Kennebec and on to Topsham. Moving on snowshoes, they endured incredible cold and hunger. He followed up this mapping trip with a journey from Quebec to the West Branch of the Penobscot in 1761. Britain was defining the edges of her new empire, and in the process helped set the eventual boundaries of Maine.

Of the Indians in the district, only an estimated 900 survived. They now formed tribes whose names became fixed. These included the Penobscots on the like-named river; the Maliseets in the interior and along the upper St. John River; the new Passamaquoddy tribe of Maliseets around the St. Croix; and Micmacs on the Nova Scotia (New Brunswick) border with Maine.

Shortly after the surrender of New France, the English military began to survey its new domain. One of the first expeditions was headed by Lieutenant John Montresor (1736–1799), who led a party from Quebec to the Kennebec in 1760 and another expedition to the Penobscot the next year. His maps of the region were later used by the American rebels. A top military engineer, Montresor spent much time on the American frontiers, served during the Revolution, and was made a colonel. His portrait was painted by John Singleton Copley (1738–1815) around 1771. COURTESY FOUNDERS SOCIETY PURCHASE, GIBBS-WILLIAMS FUND, THE DETROIT INSTITUTE OF ARTS, DETROIT, MICHIGAN

For Mainers, the end of the Seven Years' War was seen as a triumph of New England over New France, Protestantism over Catholicism. Maine, it seemed, was no longer destined to be a bloody borderland. The settlers also thought of themselves as Englishmen, in spite of occasional condescending treatment from British officials. Indeed, they had never felt so close to the mother country or its institutions. When Quebec fell, there was a Day of Thanks and the Reverend Thomas Smith wrote: "The captains of the mast ships made a great barbaque on Hog [now Diamond] Island, for a general frolic." Enoch Freeman of Falmouth composed an ode to King George III called "A New Song on the Success of 1759." It contained the deceptively edged lines: "May he defend our Laws/and ever give us Cause/to Say with Heart & Voice/God Save the King."

As a young attorney, John Adams (1735–1826) spent time riding through Maine on court business. In this pastel portrait, executed by Benjamin Blyth (1746–1787?) in 1766, Adams appears as he did on his trips to Falmouth and Pownalborough. He passed over "Roads, where a Wheel had never rolled from the Creation. . . ." Adams's generation represented the first educated group of lawyers to practice in Maine. From 1725 to 1762 the rough-and-tumble Noah Emery of Kittery pretty much had the field to himself. Once charged with calling the sheriff a fool, Emery was found guilty and fined "a pipe of tobacco." The judge then fined the sheriff "one mug of flip" for being a fool. COURTESY OF THE MASSACHUSETTS HISTORICAL SOCIETY, BOSTON

3

THE REVOLUTIONARY ERA (1763–1783)

"Contrary winds and a strong current" blew the Royal Navy sloop *Gaspee* off station in December of 1764, forcing Lieutenant Thomas Allen to put into Falmouth (later Portland) in Casco Bay. There he found, to his dismay, "Vessels arriving & sailing Daily without paying any Regard to the Regulations lately established, or without so much as taking the least note of the Custom House." Allen seized an offending vessel, but the horrified customs officials refused to act, and before the *Gaspee* could sail, a number of crewmen deserted. The lieutenant then pressed colonials into his crew, only to have his longboat seized by a mob. Forced to exchange the local crewmen for his boat, Allen struggled back to Halifax with a skeleton crew.

In an effort to pay for the Seven Years' War, the English government passed the Sugar Act, the first parliamentary law designed to raise money in the colonies for the crown. It was this regulation that Lieutenant Allen had attempted to enforce. In 1765 came the hated Stamp Act, the appearance of the Sons of Liberty, and the first in a series of crises that led to war.

Thus, a year after the Peace of Paris, colonists and English officials found a new enemy to replace the French and Indians—each other. In the ports, the point of friction was over unrestricted trade, or, as the British called it, "smuggling." Although England had trade laws in place, they were rarely enforced. Decades of salutary neglect led to a strong self-reliance among Yankee merchants and in no place did it go deeper than in the small Maine ports.

By 1760 Maine boasted some 20,000 inhabitants in fifteen towns, the largest of which was Falmouth. The solid line of settlement ran from Berwick on the New Hampshire border to the Kennebec, but extended only about twenty miles inland. A road of sorts snaked along the coast from Kittery to the Penobscot, but there was no stage service, and the postal service reached Falmouth only after 1757. Mast roads reached into the interior and were later used for transportation, but most commerce and travel moved by water, and for good reason. In 1765 attorney John Adams came to Maine on court business and recalled:

From Falmouth . . . to Pownalborough There was an entire Wilderness, except North Yarmouth, New Brunswick and Long Reach, at each of which places were a few Houses. . . . The Roads, where a Wheel had never rolled from the Creation, were miry and founderous, incumbered by long Sloughs of Water. The Stumps of Trees which had been cut to make the road all remaining fresh and the Roots crossing the path, some above ground and some beneath so that my Horse's feet would frequently get between the Roots and he would flounce and blunder, in danger of breaking his own Limbs as well as mine.

The portrait of sixteen-year-old Elizabeth Ross (1751–1831), by John Singleton Copley (1738–1815), is a rare high-style painting of a person living in Maine before the Revolution. Elizabeth was the spirited only daughter of Alexander Ross, a Falmouth merchant-shipbuilder from Scotland. Copley painted her around 1767, a year or two before her marriage to Sheriff William Tyng. As Loyalists, the Tyngs fled to New York and then to New Brunswick, and much of their property was confiscated. In the 1790s they resettled in Gorham. The Tyngs appear as characters in Kenneth Roberts's novel *Lydia Bailey* (1947). COURTESY OF M. AND M. KAROLIK COLLECTION, MUSEUM OF FINE ARTS, BOSTON

On the other hand, many frontier elements were giving way to the more cosmopolitan. In 1760 the counties of Cumberland and Lincoln joined York with elegant new courthouses appearing in the shiretowns of Pownalborough (later Dresden) and Falmouth. The latter had become the greatest masting port in North America. In 1761 its citizens built a workhouse for the poor to take care of dispersed Acadians, in 1762 the first Masonic Lodge was organized, and in 1766 a library was opened to paying members. Impressive two-and-a-half-story homes dotted the landscape from Kittery east, although most homes remained more modest. On a visit to one in Falmouth, John Adams noted: "I thought I had got into the house of a nobleman."

Adams was also impressed by the gold-laced pageantry of a York County sheriff's guard of honor, which rode out to meet the members of the Circuit Court. The large towns were all on the coast, and each had a core of merchants who owned land, built and owned vessels, traded with the West Indies, involved themselves in town business, and were generally linked to each other through marriage and trade. In an era before marine insurance, shares in a ship's cargo were sold to a number of merchants who could share in the profit or spread the loss. The loss of a vessel to privateers or weather would thus be less than disastrous. Merchants of this order had scant education, worked alongside their employees, and were much involved in local decision making. Their success was on a much lower scale than that of a Waldo or a Pepperrell, yet they dressed in scarlet cloaks with silver trim and were attended by a slave or servant during public occasions. They spent money on furnishings and, less often, on portraits. In the slack winter season, they occasionally got up sleighing parties and made the rounds of country taverns, but for the most part leisure remained unknown and unaffordable.

The most honored profession remained the

Mechios River near the Mills shows the lumber settlement of Machias, which became the easternmost hotbed of rebel activity during the Revolution. Burnham's Tavern from 1770 stands today in Machias as a reminder of that era. This image was published in 1777 and is part of DesBarres's *Atlantic Neptune*, the greatest collection of charts and plans of the North American coast published in that period. Still, as one historian noted, for all his pains, DesBarres completely omitted Northeast Harbor from his survey. COURTESY OF THE MAINE STATE MUSEUM

ministry, though attorneys and medical doctors had begun to appear. The first representatives of the latter two professions did not "have a public education," but their training continually improved. A few craftsmen, notably part-time silversmiths, appeared. Furniture, portraits, and even gravestones still came from away.

The Standing Order religion remained, though Presbyterian ministers were now replacing Congregationalists in some towns. Scots-Irish from the Ulster Plantations also made up an important part of the population. In 1765 a group of leading families in Falmouth founded an Anglican church. Aside from a Quaker meeting at Berwick in 1662 and the brief appearance of Baptists at Kittery in 1681, this was the first organized religion to flourish outside the Standing Order in established towns. Of course the Indians in old Acadia clung to the Catholic faith.

The frontier, which the Kennebeck Proprietors had so carefully nurtured during the war by building forts and bringing in settlers, provided a far richer religious blend. The Reverend Jacob Bailey, who had been ordained as an Anglican priest, in 1760 settled as a missionary at Pownalborough and found the following number of families and denominations: 25 Anglican, 23 Congregational, 15 Lutheran, 7 Catholic, 5 Presbyterian, 3 Baptist, 3 Quaker, 2 Calvinist, and 1 family with no preference. The ethnic blend included Yankees, Scots-Irish, Germans, Africans, and Huguenots.

The interior of all New England was showing signs of rapid change. The Proclamation of 1763 ruled out English settlement west of the Appalachians, thus directing New England settlers to the terra incognita of Maine, the mountains of New Hampshire, and the area that would emerge after the Revolutionary War as the Republic of Vermont. By the start of the Revolution, one fifth of New England's population lived on the Eastern Frontier. In Lincoln County and points east there were 43 settlements and 15,000 inhabitants. Indi-

Machias had been the site of various trading posts, but its real settlement began in 1763, when several men from Scarborough, Maine, came to cut hay in the marshes. In 1765 Morris O'Brien and his sons built a double sawmill. *A Sketch of Mechios Mill* was published in 1777 by J. F. W. DesBarres (1722–1824) and shows the place as it looked before the Revolution. It is probably the earliest depiction of a Maine sawmill (the first was built in York or South Berwick in 1634). COURTESY OF THE MAINE STATE MUSEUM

vidually, they ranged from poor, uneducated farm folk to those including the Reverend James Lyon, a graduate of Princeton and one of America's first published composers (*Urania*, 1761), in coastal Machias.

In the established towns, all land-holding white males shared control of local affairs through town meetings and a variety of elected offices ranging from fire-ward to hog-reeve to selectman. They imposed on themselves a variety of laws relating to hunting, fishing, keeping animals, and measuring timber. They raised taxes to build roads, schools, and bridges, sat as justices in court, and served in the militia. They were all volunteers and were used to making decisions by committee. Many of the newcomers were steeped in the same New England traditions. What this long-standing, town-based system abhorred was outside directives.

Such directives now came from two sources,

Pownalborough Courthouse was built in 1761 to serve Lincoln County, which had been established the year previous. Paid for by the Kennebeck Proprietors and built by Gershom Flagg (1705–1771), it served until Wiscasset was made the new shiretown in 1794. During its great days, the courthouse, which also served as a tavern and store, heard cases argued by John Adams and Robert Treat Paine. William Cushing, the country's first judge of the Peace and Quorum and judge of Probate, became chief justice of the Massachusetts Supreme Court in 1777 and later a U.S. Supreme Court justice. The courthouse is now a museum run by the Lincoln County Cultural and Historical Association. COURTESY OF THE MAINE HISTORIC PRESERVATION COMMISSION

British officials and absentee landholders.

The classic property holding company was the Kennebeck Purchase (the old Plymouth grant on the Kennebec). Led by such great Boston families as Gardiner, Bowdoin, Hancock, Brattle, and Apthorp, the company flourished from 1749 until its final dissolution in 1816. They faced timber pirates and squatters, fought legal battles with the surveyor-general and mast agent over the use of white pine and timber, contested other proprietors with overlapping claims, and, by the end, fought among themselves over religious and political questions. They built Pownalborough Courthouse in their company town. They evicted settlers who had no title to the land or would not meet their payments, but in the end lost the ability to control the region. Increasingly, farmers on the land resisted and joined in the revolutionary changes that were destroying proprietary control.

Farmers needed to settle quickly, clear the land, and plant crops. They did not care much for timber at first, and mast pines were a genuine problem that was dealt with by cutting and burning. Such "strip and waste" plagued proprietors and Royal officials, but it was hard to control in remote locations.

For the farmer on the land, some years proved better than others. In 1770 Moses Twitchell, the first settler in New Boston (later Gray) wrote: "The Summer before this I cut 15 load of hay but 4 loads and a half this year. I humbly pray your honers to send me sum pork and fish or else I myt be fost to sell my place to provide for my family. I owe the propryeturs sow much."

The proprietors of New Boston were also from Boston, but they were much less prominent than the Kennebeck Proprietors. They, too, wished to protect valuable tracts of timber and were appalled by "strip and waste." In the next year, the locals partly destroyed the house of a proprietary agent, and when a committee for that group met, "a Number of the Inhabitants met together in a disorderly tumultuous and riotous Manner, and carr'd a wooden Horse with four Seats, and set it before the Door of the House where the Committee had assembled, and offered other Insults and Abuses to the Committee." Such incidents were only rarely recorded, but they were part of a murky, ill-documented "Woodland Rebellion" that smoked and simmered for decades.

Other areas, such as Gorham, had entered a more lucrative phase. Elder Hugh McLellan, who had arrived in 1739, built a rude homestead. By the Revolutionary War, he owned 1,500 acres, slaves, a brick kiln, cattle that wintered on the New Hampshire border, and the county's first brick home (now on the campus of the University of Southern Maine). His timber operations were tied to Falmouth, where his McLellan cousins were ship owners and masters.

That branch of the McLellan family, along with other young, ambitious merchants, became actively involved in the cause of the Popular Party. They carried messages and goods for committees of correspondence and served on committees of inspection and safety. They carried the news of the stationing of troops in Boston (1768), the Boston Massacre (1770), the Boston Tea Party (1773), the Boston Port Bill, and the Massachusetts Government Act (1774), which led to the first Continental Congress.

The people of Falmouth and vicinity were not limited to watching. In 1767 they attacked the house of customs comptroller Arthur Savage, after he had seized a quantity of illegal rum. Finding Collector Francis Waldo there as well, the crowd adjourned to the customhouse and removed the rum. In 1771 Savage was mobbed again after he detained a schooner belonging to Sheriff William Tyng. Savage left town the next day, abandoning his elegant home, and by 1775 all customs officials were gone, save one who joined the rebels. When the Port Bill closed Boston to trade, church bells tolled all day, and communities from Berwick to

North Yarmouth sent supplies and firewood to the suffering people.

On the dark side, neighbor accused neighbor of aiding the British. In Scarborough, the well-to-do merchant Richard King was mobbed several times in 1766 and 1767 by jealous neighbors who accused him of supporting the Stamp Act. They wrecked his home and burned his papers, including their own notes of indebtedness. Though in fear, King took his neighbors to court and was ably represented by John Adams, who decried "mobocracy." But in 1774 one of King's men sold lumber to the British, and the Gorham militia marched to town and publicly humiliated King. He died early the next year leaving an impoverished family.

❖

The year 1775 proved extraordinary for Maine and the colonies. With the legality of Massachusetts government in question by the British, each town was left to act on its own, linked by committees of correspondence. The Popular Party swept local elections, and men like Judge Jonathan Sayward, who remained staunchly loyal, were ousted and placed under virtual house arrest.

The issue that finally united the back-county settlers and the maritime peoples was the mast trade. Both groups came to realize that the Royal Navy could not long function without masts. Halting the supply was a sound idea, but the rebels did so in uncoordinated and nearly disastrous ways.

In March the Falmouth merchant Thomas Coulson, a known Loyalist, was attempting to outfit his newly built mast ship *Minerva,* only to be frustrated by rebel committees who now controlled the port. Sheriff Tyng wrote for help to Vice Admiral Samuel Graves, commander in chief of the Royal Navy's North American Squadron, headquartered at Boston. Smarting from universal criticism of his weak policies and the treatment of a navy vessel at Falmouth earlier in the year, Graves dispatched Lieutenant Henry Mowat in the armed vessel *Canceaux* to bring order.

On the nineteenth of April, the shooting war began at Lexington and Concord. Maine troops and volunteers marched quickly toward the fighting, but most were turned back by officials who could not hope to supply so many. Near Bath, the rough-hewn Colonel Samuel Thompson of Brunswick started his own war by arresting the junior mast agent and effectively ending all masting in eastern Casco Bay.

The energetic Thompson had grander plans. On May 8 he landed his militia on Falmouth's Mountjoy (Munjoy) Hill, where the next day he discovered Lieutenant Mowat taking a stroll. Seizing the British captain, he made plans to destroy the *Canceaux*. Mowat's second officer threatened to bombard the town if his captain was not released.

The horrified inhabitants of Falmouth, rebel, neutral, and Tory alike, were stunned. The Woodland Rebellion had come to the seaports. Eventually Falmouth's leaders gained Mowat's parole, but his failure to return led to their own public humiliation at the hands of Brunswick and Gorham militias. "Thompson's War" ended as the *Canceaux* sailed, accompanied by the empty *Minerva*. Her cargo of masts was taken upriver and kept from the British.

As things quieted in Casco Bay, they flared up in distant Machias. That port, with its important sawmills, had been resettled in 1763. A leading merchant, Captain Ichabod Jones, appeared at Machias in company with the Royal Navy schooner *Margaretta*. He brought provisions as well as orders to bring a load of lumber to the British in Boston. The inhabitants were furious and made plans to take the navy vessel, but the commander prudently moved downriver. It would have been safer to have sailed away, for on June 12 the *Margaretta* was attacked and captured in the first naval action of the war. The rebels, some sixty in number, were "armed with guns, swords, axes,

As news of the American Revolution filtered into Europe, people eagerly sought information about events. General Benedict Arnold's march captured the popular imagination, and European engravers were quick to provide a portrait of the hero, even if they had to make one up. Once a portrait appeared, it was quickly copied by others in France, England, and Germany. This etching was produced at Nürnberg in 1777–1778. In 1831 former vice president Aaron Burr, who was part of this expedition, presented the Maine Historical Society with Arnold's Letter Book. Arnold (1741–1801) later betrayed the rebel cause, but found an apologist in twentieth-century Maine novelist Kenneth Roberts. COURTESY OF THE LIBRARY OF CONGRESS, WASHINGTON, D.C.

and pitchforks" and led by Captains Jeremiah O'Brien and Benjamin Foster. The British lieutenant, James Moore, was slain along with several of his men and two Yankees. Soon after, O'Brien and Foster went after the British schooner *Diligence* and her tender, known to be in the area. They captured both and sent the prisoners and smaller vessels to Falmouth. O'Brien's sloop, christened *Liberty*, and the *Diligence* were commissioned privateers by the state government.

On the grand scale, Ethan Allen had taken Fort Ticonderoga, the Second Continental Congress was meeting at Philadelphia, and on June 15 George Washington was appointed chief of the Continental forces.

The general arrived at Cambridge in July. Since the British were threatening from Canada, it was decided to attack Quebec. General Richard Montgomery marched from Lake Champlain, and General Benedict Arnold was to lead 1,100 men through Maine by way of the Kennebec and Chaudière Rivers. With copies of Montresor's maps, Arnold's troops left Newburyport, Massachusetts, in mid-September and sailed for Maine. The troops included such soon-to-be famous names as Aaron Burr, Daniel Morgan, and Henry Dearborn.

Proceeding from Fort Western (now Augusta), they began one of the most arduous and numbing marches in American history. They set out in 200 hastily built bateaux, which were alternately paddled and carried depending on river depth. By mid-October they entered Long Carry, between the Kennebec and Dead Rivers, where the weather turned to rain. The swampy land became flooded, boats were capsized, and much materiel was lost. Desertions began, including the withdrawal of a whole division. Those who continued faced snow, near starvation, and the fury of the Chaudière before reaching friendly French-Canadian settlements.

It was not until November 13 that Arnold crossed the St. Lawrence, and December until Montgomery appeared. On the 31st they assaulted Quebec only to have Montgomery killed, Arnold wounded, and 400 men captured, killed, or wounded. Out of this disaster Montgomery and Arnold emerged as heroes. In fact, one of the only nonsatirical plays written during and about the Revolution was Hugh Henry Brackenridge's *The*

Death of General Montgomery (Providence, 1777). In the play, Arnold's lines include: "While up the rapid Kennebec, they stem'd,/The impetuous torrent, or at the carrying place,/O'er broad morass, deep swamp, and craggy wild,/Urg'd their rough way. Thence over hill,/And dreary mountain top, to where Chaudière/Doth mix his wave, with the St. Lawrence tide." Though hardly deathless prose, these words are perhaps the earliest mention of Maine in a theatrical production.

While Arnold and his army were slogging through the grim wilderness, the largest town in Maine was engulfed in flames. Admiral Samuel Graves, tired of criticism from all quarters, determined to act decisively. On October 6 he ordered Lieutenant Mowat and a small flotilla to make "the most vigorous Efforts to burn the Towns" (Marblehead, Newburyport, Cape Ann, Ipswich, Portsmouth, Saco, Falmouth, and Machias), "and destroy the Shipping in the Harbors." Cape Ann's buildings were too widely scattered to burn. Then an intense wind carried the flotilla all the way down east to Boothbay.

On the 16th the four vessels arrived off Falmouth Neck and the next day took up position. Mowat sent an ultimatum stating his intentions and ordering the people to leave. A committee of rebels and Tories negotiated, and Mowat agreed that if all arms and ammunition were given up, he would obtain fresh instructions from Graves. The townspeople refused, and on October 18, a blood-red flag was run up to signal a sustained bombardment of the closely packed settlement. The British landed and put structures to the torch. In the end, some 400 buildings, including about 130 houses, St. Paul's Church, the courthouse, the library, a distillery, and the stores and wharves were lost. With winter coming on, people fled inland to stay with relatives or friends. Indeed, while some people remained to make the port work throughout the war, no residential building occurred until after the peace.

In the sweep of Maine history, no man has come in for more abuse than Lieutenant Henry Mowat (1734–1798), the Royal Navy officer who directed the bombardment and burning of Falmouth on October 18, 1775. As Parson Samuel Deane said of him: "If you do not like the words *execrable Scoundrel*, you may say, infamous *incendiary*. . . ." Though kidnapped by rebels earlier in the year, Mowat was following the orders of Admiral Samuel Graves, and almost certainly not seeking revenge. Later, at Bagaduce, his squadron kept a superior rebel fleet at bay until Admiral George Collier arrived to destroy it. Promoted to post captain after the war, Mowat died commanding a ship and is buried at Cape Henry, Virginia. COLLECTION OF THE MAINE HISTORICAL SOCIETY

The bombardment of the town sparked outrage on both sides of the Atlantic, primarily because the navy had not previously burned a largely white, English-speaking town before. "A few more of such flaming arguments, as were exhibited at Falmouth and Norfolk" (the Virginia

THE REVOLUTIONARY ERA 47

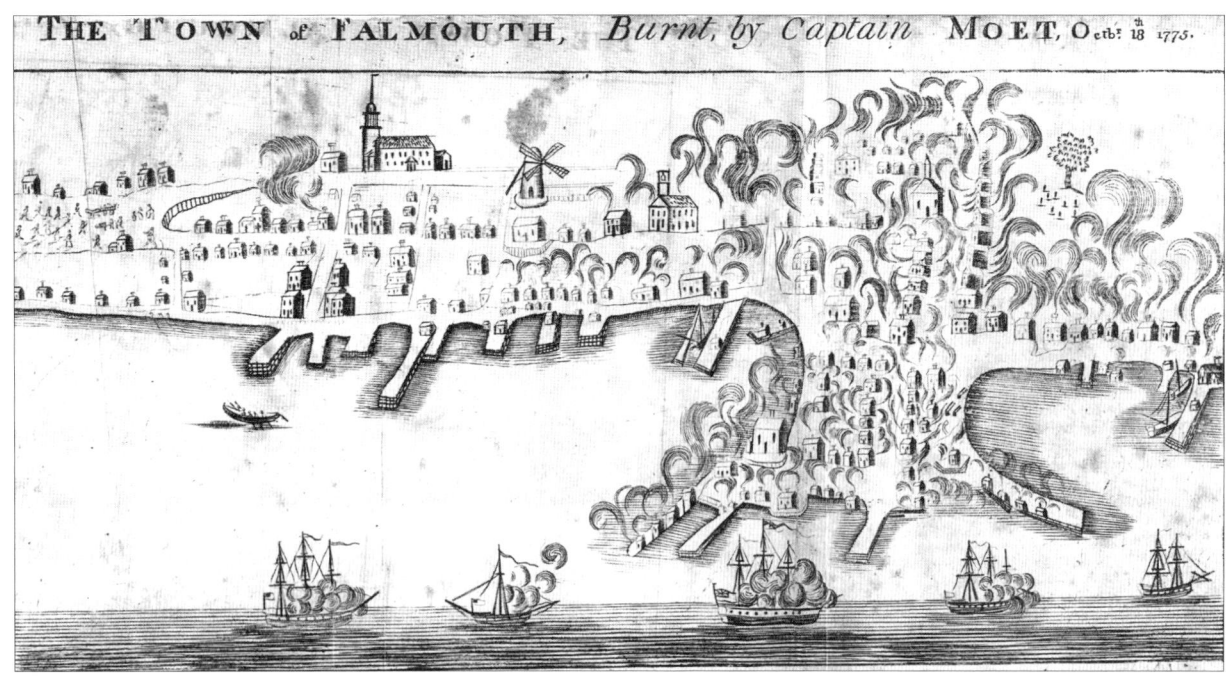

The Town of Falmouth, Burnt by Captain Moet, October 18, 1775 appeared as an illustration in James Murray's *An Impartial History of the War in America* (Boston: 1782). Probably the earliest image of the town, it shows the burning of the compact part of town around King (now India) Street, people saving their belongings, First Parish meetinghouse (Old Jerusalem), top left near windmill, and Eastern Cemetery, top right. Of the bombardment, General Washington wrote: "I know not how sufficiently to detest it."
COURTESY OF THE JOHN CARTER BROWN LIBRARY, PROVIDENCE, RHODE ISLAND

town burned during a retreat in December), noted the pamphlet *Common Sense*, "will not leave numbers at a loss to decide upon the propriety of a separation." The French foreign minister saw the bombardment as a move of "furious and boundless Despair," and the *New England Chronicle* noted that the "savage and brutal barbarity" would probably lead to a "break off of all kinds of connection with Britain. . . ." The raid also led to the makeshift building of coastal redoubts and forts.

Because they were expert seamen, the obvious way for Mainers to strike back was with privateers (privately owned vessels commissioned in war by the state or Congress to capture or destroy enemies) or letters of marque (privately owned merchant vessels authorized to do the same). For her relative size, Maine made an important contribution to the war effort. Some thirty-odd vessels sailed from Machias, Frenchman's Bay, Falmouth, York, Bristol, Saco, Kittery, and Boothbay. Local captains also journeyed to Boston, Newburyport, and Salem to take command of privateers owned in those ports.

Most of these efforts were funded by the selling of shares to members of the public, who would receive a portion of the spoils. Each colony, or state after 1776, kept a navy, and Congress created a Continental Navy. Since one of the greatest protected sources of pine lay along the Piscataqua, four Continental vessels were built along the river. Among them was the eighteen-gun sloop *Ranger*, built on Badger's Island, Kittery, in 1777. Commanded by John Paul Jones, she took many prizes and became the first man-of-war to fly the new

This painful image by John Trumbull (1756–1843) is believed to show the inhuman conditions aboard the prison hulk *Jersey*, off New York. Thousands of rebel seamen died aboard such vessels, and Daniel Tucker, a young Maine privateersman, noted: "Our most alarming apprehensions were of being imprisoned on board the old Jersey prison ship." Three members of the McLellan family alone were inmates (one died, two escaped), and young Edward Preble also found himself a captive. A Loyalist, former Sheriff Tyng was living in New York at the time and brought food, clothing, and money to his former neighbors on the *Jersey*. No one who survived forgot the horrors. COURTESY OF THE CHARLES ALLEN MUNN COLLECTION, FORDHAM UNIVERSITY LIBRARY, BRONX, NEW YORK

American flag and to be saluted by a foreign power.

The Kittery side of the Piscataqua also produced Maine's signer of the Declaration of Independence, William Whipple. A sea captain, Whipple had removed to Portsmouth at the age of twenty-nine, becoming a major slave ship captain and later a brigadier general of the New Hampshire troops and a judge of the superior court. Among other locals making important contributions were Brigadier Jedediah Preble, who declined his appointment as commander in chief of Massachusetts forces in 1775 because of age, but served in the General Court and became Cumberland County's first senator under the Constitution of 1780. Samuel Freeman joined the Falmouth Committee of Correspondence in 1775 and embarked on a career that took him to the Provincial Congress and the courts. James Sullivan, a native of Berwick, also won election to the Provincial Congress, became a judge of the superior court, and in 1783 was elected to the Continental Congress.

❖

After the excitement of 1775, Revolutionary-War

General William Whipple (1730–1785), the only Maine native to sign the Declaration of Independence, was born in Kittery. He went to sea at an early age and engaged in the slave trade. In 1760, he moved to Portsmouth. A member of the Continental Congress from 1776 to 1779, Whipple also commanded troops at Saratoga and served as a New Hampshire associate justice. Based on an earlier likeness, this portrait by Ulysses Dow Tenney (b. 1826), hangs in Portsmouth's Moffat-Ladd House where the general once lived. The John S. H. Fogg autograph collection at the Maine Historical Society, given by a native of Eliot, Maine, includes one of thirty-six sets of signatures of the signers of the Declaration of Independence. It is a singular state treasure. COURTESY OF THE NATIONAL SOCIETY OF COLONIAL DAMES OF AMERICA IN THE STATE OF NEW HAMPSHIRE

General Peleg Wadsworth (1748–1839) was a native of Duxbury, Massachusetts, and received both a B.A. and M.A. from Harvard. He came to Maine as second-in-command of the army troops in the disastrous Penobscot Expedition, where he acquitted himself well. In 1780 he was put in command of "the Eastern Parts." Well-liked by the rebels from Falmouth east, General Wadsworth proclaimed martial law and became virtual dictator of the Kennebec and Penobscot region. In 1781 he was kidnapped from his home in Thomaston, wounded in a shootout, and taken to Fort George (Castine). He managed to escape, but the war was virtually over. He moved to Falmouth where he ran a store, built a brick house (the Wadsworth–Longfellow House), began the fight for statehood, and was elected to many offices, including Congress. In 1807 he retired to his new home in Hiram. COLLECTION OF THE MAINE HISTORICAL SOCIETY

50 MAINE: THE WILDER HALF OF NEW ENGLAND

Engraving of *The Battle of the Penobscot in 1779*, after the painting by the great British marine painter Dominic Serres (1722–1793), captures the drama of the worst American naval defeat prior to Pearl Harbor. On August 14, 1779, Sir George Collier swept up behind the Massachusetts forces as they besieged Bagaduce (now Castine). Some forty rebel vessels ran upriver, where they were destroyed or lost. During the Bicentennial of the American Revolution, a number of organizations combined to excavate the privateer brig *Defence*, burned by her crew in Stockton Springs Harbor. Many of her wonderfully preserved artifacts are at the Maine State Museum in Augusta. COLLECTION OF THE MAINE HISTORICAL SOCIETY

Maine became a sideshow of greater events occurring in New York and points south. There were, however, occasional flashes of action. In 1776 Colonel Jonathan Eddy, a Nova Scotian refugee at Machias, gathered a force of Mainers, Indians, and Acadians and besieged Fort Cumberland in Nova Scotia. Vessels were taken and homes looted, but within twenty days British reinforcements scattered the invaders. This was the last attempt to enlist Nova Scotia as the fourteenth colony.

Colonel John Allan now took over the rebel forces in their attempt to hold the New Brunswick area and eastern Maine. In the six long years that followed, Allan was driven out of the St. John Valley, but as Massachusetts' Indian agent, he was most effective. In fact, the tribes were almost unanimously allied with the Americans. Among the Indian rebels were Orono of the Penobscots, Francis Joseph Neptune of the Passamaquoddy, Michael Augustine of the Micmacs, and Ambrose Bear of the Maliseets.

In 1777 Sir George Collier attacked Machias with three men-of-war and a sloop but was repulsed by a well-prepared force of settlers and Indians. As one townsman put it: "Great credit is due to the Indians for their rigid adherence to our cause; although at times the Commissary department was destitute of provisions and clothing for them."

In June of 1779, the British under General Francis McLean occupied Bagaduce, or Majabigwaduce (now Castine). There, guarding the Penobscot, he built Fort George and filled it with 700 men. They were joined by Dr. John Calef and a group of Tories. It was Calef's dream to foreshorten the borders of Yankeeland by cutting the

THE REVOLUTIONARY ERA

District of Maine in two. By holding the Penobscot, the British could check privateering raids and plant enough Loyalists (now scattered from New York to Halifax to London) to build a Royal colony to be called New Ireland.

Much alarmed, the Massachusetts General Court made bold to retake Bagaduce. To do this they assembled ships of their own navy, the Continental Navy, and privateers. They also requisitioned a number of transports, making a fleet some forty-five strong. The ships were commanded by Commodore Dudley Saltonstall and the 1,500 troops by General Solomon Lovell. After a promising first attack, the leadership of the rebel forces became divided on how to attack Fort George. Thus, from July 25 to August 14 they carried on a feeble siege. On the final day, Admiral Collier's British squadron swept up behind the Americans, driving them upriver where they were taken or destroyed. It was the worst American naval defeat until Pearl Harbor, and Saltonstall and commander-of-artillery Paul Revere had to face court-martial. The commodore was dismissed and Revere's proceedings failed to convict or acquit him. Lovell and his second-in-command, General Peleg Wadsworth, received high praise and the latter was put in charge of "the defence of the Eastern parts."

Massachusetts was bankrupted by the Battle of the Penobscot and could exercise little control

Lieutenant Jones of the Royal Navy sketched *A Southeast View of Fort George with the Peninsula and Harbor of Majabigwaduce* in 1780. The British had taken Bagaduce (now Castine) in the previous year, built Fort George, and repulsed a rebel invasion. For the rest of the war, the British divided Maine by controlling the Penobscot River and by sending out Tory privateers. Dr. John Calef and other Loyalists proposed a Royal Colony of New Ireland to terminate the Yankee border at the Penobscot, but eventually had to settle for the St. Croix and New Brunswick. SOURCE UNKNOWN, LIBRARY OF CONGRESS PHOTO-REPRODUCTION

in the district. The coast was a disaster. Early in the war, Massachusetts had ordered the evacuation of the Isles of Shoals. Some houses were rafted to the mainland and some inhabitants remained, supported by the state for their natural lives. The British uprooted the settlement at Belfast and burned Bucksport. British privateers made continual raids, as did Americans. Food was often scarce, even at Falmouth, and attempts at government price-fixing failed. When a British cartel ship under a flag of truce stranded on Cape Elizabeth in 1780, it was picked clean by leading rebels. In spite of warrants for the leaders' arrests, all got away with the deed.

Clearly, the war was in its degenerative phase. In the spring of 1780, General Wadsworth took charge at Thomaston, proclaimed martial law, and hanged a man who had aided the Tories. Thus began a nasty era in which inhabitants were pulled from their beds by armed men and charged with "treasonable & Inimical practices." This happened to Francis Rittal and Thomas Towns at Pownalborough at the hands of a rebel company, and to Wadsworth at the hands of the British. Armed with "a pair of pistols, blunderbuss, and a fusee," the general resisted, but was shot and taken to jail at Bagaduce. A month later, on March 4, 1781, a Falmouth rebel privateer raided the

This bland piece of paper is a bill of sale for a slave. Needing to equip himself for the siege of Penobscot in 1779, Captain Alexander McLellan of Gorham sold a twenty-one-year-old man named Primus to James Deering of Falmouth. In a democratic outburst, some owners freed their slaves, but others did not. Black Mainers, including London Atus, Romeo Smith, Cato Shattuck, and Prince and Plato McLellan, fought alongside white neighbors on land and sea. Still, it was not until the Massachusetts Supreme Court heard the Quock Walker case in 1783 that the hated institution was abandoned. COURTESY OF THE PORTLAND MUSEUM OF ART, PORTLAND, MAINE

THE REVOLUTIONARY ERA   53

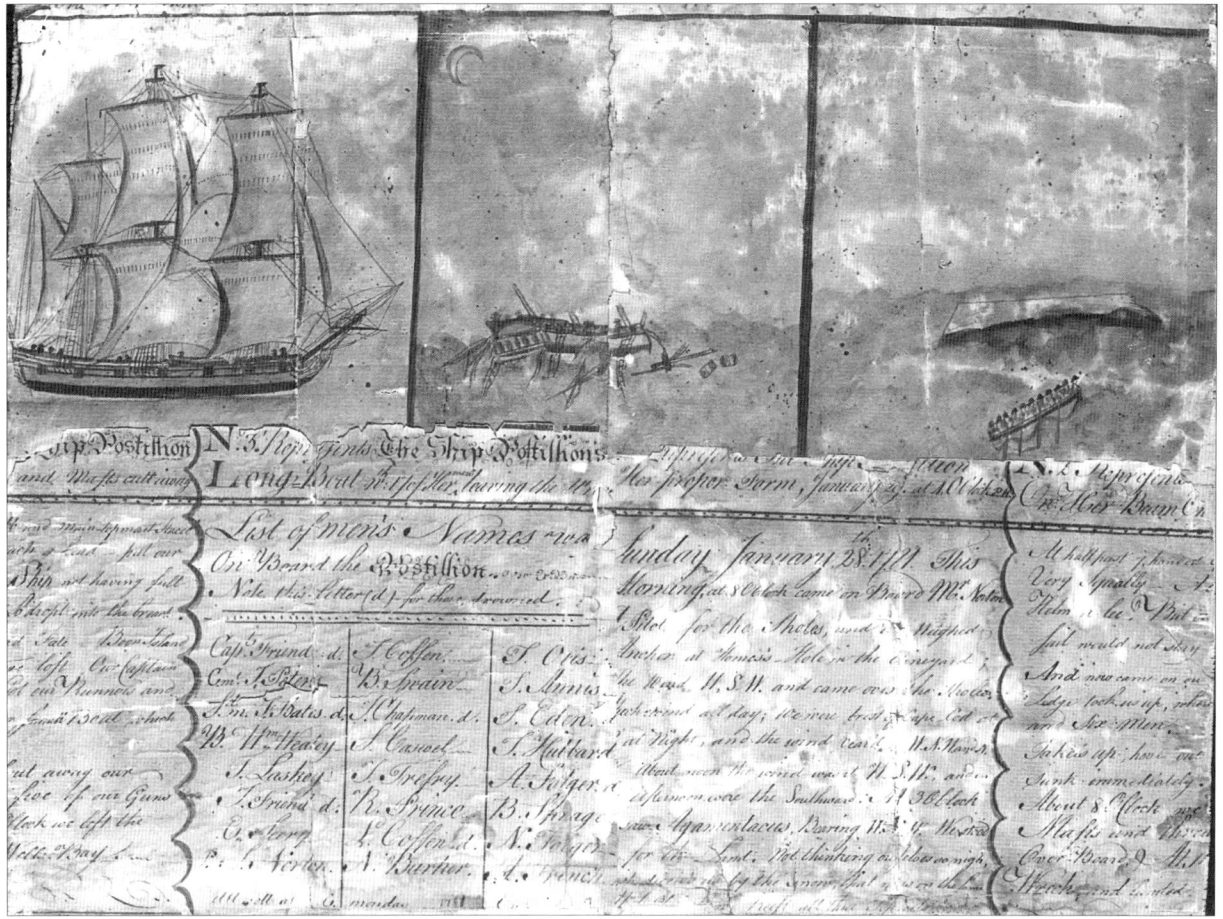

Even during wartime, wind and weather could be as tricky and punishing as the enemy. Although most of the coastal towns were devastated during the Revolutionary conflict, some vessels survived both the war and the weather. Some were engaged in purely military roles; most were a combination of merchantman and warship. A storm off Wells Beach in 1781 took the ship *Postillion* of Salem, snapped her masts, and turned her over. The painting, attributed to Ashley Bowen of Massachusetts, shows her before, during, and after the disaster. Such rigors were faced often by common seamen in the age of sail. COURTESY OF THE PEABODY MUSEUM OF SALEM, SALEM, MASSACHUSETTS

neutral settlement at Deer Isle, beat up an elderly man, and looted the settlement. A few weeks later, a group of inhabitants living between the Penobscot and St. Croix petitioned the General Court for a regional act of neutrality. In spite of war-weariness, the rebels at Machias squelched the movement. In June General Wadsworth made his famous escape from Castine, and though cheered by his neighbors at Thomaston, he could do little to continue the struggle. In October more promising news reached Maine: General Cornwallis had surrendered his army at Yorktown.

❖

Interior Maine suffered very little warfare except an Indian raid on Sudbury Canada (later Bethel) in August of 1781. This was undertaken by Indians from St. Francis, Quebec, and was the last raid on New England. Other places such as Fryeburg, the

54   MAINE: THE WILDER HALF OF NEW ENGLAND

first White Mountain town to be settled, grew and prospered. The town was one of several incorporated during the war. It seems astonishing that in spite of thousands of young Mainers serving aboard privateers, and in places from Quebec to Valley Forge to Yorktown and the West Indies, the population actually grew. According to one source, Maine began with 29,100 inhabitants in 1772, had 42,300 in 1777, and ended up with 53,321 in 1784.

Whatever the exact population, great changes were occurring. The hinterland was already filling up with new settlers seeking inexpensive public or private land on which to start a new life and raise a family. Eliot gained Maine's first Quaker meetinghouse in 1776. The older established towns such as Falmouth saw great changes as well. The traditional leading families lost, with few exceptions, their economic dominance. Some became Loyalists and fled, leaving their property to be confiscated. Those who stayed with the patriot cause saw a virtual end to the West Indies trade; most lost vessels and others property in the Bombardment of Falmouth. A generation of young go-getters with nothing to lose and everything to gain quickly filled abandoned political, social, and economic niches. In this respect there had been a true revolution—the whole economic and social structure had been turned on end.

As early as 1774, the Gorham Committee of Correspondence ended a resolve as follows: "We conclude by wishing every kind of Happiness & Prosperity to the friends of our country White or Black." In the atmosphere of liberty, several slaves were apparently freed. Others were allowed to enlist, at least one on condition he return half-pay to his former master. There was no color line, and Maine blacks served at Valley Forge and Machias, on privateers, and in the Continental Navy. Still, the institution of slavery remained until 1783, when the Massachusetts Court ruled in favor of Quock Walker, who claimed he was not property.

Maine Indians were largely responsible for keeping eastern Maine in rebel hands. Without their assistance, the border might well have been drawn at the Penobscot instead of the St. Croix. Yet they were soon confined to small areas so as not to interfere with settlement. By the end of the war, noted Louis Clinton Hatch, an early twentieth-century historian, "the Indians of Maine cease to be of political importance." Along with nearly every other observer, he was premature in that judgment, but certainly the Indians benefited the least from the Revolution.

The Peace of Paris was signed on January 20, 1783. Among the agreements was a border line that included the "height-of-land" as the boundary with Quebec and the St. Croix as a border with Nova Scotia. Within a short time, surveying teams were scurrying through the forests arguing about the meaning of the height-of-land and the location of the St. Croix. Dr. Calef's dream of New Ireland vanished, but members of the Penobscot Loyalist Organization and other Tory groups were settling on the St. Croix at St. Andrews. In 1784 the Province of New Brunswick was set off from Nova Scotia, finally dividing ancient Acadia. In the reorganization of British North America, the crown resettled hundreds of Loyalists on the borders of Yankeeland.

Though the British had been defeated, Massachusetts still dominated the district politically and economically. The Revolutionary War had been difficult for Mainers, but in surviving it, the inhabitants gained a new self-confidence. Many go-getters predicted that statehood for Maine was just around the corner. In fact, self-determination and separation from the Bay State took another forty years of struggle.

THE REVOLUTIONARY ERA

This "Fortune's Temple" lottery sign marked Major William Francis's Portland office around 1820. As great numbers of people began to arrive in Maine, men such as Francis, a land dealer, opened money lotteries. In 1784 Massachusetts had started a land lottery, and a few years after statehood, Maine began a state lottery to raise money for the Cumberland and Oxford Canal completion. The gambling instinct was strongest among immigrants. COLLECTION OF THE MAINE HISTORICAL SOCIETY

4

THE STRUGGLE FOR STATEHOOD (1783–1820)

"If we [the inhabitants of Maine] were injured, it mattered not by whom, whether by the Government of Britain or of Massachusetts, in either case duty to ourselves required immediate exertion," explained the leaders of Maine's first movement to separate from Massachusetts. On October 5, 1785, such established figures as General Peleg Wadsworth, Judge William Gorham, Stephen Longfellow, Jr., and the Reverends Thomas Smith and Samuel Deane met at Falmouth's First Parish meetinghouse to push for statehood. Though backed by the district's first newspaper, the *Falmouth Gazette* (founded 1785), the plan gained little support beyond Cumberland County. A deep and widespread desire for statehood only gradually came to predominate, as inhabitants built their towns and faced mutual challenges. Still, of all the issues faced in the period, statehood was the most recurring.

At the close of the Revolutionary War, Maine was largely a geographic term. It had some political identity as one of Massachusetts' three electoral districts, but the first political loyalty of the inhabitants was to town. Maine may have been among the earliest settled portions of New England, but its people rarely considered the idea of "ourselves" or "Maine's." They were Machiasmen, Gorhamites, or Kennebunkers. Almost as large as the other New England states combined, Maine had few roads and a scattered population. Most transportation was by water, and it was not until 1795 that a regular stage route ran from Boston to Portland.

Massachusetts, Connecticut, Rhode Island, and New Hampshire were all legitimate states under the Articles of Confederation. Vermont, though settled after 1760, had emerged from the war as a unified republic boasting its own government, army, and coinage. No such unity existed down east, a term which was coming into vogue and denoted sailing downwind from Boston. Legally, socially, and economically the towns of Maine remained linked to "the Bay."

There were also more localized attachments. The people of Kittery and Berwick gravitated to Portsmouth and the Piscataqua, just as those in Eastport and Lubec would soon interact with the Canadian side of the St. Croix. On the Kennebec and Penobscot, squatters, speculators, and Indians all looked to Boston. On the upper St. John River, Acadian settlers, distancing themselves from land-hungry Loyalists, looked to the St. Lawrence and thought of themselves as distinct from everyone else. The increasingly heterogeneous people of Falmouth were animated by a new sense of themselves as a phoenix rising from the ashes of the British bombardment. Their adventurous merchants were founding new markets and building a new infrastructure. Their leaders believed themselves destined to run Maine, and a newspaper poem in 1785 imagined Falmouth as "the mistress of a rising State." On July 4, 1786, the Neck, or

57

Taverns were an integral part of the countryside from the earliest days. They served as places of lodging and victualing as well as points of public gathering. Nearly all served as home to the innkeeper, whose trade was one of the few open to both men and women. The Black Horse Tavern in East Belfast was built in 1800 for Jerome Stephenson. Its well sweep, which survived long into the twentieth century, was an object once common along Maine's roads. Today's Seaside Inn in Kennebunkport, the fifth-oldest family-owned business in the nation, was licensed in 1667 and is run by the twelfth generation. COURTESY OF THE MAINE HISTORIC PRESERVATION COMMISSION

commercial heart of Falmouth, became the new town of Portland, and within a few years, it was the sixth largest port in the United States.

Other portions of Maine developed in different ways for different reasons. As noted, the Acadians lived a subsistence life on land granted them by the British, who thought of them as a buffer to Yankee expansion in a territory soon contested by Maine and New Brunswick. The Passamaquoddy were granted land in Washington County, and the Penobscots were given several townships, Indian Island, and some small holdings on the Penobscot River. Most observers felt that since they numbered only about 600, the Indians would eventually be assimilated into the larger American culture. The state government provided for them as objects of charity. Indeed, the origins of what became Maine's Health and Welfare Agency group can be traced back to the Division of Indian Affairs inherited from Massachusetts.

Groaning under a debt of almost three million pounds, the authorities in Massachusetts proper looked to the wild lands of Maine as a source of fiscal salvation. As early as 1783, Governor John Hancock, who had trading connections and a warehouse at York, Maine, suggested the sale of land in place of new taxes. Even earlier, a committee for land sales had been charged with the oversight of roughly 17 million acres in the District of Maine. Between 1785 and 1786, some 100,000 acres had been sold, and the following year a land lottery was tried. Too few took the gamble, so

General Henry Knox (1750–1806), hero of the Revolution and secretary of war, inherited and purchased vast land holdings in Maine. In 1793 he hired Ebenezer Dunton to design and build "Montpelier," an impressive country home at Thomaston. Standing above the St. George River, as shown in this innocent view, the structure became the center for Knox's business and the scene of lavish entertainment. Torn down in 1871, it was re-created on a new site in 1929–1930 and run by the State of Maine. The General Henry Knox Museum is now under private management. COLLECTION OF THE MAINE HISTORICAL SOCIETY

after 1790 large tracts were sold to speculators. However, most of the big speculators found "settling duties" expensive and squatters already in place. Other grants of public land were made to colleges, academies, medical societies, veterans, and even fledgling industries. Badly run and poorly organized, the Bay State's land policy caused endless legal difficulties.

Maine was the promised land, or seemed that way, and between 1783 and 1820, its population grew from 56,000 to an astonishing 300,000. This 450 percent rise meant that newcomers outnumbered native-born. The new people came from a variety of backgrounds. Some had little dreams; others had big dreams.

Three secretaries of war sought their fortune in post-Revolutionary Maine. General Benjamin Lincoln of Massachusetts served in that office from 1781 until the Treaty of Paris. He engaged in the speculation of wild lands and was nearly bankrupted, but had better luck as one of the treaty commissioners meeting with the Penobscots in 1784 and 1786. General Henry Dearborn first saw Maine on Arnold's march, and for his service was given 5,225 acres in what became Monmouth. He lived the life of a country squire until appointed secretary of war under Jefferson. His daughter, Julia, married General Joshua Wingate, a Hallowell merchant and Maine politician. The third secretary of war was General Henry Knox, a former bookseller turned Washington's chief-of-artillery. He resigned from Washington's cabinet to take

THE STRUGGLE FOR STATEHOOD 59

charge of developing his Maine lands. Henry had married Brigadier Waldo's granddaughter, Lucy Flucker, the only heir to side with the rebels. Their holdings totaled 578,000 acres along Penobscot Bay, and they constructed a great country home, "Montpelier," at Thomaston. It was, in Talleyrand's estimate, "handsome even for Europe."

From his seat at Montpelier, the corpulent, ambitious, but rather inept Knox began to speculate and build. He constructed lime and brick kilns, lumbermills, gristmills, and shipyards, and raised prize sheep and cattle. He sent surveyors throughout his realm, and when he found squatters, he tried to settle with them at reduced rates. For those who had money, it was a good deal, but many had nothing. Between 1793 and 1801 squatters, led at first by the preacher-agitator Samuel Ely, battled back, attacking agents, burning mills, and cutting log booms. But in the end, most of the claims were settled legally.

Always financially overextended, the general borrowed money from one of America's richest men, Senator William Bingham of Philadelphia. Though he visited Maine only once, Bingham was dazzled by the potential of the woods and bought some 3 million acres on the Kennebec and in Washington County. Little or no profit was realized from the huge speculations. Eventually some timberland was profitable to Bingham's heirs, the British House of Barring. They, at least, broke even with their land. When Knox died in 1806, he was insolvent, but his widow lived on at "Montpelier" in decaying splendor until her death in 1859.

Little dreams often clashed with grand ones. Indeed, Knox was not alone in facing the continued Woodland Rebellion. The most celebrated clash came in 1809 at Malta (now Windsor). A surveyor for the Kennebeck Proprietors was shot and killed. Seven men were arrested and taken to Augusta, but an armed mob dressed as Indians attempted to storm the jail. The attack was stopped, but later the men were acquitted. Within a few years the violence subsided, for there was increased legislative support for people on the land. As early as 1807 the Betterment Act was passed to protect settlers established on land for six years or more. A jury was empowered to determine the value of the property before and after it was occupied. The proprietor could then sell to the tenant at the original price or buy it at the new. The land war was largely confined to old Lincoln County with its overlapping proprietary grants.

Between the Revolution's end and the achievement of statehood, the number of incorporated towns doubled and the infusion of settlers radically changed the shape of the environment. In this age of possibilities, six new counties were formed: Washington (1789), Hancock (1789), Kennebec (1799), Oxford (1805), Somerset (1809), and Penobscot (1816). The most distant points of settlement were Houlton, settled by Massachusetts families in 1807, and Eastport (then the most eastern port in the United States), which was incorporated in 1798. Shiretowns (county seats) such as Wiscasset, Castine, and Paris Hill became prosperous places boasting courthouses, jails, and public buildings. York, once the capital of Maine, declined as a port and was replaced as county shiretown by the flourishing agricultural town of Alfred in 1802.

Most Maine farms continued to be hardscrabble affairs, one man recalling he began with a good axe and a hundred acres of land to which he had no title. Farmers grew barley, wheat, rye, oats, and Indian corn; they kept cattle and sheep, using oxen for work, and on occasion, a horse. Some grew flax for clothing. The older towns, with more settled farms, occasionally had surpluses which they took to market in Portland, and by the end of the era, wagonloads of products also arrived in Portland from northern New Hampshire and Vermont.

Woodlots proved a godsend for some farmers. In winter, a farmer and his family could cut timber for the growing number of sawmills, or harvest hemlock bark for the hundreds of tanneries, which also sought hides. There was a need for specialization in the backcountry, particularly blacksmiths, coopers, and wheelwrights. Barter and labor exchange remained parts of the whole economy, a topic well covered in Kevin D. Murphy's *Jonathan Fisher of Blue Hill, Maine* (Amherst, 2010).

Lumbering was the largest occupation east of Portland, with some seventy sawmills on the Kennebec alone. Many cutters were part-time, but others lived from payday to payday, with prices being fixed by Boston merchants. The traveler Dr. Timothy Dwight saw these men as given to "prodigality, thoughtlessness of future wants, profaneness, irreligion, immoderate behavior, and other ruinous habits." He noted that a hundred acres of wood could keep a family going for years without turning to the more civilized way of farming. The sawmills were insatiable, and by 1800 many coastal towns, including Belfast and Meduncook (Friendship), were nearly depleted of lumber and cordwood.

Religion, however, played a crucial role in the lives of most of the new arrivals from southern New England. Such people favored the newer revivalist denominations as opposed to the old Standing Order. Within a short time, Separate Baptists, Catholics, Freewill Baptists, Methodists, Quakers, Universalists, Shakers, Buzzelites, and Cocranites colored the once-bland religious scene. Politically, such people tended to be Jeffersonian (Democrat-Republican) as opposed to Federalist, and by 1805 they dominated the political life of the district. Men such as Dr. Moses Mason at Bethel took seriously their role in helping to govern, and not only controlled town government but went on to forge district-wide affiliations.

Largely ignored by the rest of Maine was the borderland Madawaska Territory on the upper St. John. The first Acadian families arrived by canoe in 1785 and were welcomed by the French-speaking Catholic Maliseet Indians. They soon established connections with Québecois in nearby areas, laid out their farms in long strips, trapped fur, lumbered on a small scale, and raised buckwheat, oats, and potatoes. In 1797 there was a famine brought on by early frost and floods. During this period the activity of Marguerite Blanche

During his many years as co-pastor of First Parish Church in Falmouth, the Reverend Samuel Deane (1733–1814) witnessed, recorded, and participated in momentous social changes. When he began his career, the Standing Order Ministry was supported by taxes and brooked no rivals, while in later years there were many self-supporting Christian faiths. Deane left an important diary, a major agricultural study, and was among the first to seek statehood for Maine. John Brewster, Jr. (1766–1859), a deaf artist who later settled in Buxton, shows the minister still wearing a powdered wig late in the Federal Period. COLLECTION OF THE MAINE HISTORICAL SOCIETY

THE STRUGGLE FOR STATEHOOD   61

St. Patrick's Church (1807–1808) in Damariscotta Mills was the heart of Maine's first Irish community and is the oldest extant Catholic Church in New England. Beginning around 1790, James Kavanagh and Matthew Cottrill settled in Newcastle and became prosperous shipbuilders and merchants. With success achieved, they hired architect Nicholas Codd to design a beautiful church. Kavanagh's son Edward became governor of Maine in 1843, the first Catholic to hold such an office in New England. The next generation of immigrant Irish in Maine, however, was not so successful nor so gently received. COURTESY OF THE MAINE HISTORIC PRESERVATION COMMISSION

Acadian settlers, distancing themselves from the newly arrived Loyalists in New Brunswick, crossed the upper St. John River into the Madawaska Territory beginning in 1785. There they founded a distinctive self-sustaining, French-speaking community. The Roy House (Maison Roy) is the finest example of a pioneer home surviving in the area. First built in what became Cyr Plantation, it was moved to the Acadian Village in Van Buren, where it joined sixteen other structures dating from different eras. PHOTOGRAPH COURTESY OF THE ACADIAN VILLAGE, VAN BUREN, MAINE

Dr. Moses Mason (1789–1866) represented a new breed of go-getter that helped transform backcountry Maine in the decades following the War for Independence. Born in New Hampshire, Mason came to Bethel, Maine, in 1799. He earned a medical certificate and ran a farm. A Baptist and Agrarian Democrat, he served as town postmaster and was later elected to the United States Congress. His portrait, painted by Chester Harding (1792–1866) in 1835, is on view in Mason's splendid home, now open to the public. COLLECTION OF THE BETHEL HISTORICAL SOCIETY, BETHEL, MAINE

Thibodeau (the wife of Joseph Cyr) became the stuff of legend. "Tante Blanche" cared for the sick, clothed those in want, and made the rounds of the settlements with provisions. In a place where families rather than government ruled, she provided the only outside relief. A museum house in Madawaska honors her today. Remotely situated, "the Madawaska" remained a prosperous world unto itself, neatly described in *The Land in Between* by Béatrice Craig and Maxime Daganais (Maine Acadian Heritage Council/Tilbury, 2009).

Fishermen, too, remained an independent-minded lot. John Adams's insistence on a fishing clause in the Treaty of Paris secured New England's right to fish anywhere in the sea used previously. Despite their poverty, Maine fishermen were able to get back in the game, aided by a government bounty. They had thirty vessels on the banks by 1790, and between 1797 and 1807, the fleet's tonnage doubled.

The most striking change in the postwar era occurred in the ports, and at Portland in particular. Even in the dull economic climate of the early 1780s, young go-getters like the McLellans were buying shares in vessels, opening the first general stores, and seeking new markets. The British West Indies and Canada were closed to trade, but they persisted in coastal and even European voyages, and were soon bartering rum, iron, and manufactured goods for country produce and lumber. With no capital, they initiated a system of paper credit (IOUs), and some companies such as John Taber & Son issued their own specie. Eventually, the federal government produced paper money as well, but it took time for people to trust its value over a neighbor's word.

❖

Though Maine was but a district of Massachusetts, she managed to influence the shape of the new Constitution through a native son, and her representatives helped tip the balance for ratification in the state convention. Ironically, it was Rufus King, son of the late accused Tory Richard King, who served as one of Massachusetts' delegates to the Constitutional Convention in 1787. Considered the finest orator on hand, King at first opposed ending the Articles of Confederation but was eventually won over to the necessity of a strong central government. He was on the committee that revised the style and presented the final draft, was one of the signers, and went back to Massachusetts to argue eloquently for passage. Of the 364 delegates at ratification, 104 were from Maine, and they included such men as General

Samuel Thompson, Captain Joseph McLellan, Sr., Samuel Nasson, and William Widgery. There was much debate and animosity between "plow joggers" and lawyers who, according to one delegate, "will swallow up us little fellows." But the final vote was 187 to 168 for the Constitution, and Cumberland County's vote probably tipped the balance. If Massachusetts (whose members insisted on passing a Bill of Rights) had failed to pass, other states might well have followed.

Rufus King (1755–1827) of Scarborough was the only Maine-born signer of the United States Constitution. A graduate of Harvard and aide to General John Glover, he served as a Massachusetts delegate to the Continental Congress and was an advocate for strong federal government. Moving to New York, he became a senator in 1789, was minister plenipotentiary to Great Britain, head of the Federalist Party, and was defeated for the presidency by James Monroe in 1816. His half-brother, William King, was Maine's first governor. COLLECTION OF THE MAINE HISTORICAL SOCIETY

Opposite: These watercolor and ink drawings from Ammi Quint's account book were done between 1803 and 1833 and show nearly every type of seagoing vessel active in Maine waters. Included are a "Top-Sail Schooner, Fishing Schooner, Sloop, 2 Sail Boats, Schooner *Industry*, Sloop *Primrose*, Ship *Dover*, Ship *Blossom*, Ship *Sally*, and Brig *Greenland*, Merchantman." COLLECTION OF THE MAINE HISTORICAL SOCIETY

Below: Seeking new markets in the Revolution's wake, Maine mariners truly became men of the world, and large Maine ports took on cosmopolitan aspects. Captain Joseph McLellan, Jr. (1762–1844), shown in this 1789 portrait attributed to Johann Baptist Hirschmann (late eighteenth century), is a case in point. Born in Portland, McLellan ran off to sea at thirteen, became a master mariner in his father's firm, and sailed to all corners of the Atlantic. His Masonic Lodge was in Dublin, Ireland. He espoused French fashion, founded the first radical Republican (Jacobin) Society of Maine, and, though not formally educated, built two respectable careers in the towns of Gray and Brunswick. COLLECTION OF THE PORTLAND MUSEUM OF ART, PORTLAND, MAINE

THE STRUGGLE FOR STATEHOOD

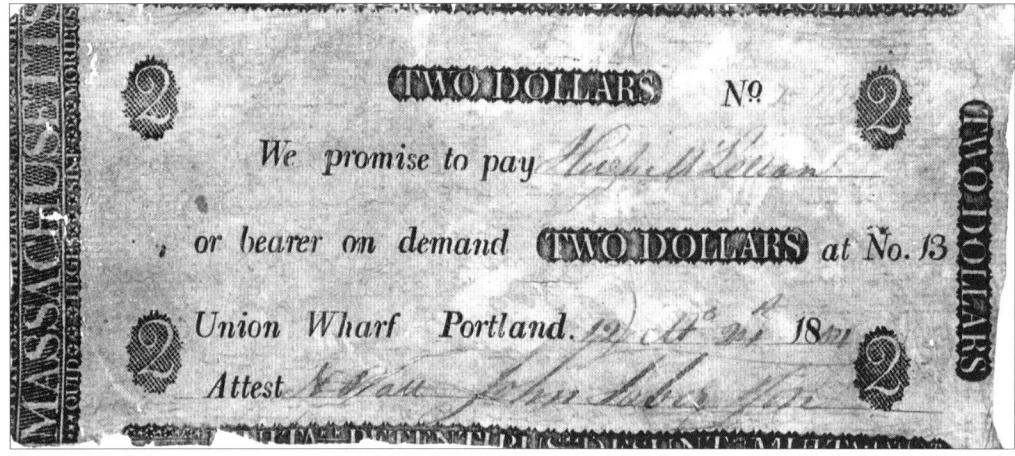

The Federal Period was a time of little hard currency. In order to expand operations beyond a barter economy, leading merchants exchanged "notes of hand" or IOUs. This system of mutual obligations included Taber Notes, privately printed paper money issued by the great Portland trading house of John Taber & Son. In 1806 the firm could not meet its obligations due to changes in Europe, and the notes became worthless. Coupled with the Embargo of 1807, such events destroyed the seacoast economy. COLLECTION OF THE MAINE HISTORICAL SOCIETY

The appearance of the federal government and its splendid start under the strong presidency of George Washington signaled a great age for coastal merchants in Maine and New England. Another major impetus to the Golden Age of Trade began in 1793, when England and France began a series of wars that lasted for decades. As neutral carriers, shipowners in Maine and ports in Massachusetts fell heir to the Atlantic carrying trade. Substantial fortunes were made in this Neutral Profits Era. Portland shipping firms built or bought vessels that took cotton from Charleston to Liverpool. There they picked up cargos of manufactured goods, which they brought home. The West Indies Trade also flourished. Most cargo was sold at Boston for high prices, and a bit was left in the owner's store. Thus much was eventually re-shipped to Portland and sold at higher prices. In 1793 a group of leading Portland merchants built the 2,000-foot Union Wharf, and in 1799 started the Portland Bank, the first bank in Maine. In 1800 the same people founded the Maine Fire and Marine Insurance Company. Great, three-story Federal-style homes were lofted by the "Nabobs," as the merchants were called. These can be found along the coast from Kittery to Wiscasset to Ellsworth and beyond.

Maine's master mariners were known in ports throughout the Atlantic, and in 1796 they founded the Portland Marine Society to collect information and assist poor seamen, widows, and orphans. Other self-help organizations, unknown before the Revolution, included the Female Charitable Society of Wiscasset (1805) and the Maine Charitable Mechanic Association (1815), which provided loans to the growing class of skilled workers and craftsmen, as well as practical instruction to poor boys.

Portland, Berwick, Hallowell, and Fryeburg founded some of the earliest academies; in 1794 Bowdoin College in Brunswick was chartered. When it opened a few years later, it was the first college in the district. Bowdoin had the support of leading Congregationalists and was able to attract top instructors, administrators, and generations of exceptional students. Proximity led many affluent families to send sons there instead of to Harvard.

In 1813 the Maine Literary and Theological Institute (later Colby College) was chartered with Baptist support. In the following year the Maine Charity School (Bangor Theological Seminary) was begun. The accumulation of wealth led sons to enter fields other than those taken by their fathers. Wealthy and middle-class women were now sent to various female academies. Indeed, well-to-do women found increasingly little to do, as families were held together by sentiment rather than economy.

The concept of leisure now became affordable, and by the teens, sailboating and island picnicking became popular in Casco Bay. In astonishingly short order, Portland's demand for entertainment was met. Columbian Hall (formerly Marston's Tavern) hosted a leopard (1809), an elephant (1816), Bradley's Museum (1817), and the Travelling Hindoos (1819). The elephant, "Old Bet," was the first to tour America, but at Alfred she was shot by an unknown person. In an age that gave little news coverage to human murder, great indignation was expressed. Today a roadside plaque marks the animal's grave. In 1794 Maine's first theater opened at the Assembly Hall on Portland's India Street, with a comedy called *The Lyar*, a song, "The Learned Pig," and a farce, *The Merry Mourners. MacBeth* was staged in 1805, and a favorite was *The Sultan, or the Captive*, which took place in Tripoli with a Maine naval hero, Commodore Preble. In 1806 self-critical Congregationalist Portlanders passed a law banning plays, and that was that until 1820.

There were also visual artists at work. Craftsmen, including silversmiths, furniture makers, ornamental painters, and carvers settled in the larger towns. Rufus Porter came to Maine in 1801, entered Fryeburg Academy, and became a decorative painter. In later years, he achieved note as an artist, inventor, and founder of the *Scientific American*. In the 1790s Bartlett Adams became the first stonecutter to settle in Portland so that gravestones of quality could now be purchased locally.

Beginning in 1783 a road show of traveling artists made trips along the east coast from Halifax to the West Indies. Included were portrait artists Dr. Josiah Flagg, Jr., John Brewster, Jr., William King, Moses Cole, John Roberts, Henry Williams, William Bache, and Nathaniel Hancock. In 1813 Canadian Moses Pierce opened a gallery in Portland after spending a year studying the important art collection at Bowdoin College. Pierce's experiment failed commercially, and there were no settled, professional artists. The town of Blue Hill, however, could boast Jonathan Fisher, the Congregational parson who was also a surveyor, writer, teacher, musician, and painter of portraits, landscapes, and genre paintings.

Music had been frowned upon by the Puritans, and the Congregationalists were not very interested, either. In the 1780s this changed in most churches, where not only hymns were sung, but organs and other instruments began to be heard. In 1785 the composer Supply Belcher settled at Hallowell and then moved on to pioneer Farmington. His collection, *The Harmony of Maine* (1794), included compositions named for local towns such as York, Readfield, Bath, New Sharon, Friendship, Farmington, and Hallowell. The latter became, along with Portland, a center for music publications and events. It was there in 1789 that the musician John Merrick first settled. In 1815, he led the new district-wide Handel Society of Maine. Among the important publications was *The Hallowell Collection of Sacred Music*, issued in 1817 by E. Goodale. Parson Jonathan Fisher began the Hancock Musical Association in 1818, and the next year saw the founding of the Beethoven Musical Society in Portland. Music became not only an enjoyment but a necessary part of middle- and upper-class family life. A very special kind of music emerged from the state's Shaker communities. Music also provided one of the first reasons to link people in associations throughout Maine.

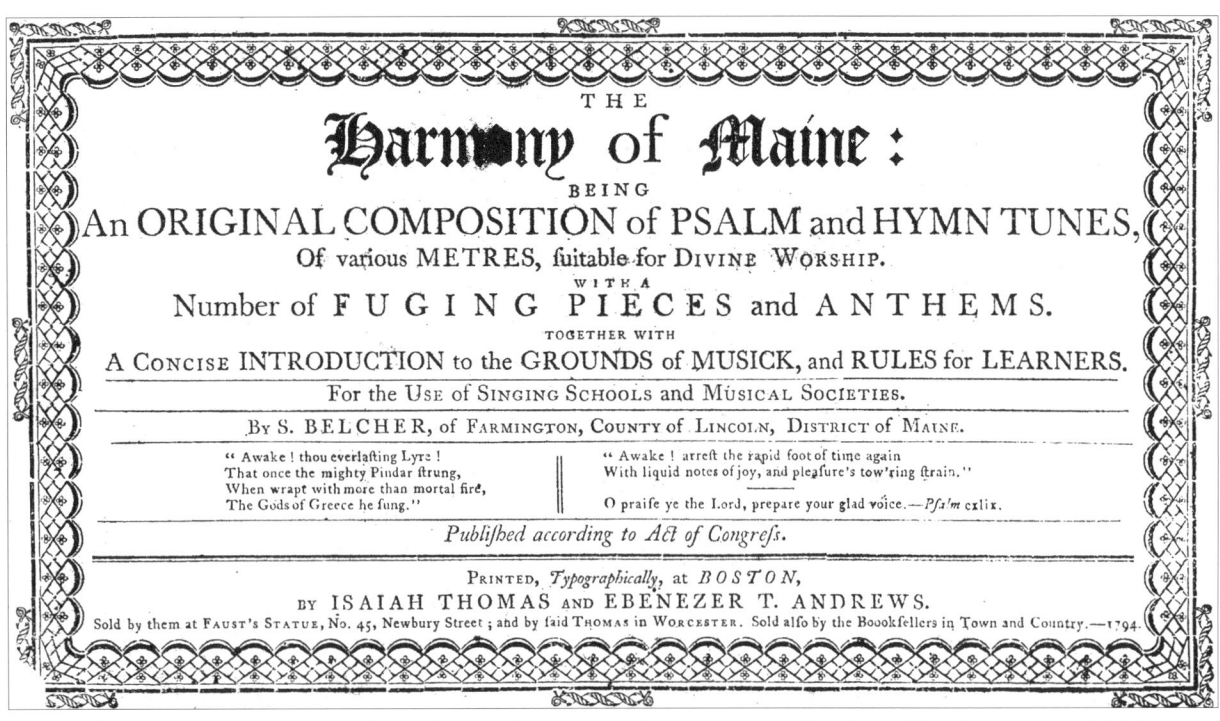

> # THE
> ## 𝔥𝔞𝔯𝔪𝔬𝔫𝔶 of 𝔐𝔞𝔦𝔫𝔢:
> BEING
> An ORIGINAL COMPOSITION of PSALM and HYMN TUNES,
> Of various METRES, suitable for DIVINE WORSHIP.
> WITH A
> Number of FUGING PIECES and ANTHEMS.
> TOGETHER WITH
> A CONCISE INTRODUCTION to the GROUNDS of MUSICK, and RULES for LEARNERS.
> For the USE of SINGING SCHOOLS and MUSICAL SOCIETIES.
> BY S. BELCHER, of FARMINGTON, COUNTY of LINCOLN, DISTRICT of MAINE.
>
> "Awake! thou everlasting Lyre! / That once the mighty Pindar strung, / When wrapt with more than mortal fire, / The Gods of Greece he sung."
>
> "Awake! arrest the rapid foot of time again / With liquid notes of joy, and pleasure's tow'ring strain." / O praise ye the Lord, prepare your glad voice.—*Psalm* cxlix.
>
> Published according to Act of Congress.
>
> PRINTED, *Typographically*, at BOSTON,
> BY ISAIAH THOMAS AND EBENEZER T. ANDREWS.
> Sold by them at FAUST'S STATUE, No. 45, Newbury Street; and by said THOMAS in Worcester. Sold also by the Booksellers in Town and Country.—1794.

Supply Belcher (1751–1836) brought out his landmark musical publication, *The Harmony of Maine* (1794), while living in Farmington, a town he helped pioneer. The son of a Massachusetts physician, Belcher ran a tavern and fought in the Revolution before suffering financial losses. He moved to the District of Maine in 1785, already influenced by musician William Billings and the Stoughton Musical Society. He hoped that his compositions, named for Maine towns, would "not only be a means of forming people into societies, but will be ornamental to civilization." COLLECTION OF THE MAINE HISTORICAL SOCIETY

In the field of writing, production lagged, but Mainers were beginning to make inroads. Some had already appeared in places distant from home. The most outstanding was Stephen Sewall of York, professor of Hebrew and Oriental languages at Harvard between 1765 and 1785. Professor Sewall, the first in a long line of down-east dons, produced a Hebrew grammar, numerous orations, translations, and some verse. Diarists such as Parsons Smith and Deane wrote clearly and well, but their stories were not published until after their deaths. Deane produced Maine's first newspaper poem, but more durable was his study, *The New England Farmer*, a practical guide that ran through three editions between 1790 and 1822. Blue Hill's Parson Fisher published a great deal,

Opposite: Maine's first newspaper, the *Falmouth Gazette and Weekly Advertiser*, appeared on January 1, 1785. Published by John B. Wait and Benjamin Titcomb, Jr., its writers espoused the concept of statehood for the District of Maine. As the issue heated up and as politics took party form, rival papers appeared to do battle. Usually the conflict was verbal, but occasionally it turned physical or economic. Other important papers during the period included the *Portland Gazette, Eastern Argus, Bangor Weekly Register,* and Bath's *Maine Gazette.* COLLECTION OF THE MAINE HISTORICAL SOCIETY

The Falmouth Gazette and Weekly Advertiser

(No. 1.)   SATURDAY, *January* 1, 1785.   (Vol. 1.)

To the PUBLIC.

FROM the generous encouragement of a number of respectable gentlemen in Falmouth, as well as in other towns of this and the neighbouring counties—we have undertaken to publish a weekly News-Paper in this place, and now present them with the first number of the Falmouth Gazette.

We hope it will meet with general approbation—and while we promise to use our best endeavours to make every future number useful and entertaining—we beg leave to express our wishes that every patron of the press will afford us that support which, in this infant country, will be peculiarly necessary to enable us to carry on the business with advantage to ourselves and those, to whom we shall devote our time and talents.

BENJAMIN TITCOMB,
THOMAS B. WAIT.

OUR Subscribers will doubtless recollect, that by the proposals for publishing this Gazette, three months advance was to be paid on receiving the first Number. If, to avoid the inconveniency of making just this sum, any Gentleman should be inclined to pay three shillings, or any larger sum, he shall be credited for the same——And, as the setting up this Press has been attended with some extraordinary expence, will be thankfully received.

Falmouth, January 1st, 1785.

THE Subscriber having lately circulated the Proposals of Messr. PETER EDES and THOMAS B. WAIT, for printing and publishing a weekly News-Paper in this place, thinks proper to inform the Public.—That Mr. EDES has lately opened a Printing-Office in Boston, and in his stead, Mr. BENJAMIN TITCOMB, a Person qualified for the business, has entered into partnership with Mr. WAIT—The Falmouth Gazette is therefore now published under the Names of the Gentlemen last mentioned.

SAMUEL FREEMAN.

Messrs. TITCOMB & WAIT,
As you intend speedily to publish a weekly News-Paper in this place, perhaps the following extract, upon "The rise and advantages of News-Papers", may not be an improper introduction. If you think it merits a place in your first number, 'tis at your service.

An intended CUSTOMER.

WHEN the new method of taxing was first made use of, under King William, people thought their ruin speedily approaching; but the more sensible were soon convinced, that the measures then taken were salutary and proper, and in little detached essays made their sentiments known to the publick. This sowed the seeds of that commendable curiosity we find so much increased. People were willing to see, and to know the reasons for laying every new tax. From desiring to know why taxes were imposed, they very naturally wished to be informed in what manner the money raised by them was expended. The people of England, by degrees, looking on themselves as the disposers of their own properties, found that the soldiers and sailors, were their servants and dependants. This incited them to inquire into their behaviour and conduct; and to procure an account of every battle, to see if matters were rightly managed abroad. Hence the rise of News-Papers, which were at first of a very singular nature.

News-Papers not only convey instruction and amusement, but, when properly conducted, secure to us the *Liberty of the Press*, which we ought at all times to cherish as a most inestimable jewel; for without it we cannot long subsist as a free people. There is another great advantage the procurers of News Papers has procured us:—Ignorance is not so prevalent; they have given a taste for reading; this occasions all useful knowledge to be cultivated and encouraged.

From the WESTMINSTER MAGAZINE.
An ADDRESS *on the* NEW YEAR.

THERE are certain occasions, when the most wicked man living cannot banish serious reflection; when he cannot help meditating on the folly of his own actions, on the importance of wisdom, and on the merits of goodness in procuring a happy life. The prospect of death is not a serious one to the good only; indeed, perhaps to them it is a happy prospect; it is not a serious prospect only to the philosopher, or man of learning, but it is an irresistible call even to the most abandoned to bethink themselves of their ways, and be wise in time. Of all other deaths, sudden death conveys most horror; few there are, be they ever so regular in their lives, who do not feel on such an occasion, that all their worldly caution and interest are very vain and unprofitable, compared with the better assurance which an unspotted conscience gives All gaiety, all grandeur, even the pomp of sophistry, and the proud reasoning of infidels and of the unprincipled rake are then at an end. On such an occasion men seem what they are.

But death, in any shape, is not the only occasion which excites the general meditations of mankind. This season opens a wide field for the most serious reflection. The commencement of the new year is, to the young a cause of merriment, but their ignorance prevents either forethought or retrospect. They are acquainted with no past events which can imbitter the present moment, and they foresee no happiness superior to that which they now enjoy, and no miseries superior to the little playful disappointments which arise from their thoughtlessness It is not so with the man of reflection. He cannot enter on the actions of a new year, without taking a review of that which is at an end. He cannot trace any action without seeing how much better it might have been done, and he cannot trace any events of his life without being conscious, that he himself was the cause of his failure, and that what happiness he has reaped, was rather accidental than merited or laboured for. At the same time too, he is apt to reflect on the many happy days and hours he formerly spent during this season of the year, and that never without sorrow, that he must no more see such days. He thinks with pain on that age, when his happiness was consciousness of innocence, and when he had neither wishes nor wants, which in innocence and moderation could not be supplied. He contrasts his present situation with the days of his childhood, and he now finds himself situated on an eminence in the world He who formerly looked up to others, is now looked up to himself. Dependent only on his own industry, he recollects the many painful doubts which the success of that industry has cost him; placed at the head of a family, or as the principal of a set of loved connections, he feels a thousand anxieties concerning himself, and at the beginning of a new year, looks back with humiliating sorrow on the little he has done. The common gaiety of the time prevents his being sunk in distress, but neither a review of the past, nor the most favourable conjectures concerning what may happen hereafter, add to his pleasures, or contribute to his happiness.

The situations of men in life, whatever those may be, whether military, civil, political or literary, are objects of the first magnitude. It is on our conduct in them, that not only our character but our peace and satisfaction depend. Yet often do we find, that when reflection comes, we are miserable on account of those situations, and like the discontented men (in Horace) wish to change situations with our neighbours. An impatience to be happy, and an ignorance of the source of happiness, produce the common

discontents. A contempt for what is solid, a neglect of what is good, and a love of the frivolous, are the common errors, and men, in the height of their folly, pretend to be in search of happiness while their footsteps go down to death.

Let all then begin, from the commencement of this year, to think for themselves with as great independence of mind as they act for themselves in the independence of trade. There is but one standard of acting, which is justice, and there is but one standard of thinking, which is religion. The one teaches us to be just to others, the second to be just to ourselves. By the one our character here is promoted to the highest estimation of the worthiest and the best of men, and by the other, our happiness is set above the vicissitudes of time, or the malice of enemies.

Let the scoffer enjoy his laugh, and the profligate consume his time, and complete his life of evil and unprofitableness yet still this truth remains unimpeached, that there is no comfort which religion does not give and allow, and there is no happiness which vice does not destroy and abuse. However we may have wasted our time, our strength, or our substance in riotous living, and useless employments, the new year is an æra from whence we may begin a better life.

In these days of political dissentions, when even the common language of the country scarce remains unpolluted by the sophisms of corrupted statesmen, when no goodness of character can stand in competition with the industry of ambition and avarice, when a desire to enjoy the emoluments of office, and a contempt for the discharge of the duties of office, militate against the prosperity of the nation, it is time for the individual to seek his stores of peace within himself; it is time for him to turn his eyes toward his own soul, and see whether there be not in it a fund of enjoyment, far superior to what prostitution of talents, or the splendour of wealth and place can give Public virtue and integrity is no longer an object in view; we look in vain for those virtues in our days, and disappointed by flatterers, and deceived by the artful, we begin to lose confidence in one another The bonds which connect men in friendship, are exchanged for the temporary bindings of interest; and as the example of high life is invariably followed by the lower ranks, we have the misery of that part of the empire which remains superadded to our disappointment in that which was left. Such views, such prospects, and such considerations are particularly necessary in this season, when people are very apt to usher in the new year, with the worst dissipations which the old year afforded.

Libertinism, whether public or private, may continue uninterrupted for a time, It may, for a time, constitute the happiness of man, and place him as an object of envy in the eyes of the ignorant and unthinking. It may, for a time, seem the ultimate end of his nature, and the essence of all his gratifications. But that time may not be of long duration. Health, even when temperance is carried to the extreme, or where prudence guides all the actions, is but a precarious tenure; and the happiness depending on dissipation is even more precarious than health itself, for it is disturbed by the petulancies of temper, and the ungovernable nature of foolish youth. It is but a short time that the strongest can boast of his strength, or the most pleasurable man of his pleasure.

Though the days of our life were as numerous as the hairs on our head, their duration could not satisfy a mind capable of comprehending eternity, or inspired with hopes of futurity. And profligacy, with all its pleasures, creates distaste

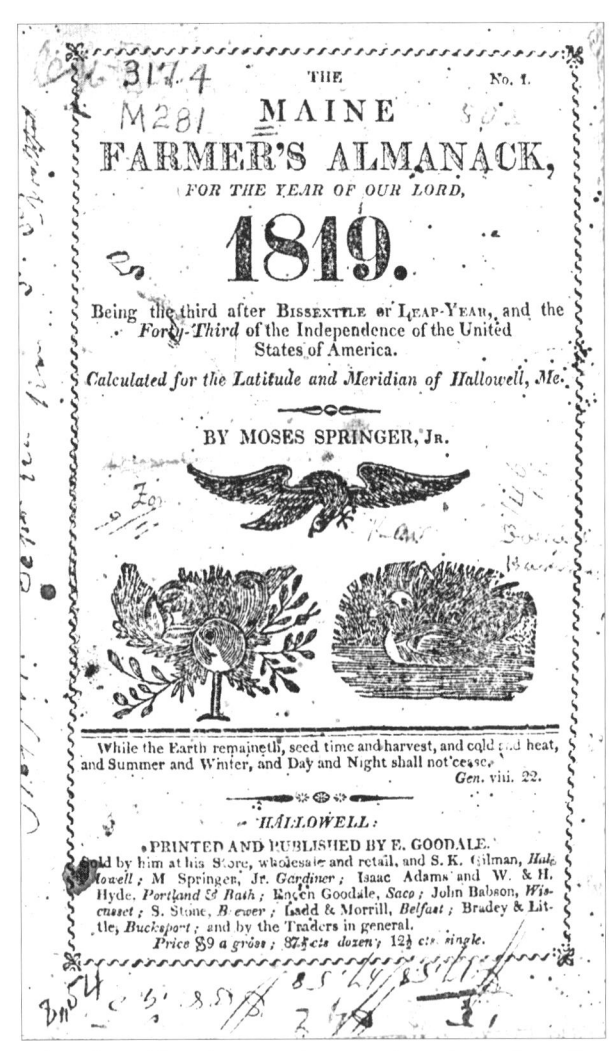

After the Bible, almanacs became the principal reading material in New England's backcountry. *The Maine Farmer's Almanack*, first published at Hallowell in 1819, provided a calendar, political information, weather forecasts, and useful tables of information. The almanac owners, faced with a shortage of paper, often used the margins to make notes or keep records. COLLECTION OF THE MAINE HISTORICAL SOCIETY

Madam Sarah Barrell Keating Wood (1759–1855), a native of York, became Maine's first fiction writer when she penned five Gothic novels between 1800 and 1827. Works including *Julia and the Illuminated Baron* and *Tales of the Night* captured male and female readers from Boston to Farmington and set the stage for the great Maine literary tradition. She lived in Wiscasset, Portland, and Kennebunk, and, as shown in this remarkable daguerreotype from about 1845, continued to dress in the old style. COURTESY OF THE MAINE WOMEN WRITERS COLLECTION, UNIVERSITY OF NEW ENGLAND, PORTLAND, MAINE and in this period brought out *The Youth's Primer* (1817) with twenty-nine of his own animal woodcuts. Published accounts of Maine were provided by such distinguished visitors as Talleyrand, the Duke de la Rochefoucault, Dr. Timothy Dwight of Yale, the Reverend Paul Coffin, and Edward Augustus Kendall. Satisfying the thirst for knowledge about Maine was the visionary future governor of Massachusetts, James Sullivan. A native of Berwick, Sullivan published his famous work, *The History of the District of Maine* (1795), a classic in its field. So, too, the appearance of publishers Thomas B. Wait and Benjamin Titcomb, Jr., and their *Falmouth Gazette* in 1785 introduced the first in a long line of newspapers. Papers served as a unique forum for dissent, rebuttal, and occasional flights of poetry.

In the sphere of fiction Sarah (Sally) Sayward Barrell Keating Wood stands virtually alone in this period. Born at York in 1795, "Madam Wood" lived in Wiscasset, Portland, and Kennebunk, married twice, and produced Maine's first novels. Included are *Julia and the Illuminated Baron* (1800); *Dorval, or The Speculator* (1801); *Amelia, or The Influence of Virtue* (1802); *Ferdinand & Elmira: A Russian Story* (1804); and *Tales of the Night* (1827). In *Dorval* she urged her neighbors into literary activity: "Hitherto we have been indebted to France, Germany, and Great Britain for the majority of our Literary pleasures. Why we should not aim at independence, with respect to our mental enjoyments, as well as for our more substantial enjoyments, I know not. Why must the amusements of our leisure hours cross the Atlantic and introduce foreign fashions and foreign manners, to a people certainly capable of fabricating their own? Surely we ought to make a return in the same way." A favorite of the younger set, who saw her as a model, Wood lived to see a more-than-favorable return in literary production.

❖

Some Mainers were living their own adventure stories. Hundreds of merchant mariners lived through unsought storms and battles with pirates or privateers. Others actually courted danger. It is doubtful that anyone had a more exotic career than Admiral George Tate of the Imperial Russian Navy, who spent his boyhood in Falmouth and then entered Catherine the Great's service in 1770. Still keeping in touch with his family, he commanded the Russian North Sea fleet in 1818 and was made an imperial senator by the tsar. The younger Edward Preble set a course that won his title, "Father of the American Navy." Commodore Preble led the American squadron against Tripoli and bombarded that city in 1804. During the siege, Lieutenant Henry Wadsworth of Portland was lost in the explosion of the *Intrepid*. Plays and panoramas depicting the campaign were popular throughout the nation. In 1807 the commodore's career was cut short by consumption.

Though not as celebrated in his day, Captain Hopley Yeaton is now honored as the "Father of the U.S. Coast Guard." Born near Portsmouth, Yeaton was active at sea and on land during the Revolution, and in 1791 became the first officer to be commissioned in the Revenue Cutter Service. For the next eighteen years, he served as captain of revenue cutters along the Maine coast. In 1792 he moved to Lubec, his base for pursuing smugglers until his death in 1812. Yeaton is buried at the Coast Guard Academy in New London, Connecticut. On a grimmer note, Thomas Bird was hanged for piracy and murder at Portland in 1790, achieving the dubious distinction of being the first person executed under the new laws of the United States.

American military and naval power was in reality quite insignificant during the post-revolutionary era. Aside from the Barbary naval actions in North Africa, the undeclared naval war with France (1798–1800), and Indian actions in the Old Northwest, peace prevailed.

In 1794 Washington began America's "First System" of defense, but the only Maine fortifica-

The first Maine-born military hero of the new Republic was Commodore Edward Preble (1761–1807), sometimes called "the Father of the American Navy." In this painting by Michele Felice Corne (1752–1845), Preble directs the bombardment of Tripoli aboard his flagship, the USS *Constitution*, in 1804. The action of the American Mediterranean squadron signaled that the fledgling Yankees would no longer allow their merchant vessels to fall victim to Barbary pirates. COLLECTION OF THE MAINE HISTORICAL SOCIETY

tion was Fort Sumner (1794) in Portland. More significant was the establishment of the nation's first government shipyard, the Portsmouth Naval Shipyard at Kittery. In 1798 the Department of the Navy had separated from the War Department, and Joshua Humphries, chief naval constructor, toured the coast and selected the site, which was purchased in 1800. Navigational improvements along the coast also became of concern to the federal government in this period. After a fatal shipwreck at Cape Elizabeth's Portland Head in 1787, the Massachusetts government began construction of a lighthouse. The project was taken over by the federal government, and the tower lighted in 1791.

In 1807 Jefferson, who had kept America neutral, began the "Second System," and Forts McClary, Preble, and Scammell were built in their first forms respectively at Kittery, South Portland, and House Island. Down-east forts were constructed at Phippsburg, Boothbay, Castine, Machias, Eastport, Edgecomb, and St. George. The Fort Edgecomb blockhouse is the finest remaining example from this period.

The great era of Federal Period prosperity came to an abrupt halt with Jefferson's Embargo of 1807, which ended all foreign trade. But even before that, the weakness of the paper-credit (IOU) system was apparent, for when England and

72   MAINE: THE WILDER HALF OF NEW ENGLAND

For years Mainers expressed the need for a lighthouse on the rocky Cape Elizabeth shore near Portland Head, the entrance to Casco Bay and Portland Harbor. After a disastrous shipwreck in 1787, Massachusetts began construction of the light. The task was soon taken over by the federal authorities. Authorized by President Washington, the first lighting took place on January 10, 1791. Eventually, some sixty-three lighthouses flashed their protective beacons from Whaleback Light off Kittery to West Quoddy Head.
COURTESY OF THE MAINE HISTORIC PRESERVATION COMMISSION

France excluded Yankee shipping in 1806, the great Portland firm of Taber & Son defaulted. This caused merchants to call in debts, at first collapsing smaller businesses and then the larger. When local vessels could no longer legally trade with other nations because of Jefferson's inept plan to avoid war, Yankees became desperate. American ships appeared in all corners of the Atlantic claiming that they had been blown off course. Smuggling became a way of life once more with little Eastport becoming one of the major hot spots.

The final nail in the coffin of Maine's maritime trade was the War of 1812. Goaded by British impressment of seamen, violations of American waters, and the blockade of certain ports, President James Madison declared a state of war with Britain. The American invasion of Canada failed, and in 1813 a blazing naval engagement was fought between the Royal Navy brig *Boxer* and the U.S. Navy brig *Enterprise* off Seguin. Both captains were killed but the *Enterprise* prevailed. Once again Mainers went privateering in such famous vessels as the *Rapid* of Portland, the *Grand Turk* of Wiscasset, and the *Dash* of Freeport. At the present site of Bremen, Maine,

THE STRUGGLE FOR STATEHOOD

Nearly every Maine coastal town saw the construction of at least a few grand, three-story Federal-style homes amid the more modest Capes during the period between 1793 and 1815. As England and France fought each other, neutral New England shipowners and builders captured the Atlantic carrying trade. The Nickles–Sortwell House in Wiscasset was built in 1807–1812 for Captain William Nickles, and is a superb example of this style. Today it is run by Historic New England as a museum house. COURTESY OF THE MAINE HISTORIC PRESERVATION COMMISSION

retired Commodore Samuel Tucker hastily improvised a war vessel and captured the British privateer *Crown*. But such victories were rare and the conflict unpopular.

In the summer of 1814, a British fleet took Eastport and landed a thousand troops. A larger fleet took Castine and soon occupied Belfast and Machias. The British also moved to capture the American corvette *Adams*, trapped up the Penobscot River at Hampden. Captain Charles Morris and his crew determined to make a stand backed by the area militia, but the troops panicked and Morris was forced to burn his ship. As a result of "the Hampden Races," Bangor was pillaged before the enemy withdrew to Castine. That town was held until April of 1815, though the peace was signed in December of 1814. The crown treated the occupied town as its own and reaped surprisingly large revenues from the customhouse.

Internal American opposition to the conflict was vocalized by Samuel Fessenden of New Gloucester, who spoke before the Massachusetts legislature about "intolerable" conditions in the abandoned district, and believed that "the sooner we come to issue with the general government the better." Some came nearer to treason. Maine sent two delegates to the infamous Hartford Convention in December of 1814, a body that flirted with

Captain Asa Clapp (1762–1848), shown in this likeness by Thomas Badger (1792–1868), was the last of the Federal Period "Nabobs" and the first of Portland's modern businessmen. Remaining loyal to Jefferson, he supported the Embargo of 1807 and through shrewd investments probably became Maine's wealthiest man. Though he never sought high office, Clapp was visited at home by luminaries such as President Monroe, General Lafayette, and future presidents Polk and Buchanan. COLLECTION OF THE MAINE HISTORICAL SOCIETY

New England secession. Few Mainers were in sympathy with such extreme moves, but the inability of the Bay State to defend the District of Maine was troubling. So was the fact that many Maine seamen languished in English prisons.

There was strong support for the fight in other quarters. Kittery's Portsmouth Naval Shipyard, under famous commandants Commodore Isaac Hull and Captain Thomas MacDonough, began the enduring tradition of shipbuilding and repair that has made the facility world-famous. Maine, to her lasting embarrassment, furnished generals Henry Dearborn, Eleazer Wheelock Ripley, and John Chandler to the regular army in Canada. In Portland, the diehard Jeffersonian merchant Captain Asa Clapp is said to have contributed half his vast personal fortune to the federal government's war effort. Indeed, few men have wielded power

The *Portrait of William King* was painted by Gilbert Stuart (1755–1828) in 1806 at the outset of King's political career. Prior to the Revolution, his father, Richard King, had been falsely accused of disloyalty and as a result was ruined. Ironically, William and his half-brother Rufus, a signer of the U.S. Constitution, became leaders of the new Republic. A self-made businessman and shipowner, William spoke for the common man and led the pro-statehood forces to victory in 1820, and, as a result of his political popularity, King was elected Maine's first governor. COURTESY OF THE MAINE STATE MUSEUM

so quietly or well as the poor farm boy from Massachusetts who served in the Revolution, married well, and became Maine's leading post-embargo capitalist. Though he never sought high office, Clapp's advice and counsel was sought by such visitors to his home as President James Monroe and future chief executives Polk and Buchanan. Clapp was an avid supporter of Maine statehood.

The separation issue surfaced again between 1791 and 1797, once more promoted by the leading Federalists. The Jeffersonian Democrat-Republican Party, however, had grown so quickly that the district became dominated by it. In 1805 James Sullivan, a Maine native and a Democrat-Republican, was elected governor of Massachusetts. At that point, the Federalists in Maine became opponents of statehood, while the Federalists in Massachusetts, hoping to rid themselves of Jeffersonian rabble, supported it. In spite of disenchantment with Jefferson's embargo, which wrecked the maritime and farming economy, and the unpopularity of "Mr. Madison's War," the Democrat-Republicans remained the majority party.

Among the leaders of the party in Maine were Richard Cutts of Saco (husband of Dolly Madison's sister Anna), John Holmes of Alfred, William Pitt Preble of Saco, General Henry Dearborn and John Chandler of Monmouth, Captain Asa Clapp of Portland, Albion K. Parris of Paris, and General William King of Bath. The latter proved the most prominent in the fight for statehood. He was another son of the accused Tory Richard King and the half-brother of Maine's only signer of the Constitution, Senator Rufus King. William grew up poor and ill-educated but ambitious and capable. He moved to Topsham and later to Bath, where he became a major shipowner and land investor. Known as the Sultan of Bath, he entered politics in 1804 as a defender of the rights of the common man. In 1808 he was successful in getting the Betterment Act passed, and in 1811 helped get the Toleration Act passed, which ended the religious tax in towns. Though not religious himself, King helped found the Congregational South Church in Bath. During the War of 1812, he served as major-general of militia and as a recruiting colonel in the regular army. Throughout the war, as in the embargo, King's vessels continued to trade, as did most of the great merchants. Smuggling, or at least subterfuges such as flying neutral Swedish colors, was carried on by King and other surviving American merchants at the same time that they fought the British. This curious dichotomy troubled few people.

As soon as the war ended, King and his fellows, many of whom had come from New Hampshire and Massachusetts seeking opportunities, began to agitate for an end to the relationship with Massachusetts. With very little preparation, they called the Brunswick Convention in 1816, but they fell short by a few votes. Members of the movement attempted to ram it through by manipulation of the meaning of "majority," but were stopped. With this surprising and inglorious defeat, the leaders regrouped. In 1818 King went to Washington to build the foundation for national support. In June of the next year, the Massachusetts legislature, anxious to be rid of the problem, passed an "Act of Separation," and in October delegates from the Maine towns met at Portland's First Parish Church to write a new constitution for the State of Maine.

As usual, however, there was another hitch. When the United States Congress was petitioned to admit Maine into the Union, the slave-free-state issue reared its ugly head. Missouri had also asked for admission at a time when there were eleven free states and eleven slave-holding states. With the North's larger population, this gave more votes to the region in the House of Representatives. After a great deal of argument, a compromise was reached. Missouri joined as a slave state, Maine joined as a free state, and slavery was excluded from the Old Louisiana Purchase north of the line 36°30′. On March 15, 1820, Maine shed her final colonial links and became the nation's twenty-third state.

Down East, 1838, by Maine's first professional landscape painter, Charles Codman (c. 1800–1842), shows an accurate view of frontier life in the post-Revolution era. Along the distant waterfall a sawmill is in operation, and in the clearing two men close a deal by shaking hands. Next to them is a load of lumber and a yoke of oxen. As timber was cut, cleared land was opened to farming and settlement. COLLECTION OF THE BOWDOIN COLLEGE MUSEUM OF ART, BRUNSWICK, MAINE

5

THE ACHIEVEMENT OF IDENTITY (1820–1861)

Dirigo (Latin for "I lead" or "I direct") was the vaunting State of Maine motto adopted by the first legislature. Citizens of the new state had abundant reason to believe in a special destiny for Maine within the Union. At birth, Maine ranked twelfth among the twenty-four states, with a population of nearly a quarter million, and as early as 1808 *The American Encyclopedia* predicted that, "Of all the northern quarters of the Union, Maine is that which will increase the fastest." There was plenty of room to expand in this half-civilized, half-frontier place, for it was almost as large in territory as the rest of New England.

In the course of the next four decades, Maine proved equal to the special destiny foreseen by so many observers. Internally, the shapes of counties took final form, except for a few minor adjustments. Most of the deep-woods hinterland was explored and surveyed and, though Mainers almost sparked a war between the United States and Great Britain over international borders, the northeast boundary was finally determined. In the same period, Bangor became the lumber capital of the world, Portland became Canada's winter railhead on the Atlantic, and Maine led the nation in the production of timber and shipbuilding.

Immigrants from Ireland, Quebec, and Germany enriched the ethnic texture, but their arrival helped fuel great social disruption as well. At the same time, Mainers took leadership roles in such causes as temperance, abolition, the treatment of mental illness, and the international peace movement. In the arts, Maine attracted and inspired many of America's finest painters and literary figures, and was the birthplace of many more, including the nation's first major art critic, John Neal, and Victorian America's most widely read poet, Henry Wadsworth Longfellow. Most significantly perhaps, Mainers achieved a unique self-identity that was recognized throughout the land.

Politics provided one of the important ways in which Maine could showcase itself within the Union. Prior to the Civil War, Maine boasted such high-caliber senators as William Pitt Fessenden, George Evans, John Fairfield, and Hannibal Hamlin. Nathan Clifford, though born in New Hampshire, made his career in Maine, moving from Congress to U.S. attorney general in the Polk administration. In 1857 President Buchanan named Clifford to the Supreme Court, where he served until 1880. Buchanan also appointed Horatio King of Paris, Maine, postmaster general. King continued briefly into the Lincoln administration. Congressman Jonathan Cilley, a graduate of Bowdoin College's famous class of 1825, won a measure of immortality when he was shot to death in a duel with Congressman Graves of Kentucky in 1838. Few Mainers caused as much controversy as Congressman F. O. J. "Fog" Smith, called by his biographer Thomas L. Gaffney "one of Maine's most prominent figures and perhaps her most magnificent failure." Among other things, Smith

This magnificent watercolor view of Portland's Congress Street was painted by Anna M. Buckman. It is the only known painting showing the first Maine State House (right corner), which stood at the corner of Myrtle Street. Next door is the Cumberland County Courthouse and the First Parish meetinghouse (Old Jerusalem). On the opposite side of Congress Street is Portland Academy, which was lofted in 1821. Portland remained the capital of Maine until the Bulfinch State House was opened at Augusta in 1833.
COLLECTIONS OF THE MAINE HISTORICAL SOCIETY AND THE MAINE STATE MUSEUM

helped build and then disrupt the Democratic Party in Maine, and, having secured Congressional support for Samuel F. B. Morse, became a partner to the latter's lasting regret.

On the state level, William King served as Maine's first governor. King attempted to usher in a local era of good feeling by bringing Federalists as well as Democratic-Republicans into the government. He also attempted to have the legislature buy all the Maine land owned by Massachusetts and to encourage industries through nominal taxation. The legislature stopped both programs, and in 1821 the frustrated King resigned to become one of the commissioners to negotiate a treaty with Spain. Sadly for King, his business and political careers proceeded on a downward spiral.

King was succeeded by the able president of the senate, William D. Williamson, who published the still-popular *History of the State of Maine* in 1832. Twenty-five men served as governor in the years

This brisk view by Portland's Charles E. Beckett (1813–1866) depicts Dr. Cummings and his prized horse "Jane Medora," an animal that once carried the mail to Canada. Mainers had enjoyed sleighing since colonial times, and the physician could also use his sleigh for house calls. Roads were improving, but even the worst roads were made better in winter. Farmers, like these in Cumberland County, spent the cropless season harvesting timber and making repairs. In 1820 oxen outnumbered horses by 48,000 to 31,000.
COLLECTION OF THE MAINE HISTORICAL SOCIETY

preceding 1861. At the outset, the Democratic-Republicans (Jeffersonians) dominated. The appearance of Andrew Jackson on the national stage transformed the party, which became known more simply as the Democratic Party. The Federalist Party collapsed and was, generally speaking, replaced by the Whig Party. The people of Maine tended to be partial to the Democrats, but in 1840 Mainers proved a bellwether by electing a Whig as governor and suggesting that William Henry Harrison and James Tyler would be victorious: This was immortalized in the contemporary political ditty:

Oh, have you heard how old Maine went?
She went hell-bent for Governor Kent,
and Tippecanoe and Tyler, too.

In the decade of the 1850s, tremendous social ferment, reflecting great national disputes including states' rights, slavery, immigration, and temperance, led to the formation of the new Republican Party. The national party was founded in June 1854 and the state party a month later. Anson P. Morrill was elected governor with Know-Nothing Party, Maine Law Party (Temperance), and Free Soil Party support. In the next election, he ran as a Republican and won the most votes, but was not chosen by the legislature. Hannibal Hamlin was the first of Maine's Republican governors, elected in 1856. Along with William Pitt Fessenden, Hamlin played a crucial role in the foundation of the party both locally and nationally.

Portland became the temporary capital of Maine and a two-story statehouse was built. Already there was a great wrangle over the location of a permanent capital, with Hallowell, Brunswick, Wiscasset, Waterville, Belfast, Augusta, and Portland emerging as prime contenders. The legislature had the final say, but most of its members looked at Portland, already the financial capital of Maine, with the same suspicion Portlanders reserved for Boston. Thus, in 1827, the tiny Kennebec River town of Augusta was chosen after Hallowell was rejected as too Federalist, and former governor William King was selected to

One of the central focuses of downtown Portland was the Elm Hotel or Tavern on the corner of Federal and Temple Streets, shown here in a broadside engraving by Fitz Henry Lane (1804–1865). The building was a popular watering place. Here, in 1828, the art critic John Neal first discovered the painting of pioneer artist Charles Codman. Until the coming of rail, late in the era, stage travel was second only to water transportation. COURTESY OF PORTLAND PUBLIC LIBRARY SPECIAL COLLECTIONS & ARCHIVES

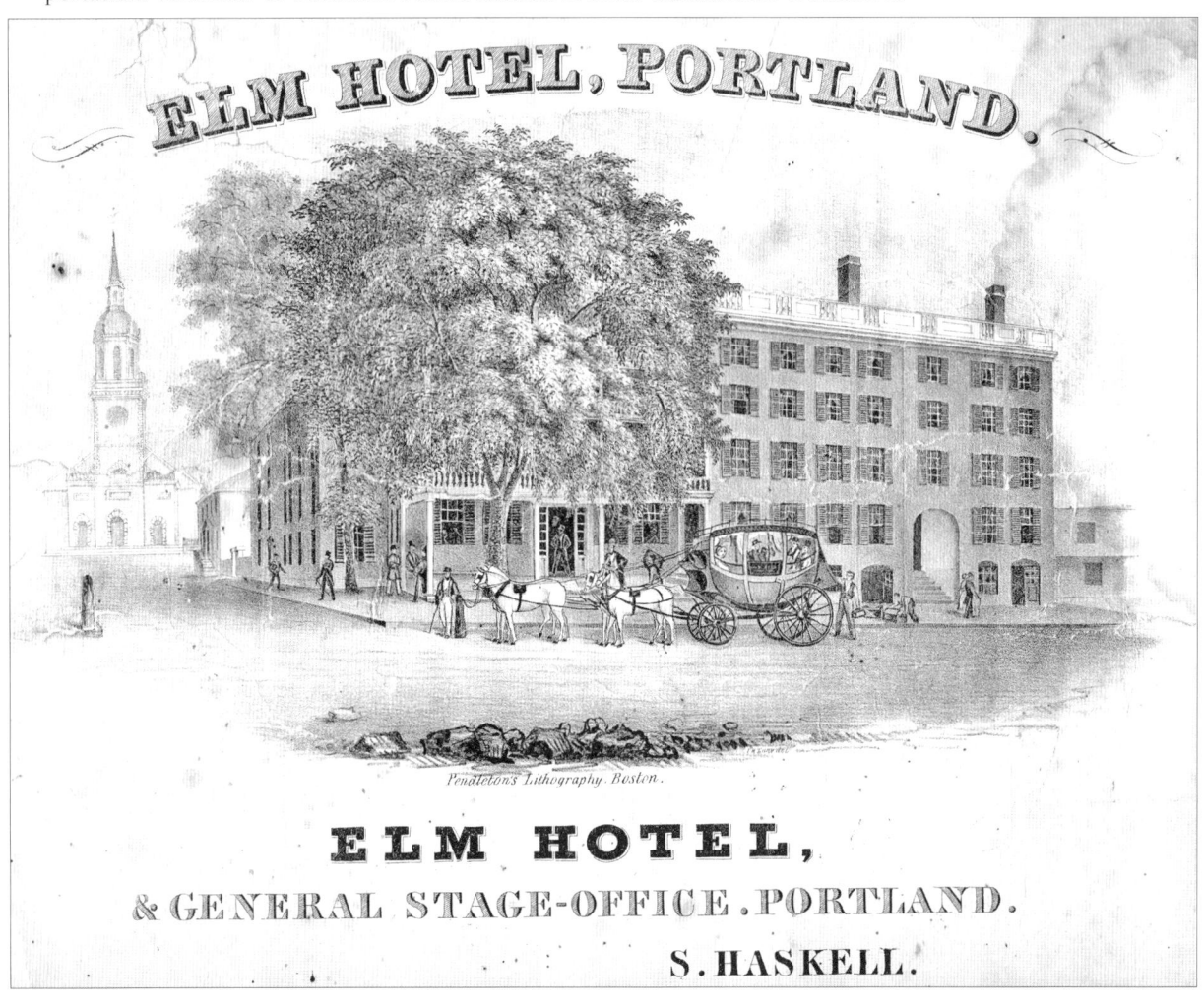

82   MAINE: THE WILDER HALF OF NEW ENGLAND

head the statehouse project. He secured the services of the noted architect Charles Bulfinch, who followed with a bold Greek Revival building of Maine granite. It was finished in 1832, and soon all functions of state government moved there. Up through 1910, numerous attempts were made to move the capital back to Portland, but Augusta remained triumphant.

The internal arrangement of counties took final shape in the decades preceding the Civil War. Franklin and Piscataquis Counties were established in 1838. Aroostook County was incorporated in 1839, and with additional lands added in 1843 and 1844, it became the largest county east of the Mississippi. Sagadahoc and Androscoggin followed in 1854 and were joined by Knox County in 1860. Aside from minor adjustments of border towns, the equation remains.

One of the major problems facing the new state government was the ownership of wild lands. In 1820 Maine and Massachusetts each owned about eight million acres. Governor King wanted to buy the Bay State's holdings, and Boston offered to sell at $.023 per acre. With the economy momentarily hitting rough weather, the legislature refused and both states continued to own the land. In the first five ranges of townships, every other township was granted to Massachusetts. In 1815 Moses Greenleaf had produced his famous *Map of the District of Maine*, followed by a statistical report. It demonstrated that nearly everything north of a line drawn between Magalloway and Vanceboro remained terra incognita. Attempts were made to understand the territory, and a basic

This view of Portsmouth Harbor in the mid-nineteenth century shows the Piscataqua River, which is shared by Maine and New Hampshire. Fernald's (Dennett's) Island in Kittery became the site of America's first naval shipyard. Its massive wooden ship houses, built over the ways to protect vessels under construction, are seen in the distance. A dozen ships, including the frigate *Congress* and steam sloop *Kearsarge*, were built in the yard during this era. In 1866 Seavey's Island was also acquired for the yard. COLLECTION OF THE MAINE HISTORICAL SOCIETY

policy for settling and selling lands appeared in 1824. With financial support from the legislature, Greenleaf published a new map and his fine volume, *A Survey of the State of Maine* (1829). In spite of the great service done by Greenleaf, he lost money on the venture. In 1837 the eminent Dr. Charles Thomas Jackson was appointed state geologist. His famous survey, which included visual images, provided better knowledge of the interior and coast but did not help the governing and disposition of the territory.

Due to major disagreements between the states and poorly kept records, much of the land remained unsold. Finally, in 1853, pressure from numerous sources led to buying out Massachusetts' remaining townships. Even then, estimates on the amount of land disposed of differed by as much as 200,000 acres. With an abundance of federal land available in the American West, attempts to attract settlers were not terribly successful. Except for the eastern part of Aroostook, much of the territory had thin topsoil and was visited by a short growing season. Farming was difficult, if not impossible, and there was the added problem of distance from markets.

Lumbering, however, flourished. As the years progressed, the timber harvesters became increasingly organized as businesses and cut deeper into the forest.

Along the ill-defined northeast boundary, timber was a major issue causing friction between Maine and Great Britain. Geopolitics played an equally important role. Maine was like a huge thumb pressed into British North America, and its existence almost led to a third war with Britain. When the St. Lawrence was frozen during the winter, Quebec's only internal route to the Atlantic was via the Temiscouata Portage to the St. John and on to Halifax. Trade and communication were also carried on with America, but during wartime, the Temiscouata route was crucial and much used by the military. Just after the War of 1812, the northeast territory began to fill up with settlers from both New Brunswick and Maine, and ownership became a real, rather than theoretical, issue.

The Peace of Paris (1783) stated that the boundary would run "from the northwest angle of Nova Scotia, viz., that angle which is formed by a line drawn due north from the source of the St. Croix River to the Highlands; along the said Highlands which divide those rivers that empty themselves into the river St. Lawrence, from those which fall into the Atlantic Ocean to the northwesternmost head of the Connecticut River." Different maps showed different rivers marked St. Croix, the northwest angle of Nova Scotia was not known, and just what constituted the Highlands was contested. In the 1790s a St. Croix commission had made some progress and a borderline had been run to present-day Amity. A new commission after the War of 1812 continued the line to Mars Hill, but after five years produced separate reports. In 1826 the king of the Netherlands was invited to arbitrate.

After the War of 1812, timber harvesters from New Brunswick had pushed into Maine, and American families from the Kennebec had settled west of the Acadians in the Madawaska region. By the 1830s, Canadian harvesters were working the Fish and Allagash River Valleys. Since the St. John flowed deep into New Brunswick, the outlet for timber in the area was Fredericton. Even American harvesters were obliged to use the route. For their part, the British authorities were anxious to get the best naval stores and mast pine for the Royal Navy.

In 1820 the lieutenant governor of New Brunswick began granting land on the Aroostook River, and in 1825 a Maine land agent appeared in the Madawaska region. Appropriately, on July 4 of that year a settler, John Baker, hoisted an American-like flag over his property. He had had trouble with provincial authorities and now asked for Maine protection. The dogged Baker was jailed

The northeast boundary controversy, which had dragged on since the end of the Revolution, flared up with new urgency as Maine and New Brunswick settlers and timber harvesters came into direct conflict in the 1820s and '30s. In 1839, the Maine land agent was arrested and the governor dispatched state troops to the border, threatening war with Great Britain. Maine built two blockhouses named for the governors, at Fort Fairfield and Fort Kent (now a National Historic Landmark) in 1839. This sketch shows the latter in 1842, the year the Webster–Ashburton Treaty (Treaty of Washington) set the border. COLLECTION OF THE MAINE HISTORICAL SOCIETY

at Fredericton as both sides exchanged verbal blasts. In 1828 the U.S. authorities established Hancock Barracks on a fortified hill at Houlton. It was garrisoned by regular army troops who built a military road to Lincoln, which was already linked to Bangor. The action moved the British to construct a similar road to Grand Falls and to appoint a warden of the disputed territory.

In 1831 the king of the Netherlands offered a boundary decision that was rejected by the Americans and put aside. During this time, lumbering increased and confrontations in the Madawaska continued. Roads were extended to attract settlers and to bolster Maine's claims. Though not directly related to the Aroostook problems, a road was constructed between the Kennebec and the Chaudière Rivers between 1817 and 1834. Now Route 201, it has remained the only highway between Maine and Quebec in spite of the long international border between these places.

Most Americans were convinced that Canada would become part of the United States or, at least

86   Maine: The Wilder Half of New England

shake free of Britain. In 1837 rebellions broke out in Upper and Lower Canada (Ontario and Quebec). In the latter, Bangor's Captain Charles Bryant became a military advisor and participant. Bryant crossed the Vermont border several times, claimed the backing of Governor Edward Kent of Maine, and became a divisional commander in the secret Hunter's Lodge Movement that failed miserably to rekindle a new revolt by Canada against Britain. Bryant drifted to Aroostook and became a military engineer for the land office.

In 1838 Maine's Governor John Fairfield received reports of stepped-up lumber-cutting by the New Brunswick interests. He called on the land agents to enter the territory with a "sufficient number of men suitably equipped, to seize the teams and provisions, break up the camps, and disperse those who are engaged in this work of devastation and pillage." Land agent Rufus McIntire hired Penobscot sheriff Hastings Strickland to lead a 200-man posse into action. They were effective until McIntire left them, was arrested, and was sent to the Fredericton jail. Fearing a large force, the posse fled. When Governor Fairfield complained, New Brunswick governor Sir John Harvey ignored his demands. Fairfield called up the militia, sent them to the border, and asked permission to draft 10,000 men. The troops took up positions, arrested the provincial warden, and shipped him to Bangor. Made up mostly of men from down-state, the militia was all for marching on Fredericton. Happily, they did not, for British regulars arrived from Quebec and the coast to back up the New Brunswick militia.

Maine was on the very edge of war with the British Empire, and if this did not daunt its citizens, it alarmed President Martin Van Buren. He dispatched General Winfield Scott with full authority to negotiate. Scott got on well with both Harvey and Fairfield, and negotiated an agreement to stand down, leaving the place as it was and under civil occupation. Daniel Webster was appointed the American negotiator and Alexander Baring (Lord Ashburton) the British negotiator. Baring not only knew a great deal about Maine, but his family retained great tracts in the state.

In the meantime, American surveyors moved across the land, finding little of interest north of the St. John. The federally funded survey, led by Captain Andrew Talcott of the Army Corps of Engineers, also produced an extraordinary group of sixteen camera-lucida watercolors taken in various sections. After a series of complicated negotiations, Maine conceded the land north of the St. John and New Brunswick gave up the south side. The Treaty of Washington was signed on August 9, 1842, and the bloodless "Aroostook War" finally ended. Interestingly, free navigation on the St. John led to cooperation between settlers, including investments and joint ventures on both sides of the border. Indeed, the natural outlet markets at Fredericton and St. John became virtually international. In the lumber trade, these ports were surpassed only by Bangor.

Bangor, the spot on the map once marking the mythical city of Norumbega, began an extraordi-

---

Opposite, top: Size and inaccessibility left Maine's northeast boundary uncertain even after statehood. Frictions with American settlers and New Brunswick timber harvesters led to a near war in the 1830s and instigated surveys. The federal Talcott Survey, completed in 1842, used a camera lucida to produce sixteen watercolor views. P. Harry made this view of relaxing surveyors labeled "Co-cum-go-muc-sis Lake—bearing from S. 15 E. to South 30 E.—and in the distance Katahdin bearing about S. 35 E.—and Spencer Mount S. 5 W.—the small lake at right is on the stream connecting Hompona." Thus were the final borders of Yankee land finally understood. COLLECTION OF THE NATIONAL ARCHIVES, WASHINGTON, D.C.

Opposite, bottom: *View from Station 212* by P. Harry, one of the first true views of the Big Woods, shows government survey workers working and clowning around to provide scale for the camera. COLLECTION OF THE NATIONAL ARCHIVES

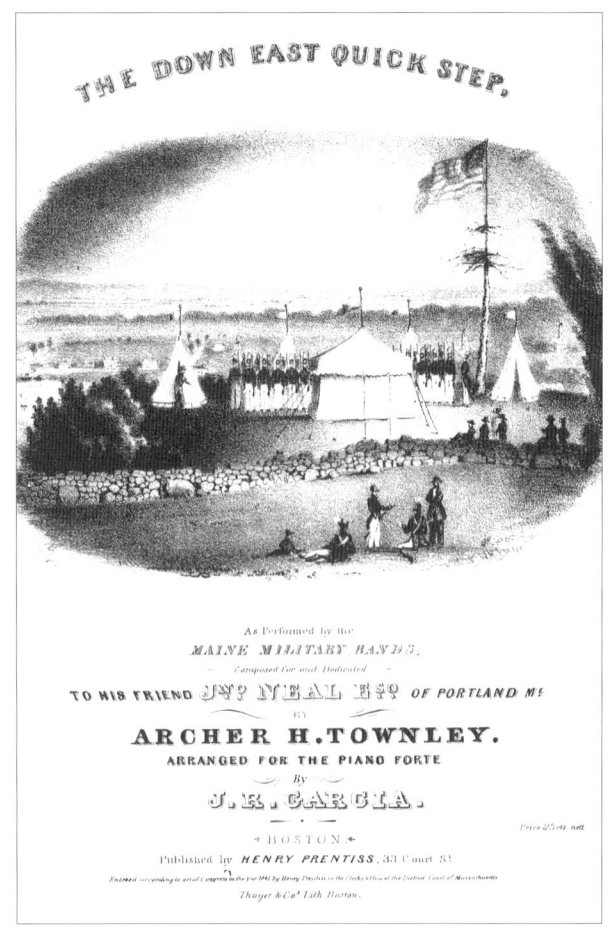

Music was a vital force throughout the period. "The Down East Quick Step" was written while the northeast boundary question still continued, and this lithographic image shows a Maine militia camp. The work is dedicated to art critic John Neal. During the so-called Aroostook War, Neal and his colleague Charles Stewart Davies (1788–1865) went to see General Winfield Scott, whom neither had met. "This gentleman," proclaimed Neal, "is my friend Charles S. Daveis, who knows all about the northeast boundary." Somewhat taken aback, Davies responded, "And General Scott, this is my friend John Neal, who knows everything else." COURTESY PRIVATE COLLECTION

General Samuel Veazie (1787–1868) was painted in his prime as one of Bangor's lumber barons; the artist was Jeremiah P. Hardy (1800–1887). The foremost painter in the city, Hardy painted at least six portraits for the Veazie family. Born in Portland, Veazie went to sea and began a career in Topsham. In 1832 he moved to Bangor and became the king of the Penobscot sawmills, with twenty saws in North Bangor, nineteen at Old Town, and thirteen at Orono. Tiring of local restrictions, he detached Bangor's seventh ward and made it the town of Veazie in 1853. COLLECTION OF THE BANGOR PUBLIC LIBRARY, BANGOR, MAINE

88   MAINE: THE WILDER HALF OF NEW ENGLAND

The *Lion*, built in Boston 1846 for the Palmer & Machiasport Railroad (later Whitneyville & Machiasport), is Maine's oldest remaining locomotive and the eighth oldest in the nation. It ran between the sawmills and the port until 1892. Railroads developed slowly in Maine, with various lines choosing different gauge tracks. It took John A. Poor, a business visionary, and the Atlantic & St. Lawrence Railroad (opened in 1852) to initiate the state's true entry into the rail era. The beautifully restored *Lion* is now on view in the Maine State Museum. COURTESY MAINE STATE MUSEUM

nary period of growth in the 1820s that produced legend-sized men and women and made the place the world's largest lumber port. Though the Penobscot iced up for part of the year, 3,376 vessels entered the port in 1860 alone. In 1834 it had become Maine's second-largest city, and in 1836 it boasted the state's first steam railway. A year before, regular steamboat service linked the city to Boston. These improvements were made possible after the opening of the state land agency in 1823.

Between 1831 and 1837 the sale of timberland attracted speculators who paid increasingly big prices for unseen tracts. In six years, Bangor's population quadrupled. Sawmills were joined by shipyards, ironworks, shoe manufacturers, toolmakers, stove companies, and furniture makers in the years before the Civil War. Shouldering their way into prominence were lumber barons such as the dapper bachelor Rufus Dwinel and General Samuel Veazie who, tiring of local restrictions,

THE ACHIEVEMENT OF IDENTITY

By 1854, when this print appeared, the city of Bangor was the flourishing crossroads of the Maine forest and the sea. Here, mariners in from long voyages and river-drivers from the Big Woods mixed it up in the watering places of Peppermint Row and Barkersville. Irish refugees came, and proud Penobscots as well as a number of visitors such as Henry David Thoreau, headed for Katahdin or the woods. The Queen City soon became the largest lumber port in the world. COURTESY PRIVATE COLLECTION

carved Ward Seven out of Bangor and made it the town of Veazie in 1853. Samuel Freeman Hersey was the greatest of them all with timber holdings as distant as Minnesota. Great fortunes were made and as quickly lost in the financial panics of 1837 and 1857.

On the waterfront, sailors in from long voyages mixed and clashed with memorable river-drivers like Joe Attien and Larry Conners in places such as Barkersville and Peppermint Row.

The Queen City offered a wide ethnic mix including Irish, Indians, and a scattering of blacks. If there was a frontier atmosphere, there was also a cosmopolitan side, which supported a population of settled artists and artisans and drew notable speakers, including Ralph Waldo Emerson (who made five visits), and actors, including Junius Booth. Norumbega Hall was opened for concerts and lectures in 1840. Bangor Academy had opened in 1820, and in 1848 both the Penobscot Musical Association and Bangor Horticultural Society were founded. Visitors included Francis Parkman, Richard Henry Dana, Frederick Douglass, (the original) Cassius Clay, and painters Chester Harding and A. G. Hoit.

Penobscot Indians down from Old Town and dressed in bright regalia adorned with trade silver caught the eye of most visitors. Indeed, such notable figures as Molly Molasses and Lieutenant-Governor John Neptune were believed to be possessed of great spiritual powers. The Maine constitution excluded Indians from the vote "not on account of their color, but [because] they have never been considered members of the body

This remarkable painting by Sir Richard R. G. A. Levinge (1811–1884) shows Maliseet fishermen spearing salmon by moonlight at Aroostook Falls in 1836. Some Indians in the more settled parts of Maine were already making a living by selling crafts and even touring with traveling theatrical companies. Up in the disputed territory, traditional occupations including hunting, fishing, and gathering continued unabated. The artist, later a member of Parliament, served with the 43rd Monmouthshire Light Infantry and wrote about his Canadian service in *Echoes from the Backwoods* (1846). COLLECTION OF THE NATIONAL ARCHIVES OF CANADA, OTTAWA, ONTARIO

politic." In 1821 the office of Agents for Penobscot and Passamaquoddy Indians was created by public law to take over the management of their property from the Massachusetts government. (It was the origin of Maine's health and welfare agency.) The Penobscot Indian Nation is near Old Town, and the Passamaquoddy have reservations near Perry, and Princeton. The loss of hunting grounds to timber cutting led many to turn to crafts like the making and selling of canoes, snowshoes, baskets, and moccasins. They made summer coastal trips camping at Kennebunk and beyond, and in the 1850s some Penobscots toured New England as part of an "Indian Exhibition." On the St. John though, Maliseets and Micmacs still carried on traditional hunting and fishing activities. Knowing the forest as they did, it was natural that Indians—including the famous Penobscot Joe Attien—hired out as guides.

Most travel was by water and the Queen City became the principal gateway to Katahdin, Maine's highest peak and one of the first recreational goals. The first known climb was accomplished by seven Bangoreans in 1804. In 1849 writer Elizabeth Oakes Smith of North Yarmouth became the first woman to reach the summit. The famous landscape painter Frederick E. Church made treks to the mountain and woods between 1852 and 1879, which inspired a number of works including his masterpiece *Twilight in the Wilderness*, 1860. Henry David Thoreau journeyed to Katahdin, Moosehead Lake, the West Branch of the Penobscot, and the Allagash between 1846 and 1857, producing his extraordinary journals later published as *The Maine Woods*. Complementing his insight into the Big Woods is John S. Springer's more pedestrian *Forest Life and Forest Trees* (1851). Springer, a native of Robbinston, reported 10,000 men cutting along the Penobscot in winter. A settler on the upper Penobscot told Thoreau of

John James Audubon (1785–1851), the artist and naturalist, came to Maine in 1832. He visited Eastport, Dennysville, Houlton, Bangor, and New Brunswick. According to historian Herbert Adams, he painted at least fourteen bird portraits based on specimens collected on the trip. Included are the Northern Phalarope, the Bufflehead Duck, the Thick-billed Murre, and the Boreal Owl. The Great Black-backed Gull, then rather uncommon, was shot at Eastport. With the spread of human habitation, that bird's numbers have actually grown.
BOWDOIN COLLEGE LIBRARY SPECIAL COLLECTIONS, BRUNSWICK, MAINE

how the growing lumber companies owned vast tracts, drove off squatters, and discouraged settlement. Interestingly, most harvesters were farmers in summer who supplemented their income by winter woods work. Still, there was a very real clash between the lumber and agricultural interests.

   The appearance of artists and other tourists in the woods was the start of Maine's vacation industry. There were other attempts to attract visitors to Maine, many successful in a modest way. In 1844 the great landscape painter Thomas Cole visited Bar Harbor to draw inspiration from the dramatic coast, and he was followed by most of the important American painters of the period. Indeed some of the best works by Fitz Henry Lane, Thomas Doughty, and Alvan Fisher depict the Maine coast. Earlier, John James Audubon explored Washington County and completed some fourteen bird portraits.

   Beginning in the 1820s, Mainers of the south, in places including Cape Elizabeth, Old Orchard, and the Isles of Shoals, turned homes into boardinghouses. In the 1830s Cape Cottage Hotel appeared in Cape Elizabeth, and in 1848 Appledore House was constructed on the Isles of Shoals. In 1850 J. S. Sargent, a Portland hotelman, built

The Pleasant Mountain House (Summit Hotel) was built atop 2,000-foot Pleasant Mountain in Denmark, Maine, in 1850. As shown in this painting by Charles E. Beckett (c. 1813–1866), the trees were burned away to create a vista, and visitors arrived by horse and oxcart. The resort included a barbershop, lookout, and bowling alley, and was given national coverage in *Gleason's Pictorial* of August 7, 1853. Together with facilities at Cape Elizabeth, Bar Harbor, and Old Orchard, resorts like this patented Maine's future as "Vacationland." COLLECTION OF THE PORTLAND MUSEUM OF ART, PORTLAND, MAINE

the Pleasant Mountain House, in Denmark, Maine. The latter had much to do with the opening of the interior by railroads and appeared prominently in *The Portland, White Mountains & Montreal Railroad Guide* (1858). Just as the Civil War began, the Ottawa House opened on Cushing's Island in Casco Bay. It was built by a Canadian for English Canadians taking the Grand Trunk Railway. In 1858 Poland Spring, which had boasted inns for years, began its life as a fashionable spa. Still, the great age of hotels and tourism was a long way off.

Mainers enjoyed more leisure time. Sailing and sailboat racing continued around Casco Bay. Bowling became fashionable in the resorts, even on Pleasant Mountain, and horseracing had begun to enjoy popularity. Baseball teams were formed, and games were played between cities, including Portland and Bangor. In winter there was sleighing, sledding, and skating. After his return to Portland in 1827, John Neal popularized the international gymnastics movement by founding gyms in Portland and exercise groups in Brunswick, Eastport, Gardiner, Saco, and North Yarmouth. Neal quit when blacks were barred and began the first athletic program at Bowdoin College. Among the highly educated German refugees arriving after the failed Revolution of 1848 was Franz Xavier Stoppel, who founded the local Turnverein, or gymnasium, which flourished for many years.

The more settled backcountry regions were undergoing great changes in farming. Areas like the intervale lands of Oxford County entered a golden age of agriculture, never to be seen again. The first statewide cattle show was held at Hallowell in 1820 by the new Maine Agricultural Society. In 1823 the Gardiner Lyceum was founded by Robert Hallowell Gardiner. This was the first agricultural school in America (the prototype of agricultural colleges). A year later, Dr. Ezekiel Holmes, called the "Father of Maine Agriculture," was appointed to the faculty. After the Lyceum folded in 1831, Dr. Holmes left and began the state's first agricultural publication, *The Maine Farmer*. Largely due to his influence, Maine formed a Board of Agriculture in 1852.

In this period Maine witnessed the beginnings of careful breeding programs and saw vast improvements in the quality of horses and cattle. In the more settled areas, commercial agriculture was replacing mere subsistence farming. Wheat remained an important crop but became less profitable in the face of western competition, which made use of the new railways. It was an age also of cattle drives, most of which crossed the Piscataqua Bridge and moved on to the stockyards of Brighton, Massachusetts. By the 1850s, railways began to lessen the need for drives.

By 1840 Maine was second among states in the production of potatoes, and starch factories flourished in Skowhegan, Mercer, Bethel, and Phillips until the blight of the 1840s caused a reversal in fortune. By the end of the next decade, resistant varieties were found and Maine was selling half the potatoes available in the United States. Apple orchards flourished and became important. New labor-saving devices were appearing in abundance, and one of them, the first "improved" or "practical" threshing machine, was invented and marketed by John and Hiram Pitts of Winthrop. North Wayne was, in 1860, the world's largest producer of scythes. The outlook in agriculture remained positive and the sector was prospering.

Other occupations were also expanding. In the first six years after statehood, Maine fisheries provided one fifth of the nation's tonnage employed in fisheries. Her vessel types included pinkies and sharpshooters (which carried eight to fifteen dories), and in 1860 the value of Maine fisheries ranked second in the United States. Granite, limestone, and slate quarries were active, and by the 1840s, Maine ice was being cut, packed in sawdust, and shipped primarily to the mid-Atlantic states. Textile mills, though small at first, began to

Sudden gales and violent weather remained a constant threat to mariners during the age of sail. On November 9, 1851, North Yarmouth skipper Levi Marston of the brig *Harriet* discovered the dismasted ship *Unicorn* wallowing off the Grand Banks. In a remarkable rescue operation, the *Harriet*, later assisted by the *Daniel Webster*, managed to save all 325 passengers. Artist Joseph B. Smith presented Captain Marston with this oil, and Queen Victoria bestowed upon him a gold medal for his heroism. COLLECTION OF THE MAINE HISTORICAL SOCIETY

take the form of huge brick complexes beginning in the 1830s. This led to the expansion of brickyards to build Biddeford's Laconia Mills and Pepperell Manufacturing in the 1840s and 1850s, the Bates Mills at Lewiston, and similar cotton and woolen mills elsewhere.

By the 1840s Maine shops were exporting shoes to the West Indies and points along the East Coast. At Gambo Falls, between Gorham and Windham, gunpowder mills flourished despite occasional disasters. At Rockland, lime burning became important, and there were potteries, foundries, and machine and furniture shops throughout the state.

Labor-saving devices improved farming and revolutionized industry. In 1831 the York Manufacturing Company found the waterpower of the Saco River a reason to locate in Saco, and in 1840 they sought a cheap source of labor among farm girls. Eight hundred young women and 200 males were employed to operate 17,800 spindles and 500 looms. The young operators were housed in com-

THE ACHIEVEMENT OF IDENTITY 95

pany living quarters, offered writing school in the evening, and provided with medical attention. It was a tightly regulated life and when pay was cut in 1841, between 400 and 500 women "turned out." They were soon fired, but the march of these women was Maine's first strike and an indication of the unpleasant side of the industry, one that would be seen increasingly in the decades to follow.

No industry caught the popular imagination more, in its day and now, than shipbuilding. In the "Golden Age of Sail" between the War of 1812 and the Civil War, Maine yards in practically every coastal hamlet produced craft from dories to clipper ships. In 1855 Maine reached her peak of 215,909 tons, or more than a third of all ship production in the nation. In this sphere, Maine led all her fellow states. Foremost builders included the Pattens of Topsham (later of Bath), the Sewalls, Houghtons, and McLellans of Bath, Edward O'Brien and Samuel Watts of Thomaston, and J. T. Southard of Richmond. These builders also managed their own fleets.

The urge for speed, stimulated by the California Gold Rush, led to the development of Maine clippers including the *Snow Squall* (part of her bow is now on display at Maine Maritime Museum in Bath), *Flying Scud*, *Portland,* and the most famous of all, the 2,306-ton *Red Jacket*, launched at Rockland in 1853. She crossed from New York to Liverpool in 13 days, 1 hour, and 25 minutes, a record for sailing ships that still holds. The panic of 1857 bankrupted many Mainers and led to the closing of many of the yards. But in its great days, the needs of the industry led to the construction of machine shops, ropewalks, and shipcarvers who produced remarkable figureheads. The town of Bath, on the Kennebec, became the center of the industry, a position it continues to hold with Bath Iron Works. Searsport boasts a heritage of ships' captains that stands unrivaled—in the 1880s they commanded a tenth of the approximately 300 full-rigged ships then under U.S. flag. Today the Maine Maritime Museum in Bath and the Penobscot Marine Museum in Searsport maintain prime collections of maritime materials and documents.

❖

Portland, which became Maine's first city in 1832, remained the state's principal commercial and artistic core. In this bright era, citizens considered themselves as equals of Boston and set forth to surpass that city. The first shot in that contest came in 1820 when Captain Arthur McLellan sold a full cargo in town rather than at Boston. The press applauded: "We hope [this example] will be followed by other capitalists in this state. We shall then be less dependent on Boston for our supplies . . . and after giving the importer a fair profit, they shall come to the consumer on better terms."

In 1821 a group of local businessmen chartered the Cumberland and Oxford Canal from Portland to Lake Sebago. It was completed in 1830, but its use dwindled and died by 1868 with the coming of railroads. Canal Bank (now Key Bank) was begun to finance the project. Between 1800 and 1851, eleven canals, three river navigations, and two ship locks were constructed. The first steamboat ran between Portland and North Yarmouth in 1822, and within a decade there was a regular passenger run to Boston. Within a short time the whole coast from Eastport to Kittery was linked up. Railroads were chartered as early as 1832 but did not operate until 1836. The Portland, Saco & Portsmouth Railroad was finished in 1842, and aside from lumber railroads, was the first important line. The first telegraph reached from Bangor to Belfast in 1848 and was extended to Portland by New Year's. Soon it continued to Eastport, and Maine had a communications network. Thoreau would observe: "We are in great haste to construct a magnetic telegraph from Maine to Texas; but Maine and Texas, it may be, have nothing important to communicate."

In fact, Maine was trading with Texas and nearly all points of the nation. Many of her sons and daughters had become teachers, farmers, mechanics, or politicians in places from Mississippi to Minnesota to Texas. Many down-easters went to California during the gold rush in 1849, while her sailing masters circled the world.

In 1846 Portland's population began to wilt as backcountry trade went to Boston, which extended its railroad lines into Vermont. But at this point Maine's great business visionary, John A. Poor, a native of East Andover, arrived on the scene. Poor fostered a remarkably outward-looking view that saw Portland's future tied to Montreal and the Canadian west. Boston interests also sought the prize. In 1845 Poor raised two million dollars locally, set out in a sleigh during a blizzard, and was able to sign an agreement forming the Atlantic & St. Lawrence Railroad. Poor's major problem was working capital, and when the 300-mile road was finished in 1853, it had to be leased to the Grand Trunk Railway. Though ownership passed into English and Canadian hands, stock immediately rose from thirty to ninety-six dollars a share. Portland, the deep, ice-free harbor a day closer to Europe than Boston, became Canada's winter port.

Though Poor's vision was never fully realized, he did found the Portland Company, which produced 628 locomotives, as well as fire engines, pulp digesters, and gunboats in its long career. Other entrepreneurs included J. B. Brown, who founded the nation's third sugar refinery and built the city's grandest home. Walter Corey turned a small furniture-making shop into one of the first mass production and marketing operations, and in 1836 T. S. Laughlin's blacksmithy began, later to grow into the world's largest manufacturer of drop-forged fittings for wire ropes and chains. The Winslow Pottery flourished and later became the huge Portland Stoneware Company. In 1849 the Portland Gas Company was founded, and soon the streets had light by night. Already the tree-lined avenues had won Portland the title of

East Andover's John Alfred Poor (1808–1871), Maine's greatest nineteenth-century business visionary, correctly predicted a future tied to Canadian grain. He raised two million dollars locally, outsmarted Boston interests, and built the Atlantic & St. Lawrence Railroad between Portland and Montreal. Because of cost overruns the line was leased to the Grand Trunk when finished in 1853; the line surrounding the port, however, remained Canada's primary winter rail connection until the 1920s, and related industries flourished. Poor was also the principal force behind the European & North American Railway, which was to have connected Bangor with the Maritimes and the Canadian west. During WW II, the Montreal pipeline from South Portland made a similar connection. COLLECTION OF THE MAINE HISTORICAL SOCIETY

"Forest City." Her stores, great wharves, banks, and beautiful Merchant's Exchange building, along with the vast Commercial Street engineering project, which extended the waterfront into the harbor, made for a bustling city.

The Portland Athenaeum was founded in 1819, and eight years later combined with the

THE ACHIEVEMENT OF IDENTITY

A guiding spirit of American culture, Henry Wadsworth Longfellow (1807–1882) became one of the most painted, sculpted, and photographed individuals anywhere. Portland's leading portrait painter, C. O. Cole (1817–1858), painted his beardless likeness in 1842. During his spectacular career as a poet and educator at Bowdoin and Harvard, Longfellow maintained close ties to Maine and enthusiastically assisted young artists and writers. COLLECTION OF THE MAINE HISTORICAL SOCIETY

Falmouth Library Association to serve as a semi-public library. It was a city that fostered education and culture, and in 1821, the nation's second high school was established.

If the city was the focus of culture, it was not alone. All over Maine, people were promoting education and societies. The Maine Historical Society, the third oldest such organization founded in the United States, was begun in 1822 at the Portland State House and later moved to Bowdoin College before returning to Portland. Bowdoin College was already turning out remarkable graduates including William Pitt Fessenden (1823); future president Franklin Pierce (1824); the remarkable Class of '25, which included authors Henry Wadsworth Longfellow, Nathaniel Hawthorne, and John S. C. Abbott; Congressman Jonathan Cilley; and Commodore Horatio Bridge. In 1826 John Brown Russwurm, the second black to graduate from an American college, began his career. He established New York's *Freedom's Journal*, and went on to become governor of Liberia's Maryland Colony. In 1824 Maine Wesleyan Seminary (later Kent's Hill Academy) was established, followed by Portland's Westbrook Seminary (now the Westbrook College campus of University of New England) in 1831 and Houlton's Ricker Classical Institute (Ricker College) in 1847. In 1846 the state of Maine established a board of education, followed by a state superintendent of schools in 1854, and a crucial "Free Public Library" law that same year. Upper- and middle-class women were also taking advantage of abundant female academies, primary schools, and seminaries in this period. By the 1820s, they were playing a major, though rarely chronicled, role in the development of Maine's social and cultural sectors.

Women of the late Jeffersonian and early Jacksonian periods were among the first groups to identify, consider, and address the problem of poverty. Colonial Mainers gave little time to the problem and did not believe much could be done about it. Portland had an almshouse, children were indentured under the direction of selectmen or overseers of the poor, and in the towns, paupers were cared for by the bidder asking the lowest amount of town support. Paupers in a person's care were expected to work for that person. By the 1830s town poor farms became popular, and many lasted until the middle of the twentieth century.

The issue of slavery captured the attention of Mainers. In 1838 the first antislavery newspaper in the state, the *Advocate of Freedom*, was published at Hallowell. Close business ties with southern ports, however, made views on abolition far from unanimous. Artist Charles Henry Granger (1812–1893) captured a poignant debate on the subject at Saco's Hanover House in the 1840s. A black man is included in the group, and though publicly overshadowed by white abolitionists, Maine blacks were active in both the antislavery and the American Colonization Society. COLLECTION OF THE SACO MUSEUM, SACO, MAINE

State government had little interest in dealing with social problems, but following national custom did build a prison at Thomaston in 1824 and a boys' reform school (now Longcreek Youth Development Center) in 1850. Hearing-impaired children and adults were sent to schools out of state. Private institutions such as the Female Orphan Asylum of Portland (1828), the Samaritan

THE ACHIEVEMENT OF IDENTITY   99

Society (1828), and the Bangor Female Orphan Asylum (1836) created a kind of social safety net. Nearly all such endeavors were run by women. By the 1850s the YMCA, the Portland School for Medical Instruction, and the Maine Medical Association were started. All were private, although occasionally town or state funds were granted for specific projects.

The federal government's role was even more slight, confined to patronage jobs in the postal system, customhouses, lighthouses, and, in the 1850s, the Life Saving Service. Most spectacular was the appearance of the government's "Third System" of forts after the War of 1812. Not only were forts like McClary in Kittery and Preble and Scammell in Casco Bay upgraded, but the impressive Forts Gorges, in Casco Bay, and Knox, guarding the Penobscot at Prospect, were begun. Shipbuilding and repair continued at the Portsmouth Naval Shipyard, where bridges built in the 1820s now connected Kittery to Portsmouth and Fernald's Island to Kittery. A hospital was constructed in 1834, a floating dry dock was operating by 1852, and twelve ships were launched in the period, among them a steam frigate and a steam sloop. Labor was rarely a problem when it came to public works and federal construction facilities.

In 1820 there were very few non-English immigrants, but that situation changed quickly. By the 1830s, stimulated by hard times and the potato famine, the Irish immigration began to have an impact on Maine. Many of the Irish contracted cholera during their passage to America. When they arrived, they were also seen as a threat to those Yankees in lower-paying jobs. As early as 1833, a clash between Irish laborers and sailors in Bangor resulted in a riot that lasted for three days. Immigrants were burned out of their residences and driven from the city. When the anti-Irish mob began to burn the homes of wealthy merchants, the militia was called out and the riot stopped. Visiting Hallowell in 1839, Nathaniel Hawthorne reported on numerous French and Irish unskilled workers who lived in shacks and frequently quarreled with each other. By the 1840s Portland's William Willis believed that the city's "increased mortality may be attributed to the influx of foreign population, drawn here by our public works." The gas company, mills, canals, and railroads all needed broad backs for jobs requiring little training. Indeed, labor-saving machinery in the hands of immigrants was putting the old skilled laborers, or mechanics, out of business. The famous black stevedores of the Portland waterfront lost out to steam winches and cheap Irish labor.

The Maine Charitable Mechanic Association and the like-named association in Bangor (1828) were designed to assist skilled workers. The former started having fairs, which included Maine's first art exhibitions in 1826, 1838, 1854, and 1859. It founded a library that still exists, gave free instruction to young men, and held a major labor parade in 1841. Organized to uplift the skilled worker in his own eyes and those of society, the association was begun as a counterbalance to the mercantile elite. But as times changed, skilled workers found themselves in conflict with the unskilled masses. More and more well-paying jobs were being lost, and to make matters worse, the newcomers were largely Catholic, the old enemy from colonial times.

Clashes between immigrants and "natives" were occurring throughout the nation, and agitators such as Ned Buntline, who flittered from St. Louis to Maine, stoked the fires. The so-called Know-Nothings (nativists) achieved political prominence, and by 1854 things were at full boil locally. Anson P. Morrill ran for governor backed by the Free Soil Party, the Maine Law Party (Temperance), and the Know-Nothings. Some 16 to 20 percent of the voters were nativist and were much alarmed by the 30,000 Catholics now estimated to be living in Maine. Portland's Catholic population rose from about 43 people in 1822 to 6,000 in

On the evening of July 6, 1854, a nativist mob burned Bath's Old South Meeting House, which was being used by Irish Catholic citizens. This was one of several outrages, including the tarring of Father John Bapst at Ellsworth, which swept Maine during the height of the nativist "Know-Nothing" movement. With the arrival of the Irish in the 1830s, immigrants began to change the ethnic texture of Maine. Firefighter John Hilling (1826–1894) accurately depicted the attack on Old South in several paintings. COLLECTION OF THE MAINE HISTORICAL SOCIETY

1866. In Ellsworth, nightly marches occurred in Catholic neighborhoods as editor William Chaney of the *Ellsworth Herald* pushed for a return to "American" values. On July 6, 1854, a night riot in Bath led to the burning of a church rented by Catholics and attacks on their homes. In October, Father John Bapst was tarred, feathered, and carried on a rail at Ellsworth, and Ned Buntline, thinking himself under attack near Bath, shot and wounded a man. By the spring of 1855, notes University of Southern Maine professor Alan Whitmore, the Know-Nothing societies in Maine listed 27,000 members. In 1854 the Diocese of Portland (which included Maine and New Hampshire) had been formed but no bishop appointed. The Madawaska remained, for a time, under a Quebec diocese. Under difficult circumstances, Father John O'Donnell struggled successfully until David

William Bacon became bishop in 1855. Soon after this, Catholic schools, orphanages, and institutions established themselves alongside those of the Yankees.

Ethnic and economic differences were not the only things to spark violence in this period. Throughout the era, there were riots aimed at houses of prostitution. The worst was Portland's King Riot of 1849, which was actually several clashes culminating in a blazing gunfight that killed one man and wounded a dozen. A crowd of a thousand burned a Munjoy Hill dancehall and was stopped from doing further damage only when the militia appeared to aid the police. Prior to 1849 there *were* no police, only a citizen's watch. Fights often occurred between sailors and young men back from college. Night-bands of musicians, often with pianos atop wagons, were paid by sleepy citizens to go away.

In this violence-prone time, Maine produced a number of important reformers who followed or led national movements. The famous Dorothea Dix, born in Hampden, spent her life addressing conditions in prisons and asylums throughout the nation and overseas. William Ladd established a model farm in Minot and founded the American Peace Society. Elijah Parish Lovejoy of Albion graduated from Waterville College (now Colby) and became a prominent journalist in the movement to abolish slavery. He was shot and killed by a mob at Alton, Illinois, in 1837, a martyr to the cause. Most famous of all was Neal Dow, the "Father of Prohibition," who got the Maine State Legislature to pass the first temperance law, the Maine Law, in 1851. By 1855 twelve other states had passed laws banishing strong drink. As mayor of Portland, Dow was the central figure in the Rum Riot of 1855, which saw the militia again called out and one rioter killed.

In these great causes, individual Mainers did lead, but their neighbors were not always in agreement. Many fortunes were made supplying illegal beer, wine, and whiskey. While most Mainers did not like slavery, they were divided on how to deal with the issue. General Fessenden was the best-known abolitionist, while others, like the color-blind John Neal, promoted the American Colonization Society, which attempted to return slaves and free blacks to Africa. The arrival of the fiery abolitionist Stephen Symonds Foster at Portland in 1842 triggered a riot at the Friends' Meeting House. Foster was beaten and had his clothing torn from his back by a mob. Only the arrival of Elizabeth Widgery Thomas and Lydia Neal Dennett, who pulled him to safety, saved him from worse. Indeed, most Mainers were not ready to force the abolition of slavery in other states. There were many commercial, social, and political ties to the South. Ruggles Sylvester Morse, for example, left Leeds, Maine, in 1816, made a fortune as a New Orleans hotelman, and, between 1858 and 1860, built Portland's lavish Victoria Mansion. The cotton trade brought wealth to shipowners. Others, including Congressman L. D. M. Sweat, had studied in Southern law offices, such as that of Louisiana's Pierre Soule. Finally, there were those down-easters such as Zebulon York of Avon who lived in the South. With his partner, York owned six plantations and some 1,700 slaves.

❖

Maine was remarkable in politics, business, and social causes, but it was in the arts that she triumphed. Prior to statehood, there was only one fiction writer of note, Madam Wood, and one serious part-time painter, Parson Fisher. Now, artists of all kinds loomed large and prosperous. Henry Wadsworth Longfellow, born in 1807 in Portland during the year of the embargo, became America's favorite and most widely read poet. In an age that loved verse, he popularized the American Indian, gave a human edge to the dour Pilgrims in *The Courtship of Miles Standish*, and wrote a most eloquent story of the Acadians dispersed at the hands of the New Englanders. Curiously, he made

Considered by many to be the finest surviving Italian villa-style home in the United States, Portland's Victoria Mansion, or Morse–Libby House, was designed by Connecticut architect Henry Austin. Built between 1858 and 1860 for the Leeds-born Ruggles Sylvester Morse, its stately brownstone exterior is matched by a breathtakingly decorated and furnished interior. Reflecting the fact that Morse made his fortune as a New Orleans hotelier, the stained-glass window in the front hall includes the state seals of both Louisiana and Maine. COURTESY OF THE VICTORIA SOCIETY OF MAINE, PORTLAND, MAINE

his grandfather's old nemesis, Paul Revere, a household name. In popularizing local and regional history, Longfellow did a great service, and his work was translated into many languages.

Historian Francis Parkman might speak of a stupid down-easter as a type on one of his several trips to Maine, but Mainers continued to help shape colleges such as Harvard. Longfellow became professor of modern languages and belles lettres in 1835; Simon Greanleaf, who grew up in New Gloucester, was given the Royall Professorship of Law in 1833, and John Langdon Sibley of Union was Harvard's librarian and author of the first three *Biographical Sketches of Graduates of Harvard University* as well as a history of Union, Maine. First-rate town historians, including William Willis, also flourished.

Talents became prolific in a short time, and two distinctive strands emerged: the native and the newcomer or visitor. Harriet Beecher Stowe is a perfect example of the latter, for it was at Brunswick, while her husband taught at Bowdoin, that she wrote the widely influential novel *Uncle Tom's Cabin* (1852). Charles Codman, Maine's first settled landscape painter, was born in the Boston area before appearing at Portland in 1822. Yet he became the co-founder of a strong, local visual arts tradition. The first generation included William Mathew Prior of Bath, Charles O. Cole, J. T. Harris, C. E. Beckett, and Frederic Mellen, all of whom worked in the city.

John Neal, born at Portland in 1793, became an itinerant artist, read for the law in Baltimore, learned to box, fence, and write novels, lived in the household of English philosopher Jeremy Bentham, and wrote the first criticism of American art in English magazines during the 1810s and 1820s. Returning home in 1827, Neal was met by a mob whose members took issue at finding themselves in one of his novels. After knocking one tormentor about, the combative Neal stayed to forge an alliance of writers and artists. Working from Portland, he published a literary magazine, *The Yankee* (1828–1829), and helped promote or discover Poe, Whittier, Rembrandt Peale, and others, including the next generation of Maine artists. Among them were sculptors Benjamin Paul Akers and Franklin Simmons and painters Maria à Becket, Harrison Bird Brown, and J. R. Tilton.

THE ACHIEVEMENT OF IDENTITY

Next to Longfellow, John Neal (1793–1876) was Maine's best-known literary figure of the time. An attorney, novelist, and boxer, he became America's first art critic in the 1820s. He helped make Portland an art center that drew talent from the backcountry. At times Portland rivaled and employed more artists than Boston. Neal founded a literary journal, *The Yankee*, demanded full rights for women, and was "the Father of Athletics in Maine." COURTESY PRIVATE COLLECTION

Several of these people had extraordinary careers in America and abroad. Neal wrote novels including *Seventy-Six* and *The Down-Easters*, but aside from his reviews and autobiography produced no masterpieces. As America's first art critic, however, and a talent scout and social activist supporting total equality for women, he loomed large.

Together with Neal, there were a number of popular artists who won national or even international fame. Ann S. Stephens, a Neal protégé, published and edited the *Portland Magazine* and *Portland Sketchbook* in the 1830s. Those volumes drew together Longfellow, Neal, Codman, and a half-dozen other important talents. Stephens went on to New York, where she edited and later published monthly magazines and also wrote highly successful dime novels. Portland's N. P Willis became a notable journalist, travel writer, and member of the Knickerbocker group in New York. His sister, Sara Payson Willis Parton, wrote best-selling books under the pen name "Fanny Fern." In 1855 she was making the then-remarkable sum of a hundred dollars a week writing for the *New York Ledger*. Elizabeth Oakes Smith was yet another Mainer whose journalism enjoyed national popularity. Her feminist works are of particular importance. Two brothers from Maine, Jacob and John S. C. Abbott, also turned to writing, The first produced some two hundred works, most notably the "Little Rollo" stories for children, while John's most noted book was a much-read biography of Napoleon. Isaac McLellan, Jr., was a favorite of the small but growing contingent of outdoorsmen and won the title "Poet of Rod and Gun."

Nearly every town produced a visual artist or two. Sculptor Edward Augustus Brackett, whose *Drowned Mother and Child* was a sentimental favorite, came from Vassalboro. His brother Walter, a noted painter of game fish, was born at Unity. Saco was home to genre artist Charles Henry Granger, and Rumford home to the Ward-

In 1830 the artist James Osborne (n.d.) painted this unusually fresh watercolor as a genealogical record of Scarborough's Libby family. These well-to-do country folk are dressed in all their finery. Beneath them is their home, a fine early example of Maine Connected Architecture. Throughout the period, agriculture remained the primary occupation of most Mainers. COLLECTION OF THE MAINE HISTORICAL SOCIETY

well family of painters and craftspeople. Bangor and Brewer, where the art scene was rivaled only by Portland, was famous for painter Jeremiah Pearson Hardy, his sister Mary Ann, and second and third generations of artists, photographers, and writers. The first daguerrotypist visited Maine in 1840, and by 1860 there were eighty-nine resident photographers. The famous genre artist Eastman Johnson hailed from Lovell and produced some of his best works in Maine. During this period, the State of Maine's citizens reached an unparalleled height of self-confidence.

Through the 1860s, no one city dominated the American art scene. There were a number of small markets scattered across the land, and Portland and Bangor were counted as important. Not only did they produce impressive figures and patrons, but they attracted major artists, actors, and traveling exhibitions. For example, William Dunlap's large oil painting, *The Christ Rejected* (1822), had failed to attract interest in Boston. Depressed, the artist recalled: "I shipped my picture further east, to Portland where the tide of fortune turned." In a short time he made, above expenses, between two and three hundred dollars. Thomas Sully's famous *Passage of the Delaware* (1822) and Hiram Powers's marble masterpiece *The Greek Slave* (1851) were also exhibited in Portland to acclaim.

In 1829 a theater was built in Portland and it drew first-class actors such as Edwin Forest.

Persis Sibley Andrews Black (1813–1891) was a first-rate diarist. A native of Freedom, she lived in various Oxford County towns. Her first husband was Charles Andrews, her second Congressman Alvah Black. This image of Persis and her first child was painted at Dixfield in 1844 by Rumford itinerant Caroline Wardwell (1822–1896). In her diary, now in the Maine Historical Society, Persis noted: "Miss Wardwell paints as well as any Miniature painter I ever knew tho' she is a beginner & almost entirely self taught. She has boarded with us & asks only $5.00. Her company more than pays for a week's board." COLLECTION OF THE MAINE HISTORICAL SOCIETY

Bangor followed, attracting similar talents. The strange Professor F. Nicholls Crouch, composer of *Kathleen Mavourneen*, headed up Portland's Sacred Music Society, causing little but disharmony. Hermann Kotzschmar left Germany after the Revolution of 1848 and became the veritable music tsar of Maine for the next forty-seven years. Under his strong direction, major touring musicians made Portland a must stop.

Perhaps the most famous Mainer of the period was not a person, but a character escaped from the imagination of Buckfield journalist Seba Smith, husband of Elizabeth Oakes. The character was Major Jack Downing, who first appeared in the *Portland Courier* in 1830. A rural down-easter, Major Jack blundered into Portland and on to Washington where, by a series of happy accidents, he became an advisor to President Jackson. People from other regions recognized themselves, or elements of themselves, in the attitude and local dialect of this everyman from "jest about the middle of down east." For their part, Mainers found a specific identity that they could laugh at and be proud of simultaneously. Smith produced two books: *The Life and Writings of Major Jack Downing of Downingville* (1833) and *My Thirty Years Out of the Senate* (1859). The character was pirated by other writers, and the major showed up at the elbow of Jackson in all the best political cartoons of the day. Seba Smith made little money on the idea, but he initiated a Maine tradition of humor that, for better or worse, continues into the present. Together with the poems of Longfellow, the scenes of Eastman Johnson, the political prominence of Hannibal Hamlin, the observations of Fanny Fern, and the appearance of ships such as *Red Jacket*, Maine and Mainers had assumed a positive national identity.

Major Jack Downing was born in the pages of the *Portland Courier* during the 1830s. The original down-east character was the creation of Buckfield's Seba Smith (1792–1868), and within a short time, Major Jack became America's symbol for the backwoods Jacksonian. Smith wrote *The Life and Writings of Major Jack Downing* (1833) and *My Thirty Years Out of the Senate* (1859), from which this illustration was taken. His character, however, was pirated by other journalists, including Charles Augustus Davis of the *New York Advertiser*. The Major became an almost essential element of the era's political cartoons. COURTESY OF PORTLAND PUBLIC LIBRARY SPECIAL COLLECTIONS & ARCHIVES

ON THE ROAD TO PORTLAND.

Lovell-born Jonathan Eastman Johnson (1824–1906) had dropped his first name and already achieved national status when he returned to paint at Fryeburg in 1860. *Corn Husking* gives a unique, intimate view of the richness of Maine farm life on the eve of war. On the barn door is the misspelled message "Lincoln and Hamlon," the Republican ticket with Hannibal Hamlin as vice president. The Currier and Ives lithograph published during the war changed the words to "The Union Forever." COURTESY OF THE EVERSON MUSEUM OF ART, SYRACUSE, NEW YORK

6

MAINE AND THE CIVIL WAR (1861–1865)

"If you read the Newspapers you will see that we are in for a season of trouble," wrote Henry Wadsworth Longfellow in the first days of what became the Civil War. "It is an evil now," the poet continued, "but I trust that a great good will come out of it." Not all Mainers were in sympathy with that view, for as soon as South Carolina's forces had reduced Fort Sumter, Portland's powerful newspaper, the Democratic *Eastern Argus*, was squealing "The Calamity is upon us!" asking, "What is to be gained by War?" and terming the action "President Lincoln's War." Others quickly organized volunteer troops in answer to Lincoln's call. Indeed, the Second Maine Regiment organized at Bangor may have been the first in the nation. Whatever the view, nobody could have predicted the brutality and cost of the conflict to come, nor the fact that it marks such an extraordinary watershed in the history of Maine and the nation.

In 1860 Maine was still largely an agrarian state with 64,843 farmers and 15,865 farm laborers. Other important occupations listed in the 1860 census included 18,734 laborers, 13,371 servants, 11,370 mariners, 5,209 teachers, and 4,607 fishermen. There were 3,032 merchants, 2,777 blacksmiths, 1,460 lumbermen (presumably full-time), 2,384 seamstresses, 1,982 ship-carpenters, and 1,215 traders among the major employment groups. Interestingly, there were 111 artists, 52 musicians, 4 actors, and 3 authors, again all presumably full-time. In spite of reverses in shipbuilding, pre–Civil War Maine was vibrant and its citizens optimistic about the future of the nation and their place in it.

In 1860 the great genre artist Eastman Johnson visited the haunts of his Oxford County boyhood and produced one of his most enduring images, *Corn Husking*. The scene was painted using the barn of Ebenezer Day in Fryeburg and shows Maine farmers at a high point of confidence and productivity. A sturdy laborer carries a basket of corn from the barn while behind him are a young couple and an old man with a toddler. A gun, dog, brace of ducks, and the words "Lincoln and Hamlon [sic]" written on the door complete the scene. Few works better foreshadow the coming war.

Indeed, Mainers took pride in the fact that their favorite son, Hannibal Hamlin, had become the Republican vice-presidential candidate in May of 1860. His participation gave Abraham Lincoln a much-needed boost in a split field that included Democrat Stephen A. Douglas, Constitutional Union candidate John Bell, and the southern favorite John C. Breckenridge. In November Lincoln and Hamlin won the electoral vote, and the die was cast.

South Carolina, a state with close commercial ties to Maine, seceded from the Union in December of 1860, and by February of 1861, ten states had followed in the creation of the Confederate

Lincoln's first vice president, Hannibal Hamlin (1809–1891), was born at Paris Hill, Maine, studied law in the office of Fessenden & Deblois, and practiced in Hampden. He served in Congress and the Senate as a Democrat, but became a Republican in 1856, announcing the change on the floor of the Senate. He won election as governor that year. He returned to the Senate, became Lincoln's running mate, and later became a private soldier in Maine. In the postwar era he was re-elected to the Senate, serving until 1881. COURTESY PRIVATE COLLECTION

Governor Israel Washburn's first call for ten companies of volunteers produced only six, for Maine was largely unprepared. By the war's finish, however, Maine had supplied 70,107 men, more in proportion to its population than any other northern state. COLLECTION OF THE MAINE HISTORICAL SOCIETY

States of America. Jefferson Davis was made president of the new nation, and federal installations and arms were seized in the sad last days of the Buchanan administration. Under heavy guard, Lincoln and Hamlin were sworn into office on March 4, 1861. Then, on the 12th of April, Confederate forces bombarded and forced the evacuation of Fort Sumter. With the fall of the fort, Lincoln called for 75,000 volunteers.

Like many northern states, Maine was ill-prepared for combat. Although she had militia orga- nizations dating back to the earliest times, many were little more than social clubs. Historian William B. Jordan, Jr., estimates that of the 60,000 men enrolled, only 12,000 were regular attendants at muster. Some Mainers had seen service in the Mexican–American War, but that conflict was short and had little impact on the state. Governor Israel Washburn's first call for ten companies of volunteers produced only six. Organization at the outset was bungled, although a few existing companies, such as the Lewiston Zouaves, the Bangor

110   MAINE: THE WILDER HALF OF NEW ENGLAND

U.S. Supreme Court Justice, Nathan Clifford (1803–1881) of Rumney, New Hampshire, moved to Maine at the outset of his legal career and became the most prominent Maine Democrat of the Civil War era. He served in Congress, was U.S. minister to Mexico and negotiator of the Mexican War Treaty, and served as attorney general in the Polk administration (1846–1848). President Buchanan appointed him to the Supreme Court, where he served until his death. COLLECTION OF THE MAINE HISTORICAL SOCIETY

There were four Maine governors between 1861 and 1865, all Republicans. Abner Coburn (1803–1885), a "lumber king" from Skowhegan, gained the office with a bit of maneuvering by the rising state Republican Party chairman, James G. Blaine, in 1862. A dour, rough-hewn character, Coburn kept his sizable fortune close until his death, when he made generous bequests to the Maine General Hospital, Colby College, and the University of Maine. COURTESY PRIVATE COLLECTION

Light Infantry, and the Portland Mechanic Blues, could be considered elite. As things began to take form, enthusiasm grew. With a first loan of one million dollars assumed by the state, new uniforms, bands, and banners were the order of the day. Civilians responded as women rolled bandages and railroads and steamboats took soldiers south without charge. Bangor's Samuel Veazie gave $50,000 to the war effort. "On to Richmond!" was the hopeful cry heard in the streets and town squares. The disaster of Bull Run, late in July of 1861, came as a blow and suggested a longer and bloodier effort. A few weeks later, a peace convention was held in Bangor, and a patriotic backlash led to the destruction of Marcellus Emery's *Bangor Democrat* newspaper.

Antiwar Democrats, called "Copperheads" by their detractors, remained prominent throughout the conflict. Only one Maine Democrat, Lorenzo De Medici Sweat, was elected to Congress during the war. All governors in the period were Republican. Lot M. Morrill finished his term in 1861 and

William Pitt Fessenden (1806–1869) was born in New Hampshire but grew up in Maine with his natural father. Graduating from Bowdoin in 1823, he became an attorney and Whig politician. His antislavery stance brought him to prominence in the new Republican Party. As a senator, he chaired the Finance Committee and became Lincoln's secretary of the treasury in 1864. During the impeachment trial of President Andrew Johnson, Fessenden's courageous "not guilty" vote saved Johnson and led to Fessenden's public denunciation. COLLECTION OF THE MAINE HISTORICAL SOCIETY

was followed by Israel Washburn, Jr., Abner Coburn, and Samuel Cony. The U.S. senators from Maine were Augusta's Lot M. Morrill, Rockland's Nathan A. Farwell, and Portland's great William Pitt Fessenden. Interestingly, Maine-born men served as wartime governors in Massachusetts and New Hampshire. Governor Washburn's brother Elihu was a congressman from Illinois and his brother Cadwallader a congressman from Wisconsin who resigned to become a major general.

On a national political level, Mainers continued to fill important positions. The most conspicuous was Vice President Hamlin, but he had little power. In an effort to gain support in the border states, the Republican Party chose to replace Hamlin with vice-presidential candidate Andrew Johnson during Lincoln's second campaign. In 1865, Hamlin was again disappointed in a bid to become senator, but he would resurface again after the fighting was over. More crucial to the grand scheme was Senator William Pitt Fessenden, the powerful chairman of the Finance Committee, which was in charge of both revenue and appropriation bills. In June of 1864, Lincoln talked Fessenden into serving as secretary of the treasury, a cabinet position previously held by Salmon Portland Chase. Until he returned to his Senate seat, Fessenden's financial skill helped guide the nation. Fessenden's hand-picked successor as secretary was Hugh McCulloch, a native of Kennebunk.

It was also during the war that James G. Blaine, soon to be known as "the Man from Maine," began his rise to power. Actually, Blaine was a native of Pennsylvania who came to the state in 1854 after marrying Augusta's Harriet Stanwood. In 1862, as chairman of the Republican Party, he assisted in the nomination and election of lumber baron Abner Coburn as governor. The following year saw Blaine elected to Congress, where he would achieve subsequent fame.

Political influence was augmented by literary productions. Lincoln, like most Americans, was

Artemus Ward, "the genial Yankee showman," was the creation of Charles Farrar Browne (1834–1867) of Waterford, Maine. The earthy character, a descendant of Major Jack Downing, first appeared in Ohio newspapers and then moved to the theater and books. During the struggle for the Union, Ward became a favorite of the public and Lincoln himself. This illustration appears in *Artemus Ward, His Book*, 1862. COURTESY OF PORTLAND PUBLIC LIBRARY SPECIAL COLLECTIONS & ARCHIVES

fond of Longfellow's verse, and the president claimed that most of his "historical knowledge" derived from the books of Brunswick's John S. C. Abbott. When Lincoln was presented to Harriet Beecher Stowe, he is supposed to have responded, "So this is the little woman who wrote the book that made this big war." *Uncle Tom's Cabin* was followed by Stowe's best Maine novel, *The Pearl of Orr's Island* (1862). Stowe's home in Brunswick remains a point of interest for many tourists.

Following in the tradition of Seba Smith and his character Major Jack Downing was Charles Farrar Browne of Waterford, Maine, and his creation, Artemus Ward, "the genial Yankee showman." After working as a printer for a Skowhegan newspaper, Browne ran through a series of jobs. While working for the *Cleveland Plain Dealer* in Ohio, Browne introduced a letter to the editor from the showman "Artemus Ward." The character caught on, leading to national articles, a tour of the United States and Europe, and several books. *Artemus Ward, His Book* (1862), complete with "ingrammaticisms," sold an immediate 40,000 copies and was a favorite of the president, who read Ward to the cabinet before telling them he had signed the Emancipation Proclamation. During the war, the showman was a great supporter of the Union cause.

Artemus Ward toured Maine, where lectures, concerts, and plays continued unabated. At the time of Fort Sumter's bombardment, for instance, John Wilkes Booth was in Portland appearing in *Rafaelle, the Reprobate* and *The Corsican Brothers*. The next day he absconded without paying his newspaper advertising bill. The theatrical atmosphere was brightened considerably when America's celebrated actress, Charlotte Cushman, arrived a few weeks later to play Lady Macbeth.

Miss Cushman had close connections to critic John Neal and the sculptor Benjamin Paul Akers. The latter had formally exhibited his neoclassic masterpiece, *The Dead Pearl Diver*, at the Maine Charitable Mechanic Exhibition and Fair in 1859–1860. His place as leading sculptor was taken by Franklin Simmons, a native of Webster, Maine, who became one of the chief artistic beneficiaries of the war. Simmons began with a full-length statue of Rockland's General Hiram C. Berry, who was killed at Chancellorsville. Probably aided by William Pitt Fessenden, Simmons produced a series of portrait medallions of Lincoln's cabinet. From that point until decades later, the sculptor continued to meet the demand for images of fallen heroes and rising politicians. A few artists, including Gardiner's Elbridge Wesley Webber and Portland's J. B. Hudson, Jr., entered the army and produced paintings. The once-healthy market for landscape and portrait painting, however, was drying up. Photography and prints were becoming more available, affordable, and desirable.

For the most part, life on the home front remained productive. Portland, in particular, was growing. It boasted its first street railway with horse cars. There was also a new 10,647-book athenaeum. In 1864 the venerable Bangor Historical Society got off to a start. The previous year, William Willis completed his *History of the Law Courts and Lawyers of Maine*. In 1861 Lemuel Cushing of Chatham, Canada, opened the Ottawa House on a Casco Bay island renamed for himself. Cushing anticipated the arrival of affluent summer visitors via the Grand Trunk. J. B. Brown, Portland's leading capitalist, combined with others to open the Portland Glass Company in 1863, and soon it was producing 5,000 pieces of pressed glass a day. The arrival of soldiers and sailors in number made a rowdy town even more so, and there were numerous clashes between the authorities and patrons of bawdy houses.

Many industries turned directly to the war effort. In Rockland, sail lofts were converted to tent-making spaces, while the growing factory complexes at Biddeford and Lewiston were producing blankets and other textiles for the armed forces. Still, Maine ranked fifth in New England in the number employed in cotton manufacturing and sixth in woolen. In 1860 some 7,000 French-

While rebel guns pounded Fort Sumter into submission on April 13, 1861, Portlanders were enjoying the acting of John Wilkes Booth (1838–1865) in *Rafaelle*, *The Reprobate*, and *The Corsican Brothers*. This rare broadside announces his earlier performance as Macbeth, which was repeated on April 11 with an extra attraction, *Brothers and Sisters, or The Soldiers of Fort Sumter*. The Portland Theatre stood on the site of the Fidelity Bank Building, next to the present Portland Public Library. Information on Booth in Portland was gathered by Herbert Adams. COURTESY OF THE COLLECTION OF ARTHUR F. LOUX, STILWELL, KANSAS

Mainers followed the events of the Civil War largely through newspapers. Combat artists such as Winslow Homer (1836–1910) focused on the great and small events of army life. This illustration from *Harper's Weekly*, May 17, 1862, shows Homer sketching two six-foot-seven privates from Company F of the 1st Maine Regiment, apparently John J. Handly of Wilton and Edwin Farrar of Bethel. COURTESY PRIVATE COLLECTION

MAINE AND THE CIVIL WAR   115

BUILT FOR THE UNITED STATES
GOVERNMENT IN 1864

The durable Portland Company, started by John A. Poor as a sideline to his railroad project, was active in the war effort, producing the gunboats *Pontoosic* and *Agawam*, fifty eleven-inch rifled cannon, and several locomotives for use by the government. Number 251 was completed in 1864 on government contract.
COLLECTION OF THE MAINE HISTORICAL SOCIETY

Canadian textile workers were in the state. Most had arrived in the last decade. Shipbuilding had declined 80 percent between 1855 and 1859, and the war did little to help. Boots and shoes were in demand, and many small and medium-sized factories flourished along with the tanning industry.

Horses were crucial to the war effort both for the cavalry and as a means of transporting supplies. This broadside, posted at Houlton, speaks to that need. Several Maine fortunes were made by selling horses to the army. COLLECTION OF THE AROOSTOOK COUNTY HISTORICAL AND ART MUSEUM, HOULTON, MAINE

ARMY HORSES WANTED!

FROM 50 TO 60 HORSES
FOR THE CAVALRY, will be purchased at HUNT'S HOTEL, on
MONDAY, TUESDAY, & WEDNESDAY!
Nov. 16th, 17th and 18th. The Horses must be sound, from 5 to 9 years old and well shod. All Colors taken.
T. S. PALMERS,
A. H. GOODSPEED.
Houlton, Nov. 18. 1863.

The Oriental Powder Company in Gorham-Windham was producing 2,500,000 pounds of gunpowder a year for the government. The Portland Company, founded by John A. Poor, turned out more than fifty eleven-inch rifled cannons, several locomotives under government contract, and the gunboats *Pontoosuc* and *Agawam*. Both vessels saw dramatic action.

The Portsmouth Naval Shipyard saw its greatest activity to that date as twenty-six vessels were launched between 1861 and 1865. Among them were the steam sloop *Kearsarge*, which bested the Confederate raider *Alabama* off Cherbourg, France, in 1864, and the ironclads *Passaconaway* and *Agamenticus*. At the height of production, over 2,000 workmen were employed at the yard.

Fear of coastal attack was expressed early in the war when Governor Washburn wrote Lincoln: "Should war again occur with any leading European power, Maine must fall at once into the hands of the enemy, unless means of defense are provided." Soon Portland's harbor forts were being refurbished, Kittery's Fort McClary reinforced, and Fort Popham at the mouth of the Kennebec put under construction. None of these

116   MAINE: THE WILDER HALF OF NEW ENGLAND

Above: The extensive textile mills at Lewiston, shown in this photograph, provided blankets for the federal troops and attracted a growing number of French-speaking workers from Quebec. Many of the early Canadian laborers came with the idea of making money and returning to their farms, but in time, thousands became citizens of Maine. The French Americans soon became the largest non-English ethnic group in the state. Courtesy of the Maine State Museum, Augusta, Maine

Below: The most awesome of Maine's coastal fortifications remains Fort Knox, above the Penobscot River at Prospect. Begun in 1844, it took twenty years to finish the gigantic granite structure, which was intended to mount 137 guns. The state supplied 40 companies of infantry and 3 of artillery for coastal defense. Fort Knox, shown here by Brunswick military painter Seth Eastman (1808–1875), was garrisoned, but never fired a shot in anger. Courtesy of the Library of Congress

Portland marine artist Harrison B. Brown (1831–1915) captured the blowing up of the U.S. revenue cutter *Caleb Cushing* by Confederate raiders under Lieutenant Charles W. Read. On the night of June 26, 1863, the rebels slipped in between the harbor defenses of Portland, captured the cutter, and sailed away. When the wind died and they were overtaken by angry citizens in the steamboats *Chesapeake* and *Forest City*, they chose to destroy the prize and surrender. COLLECTION OF THE MAINE HISTORICAL SOCIETY

magnificent granite defenses was ever fully completed, but they were garrisoned and taken quite seriously. Although the Confederacy attempted to attract help from England and France, such a plan never materialized. On April 17, 1861, however, President Jefferson Davis authorized the licensing of privateers to prey upon United States–flag vessels. Taking this to heart, many American shipowners sold or re-flagged their vessels under other national flags.

The Confederates lacked a large ocean navy, but their raiders proved remarkably successful. Vessels including the *Alabama*, *Florida*, *Tallahassee*, *Sally*, and *Sumter* became famous. In the course of the conflict, eighty-eight Maine vessels were captured or destroyed. The carrying trade was damaged, insurance rates rose, and ships from Norway, Italy, France, and England began to take over commerce. Incidentally, the bounty on codfish was dropped during the war, nearly destroying the Grand Banks fishery in Maine.

The Southerners made several strikes down

east. In the summer of 1863 Lieutenant Charles W. Read, CSN, and a crew of twenty men cut a swath from Cape Hatteras to Portland. Beginning with the captured brig *Clarence*, he transferred to the bark *Tacony* and finally the schooner *Archer*. In the process he sank everything from large ships to fishing schooners. A $10,000 reward was offered for the capture of the audacious privateer who now headed down east. Quietly slipping between Portland's imposing harbor defenses, the rebels boarded and captured the U.S. revenue cutter *Caleb Cushing* and took her out to sea. It was a flawless exercise worthy of Read's training as an Annapolis cadet, but the wind soon died and the steamers *Forest City* and *Chesapeake*, crammed with angry and armed Mainers, soon hove into view. Read abandoned and blew up the cutter and was sent to Fort Warren in Boston Harbor. Several rebels made escape attempts, and two actually made the Maine coast before being caught.

In December of 1863, the *Chesapeake*, on its run from New York to Portland, was hijacked by the terrorist John Clibbon Brain. Arrested earlier in the war for organizing a secret society, Brain claimed British citizenship and was released on condition he not take up arms again. But Brains's unauthorized actions continued, and his men killed a crewman on the *Chesapeake* before taking the vessel to Canada. There she was recaptured by the USS *Malvern*. Canadians had mixed feelings about the war. In 1861, a pro-Southern mob wrecked a pro-Union newspaper in St. Stephen, New Brunswick. In July of 1864, four armed rebels left New Brunswick under the command of Lieutenant William Collins, intending to rob the Calais Bank. Authorities were forewarned by the intelligence network of James Quay Howard, the U.S. consul at St. John, and by Collins's Unionist brother John, who lived in York. Sent to the Maine State Prison at Thomaston, Lieutenant Collins escaped and was helped along the way to Canada by sympathetic or ambivalent Maine farmers.

Ironically, Maine gave birth to more Confederate generals than did Texas, and the only man ever hanged for slave trading under the laws of the United States was a Portlander. A number of Maine men and women had settled in the South and were supportive of the Confederacy. General Danville Leadbetter, a native of Leeds, Maine, graduated from West Point in 1836 and became a prominent army engineer. In 1857 he became Alabama's state engineer. During the war he constructed the fortifications on Mobile Bay and the defenses on Missionary Ridge, and at war's end fled the country with General Joseph Shelby. General Zebulon York was born in Avon, Maine, and went to college in Kentucky. He graduated from Louisiana University with a degree in law before becoming one of the largest slave owners in the South. He fought in a dozen battles, led a regiment at Gettysburg, and lost an arm in the Shenandoah campaign.

Captain Nathaniel Gordon's career was anything but romantic or honorable. A native of Portland, he loaded 900 African slaves aboard the ship *Erie* at the mouth of the Congo River in 1860. The slaver was soon captured by the USS *Mohican*, the captives released in Liberia, and Gordon taken to trial in New York. Though the laws had been on the books for decades, no white man had ever been convicted and executed for man-stealing (piracy). Gordon's timing made him a symbol, with Ralph Waldo Emerson and the Reverend Henry Ward Beecher crying for his death after the jury found him guilty. The war had just begun; Lincoln, under much pressure, refused to sign a reprieve, and in February 1862 Gordon went to the drop. Between 1808 and 1860, it is estimated that one and a half million Africans were smuggled into the United States in ships like Gordon's. Still, there was some sympathy for Gordon, and many down-easters blamed the abolitionists for the war.

In 1861 Robert Elliot of Freedom, Maine,

One of the most dashing officers of the First Maine Cavalry was Captain Black Hawk Putnam (1838–1909) of Houlton, who recruited and led Company E, a unit that lost forty-two men in the Battle of Middleton. Wounded and captured, Putnam escaped to the mountains of Virginia and eventually made it to Union lines. In later years, he was a leader in the Grand Army of the Republic veterans' organization, and is shown riding tall in the saddle in his old age. The Aroostook County Historical and Art Museum's excellent collection boasts much Putnam material, including his boot with the bullet hole suffered at Middleton. COURTESY OF THE AROOSTOOK COUNTY HISTORICAL AND ART MUSEUM, HOULTON, MAINE

organized a company of over forty men opposed to the draft and war taxes. Elliot was arrested and went to prison. In 1863 Congress mandated conscription. The draft proved widely unpopular and was certainly unfair. Those who were wealthy enough could pay a $300 commutation fee or hire a substitute. A number of public figures did so, while supporting the idea of the war. In Kingfield a mob destroyed draft notices, and "Skedaddler's Ridge," across the New Brunswick border near St. Stephen, became a famous point of exit for draft dodgers. On July 4, 1863, some 15,000 people gathered for a peace demonstration led by Anson Burlingame in Garland, Maine. That same summer, Dr. James Rowse, a fiery promoter of peace, got into a broil with the pro-Union Cornelius Hanrahan at Thomaston. As his closing argument, Rowse drew a pistol and shot Hanrahan dead. The doctor was jailed, but escaped to the west.

The majority of the state's citizens remained loyal, at least to the cause of Union. Indeed, few states made greater sacrifices. Maine-born Dorothea Dix was put in charge of the Union's military nurses. Other women, including the valiant Sarah J. Milliken of Baldwin, Hannah E. Starbird of Skowhegan, and Amy Morris Bradley of East Vassalboro, provided extraordinary nursing duty. Miss Bradley, principal of a grammar school in Gardiner, became superintendent of the hospital ship *Ocean Queen* and relief agent at the hospital camp near Alexandria, Virginia. Horrific wounds and casualties in numbers never dreamed of pushed the medical establishment beyond its limits. The U.S. Sanitary Commission, assisted by fundraising fairs, was begun and temporary hospitals constructed. Relief societies were formed to send food, clothing, and medical supplies to the suffering troops, at home and on the front.

Young men from Yankee, Irish, and black families scattered across the map flocked to arms. Maine sent thirty-two infantry regiments, two cavalry regiments, seven batteries of field artillery, one heavy artillery regiment, and a company of crack sharpshooters into battle. She provided more than five thousand sailors and marines and, for garrison duty on the home coast, forty companies of infantry and three companies of artillery. There were heroes like the First Cavalry's Black Hawk Putnam of Houlton. Leading Company E, Captain Putnam was wounded and forty-two of his men were killed at the Battle of Middleton. He and his surviving men soon escaped, and his boot, with a bullet hole, remains an object of admiration on view in the Aroostook County Historical and Art Museum. Others were not so lucky. The 1st Regiment of Maine Cavalry suffered the heaviest losses of any Union cavalry regiment with 174 slain, 334 dead of disease, and 145 captured. Historian Kenneth E. Thompson lists twenty-nine Maine soldiers and twenty-one Maine sailors who earned the Medal of Honor during the War of the Rebellion. John Anglin (1850–1905), the fourteen-year-old son of immigrants at Portland, served as a cabin boy on the USS *Pontoosuc* during the capture of Fort Fisher in 1864–1865 and became the second-youngest recipient "for carrying out his duties faithfully" and for "his cool courage while under enemy fire."

Thirty-one Union generals claimed Maine as their birthplace, as did a number of prominent navy officers. Neal Dow, the former mayor of Portland and temperance leader, organized the 13th Maine as a model, clean-living "Prohibition Regiment." The 13th saw action in Texas and Louisiana, and Dow, promoted to brigadier general, Department of the Gulf, was wounded, captured, sent to Libby Prison, and later exchanged for General Fitzhugh Lee. Other officers included Denmark's General Rufus Ingalls, the quartermaster-general of the Army of the Potomac; Rockland's Adelbert Ames, later Reconstruction governor of Mississippi; Augusta's General Seth Williams; and Bethel's General Cuvier Grover. Nor

Neal Dow (1804–1897) served as colonel of the 13th Maine Regiment, which was dedicated to temperance and clean living. As a brigadier general, he was captured and sent to notorious Libby Prison. Before the war he spearheaded the "Maine Law," prohibiting the sale and manufacture of liquor, and as mayor of Portland was the focus of the 1855 Rum Riot. In 1880 the "Father of Prohibition" made a presidential bid. His home in Portland is a National Historic Landmark administered by the Maine Women's Christian Temperance Union.
COLLECTION OF THE MAINE HISTORICAL SOCIETY

MAINE AND THE CIVIL WAR   121

"Damn the torpedoes!"—Admiral Farragut's famous command at the Battle of Mobile Bay was directed at a Maine man, Captain James Alden (1810–1877). Commanding the *Brooklyn*, Alden brought her and the whole line to a stop when the monitor *Tecumseh* exploded on a mine or torpedo. The battle was quickly resumed, and in spite of his brief hesitation, Alden ended his career as a rear admiral. This portrait was painted by Francois Antoine Cavalli (1835 to after 1878). COLLECTION OF THE MAINE HISTORICAL SOCIETY

The name of Joshua Lawrence Chamberlain (1828–1914), soldier, educator, and politician, will always be linked to Gettysburg, where he commanded the 20th Maine at Little Round Top. His audacity and the valor of the regiment probably turned the tide of battle. A graduate of Bowdoin and the Bangor Theological Seminary, the Brewer-born Chamberlain taught at Bowdoin before the conflict. He served as governor from 1867 to 1871, and for twelve years was president of Bowdoin. His home in Brunswick is maintained by the Pejepscot Historical Society. COLLECTION OF THE MAINE HISTORICAL SOCIETY

should one forget General Benjamin Butler, graduate of Waterville (Colby) College and later controversial governor of Massachusetts.

On the sea, Mainers continued the great tradition of O'Brien and Preble. Admiral Thomas S. Phelps commanded units on the Potomac and York Rivers. George Henry Preble, nephew of Edward Preble, commanded the gunboat *Katahdin* and later the steam sloop *Oneida* in the Gulf of Mexico. He allowed the Confederate cruiser *Oreto* (*Florida*) to get by the blockade, an action that led to his dismissal. Later reinstated, he distinguished himself and was eventually promoted to rear admiral. James Alden, also of Portland, was a career officer who had served in the famous Wilkes Exploration of the Pacific and in the Mexican War. In the Civil War he helped clear the Mississippi, but as commander of the *Brooklyn* at the Battle of Mobile Bay, stopped his ship when the monitor *Tecumseh* hit a mine (torpedo). It was to Alden that Admiral Farragut directed the historic words: "Damn the torpedoes!" Aside from this

The 5th Maine Battery blasts the flank of the attacking Louisiana Tigers at Gettysburg's Cemetery Hill in this sweeping view by Peter Frederick Rothermel (1817–1895). Though Maine was represented in most of the battles of the war, it was perhaps at Gettysburg that her troops performed most brilliantly. Not only did Joshua Chamberlain and O. O. Howard serve the Union well, but the Maine-born general Zebulon York commanded the Louisiana Regiment. COURTESY OF THE STATE MUSEUM OF PENNSYLVANIA, PENNSYLVANIA HISTORICAL SOCIETY AND MUSEUM COMMISSION, HARRISBURG, PENNSYLVANIA

moment of hesitation, Alden was a brave and daring officer who became a rear admiral in the next decade.

The two most famous fighting generals born in Maine were certainly Oliver Otis Howard of Leeds and Joshua L. Chamberlain of Brewer. General Howard, a graduate of Bowdoin College and West Point (class of 1854), was the only Mainer to command an army. He fought in twenty battles, lost an arm at Fair Oaks, and was in charge of Sherman's Right Wing in the march through Georgia. After the war, he headed the Freedman's Bureau, and his interest in black education led to his role in founding Howard University and Lincoln Memorial University. Later he served as superintendent of West Point. Howard also became a negotiator of skill with the Apache and Nez Perce Indians. Equally scholarly and capable, Chamberlain was also a Bowdoin graduate. Unlike Howard, Chamberlain was an ordained minister and a graduate of the Bangor Theological Seminary. Prior to the war he taught rhetoric, moral philosophy, political science, and modern languages at Bowdoin. From 1867 to 1871 Chamberlain was governor of Maine, and for the next twelve years, president of Bowdoin.

The Battle of Gettysburg marked the turning point in the war and it saw both officers at their best. At Cemetery Hill General Howard's 11th Army Corps withstood a massive Southern charge, and Lieutenant Colonel Chamberlain's unflinching 20th Maine drove off two attacks by the rebels at

This wonderful photograph shows the return of the 10th Maine Regiment to Augusta on June 7, 1865. The Bulfinch capitol building is seen in the distance as the men line up before admiring citizens. This infantry regiment saw action at the Battles of Winchester, Cedar Mountain, and Antietam. COURTESY OF THE MAINE HISTORIC PRESERVATION COMMISSION

Little Round Top. Many have viewed that heroic action as the turning point in the battle, which occurred during the first three days of July 1863.

The Emancipation Proclamation had been delivered on January 1 of the same year, making an end of slavery the goal in common with saving the Union. The battle would continue to rage, but dwindling Southern resources and swelling Northern armies were making the outcome all but certain. On November 8, 1864, Lincoln won reelection, and on April 9, 1865, General Robert E. Lee surrendered at Appomattox Courthouse. While some rebels held out until May, and while Lincoln would be assassinated by John Wilkes Booth on April 14, the conflict was for all intents over. Chamberlain, now a general, was given the honor of being present at Lee's surrender and recorded:

> On our part, not a sound of trumpet more, nor roll of drum; not a cheer, nor word nor whisper of vain-glorying . . . but an awed stillness rather, and breath holding, as if it were the passing of the dead. They tenderly folded their flags, battleworn and torn, and laid them down, and then only the Flag of the Union greeted the sky.

124   MAINE: THE WILDER HALF OF NEW ENGLAND

For that privilege, 350,528 Union soldiers had died and 275,175 had been wounded. There were 258,000 Confederate dead and at least 100,000 wounded. In proportion to its population, Maine supplied more men than any other northern state—70,107. Another 2,007 paid commutation. There were 3,184 troops killed in battle, 5,257 who died of disease, and with other causes total deaths reached 9,398. Of all the army's 2,047 regiments, the 1st Regiment Maine Heavy Artillery sustained the greatest loss in combat—423 killed, and at Petersburg alone they sustained 66.5 percent casualties.

Perhaps the worst part concerned an estimated 11,000 wounded and disabled young men who returned home. Some could never again support themselves or their families. Indeed, the army founded the National Home for Disabled Soldiers at Togus in 1866, and the state assisted in opening the Bath Military and Naval Orphan Asylum that same year. Dependent children and broken families had been created by the war. The asylum was one of the state's first tentative moves into the field of dependent care, but it did not become a true state facility until 1929.

Some small towns never really recovered. Little Cyr Plantation sent twenty-five men to the war and eleven died, while Chelsea lost twenty-eight of her ninety-eight soldiers. Forty-nine Mainers received the Congressional Medal of Honor, as did nineteen others with Maine ties, according to Kenneth E. Thompson. The birthrate decreased, and many veterans returned down east only long enough to move their families to the west or to bustling cities. Finally, the state government had saddled itself with a massive $18 million war debt. In 1865 things looked very bleak.

In 1866 Portland, a city of 30,000, ranked fourth in imports and fifth in exports among the nation's seaports. Then, on the afternoon of July Fourth, a carelessly tossed firecracker started a blaze that destroyed over 1,500 buildings and left 12,000 homeless. As the largest urban fire in American history to that date, it galvanized the new National Board of Fire Underwriters. A new, attractive, Victorian city of brick, with a water system and parks, rose from the ashes, but Portland never again rivaled Boston in trade or the arts.
COLLECTION OF THE MAINE HISTORICAL SOCIETY

7

DIMINISHING EXPECTATIONS (1865–1914)

"The fact of the matter is, that in our way of doing business Maine has become an old and exhausted State, before her true wealth has begun to develop," warned Joshua L. Chamberlain in 1877. In preserving the Union, the state lost more than 9,000 young men and had as many as 11,000 wounded or debilitated, while incurring a debt of $18 million.

Now young people left Maine to seek opportunity as old industries failed and new ones proved less lucrative. In time they were replaced by immigrants from Quebec and Europe and by an infusion of summer people and artists seeking an inexpensive, pressure-free environment. Internally, the forward-looking attitudes of John A. Poor and others who saw Maine as a rival of Boston evaporated as Maine became reactive. Still, she managed to boast such outsized figures as James G. Blaine and "Czar" Thomas Brackett Reed in politics, Sara Orne Jewett in literature, Winslow Homer in painting, Madame Nordica in music, and Admiral Robert E. Peary in the field of arctic exploration. In an odd way, the national image of romantic Maine woods and coast was fixed in this era of diminishing expectations.

Arriving at an overview of this contradictory period is made difficult by the lack of historical studies and the growing scale of change as Maine became increasingly part of national trends. Still, an examination of changes in economics, transportation, immigration, lifestyle, culture, education, attitude, and politics provides a framework for consideration.

Fresh from the surrender at Appomattox, General Joshua L. Chamberlain proved an excellent choice as Maine's first postwar governor. He brought intelligence and strong leadership in a time of debt and exodus. The 1870 census showed that for the first time since the Revolutionary War, Maine's population had actually dropped from 628,000 to 627,000. This so alarmed the legislature that William Widgery Thomas, Jr., of the important Portland banking family, was empowered to recruit new settlers from Sweden. He returned successfully with a small group that founded the Aroostook town of New Sweden. Though colorful, the experiment was small in scale and had little overall impact. The opening of Aroostook County—and its eventual connection to the rest of Maine by rail—was the great agricultural bright spot of the period. New England's last frontier had opened. Overall though, Chamberlain's warning about Maine being "old and exhausted" was on the mark.

Since the Revolution, Portland had served as the cultural and commercial heart of Maine, and it had been the focus of such visionary leaders as John Neal and John A. Poor. It had produced businessmen, authors, and artists and, in 1865, the attorney William Willis completed his final edition of *The History of Portland*, a classic of its type, which sold out in a few days. Important Maine historians would soon include James P. Baxter, Henry Burrage, and Joseph Williamson.

Suddenly, on July 4, 1866, Portland was dealt a blow to its confidence and direction. It was a day of celebration that saw the Una rowing club sweep to victory, the Eon baseball team lose to the Massachusetts Lowells, and the trotter, Portland Boy, outdistance his rivals at Presumpscot Park. Then a carelessly tossed firecracker touched off the worst urban fire yet seen in the United States. Twelve thousand were left homeless, and damage was estimated at between five and ten million dollars. Several insurance companies failed, and a National Board of Fire Underwriters was hastily reorganized to protect against future disasters. A modern water system bringing water from Lake Sebago replaced wells, ponds, and cisterns, and a new brick Victorian city was born.

The new Portland, which renewed the phoenix as its symbol, never recovered its competitive edge with Boston. "Portland Beautiful" became the new focus, with the Deering family giving Deering Oaks Park in 1879 and Mayor James Phinney Baxter acquiring land around Back Cove and hiring the Olmsted firm to create a unified park system. In 1882 the Portland Society of Art was founded just as the art scene began to fade, and in 1911 that group opened the L. D. M. Sweat Memorial (now the Portland Museum of Art). It was made possible by the generosity of writer Margaret Jane

The horrors of the Civil War, with its modern weapons and traditional tactics, had caused numerous medical problems. Prior to war, hospitals—where they existed at all—were for the poor. Now, as modern medical techniques began to emerge, they became a place for sick people of all economic backgrounds. In 1867 Dr. Samuel H. Tewksbury of the Maine Medical Association suggested that a hospital be constructed in Portland, and the Maine General Hospital was soon incorporated. Designed by Portland Architect Francis H. Fassett (1823–1908), it was built with help from the state and opened in 1874. As Maine Medical Center, it remains the largest medical facility in the state. COLLECTION OF THE MAINE HISTORICAL SOCIETY

Mussey Sweat. (Curiously, all Maine museums before World War II were founded by women and named for men.) In 1889 the city's first fully public library was opened courtesy of Mayor Baxter, whose own scholarly work focused on the Maine Historical Society's publication series. Bangor's Public Library had opened six years earlier.

In business, John A. DeWitt brought Union Mutual Life Insurance Company (now UNUM) from Massachusetts to new corporate headquarters in Portland. It has remained a key part of the economy. Businesses with origins in the era include Burnham & Morrill, Hannaford Brothers, Deering Ice Cream, retailer Owen Moore, and the Guy P. Gannett Publishing Co. For a time, John Curtis made the city the "Chewing Gum Capital of the World," and Star Match had the second-largest match factory in New England. Beginning in 1891, Thomas Bird Mosher pioneered "modern fine printing in the U.S.," bringing international fame to Portland. The Portland Company continued to produce locomotives and machinery, and in 1910 the Fidelity Building on Congress Street became, briefly, the tallest building in New England.

On the other hand, few improvements were

The Canadian Illustrated News of November 4, 1871, along with papers in the United States, devoted much space to President Ulysses S. Grant's appearance at the opening of the European & North American Railway. Here, Grant leaves the historic Bangor House, designed by Isaiah Rogers in 1834, amid cheering crowds and military units. Unfortunately, the railway—John A. Poor's last dream of competing with Boston—was a failure and had to be leased to the growing Maine Central. COLLECTION OF THE BANGOR HISTORICAL SOCIETY, BANGOR, MAINE

The amount of lumber surveyed at Bangor, after coming down the Penobscot, reached new records in 1866, 1868, 1871, and 1872 in a time when spruce replaced pine. The river-drivers, romanticized by camp poets and later by Holman Day, were as tough a group of men as ever assembled. The work was difficult and risky, necessitating special equipment (steel-calked boots, pick-poles, and peaveys) and guts. The images of these postwar "knights of the spiked-soled boots" speak for themselves. COURTESY PRIVATE COLLECTION

made to the port, and shipping and the West Indies trade went into decline. Factories including Walter Corey's furniture business were never rebuilt after the Great Fire, while Portland Glass manufacturing and J. B. Brown's sugar refinery were soon put out of business by larger, distant competitors.

With the age of commercial mobility finished, more Yankees stayed home. Increasingly the place became more heterogeneous, filling with Irish, German, Jewish, Armenian, Italian, and Scandinavian citizens. Politically and commercially, the Yankee leadership looked inward, touting the community as "Convention City" and a nice place to visit. Summing it up in 1889, the *Sunday Telegram* noted: "We know that this is a too frequent characteristic of Portland people to deem everything which emanates from our city inferior." Such an attitude was a statewide phenomenon that would have horrified Messrs. Neal and Poor.

John A. Poor's last great vision focused on

130   MAINE: THE WILDER HALF OF NEW ENGLAND

In the Warp Room at the Pepperell mill in Biddeford, around 1890 or 1900, female employees wind yarn from cones on a creel onto back beams. In the foreground second hands, or foremen, with watches and ties, go over notes. By this time, 55 percent of the labor force at Pepperell was French-speaking. For excellent insight into the time and place, see Dr. Michael J. Guignard's *La foi, la langue, la culture: The Franco Americans of Biddeford, Maine* (1982). COURTESY OF THE SACO MUSEUM, SACO, MAINE

Bangor, which he wished to connect to St. John, New Brunswick, through a new railroad, the European & North American. He waged a battle to keep only broad gauge, which corresponded to Canadian tracks, and thus kept Boston interests out of state. His new plan again lacked cash and was plagued by problems that led to his ouster. Poor died fifteen days before the line was finished in 1871. The European & North American failed to make money or to stimulate the northern Maine economy in the way it was hoped. Bangor continued to flourish, from boom to bust. The lumber capital still attracted river-drivers and sailors to the notorious "Devil's Half Acre" and the famous madam, Aunt Hat. The port was also the entrance to the Big Woods.

In the same period, the Queen City enjoyed good lectures, plays, and music, as noted in the delightful published journals of Judge John Edwards Godfrey. Covering the period between

Livermore, Maine, boasts a remarkable grouping of buildings on the Washburn estate known as Norlands, including a school, a Universalist Church, a library, and the house shown in this nineteenth-century photograph. The seven sons of Israel and Martha Washburn grew up on a hardscrabble farm, went on to accomplish great things, and built this house for their father in 1868. Israel Jr. was governor of Maine; William Drew was U.S. senator from Minnesota; Elihu was U.S. Secretary of State and congressman from Illinois; Cadwallader was governor and congressman from Wisconsin, and with his brother William founded the mills that would become General Mills; Samuel Benjamin was the captain of a gunboat in the Civil War; and Charles Ames a writer, editor, and diplomat. Today the Washburn–Norlands Foundation runs the estate as a living-history museum that provides rare insight into rural Maine in the last century. COURTESY PRIVATE COLLECTION

1863 and 1884, they show the vivid, aspiring side of city life. One entry reads: "Last Tuesday evening your Ma and I went to the Opera House to hear Oscar Wilde, a young aesthetic Englishman who came to this country last winter to teach us aesthetics and make some money." Like Portland and most other major cities, Bangor suffered periodic fires, and the worst, which destroyed much of the historic business section, occurred in 1911.

❖

Though Bangor and Portland, along with smaller coastal cities, enjoyed some manufacturing in the period, it was in the river cities of Biddeford-Saco and Lewiston-Auburn that the classic textile communities, with their enormous brick factory complexes, continued to take shape. Begun prior to the war, they prospered during the conflict only to face a major labor shortage. French-speaking Canadian workers using the Grand Trunk Railway came as laborers expecting to return, but many stayed. In 1870 12 percent of Biddeford's population was French-speaking, 31 percent in 1880, and by 1900 there were 11,000 French Canadians in a city of 18,000.

In 1873 the Maine Department of Industry concluded: "Maine has entered upon a new era of prosperity. . . . Wonderful progress has been made under a State policy which is so favorable for the establishment of manufacturing enterprises." Indeed, other cotton or woolen mills flourished in Augusta, Sanford, Waterville, Lisbon, Brunswick, Skowhegan, and other river towns. As one historian observed: ". . . it will be noted that [cotton] mills are in operation only within a very small area when compared with the size of the state; Cumberland, York, Kennebec, and Androscoggin counties being the only four represented." Woolen mills were smaller and more scattered. Unlike traditional farms and old commercial operations, the manufacturing industries brought a series of health and safety problems and led to serious labor abuses that would necessitate state action.

The labor movement had origins dating from C. H. P. McLellan's *Workingman's Advocate* (1835), but really got under way in 1882 with the arrival of the Knights of Labor. By 1887 the order claimed 27,900 members in Maine, but it declined rapidly and was partially replaced by the American Federation of Labor. In 1891 the state began to celebrate Labor Day. The Panic of 1893 caused economic dislocation and hard times, and the state branch disbanded in 1897. But by 1903, Maine counted 174 unions in 35 locations with around 13,000 members, and new state branch of the AFL was formed in 1904.

Following the 1860s, Maine became a leader in the canning industry, tinning everything from sardines to lobster, corn, beans, squash, and blueberries. The Portland Packing Company, founded by James Phinney Baxter, Samuel Rummery, and W. G. Davis, became the largest food packer in the world, Burnham & Morrill's baked beans appeared on the market, and by 1914 there were seventy-six corn-packing plants alone. The canning industry connected manufacturing, agriculture, and transportation in unique ways and was spread from York to Washington Counties.

In the same period other industries flourished. The manufacture of boots and shoes grew around

Canning really took off in the wake of the Civil War, creating unskilled jobs along the coast and making Maine products such as corn, blueberries, salmon, and lobster famous. Isaac Winslow of Maine began experiments in 1839, and he assigned patent rights to his nephew John Winslow Jones in 1862. A few years later, he sold some of his patents to William G. Davis and James Phinney Baxter. They formed the Portland Packing Company, which became the largest food packer in the world. COLLECTION OF THE MAINE HISTORICAL SOCIETY

the tanning industry, with Maine's ready supply of hemlock trees. By the end of the century, the new chrome tanning process (which remains dominant) replaced vegetable tanning, but the shoe factories grew, employing 6,432 by 1900. Among the most enduring companies was G. H. Bass, which began in 1876 and has provided everything from leg boots and plow shoes for farmers to calk-soled boots for river-drivers, growing to become a worldwide company by the mid-twentieth century.

Quarrying and stonecutting made Maine and such places as Hurricane Island, North Jay, and Hallowell famous. Indeed, the granite facings for the Washington Monument, the Library of Congress, and the Suffolk County Courthouse in Boston all derive from Maine bedrock. Italians, Finns, Irish, Swedes, and Scots were among the many immigrants employed. Some men, like finish stonecutters A. S. Falconi and Protorio Neri, were master craftsmen, while others were unskilled and low-paid. Paternalistic General Davis Tillson, known to his workers as "Bombasto Furioso," had Hurricane Island turned into a separate town (1878 to 1922) to better control his company.

The ice industry, a wonderful Yankee harvest, began in the 1840s and reached its peak of three million tons in 1890. Frozen lakes and tidal rivers were harvested as soon as ice became a foot thick. A canal was cut to transport the cut blocks to the icehouse, where they were stored in sawdust. This was great work for men and boys during the slack winter season. The blocks were shipped to the cities and used in iceboxes. Bath's noted speculator-promoter Charles Wyman Morse formed the American Ice Company, which controlled the price of New York's ice supply. Before the bubble burst, he withdrew, collapsing the market and making an estimated twelve million dollars. Refrigeration soon destroyed much of the remaining business, though ice continues to be cut on a smaller scale.

❖

America's deepwater fleet declined before foreign competition, but its primarily Maine-built square-riggers, later termed "Down Easters," were arguably the best wooden merchant ships ever built. They were in large part commanded by Maine captains who often took wives and children

The great six-masted schooner *Wyoming*, the largest fore-and-after ever constructed, awaits her launching at Bath's Percy & Small shipyard in 1909. She was lost with all hands during an Atlantic storm in March of 1924. It is appropriate that the Percy & Small yard is now part of the grounds of the Maine Maritime Museum. COURTESY OF THE MAINE MARITIME MUSEUM, BATH, MAINE

to sea with them. In 1889 Searsport alone had seventy-five captains in service. Crews were increasingly made up of non-Americans, for wages were frozen around fifteen to twenty-five dollars a month. Crews were difficult to assemble and were often shanghaied from waterfronts cities. Those who complained on waking aboard ship were answered by the billy or brass knuckles of a bucko-mate. The National Seamen's Union of America kept the *Red Record*, a list of alleged brutality. They listed Captain Joseph Ellis Sewall of Bath fourteen times and termed him "one of the most notorious brutes in charge of an American ship." For his part Sewall disdained the crews, noting "ships are not safe at sea with cattle manning them." Gone were the days when crewmen were neighbors or even partners with a master.

The wooden, square-rigger though less graceful than the earlier "clipper," was nearly as swift. It was designed to carry more freight with a smaller crew. As the fleet of deepwater square-riggers declined, the coastal sailing fleet—primarily Maine-built schooners of ever-increasing size and masts—rapidly expanded and was the world's best. In 1894 the first American steel-hulled square-rigger was launched from the Sewall yard at Bath, signaling the twilight of wooden ships. The Percy & Small yard in Bath is today part of the Maine Maritime Museum. That institution, along with Searsport's Penobscot Marine Museum and smaller groups, well preserves this heritage.

Bath remained Maine's most important shipbuilding and ship-owning community, and special mention needs to be made of what became Maine's most enduring contribution to American shipbuilding—Bath Iron Works. This company was started by General Thomas W. Hyde in an effort to make a transition from wood and sail to steam and steel. The first contract was signed in 1888. Soon the yard was producing gunboats for the navy and steel yachts for the wealthy. The U.S. Naval Academy training ship *Chesapeake* of 1899 was the last full-rigged ship built in this country. The general's death in that year brought, successively, two sons to the head of the company. High profits attracted other investors, and in 1917 ownership passed to a syndicate.

❖

The loss of the federal bounty had all but ruined Maine's Grand Banks fishing industry and towns including Castine. However, demand by consumers in coastal cities and the use of ice as a preservative led fishermen in new directions. By the 1870s haddock, formerly a trash fish, became marketable. Small herring, caught in seines and weirs, were packed as sardines in Eastport in 1875, and by the turn of the century there were sixty-eight plants with six thousand workers, including men, women, and children. There was a boom in the fish-oil business between 1864 and 1878, but soon after, the menhaden, for reasons unknown, deserted the coast. Shellfish, lobsters, and clams also provided a living to coastal settlements and, with the arrival of summer people and hotels, grew in importance. These marine industries continued to provide a living to coastal families able and willing to pursue such a rigorous but independent life.

In the field of agriculture, great changes took place. In 1874 an observer in Greene wrote: "Within sight of my home are nine empty farm houses. They are comfortable, tasty residences on good, productive farms." The owners had vacated them for the West or more lucrative jobs in factories in the cities. Millions of acres of improved land returned to woods between 1865 and 1914. Some of it was good land, while much was marginal and should not have been farmed to begin with. Thousands of people flocked to the rich lands of Aroostook, which was made accessible to market first by Canadian railroads and then, in 1894, by the Bangor & Aroostook. The potato crop and related starch factories brought "The County" into a leadership position in the state and

136   Maine: The Wilder Half of New England

Opposite, top: The loss of the federal bounty hurt the Maine fishing industry, but in the 1870s the popularity of finnan haddie made haddock a sought-after fish. In the same period, Maine sardines began to be caught and canned in Eastport and in other coastal settlements. This man is bailing herring from a "reach boat" in the 1880s. COURTESY OF THE MAINE STATE ARCHIVES

Opposite, bottom: The canning industry became an important element of the state's economy and children, such as these girls shown processing sardines at Jonesport, were often employed. As the nineteenth century faded, stronger child labor laws as well as a new group of child-saving institutions came into being. These changes were reinforced by the appearance of compulsory education laws. Ironically, at the outset of the twenty-first century, child labor laws were under threat. COURTESY OF THE WILLIAM UNDERWOOD COLLECTION, FOGLER LIBRARY'S SPECIAL COLLECTIONS DEPARTMENT, UNIVERSITY OF MAINE AT ORONO

the nation. Also, with the arrival of refrigerated railroad cars around 1900, Maine became one of the leading dairy states.

Several forces were aware of problems in agriculture, especially the transition from subsistence farming to businesslike operations. The Grange established itself in the early 1870s and continued as a force for change, supporting uniform textbooks and the growth of agricultural education and information. It opposed the power of railroads. The State Board of Agriculture (Department of Agriculture in 1902) pushed for and got change. The federal Morrill Land Grant of 1862 opened the way for the legislature to establish a state school. The Maine State College of Agriculture and the Mechanic Arts opened at Orono in 1868. In spite of poor support from the legislature, the institution prospered to become the University

The federal Morrill Land Grant of 1862 opened the way for the state legislature to establish the Maine State College of Agriculture and the Mechanic Arts at Orono in 1868. Despite only intermittent assistance from the legislature, the college endured, becoming the University of Maine in 1897. Here, intent young botany students attend a laboratory in the 1890s. Though the liberal arts had come to stay, agriculture was still spotlighted through coursework, the Experiment Station (1885), and the Department of Extension (1907). COURTESY OF THE FOGLER LIBRARY, UNIVERSITY OF MAINE AT ORONO

DIMINISHING EXPECTATIONS

EAST OXFORD AGRICULTURAL SOCIETY.

Cattle Show, Fair and Horse Trot

THE THIRTEENTH ANNUAL EXHIBITION

Of the East Oxford Agricultural Society, will be held on the Fair Ground of said Society,

IN DIXFIELD VILLAGE, WEDNESDAY, THURSDAY AND FRIDAY,

October 1, 2 & 3, 1873.

ORDER OF EXERCISES.

WEDNESDAY.—Exhibition of Stock. Examination by the Committees in the forenoon. Plowing Match at 2 o'clock P. M. Trial of Strength and Discipline of Oxen at 3 o'clock P. M. Meeting of the Members of the Society for the Choice of Officers and other business of the Society at Jackson's Hall, at 6 1-2 o'clock P. M.
THURSDAY.—Examination of Horses and Colts in the morning. ADDRESS at 11 o'clock A. M., by

R. P. THOMPSON, ESQ., of Jay.

The First Purse for Trotting of Horses owned in the limits of the Society at 1 o'clock P. M. Report of Awarding Committees at 3 P. M.
FRIDAY.—Trotting of Horses.

COMMITTEES AND LIST OF PREMIUMS.

MARSHAL, D. P. STOWELL.

[Detailed list of committees and premiums for: Matched Oxen, Matched Steers, Town Teams of Oxen, Disciplined Steers, Town Teams of Steers, Steers, Bulls, Beef, Cows and Heifers, Sheep, Swine, Horses, Colts, Matched Horses, Poultry, Draft Oxen, Plowing, Dairy, Grain, Potatoes, Fruit, Farming Tools and Carriages, Miscellaneous and Fancy Articles, Spinning, Hops, Boots, Horse and Ox Shoes.]

Horse Trotting.

☞ On Thursday, at 2 o'clock P. M., a Society Purse of $25.00.

Open to all Horses owned within the limits of the Society for one year, that have never beaten three minutes; $12 to first, $8 to second, $5 to third.

Thursday, at 4 o'clock P. M., there will be a Slow Race for a dash of one mile,

$5 to the slowest, $3 to the second, $2 to the third; each Horse to be driven by his opponent, or no man allowed to drive his own Horse.

Friday, at 9 o'clock A. M. a Purse of $40.00.

Open to all Horses that have never beaten three minutes; $25 to first, $10 to second, $5 to third.

A Purse of $25.00.

Open to all Horses owned and raised within the limits of the Society; $12 to first, $8 to second, $5 to third.

A SWEEPSTAKES PURSE OF $60.00.

Open to all Horses; $35 to first, $18 to second, $7 to third.

Committee.—CHARLES A. KIMBALL, WM. W. SMITH, THOMAS REYNOLDS.

All the above races are mile heats, best 3 in 5 to harness, catch weight, and governed by the Rules of the National Association. Entrance money 10 per cent, which must accompany nominations in all cases. All entries must be made to C. W. Ellis, Dixfield, in sealed envelopes, stating class of purse, with color and name of Horse. Not less than three to enter and two to start. All entries for the last day's trotting to be made before 9 A. M. of the day previous to the trot. Any Horse distancing the field will be entitled to the first money only.

☞ All Neat Stock must be entered with the Secretary by 10 o'clock A. M., of the first day, and all other articles intended for the Ladies' Fair, and Agricultural Products, and Mechanical Implements and other things except Horses and Colts, by 12 o'clock of first day, all Horses and Colts for Exhibition, by 10 o'clock of second day. Persons applying for premiums on Dairy Products, and all Crops of Hops, Grain or Vegetables, must present a specimen sample, and make their application in writing, giving a full account of the process pursued, and all items of interest to the Committee, in order to obtain a Premium. All entries must be made in the owner's name. Any driver of Horses or Oxen who shall abuse either, or use any profane language, shall be immediately ordered off the ground. No teamster to be allowed over ten minutes to draw his oxen at one time.

ADMITTANCE FEE TO FAIR GROUND.

Family Ticket for first two days, $1.00. For Single Horse and Carriage, 50 cts. per day. For each person, 25 cts. per day. Children under 12 years of age, 10 cts. per day.

JOURNAL PRESS, LEWISTON.

PER ORDER OF TRUSTEES.

Opposite: The first statewide cattle show was held at Hallowell in the autumn of 1820, sponsored by the Maine Agricultural Society. Within a few years the idea grew, and town and county fairs became part of Maine life. The original idea was educational, a chance to show off and compare agricultural products, but in time fairs included entertainments such as harness racing, as advertised in this 1873 broadside. The tradition continues in fairs from Bangor to Presque Isle to Fryeburg to the Common Ground Fair in Unity. COLLECTION OF THE MAINE HISTORICAL SOCIETY

Below: Non-English-speaking immigrants were met at the docks, offered jobs, and put on trains that took them to the new paper-manufacturing towns of Rumford and Millinocket. Workers such as these Italian men in Rumford built crude temporary shelters to house themselves and were often scorned by Yankees who forgot that their own immigrant ancestors had first lived in similar shelters. COURTESY OF THE RUMFORD AREA HISTORICAL SOCIETY, RUMFORD, MAINE

of Maine in 1897. Its existence added to the development of agriculture through courses in veterinary science, horticulture, and animal husbandry, and through the Experiment Station (1885) and Department of Extension (1907). The university then opened doors to the liberal arts and other fields, and in the 1880s opened a law school in Bangor.

While many communities withered and died in the period, two huge (by Maine standards) cities appeared full-blown in the wilderness. Industrialist Hugh J. Chisholm picked an uninhabited spot below Rumford Falls, imported hundreds of workers representing a half-dozen nationalities, and, between 1890 and 1900, the city of Rumford went up like a Hollywood set. Even more spectacular was the construction of Millinocket, "the magic city of the North," between 1899 and 1900. Again, European immigrants were imported and set to work, and within a short time the Great

DIMINISHING EXPECTATIONS

This rousing photograph shows lumbermen playing hard in their bateaux, probably on the Fourth of July or Saint-Jean-Baptist Day. Such workboats were commonplace throughout the rivers of the Big Woods. The Lumbermen's Museum in Patten includes buildings, tools, photographs, machines, and paintings relating to the industry. COLLECTION OF THE LUMBERMEN'S MUSEUM, PATTEN, MAINE, COURTESY OF FRANK PELTIER

Northern Paper Company was in operation, turning out 240 tons of newsprint a day.

The pulp and paper industry, which replaced textiles as Maine's largest industry in 1914, began after the Civil War when a commercially successful process for making paper out of wood was developed. Before that rags were used, but that was increasingly expensive as demand for newspapers, books, and the like grew. By 1870 S. D. Warren's big plant at Westbrook was producing a million dollars' worth of paper a year, and during the 1880s it was the largest such plant in the world. Pulp and paper made great demands on the forest, and the industry still plays a controlling role.

The lumber business, which shifted from pine to spruce harvesting, experienced its biggest growth years in the decades before and after the turn of the century. In the woods, cutters from Maine, New Brunswick, and Prince Edward Island lived a rugged existence preserved in the songs of Larry Gorman and novels of Holman Day. Wages were low, food was basic, and accidents common. Horses began to replace oxen, but axes were used throughout the period. River drives continued apace, but there were changes brought on by railroads and improved equipment. In 1899, for example, Alvin Lombard of Waterville invented the steam log hauler with its tread propulsion.

The SS *State of Maine*, shown here in an 1893 painting by Antonio Jacobsen (1850–1921), was a classic side-wheel passenger steamer. Launched at Bath in 1881, the elegant vessel was part of a coastal marine transportation network that has never been equaled. Occasionally there was a disaster, such as the loss of the steamer *Portland* in 1898 with more than 160 passengers. For a time before 1907, Bath's Charles W. Morse (1856–1933) gained a monopoly on all coastal shipping from Texas to Maine.
COLLECTION OF THE MAINE HISTORICAL SOCIETY

Sawmills and woodworking shops were a vital part of rural towns and continue to be in the present.

Maine's abundant waterpower, which had attracted settlers since the earliest times, found a new use: the generation of electricity. The first electric lights came to Maine in the 1880s, set up by a variety of small companies. In 1899 Walter S. Wyman of West Waterville bought the Oakland Electric Light Company. With Harvey Eaton, he began to buy up other companies, becoming Central Maine Power in 1910. Perhaps the last major impediment to the growth of the company was the Maine legislature's Fernald Law of 1909. This law forbade the export of electrical power beyond state lines. This was a reaction to outside industries and the fear they might come to control the hydro resources; it was hoped that industries would be forced to locate within the state. The law became a point of controversy in the decades that followed.

The first telephones appeared in Portland in 1879, and in the next year the National Bell Telephone Company of Maine (the start of the New England Telephone Company) was founded. Gas companies were already in operation, and running-water and sewage systems were appearing in the larger towns.

In the field of transportation, Maine became swept up in great national trends. In the age of steam and sail, Eastern Steamship Company of Boston linked the major Maine coastal and river towns with Boston, New York, and the whole east coast. In spite of the occasional disaster, such as the loss of the *Portland* with all aboard in 1898, these steamers ran regularly and provided unsurpassed comfort to the traveler. Bangor began its first electric trolley service in 1887, and Portland followed in 1891. Soon a network connected the major cities with small towns like Freeport and opened them to business and recreation. Maine's railroads had been somewhat retarded by quarrels over gauges, which meant that passengers and freight had to change cars at some junctions. In 1873 standard gauge was established. In 1870 Maine had 772 miles of rail. This increased to 1,322 in 1889 and grew until the 1920s. As never before, Maine towns became linked to each other and to the rest of the nation through an unparalleled network of transportation. Fees were light and accommodations generally comfortable.

In the last years of the nineteenth century the first automobiles appeared, and Maine soon contributed to the new mode of transportation through several small companies. The most important was the Stanley Steamer, invented by Francis E. and Freelan O. Stanley of Kingfield in 1898. For the first decade, the automobile was a novelty, but soon mass-produced, gasoline-driven cars were becoming part of the fabric. Maine was forced to establish a Division of Motor Vehicles in 1905.

❖

The state's vast tracts of public land began to undergo significant changes at this time. Even before the Civil War, Maine's land agent was selling the rights to cut and harvest timber. Now, as wood-pulp paper replaced rag as the stuff of newsprint, a new industry was created. By 1900 there were thirty-five paper mills in Maine, which led the nation in that field. Between 1912 and 1914, pulp and paper became the state's leading industry (and remained so, although now it would seem that tourism has trumped it). Since the Big Woods

The Maine Woods attracted not only loggers but sportsmen seeking relief from the city. They spawned a growth industry that came to include hunting camps and lodges, guides including Bill Sewall, Joe Mell, and Cornelia Thurza "Fly Rod" Crosby, and the *Maine Woods* magazine. These "rusticators," John Hall and Herbert Washington, are canoeing on Ragged Lake around 1900. The photograph comes from the remarkable John W. G. Dunn Collection. COLLECTION OF THE MAINE HISTORICAL SOCIETY

remained unsettled, the legislature willingly turned their basic operation over to lumber barons and later to big corporations. Such companies came to control and manage roads, dams, and all facilities, including timber and hay. Still, by the 1880s there was much debate over how the holdings were being managed. In 1891 the position of forest commissioner was created by the state to take the place of the old land agent, and soon men such as Commissioner Edgar Ring, fieldworker Austin F. Cary, and novelist Holman Day, author of *King Spruce* (1908), were bringing ideas and practices of conservation and scientific forestry to Maine.

Forests, fields, and streams also attracted a new class: the sportsman. While the Department of Inland Fisheries had been formed in 1850, and a few fish and game wardens appointed before that, enforcement was very poor due to virtually no funding. By the 1870s market-hunting on a large scale was being stimulated by the growth of railroads and the demand for fresh game in distant cities. Natives, turned poachers of moose, deer, and caribou, could improve their living a good deal and resented state intrusion. Slowly, a system of fish, game, and fire wardens was backed by stronger laws, licenses, and bag limits. However, in 1886 Warden Lyman Hill and Deputy Charles Niles were shot and killed by illegal hunters west of the Machias River. Securing control over largely unoccupied regions became, ever increasingly, a part of state government.

Railroads actively promoted the benefits of the outdoors, and a variety of camps, lodges, and hotels took root. Some were posh, Gilded Age resorts such as Poland Spring and Mount Kineo. Others were modest affairs such as the Mount Abram Hotel, established at Locke's Mills to cater to salesmen or the occasional hunter. By the 1870s national newspapers were singing the praises of the Rangeley Lakes and the large trout to be had for the taking. Deeper in the woods were places like Kidney Pond Camps, accessible by growing rail links only. In small towns like Hanover, rustic sporting retreats such as Indian Rock Camps appeared in the 1890s. A whole hierarchy of guides, hunters, provisioners, and campground personnel came into being. Bill Sewall of Island Falls was young Theodore Roosevelt's guide in the 1870s and remained a lifelong comrade. Maine Indians, including Joe Mell, achieved similar fame in guiding visitors, but perhaps the most celebrated guide was Cornelia Thurza Crosby. Known as "Fly Rod" Crosby, she spoke at sports shows, wrote colorful articles for the *Maine Woods* magazine, and guided parties through the Rangeley region. Greenville's D. T. Sanders & Son, founded in 1857, became famous outfitters. In coastal Freeport, L. L. Bean started a mail-order business in 1912 that would grow to fantastic proportions in later years. The mystique of Maine, an idea sometimes lost on its residents, was given an additional nudge in 1914, when the first Paul Bunyan story reached print and quickly grew in the popular imagination. Tales of the woods became staples of camps for boys and girls. One of the earliest of these was Camp Wyonegonic at Moose Pond in Denmark, founded in 1902. Soon the era of Boy Scouts, Girl Scouts, and other such organizations was underway.

The rocky Atlantic shore had beckoned even earlier to artists and the well-to-do vacationer. But it was transportation improvements that led to a boom in the late nineteenth century. Bar Harbor became one of America's premier summer resorts. By 1872 there were fifteen hotels, but it was the luxury "cottages" of the very rich that distinguished the spot. Here, great architects concocted "Elsinore" for Hugh McMillan, "Sonogee" for Atwater Kent, "Stanwood" for James G. Blaine, and "Chatswold," which was owned by Joseph Pulitzer. By 1890 the summer colony was deeply entrenched, and the dichotomy of "summer people" and "natives" has continued. Former vice president Nelson A. Rockefeller was born at Bar

Above: Old Orchard Beach, with its sweep of white sand, became an independent town in 1883 and pursued a destiny rare in Maine—that of a summer amusement town. Stately hotels and a rustic nature walk were replaced by ferris wheels, funhouses, and, in 1889, by an 1,800-foot steel pier with a miniature locomotive and train. Each generation of children treasures its own image of this resort for everyman. COLLECTION OF THE MAINE HISTORICAL SOCIETY

Right: Though under great pressure from the dominating culture, Native American tribes in Maine were able to endure and preserve many of their own ways. This portrait of Joe Francis of the Penobscot Indian Nation, in formal garb, was taken at Old Town in 1912. COURTESY PRIVATE COLLECTION

Harbor in the summer of 1908 and returned each year to Seal Harbor.

Islesboro was first discovered by wealthy Bangor vacationers in 1868. But in 1888 it began to attract some of the nation's great families, along with notables including illustrator Charles Dana Gibson and tennis champion Richard D. Sears. In 1901 a Belfast newspaper gushed: "Imagine an island, barren save a few scattered houses and settlements three or four years ago, to have grown to be a beautiful villa-dotted paradise where $500,000 has been expended for summer cottages alone." Names including Rothschild, Auchincloss, and Dillon still predominate at Islesboro. Indeed, from the summer home of author-editor William Dean Howells in Kittery to Franklin Roosevelt's retreat at New Brunswick's Campobello (now an international memorial park), the coast had an annual ebb and flow of visitors.

Old Orchard, with its stunning crescent of white sand, beckoned to the less affluent, who could easily make the journey from southern New England or Canada by rail. The Ocean Park section became famous as a Protestant religious retreat by the 1880s, while to the west the midways and amusements began to rise among the

144   MAINE: THE WILDER HALF OF NEW ENGLAND

Improved transportation during the era made Bar Harbor a destination for the rich and famous as well as for the artists drawn there since the days of Thomas Cole. The busy summer harbor included workboats, steamers, and increasingly, pleasure boats. Great cottages were owned by such distinguished people as Joseph Pulitzer, Alice Pike Barney, Beatrix Farrand, A. Atwater Kent, Mrs. Potter Palmer II, Mrs. Henry F. Dimock, and Senator James G. Blaine. COLLECTION OF THE MAINE HISTORICAL SOCIETY

beachfront hotels. The first Old Orchard Pier was built in 1898.

In his 1875 *History of Maine*, John S. C. Abbott remarked: "The flood of foreign immigration is not pouring into Maine as into some other parts of the union. But this saves the State from a vast amount, in inebriation, vagabondage, crime, and pauperism. And those who do select Maine as their home generally come from those countries in northern Europe where intelligence and piety prevail."

Few observers have ever been so self-assuredly incorrect. Maine was becoming quite heterogeneous. In spite of being confined to small reservation areas, and roundly neglected, Native American tribes in Maine were able to retain their cultural identities. A number of Irish Americans had inched their way up in the economic order, and by World War I the Catholic Church ran seven orphan asylums and played a major welfare role. Jewish people were arriving in some number, particularly in the larger communities, and by 1906 Portland had a United Hebrew Charities. Scatterings of Greeks, Poles, Armenians, Lebanese, Italians, and others came to stay. In the mill towns, Franco-Americans were able to preserve their culture and language for generations through the agency of their parishes, social clubs, families, and newspapers such as *Le Messager* (1880–1910) and *La Justice* (1896–1950). The newcomers from Quebec reintroduced snowshoeing as a winter sport and later helped found the first credit unions. They were slow in being absorbed into the larger culture, however, and New Englanders feared them and their lifestyles.

On the other hand, Yankee industrialists welcomed immigrants of all backgrounds, and they shipped them in from large ports of entry. Immigrants were an inexpensive source of labor for the machine age. Often bosses would play one group against another, and the first arrivals in some interior towns had to build their own shacks. In some cases, such as the paper mill of S. D. Warren in Westbrook, housing was provided and relatively good care taken of workers. In the 1880s the labor movement revived with the Knights of Labor, but the Conspiracy Law of 1881 and the Panic of 1893 (brought about by the British Baring Brothers firm's collapse) hit labor hard. The movement would continue, and the children of immigrants were growing up, about to give a new twist to the meaning of the name "Yankee."

In 1912, sparked by the worldwide "eugenics scare" and local considerations, Maine's governor evicted some forty-five citizens from Malaga Island in Casco Bay. The people, three of whom are shown in their dooryard, were a mixture of African Americans, Yankees, Irish, and Portuguese who had settled nearby in the late eighteenth century. Judged unable to care for themselves, they were scattered or institutionalized. Malaga was not the only instance of state efforts to root out what the politicians, press, and medical authorities saw as pockets of crime, insanity, and poverty. COURTESY PRIVATE COLLECTION

Women took the lead in building a variety of social institutions. This era saw the establishment of the Young Men's Christian Association, Young Men's Hebrew Association, the Children's Aid Society in Belfast (1893), the Little Samaritans (Maine Home for Boys, 1893), and Opportunity Farm in New Gloucester in 1910. In the 1880s Portland had a social settlement house for immigrant children. Though not a tightly woven safety net, the individual charities did a great deal for children and adults in a period of sparse government aid.

But things could go badly in spite of the best of intentions. The "eugenics scare" preached the gospel of heredity and claimed that "decaying families" and "retrograde stock" were spreading crime and disease. From the 1870s on, Mainers began to look at rural families and individuals in need. One of the most publicized "problems" focused on Malaga Island in Casco Bay, where people lived a rugged life. The inhabitants were Irish, black, and Yankee. Attempts by private groups to build schools and provide help failed. In 1912 the state forcibly removed the inhabitants of Malaga, tore down or removed the houses, and dug up the cemetery. The people were scattered, though many were placed in the Maine School for the Feeble-Minded at Pownal, where they could be segregated from society.

In a state that seemed to provide fewer traditional opportunities, youngsters of all ethnic backgrounds found a new arena of possibilities in sports. The growing middle class, with leisure time on its hands, took up a variety of recreational activities including bicycling, canoeing, beach bathing, tennis, and golf. New activities led to an appreciation of the Maine environment and of athletes. One of the first to gain national attention was Edward Payson Weston, who sparked "the Pedestrian Mania" by walking from Portland to Chicago in 1867. Soon Weston and others were grabbing headlines by setting record times between various places. Harness racing continued to color the era. Horses, such as "Nelson," of Waterville, became famous. William E. O'Connell and John P. Buckley of Portland won the world double-sculling championships in 1882 and 1883, and in 1893 and 1899 the winning *America*'s Cup defender was crewed by Mainers.

On the beach at Old Orchard, Barney Oldfield and other legendary racecar drivers competed in the decade before World War I. Jack McAuliffe, who grew up on the tough Bangor waterfront, punched his way to the World Lightweight Championship, and Mysterious Billy Smith of Eastport took the World Middleweight belt. Andrew Sockalexis of Old Town, a Penobscot, ran second in the Boston Marathon and was on the 1912 U.S. Olympic team. His cousin, Louis Francis Sockalexis, was one of a number of professional baseball players from Maine and is said to be the reason for Cleveland's team being called the

This photograph shows Bangor's Congregation Beth Israel. In 1849 a Congregation Ahawas Achim appeared in the same city but did not last. The Beth Israel Society was formed in 1888, and a cornerstone for a synagogue laid in 1897. The building burned in 1911 and was replaced by this remarkable temple in 1913. Though small in number, Jewish people have contributed enormously to Maine life in medicine, business, law, education, the arts, and other fields. COURTESY OF THE BANGOR HISTORICAL SOCIETY, BANGOR, MAINE

Maine claimed a number of splendid athletes in this period, including baseball pitcher John Wesley Coombs (1882–1957). Though born in Iowa, Coombs was raised in Freeport and graduated from Waterville's Colby College in 1906. Five days later "Colby Jack" was pitching for the Philadelphia Athletics. He led the league in 1910 with thirty-one wins and the next year with twenty-eight. He retired in 1920, having played for Brooklyn and Detroit and coached on the college level. Summers were spent in Kennebunk. This photo was taken at Freeport in 1902, and Jack is second from the left. COURTESY OF THE FREEPORT HISTORICAL SOCIETY

Indians. Others who pioneered baseball include George F. "Piano Legs" Gore of Hartland, Frederick Alfred "the Flying Frenchman" Parent of Biddeford, Bill "Rough" Carrigan of Lewiston, and the great pitcher John W. Coombs, who grew up in Freeport, graduated from Colby College, and led the American League in games won during 1910 and 1911.

At Portland High School, John "Bull" Feeney, one of thirteen children born to Irish parents, was making a name for himself on the football field.

After graduating in 1914, he would enlarge on his celebrity in Hollywood, where he changed his name to John Ford. The same year saw Bucksport's Dustin Farnham star in the silent films, *The Virginian* and *The Squaw Man*.

❖

Winslow Homer's enduring images of the Maine coast captured the imagination of the public. He moved to Prout's Neck, Scarborough, in 1883 and built a studio. Indeed, generations have come to know the state largely through his much-reproduced and imitated images. His arrival signaled the seasonal appearance of established artists "from away" who found a beautiful, pressure-free, inexpensive workplace. Arriving as full-blown successes, the new artists had little to do with the "native" artists. As late as the 1870s, critic John Neal had welcomed the English-born watercolor painter Elizabeth Heaphey Murray as one of the Portland Painters, but in contrast, John T. Hull's 1889 *Handbook of Portland*, refers slightingly to "that New York painter Winslow Homer."

The once-rich Portland art scene was failing by 1880. Old painters such as Harrison B. Brown clung to the few remaining patrons; marine painter Franklin Stanwood lived hand to mouth but produced admirably; landscape painter Charles F. Kimball turned amateur to produce his best work; and youngsters such as Walter Griffin, Auburn sports painter Scott Leighton, and Brewer sculptor Charles E. Tefft made their careers out of state.

In Brunswick, Kate Furbish achieved fame as a botanical painter and the discoverer of two plants, one of which was subsequently named Furbish's lousewort. Annie Eliza Hardy continued to paint and survive at Bangor, and jack-of-all-arts Harry H. Cochrane did so at Monmouth. In most towns, photography became the supporting visual-art form. Still, it is only recently that works by Kingfield's Chansonetta Stanley Emmons, Amity's Isaac Simpson, Bath's Emma D. Sewall, and Norway's Minnie Libby have gained special recogni-

John Calvin Stevens (1855–1940) was Maine's foremost architect of the era. A native of Boston who grew up in Portland, Stevens studied with Francis H. Fassett, whose firm he joined. In the 1880s Stevens moved from the Queen Anne Style to the Shingle Style, which expressed his work to the fullest. In his hands and those of others, Shingle-Style homes graced the coast and came closest to what might stand as a regional form. This drawing depicts his own home in Portland and appears in *Examples of American Domestic Architecture*, which he produced with Albert Winslow Cobb in 1889. COURTESY OF THE MAINE HISTORIC PRESERVATION COMMISSION

tion. In the period, collecting institutions including the Walker Art Gallery at Bowdoin and the L. D. M. Sweat Museum (Portland Museum of Art) appeared. The latter, along with the Bangor publication, *Leaflets of the Artists* (1893), preserved much of what was best of the earlier nineteenth-century flowering of local talent.

Most outside observers saw Maine through the work of newcomers such as Homer at Prout's Neck, or Childe Hassam at the Isles of Shoals. Beginning in the 1880s, Charles Woodbury turned Ogunquit into a popular beachside location for his landscape-painting classes. Soon he was in competition with the modern painter-critic Hamilton Easter Field, and "art colonies" also appeared at Bridgton, Poland Spring, Boothbay, Monhegan, and Eastport. Before long, the likes of Maurice Prendergast, Rockwell Kent, Robert Henri, George Bellows, and illustrators N. C. Wyeth and William H. Foster were also discovering the coast. At the century's turn, a few young Mainers, most notably Lewiston's Marsden Hartley, were at the outset of visual arts careers.

Architecture became an honored profession in this era, which witnessed a profusion of tastes including Queen Anne, Shingle, and Colonial

DIMINISHING EXPECTATIONS

Maine produced some remarkable voices during the period, and three of the state's women, Annie Louise Cary of Wayne, Emma Eames of Shanghai, China, and Bath, and Madame Nordica of Farmington, achieved world renown in opera. Born Lillian Norton (1857–1914), Nordica made her debut in Italy and performed at the Metropolitan Opera House, where her portrait by S. B. Baker (1882–1967) hangs. It was a gift of Norman Kelly, the first Maine man to receive a Met

Revival styles. Maine's foremost architect from the 1880s on was John Calvin Stevens, a pioneer of the Shingle Style, perhaps the most successful domestic form ever to grace the coast.

In the cities, large apartment buildings rising three and four stories became an enduring element of life, along with larger school buildings and a delightful array of picturesque public libraries in towns from Calais to Kittery to West Paris.

The end of the period also saw the rise of impressive public buildings in Maine granite. A good example of such work appears near Portland's Lincoln Park. The Cumberland County Courthouse (1910), Judge Edward T. Gignoux Federal Courthouse (1911), and Portland City Hall (1912) bespeak continuance, order, tradition, and civic duty.

Parks, fountains, bandstands, and war memorials in great number were also a feature of the era, along with open-air concerts. The oldest bands include La Fanfare Painchaud, organized at Biddeford in 1872, and Chandler's Band, begun at Portland in 1876.

Music flourished in societies led by such indomitable figures as Hermann Kotzschmar and George W. Marston, and marching bands in military dress were ready on all public occasions. When Ignace Jan Paderewski gave a piano recital at Portland in 1892, he was stunned by the size and warmth of his audience. Kotzschmar had seen to it that musicians from all over Maine were in attendance. The Bangor Opera House opened in 1882 and drew first-run performers. In 1896 the Bangor Symphony, the nation's second oldest continuous symphony, was founded, and in the next year the Maine Music Festival, under William R. Chapman, began its fruitful life. John Knowles Paine, of the Portland music family, studied with

contract. The Nordica Homestead in Farmington is open to the public and contains objects, documents, and recordings relating to the diva's life. COURTESY OF THE METROPOLITAN OPERA HOUSE, NEW YORK

Kotzschmar, became America's most noted composer of the day, and in the 1860s was appointed director of music at Harvard. In 1875 he became a full professor, occupying one of the country's first chairs of music at a university.

Down-east women contributed to the success of American opera. Annie Louise Cary, from Wayne, Maine, appeared in the American premier of *Aida* in 1873 and toured the world. Madame Nordica (Lillian Norton) of Farmington made her debut in Milan and achieved world fame as a prima donna, including twenty-one roles at the Metropolitan Opera. Her home in Farmington is now a museum house. Emma Eames was born in Shanghai but grew up in Bath. Her operatic debut in Paris caused one critic to write that she possessed the "finest soprano voice I had ever heard." The fourth figure, Madame Scalar (Minnie Plummer Stephens) of West Paris, Maine, had a successful career as a prima donna in Europe before retiring to her home state.

Theater can only be touched on, but Portland

The Country of the Pointed Firs (1896) by South Berwick's Sarah Orne Jewett (1849–1909) combined clarity of style with a unique understanding of coastal life and custom. It is often seen as the finest work of prose fiction to emerge from nineteenth-century Maine. This 1910 edition, illustrated by Marcia Oakes Woodbury (1865–1913), also of South Berwick, shows Mrs. Todd, the central character in the novel.
COLLECTION OF THE MAINE HISTORICAL SOCIETY

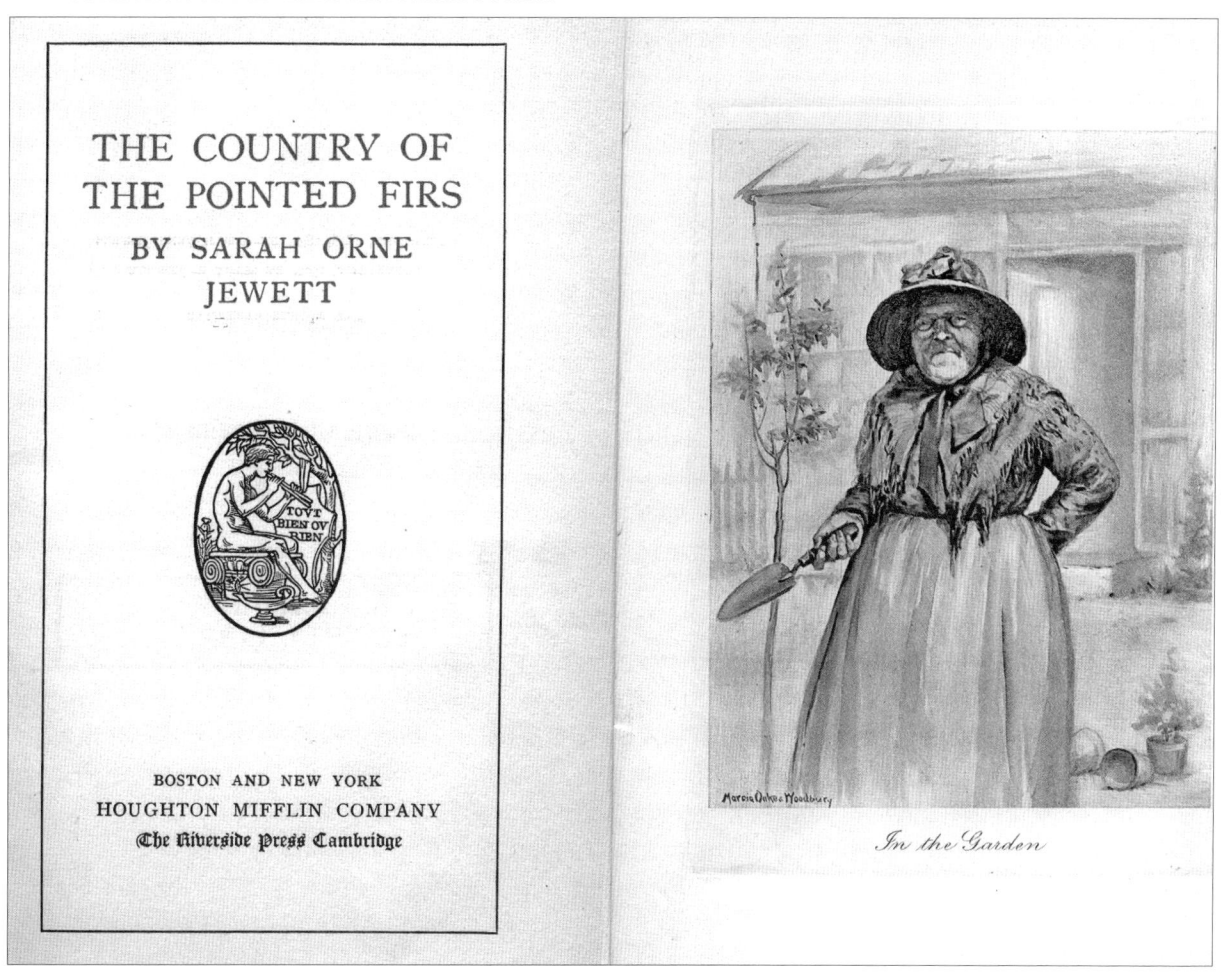

DIMINISHING EXPECTATIONS   151

The Ring and Dunn cousins of Orono, Maine, sit impatiently in 1908. The cart and later-to-be-famous burro were gifts from another cousin, Blue Hill writer Mary Ellen Chase (1887–1973). In 1964 Chase would write *Richard Mansfield, Prince of Donkeys*. The little girl with the white bow (center) is Elizabeth Ring, who graduated from UMO with an MA and became one of the first individuals to study Maine history and to teach it as a subject. Among her many students are historian Earle G. Shettleworth, Jr., former CMP president David Flanagan, and the amazing novelist E. Annie Proulx.
COLLECTION OF WILLIAM AND DEBRA BARRY

and Bangor continued to get the best dramatic and vaudeville performers. By the turn of the century, summer theater at Cape Elizabeth, Peaks Island, and Skowhegan's famous "Lakewood" caught on. Some films were shown in the 1880s, and the first movie houses were in operation at Portland by 1907.

The era abounded in writers, though Sarah Orne Jewett of South Berwick was the standout in terms of clarity of style and as a skilled observer of everyday Mainers. Her short stories, particularly those collected in *The Country of the Pointed Firs* (1896), remain American classics. Longfellow, still internationally revered, died in 1882. Portlanders erected a full-length seated statue of the poet on Congress Street in 1888, and in 1907, his boyhood home was opened to the public. Maine could still claim major figures in literature such as William Dean Howells, the Father of American Realism, who entertained the likes of Mark Twain and Henry James at his summer home in Kittery Point. Celia Thaxter, even earlier, made Appledore a seasonal scene and had written *Among the Isles of Shoals* (1873) and *My Island Garden* (1894). Laura E. Richards of Gardiner was a national social activist and author of *Captain January* (1890), and Calais's Charles Townsend was a distinguished professor of writing at Harvard. Harriet Prescott Spofford, also of Calais, was a frequent contributor to *Atlantic Monthly*, while Bill Nye of Shirley and William Robinson Pattangall of Pembroke continued the tradition of Maine humor. Waiting in the wings was the hardworking poet Edwin Arlington Robinson of Head Tide and Gardiner. Brewer's Fannie Hardy Eckstorm produced important nonfiction relating to the Maine woods and Indian culture, and James Phinney Baxter proved a dogged gatherer of manuscripts and a scholar of Maine history.

Young adult and children's writers flourished. Kate Douglas Wiggin wrote at Hollis and created *Rebecca of Sunnybrook Farm* (1903), while James Otis Kaler, a native of Winterport and superintendent of schools in South Portland, wrote the delightful *Toby Tyler* (1880). For decades, Clarence E. Mulford worked at Fryeburg and is best known for his cowboy hero Hopalong Cassidy. Rebecca Sophia Clarke of Norridgewock penned the "Dotty Dimple" and "Flaxie Frizzle" stories, winning the nickname Dickens of the Nursery. The Reverend Elijah Kellogg, Jr., entertained a generation with his tales of the Maine coast, Dr. Charles A. Stephens of Norway wrote for six decades as an adventure author for the *Youth's Companion*, and Gilbert Patten of Corinna was the creator of boy-hero Frank Merriwell. Vassalboro's Holman Day also began as a juvenile author before turning to journalism and books about Maine lumbering and liquor smuggling.

Real-life adventure was embodied in the person of arctic explorer Robert E. Peary, who grew up in South Portland, attended Bowdoin, and made his vacation home at Eagle Island in Casco Bay (now a museum house). In April of 1909, he claimed victory in the effort to reach the North Pole. The Peary–MacMillan Arctic Museum at Bowdoin College illustrates his productive, controversial career. Other achievers in distant places included Cyrus Hamlin, who founded Robert College in Constantinople and wrote *Among the Turks* (1878). Edward Sylvester Morse was a scientist, artist, teacher, and creator of lasting cultural ties with Japan, and Sanford Dole, the son of Maine missionaries, became president of Hawaii in 1894.

Mention should also be made of businessmen of note. Cyrus H. K. Curtis of Portland left the state to found the *Saturday Evening Post, Ladies' Home Journal,* and other Curtis publications. He did much for Maine, including the gift of the Kotzschmar Memorial Organ at Portland City Hall. In 1869 E. C. Allen founded the *People's Literary Companion* and rapidly turned Augusta into the mail-order capital of the nation. William Howard Gannett of the same city started *Comfort Magazine,* the country's first million-circulation publication.

In politics Maine continued to be represented by extraordinary figures. When the dominant Radical Republicans impeached President Andrew Johnson in 1867, Senator William Pitt Fessenden was faced with his most difficult decision. As majority leader, he was pressured from all sides to vote to remove the unpopular Johnson. With rare courage, Fessenden replied: "The opinions and wishes of my party friends ought not to have a feather's weight with me in coming to a conclusion." His vote of not guilty helped keep Johnson in the White House but generated a whirlwind of invective around the senator. While working to gain the Senate seat again in 1869, Fessenden died. Hannibal Hamlin returned to the Senate, where he supported the Radical Republicans until his retirement in 1881. His statue, along with that of Governor William King, represents Maine in the United States Capitol.

The rising star of the post–Civil War era was James G. Blaine, a Mainer by choice, former editor of the *Kennebec Journal,* and chairman of the Republican state committee until 1881. He served in the U.S. House of Representatives from 1863 until 1875, and he was elected Speaker in 1869. From 1876 to 1881 Blaine served as senator from Maine. Popular in the West, he was nominated for the presidency in 1884, but lost in a tough election to Grover Cleveland. The expression "rum, Romanism, and rebellion," used by a Blaine supporter, helped swing the large Catholic vote against him. There was also the question of his wealth, which opponents suggested grew without a means of income. The Plumed Knight, as he was known, served well as secretary of state under James Garfield and Benjamin Harrison. In fact, he was one of the few Americans of his day with a real understanding of how to conduct foreign affairs.

Even more formidable was Thomas Brackett Reed. Born in Portland, Reed graduated from Bowdoin in 1860, served in the navy, and soon entered local politics. He entered the U.S. House of Representatives in 1876 and remained there until 1898, becoming one of the most powerful and respected members of the body.

As Speaker of the House, his honest but heavy-handed leadership earned him the title Czar Reed. He did much to strengthen the party, presided over the first "billion dollar Congress," and became a player in the Republican presidential nominations of 1896. Weighing in at 275 pounds, Reed was both physically and mentally imposing. He once

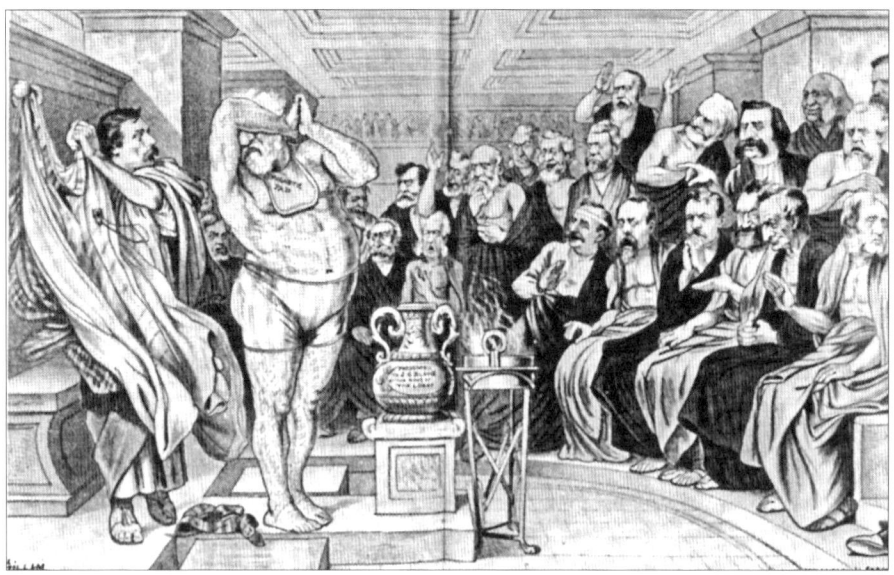

James G. Blaine (1830–1893), "the Plumed Knight," was Maine's most powerful political figure of the postwar period. From 1859 to 1881, he remained chairman of the Republican State Committee and was Speaker of the U.S. House of Representatives from 1869 to 1875. Moving on to the Senate, he twice served ably as secretary of state and was the GOP presidential candidate in 1884. This cartoon, which substituted the lumpish, tattooed Blaine for a comely Greek heroine, so enraged Blaine that only close friends could dissuade him from suing the magazine that ran it. COURTESY PRIVATE COLLECTION

complimented Theodore Roosevelt on the latter's "original discovery of the ten commandments," and when a congressman stated that he would rather be right than president, Reed assured him, "You'll never be either." Honest and blunt, Czar Reed could not stomach the Spanish-American War, which he saw as imperialistic and wrong. Soon after reelection, he resigned from Congress. He continued to practice law in Portland and New York, and was visited in Maine by President Roosevelt in 1902.

The political muscle did not all belong to the Republicans, for President Cleveland appointed Augusta-born Melville Weston Fuller chief justice of the United States Supreme Court. Indeed, Fuller ran a Democratic newspaper in opposition to James G. Blaine before moving to Chicago. He served as chief justice from 1888 until his death at Sorrento, Maine, in 1910. He was a much-liked man, a top-notch manager of court business, and rendered over 850 opinions. Also, in 1896, Bath shipbuilder Arthur Sewall became William Jennings Bryan's vice-presidential running mate in what proved a losing cause.

But a visitor to Washington, D.C., in 1889 might have assumed that Maine was still a large and powerful state. Blaine was secretary of state, Reed Speaker of the House, Nelson Dingley chairman of the powerful Ways and Means Committee, Fuller chief justice, and Lewiston's William P. Frye a leader of the Senate. At least three important congressional committees were controlled, as well, by down-easters.

Other Maine-born figures were also cabinet members in the period. Elihu B. Washburne served as secretary of state under Ulysses S. Grant in

Thomas Brackett Reed (1839–1902) of Portland was probably the most distinguished and effective Maine political figure in the last decades of the century. A physical and intellectual giant, "Czar Reed" served as U.S. Speaker of the House in 1889–1891 and 1895–1899 and wrote *Reed's Rules of Order,* which greatly facilitated business on the Hill. Cartoonists delighted in depicting Reed as Gulliver dominating a Congress of Lilliputians. Here the czar confers with Maine congressman Nelson Dingley, Jr., a giant under ordinary conditions. COLLECTION OF THE MAINE HISTORICAL SOCIETY

1869, and Lot M. Morrill and Hugh McCulloch each stood as secretary of the treasury under Grant and Chester A. Arthur respectively. T. O. Howe was postmaster general in 1881–1882. Under ordinary circumstances, such capable and important figures as William P. Frye (congressman from 1871 to 1881 and senator until 1911); Nelson Dingley, Jr. (congressman from 1881–1911); and Eugene Hale (senator from 1881–1911) would have loomed larger.

❖

The impact of the federal government on Maine and other states remained relatively slight. The government continued to build and maintain customhouses, lighthouses, forts, lifesaving stations, a Marine Hospital at Portland, and a military home at Togus. During the Portland Fire of 1866, the army provided tents and material assistance to the sufferers. But the Great Fire was an unusual event. Coastal fortification fell into disrepair after the war, and it was not until the mid-1880s that Congress moved to upgrade the situation. By 1890 the Endicott Plan to fortify coastal defenses was underway, and by 1910 it was largely completed. In between, the battleship *Maine* blew up in Havana Harbor, plunging the United States into a short war with Spain and leaving America with a colonial empire. Nearly a thousand Spanish prisoners were housed in a stockade at the Portsmouth Naval Shipyard (located in Kittery) and thirty-one died there. Indeed, the period saw the building of a huge dry dock, construction of submarines, and in 1905, the greatest manmade explosion of that time occurred as engineers deepened the channel off Henderson Point. In the same year President Roosevelt hosted Russian and Japanese signers of the Treaty of Portsmouth, focusing world attention on the naval yard.

"As Maine Goes, So Goes the Nation" served as the bellwether maxim of national politics from 1888 to 1932, when elections in Maine were held in September. Locally, the Republicans tended to dominate, but their power was never completely certain. Joshua L. Chamberlain was elected governor three times after 1867. The Grand Old Party triumphed in that office until 1878. In that year, the Greenback Party, led by the great crowd-pleaser Solon Chase, a farmer from Turner, waged a spirited campaign. In the end, the people had failed to elect a governor, and the state senate

Solon Chase (1822–1909) stands with "Them Steers," a pair of oxen that he exhibited from town to town to illustrate the evils of currency deflation and its effect on the price of cattle. A native of Turner, "Uncle Solon" was the father of the powerful Greenback Party in Maine and a figure of national stature within the movement. He cultivated his image as a shrewd, honest, dirt farmer (much in the literary tradition of "Major Jack Downing"), published *Chase's Chronicle,* and the success of his party allowed the Democrats, or Fusion Party, to twice capture the Blaine House. COURTESY OF THE BETHEL HISTORICAL SOCIETY, BETHEL, MAINE

decided a Democrat was the lesser of two evils. Governor Alonzo W. Garcelon of Lewiston, a Bowdoin graduate and physician of stature, served a term, but in 1879, the election had the same result. Amid cries of fraud in counting the vote, armed men moved on Augusta causing Garcelon to call out the militia and to appoint General Chamberlain to "protect the public property and institutions." This near civil insurrection in Maine grabbed national headlines and caused a sensation. A Republican was appointed, but in the next election, the Democrats and Greenbackers combined as the Fusion Party to elect Harris W. Plaisted.

The Republicans won the position in 1883 and hung on strong. By the turn of the century, however, the balance began to shift. The Democrats were able to picture the GOP as spendthrifts who

Great excitement erupted in the chambers of the Maine State House in the wake of the disputed election of 1879, as depicted in *Frank Leslie's Illustrated Newspaper* of January 24, 1880. Here, Governor Alonzo Garcelon administers the oath to state senators that he had certified. For several elections, the Democrats were able to use the Greenback Party votes to fight the Republicans, resulting in one Democrat and one Fusion chief executive. In this instance, a near civil insurrection was narrowly averted. General Chamberlain took charge of Augusta, and later a Gatling gun guarded the State House. COURTESY OF THE MAINE HISTORIC PRESERVATION COMMISSION

were unable or unwilling to enforce Prohibition laws and who did not support national efforts to reform the party. Thus in 1910, the Democrat Frederick W. Plaisted (son of the Fusion governor) was elected, along with a Democratic legislature. Two congressmen were elected from the party, and the legislature filled two U.S. Senate seats with Democrats. One of the latter, Obadiah Gardner, was a former master of the Maine Grange. Once again this election proved a bellwether for the rise of the Progressive Movement nationally and the election of President Woodrow Wilson in 1912. "As Maine Goes, So Goes the Nation" proved correct, as that year saw the first Maine electoral votes cast for a Democrat since the time of Franklin Pierce.

Republican gubernatorial candidate William T. Haines defeated Plaisted that year but was himself vanquished by Democrat Oakley C. Curtis in 1914. Then the Democratic interlude ended for a time.

❖

One of the most trying legislative issues was that of Prohibition, backed by the aging Neal Dow and an army of women under the banner of the Women's Christian Temperance Union. Perhaps the most forceful of these workers was Portland's Lillian M. Stevens, also a power in the growing suffrage movement. In 1871 laws forbidding the sale of liquors were extended to cider and wine. Finally, in 1884, an amendment to the state constitution forbade the manufacture of liquors except

DIMINISHING EXPECTATIONS   *157*

In 1907 the Maine Historical Society opened its new library and headquarters beside Portland's Wadsworth–Longfellow House (about 1785–1886), which had been willed to the organization by the poet's sister Anne Longfellow Pierce (1810–1901). Interest in local history and an appreciation of objects and documents were heightened by the Centennial Celebration in 1876. In the decades to come, many historic Maine buildings were saved and opened as museum houses by a variety of historic and preservation groups. This scene shows the Maine Historical complex around 1907. COLLECTION OF THE MAINE HISTORICAL SOCIETY

Beginning with the centennial of the American Revolution in 1876, Americans began to appreciate and collect objects from their past. Historical societies were formed and antique dealers appeared upon the scene. Improved transportation, including trains and automobiles, allowed quaint, job-poor villages to flourish. Among the first dealers was Fred Tuck, who started at Kennebunkport in 1893. His "Old Curiosity Shop" in Union Square, photographed around 1897, boasted old, new, and used furniture, china, and other locally acquired objects. He would later expand to include an ice cream parlor, a career documented in Joyce Butler's *Kennebunkport Scrapbooks* and in Dean Fales's *Antiqueman's Diary*. COURTESY OF THE BRICK STORE MUSEUM, KENNEBUNK, MAINE

for cider. Two years before, General Dow had been the Prohibition Party candidate for president. It is curious to observe that while most Mainers wanted Prohibition, great numbers of them continued to make, sell, and drink the stuff. A number of individuals made a living off the trade and virtually nothing was done to enforce the laws. Rural and urban kitchens became taverns, winked at by the law. When the artist Elihu Vedder visited this drinkers' desert in 1894 to place his mural at the Walker Art Building, he had no trouble finding a drink. The waitress at the hotel directed him to a spot in Robinhood.

The role of state government only gradually and grudgingly extended into new areas between 1865 and 1914. Neither party, in fact, wished it and they constantly chided each other for overspending. A year after the Civil War, the legislature

helped fund an orphanage for children of military men, but it was among the nation's smallest and not fully under state control. At the same time, following national trends, they sponsored the construction of Maine General Hospital in Portland. Previously, hospitals had been for the poor, but the Civil War brought great advances in the field of health care. Improvements were made at the prison in Thomaston and at the reform school, but as yet there was no separate prison for women. In 1885 a State Board of Health appeared, but not until 1887 did it get underway, ordering towns to appoint their own boards and officers. Gradually, an umbrella of state laws was opening. In 1907 the State School for the Feeble-Minded (later Pineland

158 MAINE: THE WILDER HALF OF NEW ENGLAND

In 1907, the problem of inadequate space again brought to debate the question of moving the capital. It was subsequently decided to remain in Augusta, and architect G. Henri Desmond (1876–1965) won the design competition to enlarge the State House. He added two wings and the 185-foot dome, shown under construction in 1910. After the fourth attempt to move the capital, an amendment to the Maine Constitution assured that Augusta would always be the seat of Maine government. COURTESY OF THE MAINE HISTORIC PRESERVATION COMMISSION

Center) was begun at Pownal. A State Board of Corrections was started in 1913. In the 1880s clear abuses of children in the workplace led to child labor laws. In 1911 the National Child Labor Committee sent Lewis W. Hine to photograph Maine children at work. Gradually a more humane ethic began to develop. In agricultural Aroostook, children were dismissed from school to help with the harvest, a practice that lasted until 1990.

In the field of education, the university was founded along with normal schools (teaching colleges) in Farmington, Castine, Gorham, Fort Kent, Presque Isle, and Machias. Free high schools and free textbooks derived from increasingly stronger compulsory education laws.

❖

In 1910, after repeated attempts to move the capital to Portland, Augusta was reconfirmed. In the same year, architect G. Henri Desmond's new designs for the State House were carried out. While the Bulfinch portico remained, a new dome and impressive north and south wings changed the building forever. Gardiner sculptor W. Clark Noble's allegorical female figure, *Wisdom*, was then placed atop the shining dome. Mainers, like their counterparts throughout the United States, would soon face the challenges of the twentieth century and the horrors of world war.

DIMINISHING EXPECTATIONS   *159*

As the First World War was breaking out in Europe, guests at the Poland Spring House remained ambivalent and uninterested. The grand hotels would continue to attract people, and even President Warren G. Harding motored in from Portland in 1921. Increasingly, though, ordinary Americans would travel by automobile, staying at less expensive roadside cabins or motor courts. COURTESY OF THE MAINE HISTORIC PRESERVATION COMMISSION

8

THE EARLY TWENTIETH CENTURY (1914–1941)

In 1914 most Mainers looked forward to what they believed would be a century of technological progress and modest growth and prosperity. Few, if any, were prepared for the fits and starts of the twentieth century. First came the burst of patriotism and economic surge of World War I, only to be followed by a sharp business decline. The decade of the 1920s brought a rise in economic expectations stimulated by the automobile, tourism, and conservation, tempered by another virulent round of nativism, this time in Ku Klux Klan sheets. The Great Depression and the end of Canadian grain shipments through the Grand Trunk brought hard times countered by a resurgence of the Democrats, the initiation of large federally supported projects that changed the role of government, and a start toward recovery. As ever, Maine continued to produce many original personalities—Marsden Hartley, Edna St. Vincent Millay, L. L. Bean, Governor Percival P. Baxter, and Guy Gannett among them. Indeed, it was through such personalities that many observers came to define Maine.

As the nations of Europe marched off to war in 1914, Mainers were still enjoying the benefits of the Progressive Era. After years of Republican dominance, a Democrat, Woodrow Wilson, occupied the White House. The Progressive break with the GOP was mirrored in Maine where Democrat Oakley C. Curtis was elected governor. When the Progressive Republicans rejoined the party in 1916, they again became dominant under popular Governor Carl E. Milliken, a lumber manufacturer from Island Falls. That year also witnessed Maine's first primary election of U.S. senators and personal victory for Frederick Hale, Maine's first popularly elected senator.

The teens also brought the formation of the Maine Public Utilities Commission (1914), the establishment of Sieur de Monts National Monument (1916), the opening of Sweetser Orphan Asylum (1917), and the start of the Mother's Aid Program and the new Maine Department of Health (1914). There was an increase in awareness of social problems marked by state and regional conferences focused on education, child labor, and working women. St. Joseph's College, the first Catholic institution of its kind in Maine, was established in 1915. In Portland a major street railway strike occurred in 1916. The year 1918 marked the culminating year of two decades' worth of strengthened education laws, tougher qualifications for teachers and administrators, and the extension of health care into public schools.

❖

Perhaps the most remarkable thing about the teens was the shift in attitude from total disinterest in the "European war" to a wave of anti-German sentiment and enthusiastic entry into battle. This, in fact, reflected national trends marked by President Wilson—who was elected on the slogan "He Kept Us Out of War"—asking Congress to declare war. The changes were inspired by Germany's use

The Bath-built bark *William P. Frye* is sent to the bottom of the South Atlantic on January 27, 1915, by a German raider, *Prinz Eitel Friedrich*. The *Frye* had been carrying a cargo of wheat to Queenstown when overtaken. Her crew was removed by the raiders and the vessel dynamited. Not since the Civil War had downeasters faced this kind of challenge. As the conflict progressed, demand for Maine-built ships grew. It was to be the last such building boom; the age of sail was ending.
COURTESY OF THE MAINE MARITIME MUSEUM, BATH, MAINE

of unrestricted submarine warfare, growing reports of atrocities by the Central Powers, and the wish to protect a growing number of loans made by American investors to England and France.

In January of 1915, the four-masted bark *William P. Frye* became the first American merchant vessel to be sunk by the Germans. The Bath-built vessel was carrying grain from Seattle to Queenstown when she was stopped by the commerce raider *Prinz Eitel Friedrich* in the South Atlantic. Unable to remove the cargo and wanting to keep it from the British, the Germans removed

H. O. PHILLIPS
Formerly War Stamp Chairman for Cumberland County

Sing a song of quarters, a pocket full of rye,
Fifteen million dollars' worth of stamps in a pie,
Stuff it full of war stamps as tight as you can cram;
Reckon that'll be some dish to hand our Uncle Sam.

In April of 1917 the United States entered the First World War, and in July the Second Maine Regiment was mobilized and soon sent to France as part of the famous 26th Division. On the home front, civilian leaders organized fund drives and Red Cross activities of all kinds. The book *Mother Goose Comes to Portland* (1918), by Frederic W. Freeman, provides caricatures of various leaders. Here, grain store president Herbert Owen Phillips sells war stamps. COLLECTION OF THE MAINE HISTORICAL SOCIETY

the crew and dynamited the *Frye*. A diplomatic protest was made and Yankee captains kept sharper watches, but the event caused less excitement than might be imagined. America's merchant marine, in a sorry state since after the Civil War, realized a sudden windfall and an unexpected

Parades had been a part of Maine life since the Federal Period. Here, Red Cross and Red Star nurses lead the Third Liberty Loan march in Portland in April of 1917. In the fall of the next year, their services were needed more than ever as the influenza epidemic swept the state. COLLECTION OF THE MAINE HISTORICAL SOCIETY

extension of the age of sail. With the Germans blockaded and the British using merchant vessels for wartime tasks, neutral ships were needed. Shipping rates climbed, and anyone with a vessel could realize tremendous profits. Maine was one of the few places with a workforce skilled in wooden shipbuilding. Long-defunct yards suddenly surged with activity; in East Harrington alone a half-dozen schooners were launched. In 1916 Congress passed the Shipping Act to try to reestablish a viable merchant marine.

The wish to recapture the Atlantic carrying trade was paralleled by growing diplomatic rifts between Berlin and Washington, as the sinking of vessels continued and, increasingly, America became the "paymaster of the Allies." A change was in the air by 1916 as attitudes shifted from neutrality to jingoism, strengthened by an effective anti-German campaign in the press. War was declared on April 6, 1917, and the opposition was effectively silenced. Newspapers carried unflattering portrayals of "the Hun," and local artists were active in producing war cartoons and posters, such as the one by William Wallace Gilchrist, Jr., still on view at Brunswick's Curtis Library. Under the administration of President Robert G. Aley, the University of Maine took on a martial look as the Student Army Training Corps regulations spilled over into daily life, study of the German language was dropped, and the law school dean was dismissed for alleged German sentiments.

On the home front, Maine men, women, and

THE EARLY TWENTIETH CENTURY

children were actively involved in Liberty Bond, War Savings Stamp, and Red Cross activities. Almost $16 million in loans and contributions was raised in Maine. At South Portland, wooden freighters were built and sent into action. By 1917 Bath Iron Works was already "the premier builder of destroyers in the nation" and supplied other yards with plans and technical assistance. At the Portsmouth Naval Yard, *L-8*, the first submarine built at a U.S. naval facility, was launched and five other subs were underway. This was the start of a grand Kittery tradition and, at the same time, 122 ships were repaired by a workforce of 5,722. Pay rates rose, as did the cost of living.

As soon as Governor Milliken delivered his war message, the legislature authorized the issue of state bonds to the amount of $1 million. The 2nd Maine Regiment was mobilized and quartered in Augusta. Under Colonel Frank M. Hume of Houlton, it became part of the 103rd Regiment of the 26th Division and saw heavy fighting in France. Other Maine units followed and citizens joined all manner of army and navy operations. Interestingly, Mainers were among the first American troops ever to parade in London. There was some draft evasion, with searches of Portland and various shipyards undertaken, but most citizens supported the fight and there were ample volunteers. Some 35,214 of the state's men and women served. Deaths from all causes numbered 1,073, with 228 killed in battle. Much of the old state imprint had been erased, for as historian Glenn Wendell Starkey noted in 1920: "The great inclusive method of training our soldiers in the war adopted by the government made it impossible for state units to be recognized and the regiments formed and named so that each state could retain its personal touch and feeling of ownership in them."

❖

During the conflict, Lieutenant Walker Blaine Beale, a grandson of James G. Blaine, offered the Blaine House in Augusta to the Maine Committee of Public Safety, and it became the nerve center of emergency activity. In 1918 Lieutenant Beale was killed in the St. Mihiel offensive, and his mother presented the Blaine House to the state. It was accepted as the official governor's mansion and has remained so ever since. War's end saw the organization of the American Legion (1919) and the establishment of fifty-four posts in Maine that year. The legislature also passed a soldier's bonus of one hundred dollars.

The war had established the United States as a world leader, but within a few years the bloom faded. America failed to realize its dream of recapturing the Atlantic carrying trade, only Finland paid back its war debt, and, disgusted with Europe, America kept out of the League of Nations. The shift to a peacetime economy caused immediate hardships in the days following the armistice, but the Roaring Twenties were generally productive.

Several big issues grabbed the country's attention. The ratification of the Eighteenth Amendment, which prohibited the making, sale, and shipment of liquor, occurred on January 29, 1919. The entire nation was drawn into an experiment that Maine had begun in the days of Neal Dow. It was to have disastrous consequences and end in failure before the Second World War. Of lasting importance was the ratification of the Nineteenth Amendment guaranteeing women the vote, which occurred on August 26, 1920, and which had earlier been approved by the state legislature. John Neal's call for total equality of the sexes, though not completely answered, had crossed a major threshold. Crucial to the movement in Maine were Laura J. Curtis Bullard, Isabel Greenwood, Deborah Knox Livingston, Maude Maywood Park, and attorney Gail Laughlin of Robbinston.

Historian Elizabeth Ring termed this "the arid but not-so-dry twenties," noting that the decade produced "the speakeasy, the hip flask, and flaming youth," and in Maine "the Klan, the crusading zeal of the WCTU, and the fight against the Insull

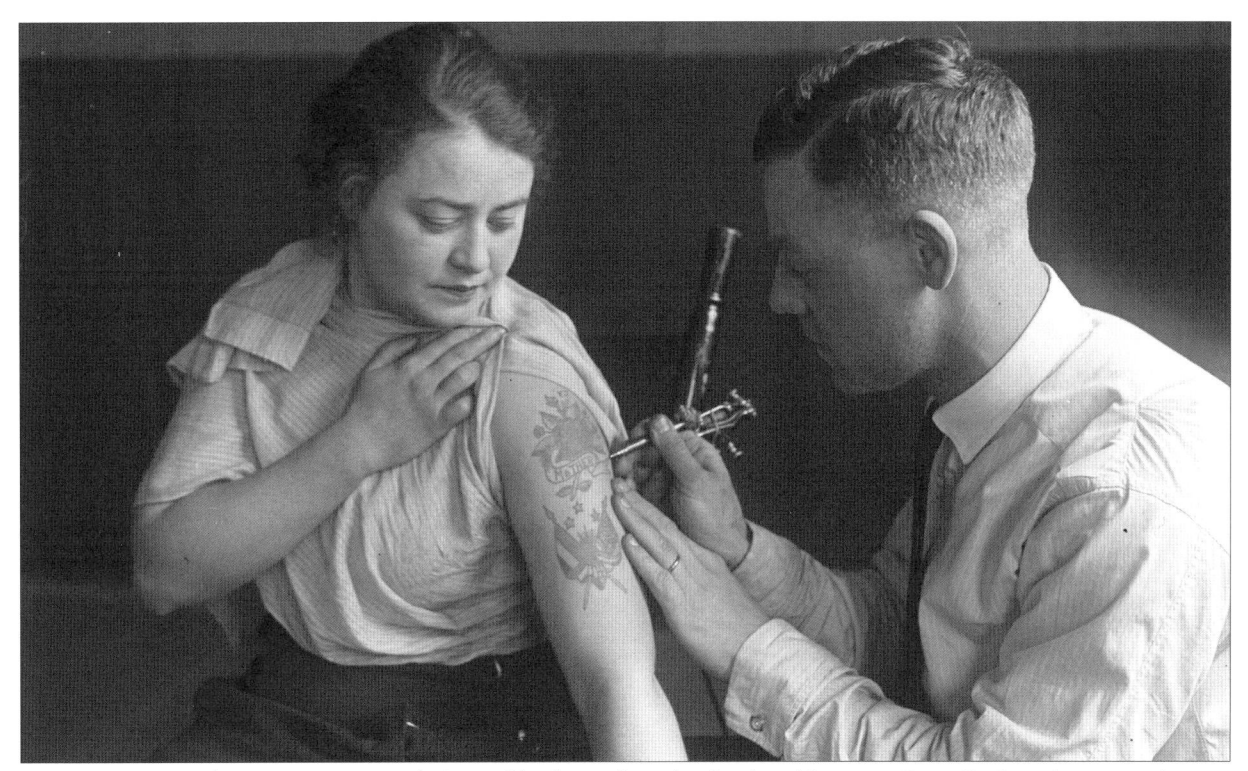

Yvonne Jongeleen gets an unusual piece of body art from her husband in 1925. Peter D. Jongeleen, a native of the Netherlands, offered "electrical tattooing" from his shop at 320 York Street, Portland. COLLECTION OF THE MAINE HISTORICAL SOCIETY

interests determined to repeal the Fernald Law of 1909." In these get-rich-quick years, the Republicans dominated to the point of excluding Democrats from all congressional seats and the Blaine House. Of the governors in the twenties, the most outstanding was certainly Percival P. Baxter and the most controversial, Ralph Owen Brewster.

Governor Percival P. Baxter was the son of Mayor James Phinney Baxter of Portland, the noted builder of city parks and donor of public libraries in Portland and his birthplace of Gorham. Percy graduated from Bowdoin and Harvard Law before entering the family canning business. Elected to the state legislature in 1905, he became senate president in 1917 and succeeded Governor Frederick Parkhurst on the latter's death. A Maine original, Baxter lowered the statehouse flags upon the death of his Irish setter and traded harsh words with Kenneth Roberts over the appropriateness of billboards along highways. More significantly, he was the first chief executive to bring women into state government and was an outspoken critic of the Ku Klux Klan.

In Maine the Klan was generally anti-Catholic and anti-Semitic but did not scruple at hating the occasional African American. It took hold for the same reasons that had generated the Know-Nothings a century before. Some Yankees, and established ethnic groups as well, tended to see the new immigrants as a threat to jobs and morals, and favored exclusionary legislation. Indeed, in the peak year of 1913, some 26,000 immigrants had come through the Portland inspection station. While many of these people went on to Canada, they were still feared. By the mid-1920s, some 40,000 Mainers had joined the Klan. In his race

Dapper Governor Percival P. Baxter (1876–1969) visits Boothbay for the departure of the schooner *Bowdoin* for the Arctic in 1921. The son of businessman-scholar James Phinney Baxter graduated from Bowdoin and Harvard Law School before entering politics; he served as governor from 1921 to 1925. Baxter is remembered for his purchase of Katahdin and environs and the creation of Baxter State Park, which he virtually forced on the legislature along with millions to provide for the wilderness area. COURTESY OF THE MAINE HISTORIC PRESERVATION COMMISSION

for the governorship, Ralph Owen Brewster of Portland drew strong support from and failed to disown the Kluxers. He also favored an amendment to withhold funds from private schools, a fact that helped bring French Canadians and other groups into the election process as opponents. On a town and city level, leaders entered the system from a variety of ethnic pools. The personal demise of the Klan's charismatic leader, Eugene "Doc" Farnsworth, led to the failure of the organization after marches in Brewer and Portland and cross-burnings in Mexico. More sinister were responses from the intellectual community, including Kenneth Roberts's book, *Why Europe Leaves Home* (1922). The Kennebunk native believed that "America is confronted by a perpetual emergency as long as her laws permit millions of non-Nordic aliens to pour through her sea-gates."

In terms of social welfare, the trend begun in the Progressive Era to move from traditional charity to professional social work was slowed. Locally, institutions such as the Female Orphan Asylum of Portland (Children's Home of Portland) strengthened their positions. Consolidation was also the name of the game in industry and business. The big retail stores, which appeared first before the turn of the century, reached their ultimate look of stylishness in this era.

In 1921 Portland had three rival newspapers. That year, Guy Gannett purchased the *Portland Press*, the *Portland Herald,* and the *Waterville Sentinel,* and by the mid-1920s was building a news-

The Ku Klux Klan parades in full regalia through the streets of Brewer, Maine, in 1924. Led by the charismatic F. Eugene "Doc" Farnsworth, the Klan claimed 40,000 members in the state between 1922 and 1925. A huge Klan headquarters arose on Forest Avenue in Portland, where it supported new council-manager government, as opposed to the ward system, which it saw as controlled by Catholics and Jews. The hysteria soon died down, and the local and national popularity of the Klan faded. COURTESY PRIVATE COLLECTION

paper empire. Gannett's lock on Portland's morning, evening, and Sunday newspapers drew criticism along with charges of close ties to utility magnate Samuel Insull's spreading network of power companies. In 1923 Maine was the third largest producer of power in the country, and the Portland papers led the fight to unplug the Fernald Law. Guy Gannett's close ties with Central Maine Power infuriated many individuals on a local and national level and brought Dr. Ernest Gruening to do battle as editor of the new *Portland Evening News* between 1927 and 1932. Previously managing editor of *The Nation*, and subsequently "the Father of Alaska Statehood," Gruening's high-power status was a measure of the intensity of feelings generated by the power controversy and newspaper monopoly charges.

Mainers were also experiencing a new kind of communication and entertainment in the form of radio. The state's first broadcast came from a Bangor church in 1922, and three years later WCSH in Portland was granted a commercial license. In 1925 Dover-Foxcroft got a station, which was soon transferred to Bangor, the site of WAIB. Maine also pioneered national radio religious programming with the First Radio Parish Church of America, formed by the Reverend Howard O. Hough in 1926. Geography played the major role in the selection of Houlton for America's premier long-wave trans-Atlantic telephone receiving station in 1927.

As radio changed the way people got information and ordered their time, automobiles and trucks brought even greater changes. In 1919 Mainers approved an $8 million bond issue in order to match federal highway funds, and in 1923 the legislature approved a one-cent-per-gallon tax on gasoline. Maine was now open to a new, growing class of physically and financially mobile Americans with private cars. Motor courts ranged from a crescent of one-room cabins to Scarborough's elaborate Danish Village of 1930.

Route One, which stretched along the coast and on to Florida, would soon boast a variety of roadside attractions such as Perry's Nut House in Belfast and the Desert of Maine in Freeport. Automobiles made it possible to get to historic places such as Stroudwater's Historic Tate House (1935) and the Penobscot Marine Museum (1936). It was an era of diners, roadhouses, and above all, gas stations. It was the classical era of the L.L. Bean store and illustrated catalog. Hunting, fishing, and camping, once largely the realm of wealthy sports or locals, were now appealing to many. Already George Bucknam Dorr and Harvard's president Charles Eliot had influenced the buying up of land on Mount Desert for preservation. They organized the purchase of 15,000 acres around Cadillac Mountain, which the federal government accepted as Sieur de Monts National Monument (1916) and as Lafayette National Park in 1919. The first national park east of the Mississippi grew, and in 1928 was renamed Acadia National Park, currently the system's second-most-visited facility.

In winter much of Maine's transportation was still moving on runners, as demonstrated by this photograph of Fort Kent in 1936. The vehicle on the right is a school cart, forerunner of a school bus. In the 1920s the absence of public plowing led transportation pioneer A. J. "Allie" Cole to send out his own plowing crews. In the next decade the state finally began extending the service. Not until 1945 did the highway commission assume responsibility for Aroostook. COURTESY OF CAROLE L. WEEKS FOR MARGARET LOVELY MCATEE, PHOTOGRAPH BY JAMES W. SWANSON

Other forms of transportation continued, but most were in some sort of difficulty. In 1924 Maine witnessed the growth of its rail miles to 2,379 in spite of growing financial problems. Thereafter, the miles began to decline. For seventy years, Portland had served as Canada's winter port for grain export, but in 1923 the Grand Trunk was absorbed by government-owned Canadian National. Political pressure brought preferential treatment to the ports of Halifax and St. John at Portland's expense. Tariffs made it impossible to afford the Maine route, and grain imports fell rapidly, ceasing altogether in 1934. Aside from the local construction of the Maine State Pier, the Portland waterfront began to languish and decay. Congress Street, already studded with department stores, became the city's unquestioned main street. The agricultural expansion in the Aroostook potato made the Bangor & Aroostook line more successful, though the County's market was subject to boom and bust periods.

Rum also traveled by back roads, which were ill-patrolled. Highways grew in importance, and in 1925 the Maine State Police was established to handle responsibilities previously handled by county sheriffs' departments. In 1927 the state also took charge of highway snow removal in the most-traveled portions. In the north, trucker A. J. "Allie" Cole of Enfield set his own crews to clearing snow beyond Lincoln, and later he extended service into Presque Isle. Not till 1945 did the state extend service into Aroostook. Cole had pioneered trucking in 1917—indeed, he started with wagons and soon had a fleet of gasoline-driven vehicles. Today, Cole's Land Transportation Museum in Bangor showcases trucks, trains, and all forms of

In the 1920s and '30s, Old Orchard Beach became a natural runway for airplanes of all sorts. The dashing Harry Jones had a hangar that became a stopover for some of the world's best aviators. Three flyers made the transatlantic flight from there prior to 1939; Jean Assolant's *Yellow Bird* was the first to fly from the U.S. to Spain in 1929. COLLECTION OF THE MAINE HISTORICAL SOCIETY

vehicles. In the south, Paul E. Merrill of Cumberland Center entered the same business in the inauspicious year of 1929 with one Reo truck. He, too, built a transportation empire, which continued strong to the end of the twentieth century.

❖

The newest form of transportation was by air, and the sands of Old Orchard made a superb natural runway. The dashing pilot Harry Jones built a hangar on the beach, which became a stopover for some of the world's best pilots including Colonel Charles Lindbergh, fresh from his conquest of the Atlantic. Eight attempts to duplicate his feat were begun from the beach before 1939. Three adventurers, including Jean Assolant in the *Yellow Bird*, made the passage. Two others vanished en route.

In 1923 the entire U.S. Army Air Corps, under General Billy Mitchell, landed at Bangor. Merl Fogg of Howland, one of the state's first licensed pilots, was active around Bangor. Bush pilots soon opened up the North Woods of Maine, and as the Maine Warden Service took on its modern form under commissioner of Fish and Game George Stobie, the latest equipment was utilized. He was particularly interested in using aircraft to cover the wilderness. In 1939 Bill Turgeon, a World War I flyer, former state aviation advisor, and owner of a small airline out of Lewiston–Auburn Municipal Airport, became the warden service's first pilot. In 1936 Maine could claim twenty-nine airfields and sixty-two flyers.

Bangor Airport had opened in 1931, and commercial flights to Maine began in 1934 on the railroad-owned Boston–Maine Airways. The service linked Boston with Portland and Bangor. In 1938 Portland purchased the city airport; it was later improved with WPA funds. Bangor and Portland continue to maintain important facilities.

The great white coastal steamers, which had connected the ports of Maine with Boston for nearly one hundred years, began to phase out in this era. The stranding of the *City of Rockland* in the Kennebec during the autumn of 1923 ended continuous service from Bath to Boston. In 1935 service to the Penobscot and St. John terminated, and only a few smaller runs between ports survived until the war. Shipbuilding, too, appeared dead. In 1926 Bath Iron Works Ltd., which had lost its navy contract in 1920, went bust. In the following year, it was purchased by William Stark "Pete" Newell, a former draftsman and manager who was to prove one of the most remarkable figures in the history of Maine business. Newell surrounded himself with the best workers, engineers, and promoters and went after anything he could get, including the contract for J. P. Morgan's gargantuan yacht *Corsair* in 1929.

During the 1920s, some 2,000 workers were active at the Portsmouth Naval Shipyard, where more than a dozen submarines were launched. In 1923 the chief of naval operations reported: "Submarines can be more economically and expeditiously overhauled at Portsmouth than at any other eastern yard...." Thus Maine hung on to shipbuilding. Boatbuilding was another matter, and yards met the demand for swift motor vessels for Coast Guard and rumrunner alike.

Liquor traffic became a growth industry in the wake of national prohibition, and some Mainers returned to the well-known patterns of smuggling laid down prior to the Revolution. The nature of the contraband had changed along with the speed of boats and radio communication, but the basic methods and desire to buck the system and turn a profit endured. Beyond the twelve-mile limit the silhouettes of the *Ocean Maid*, *Kathleen Conrad*, and *Maude Thornhill* became the focus of local traffic, and places like Hills Beach in Biddeford became nighttime ports. Each town had its rum room for the destruction of the contraband. Ingenious ways to hide drinks of all sorts were devised, much to the dismay of the WCTU.

Traditional industries continued apace. In 1917 the Commission of Sea and Shore Fisheries

Few Mainers could imagine a lifestyle like that of Anne Paul Nevin, wife of composer Ethelbert Nevin. Her estate, "Arcady," at Blue Hill was named for her husband's once-famous composition "In Arcady" and was, with its extraordinary formal gardens, considered a monument to his work. Well into the 1920s, summer residents lofted sumptuous cottages along the shore. COLLECTION OF THE MAINE HISTORICAL SOCIETY

replaced a single commissioner. In 1931 the importance of the fisheries rated a department with its own commissioner. Lobstering, now carried on in motorized vessels instead of under sail or by oar, continued, and gill-netters and trawlers appeared. Draggers from Massachusetts plied the Gulf of Maine and sold their catch in Portland. Most were operated by Italian Americans, and one account noted: "The bright green and blue hulls of these out-of-state boats lend an almost European touch to the everyday scene."

The University of Maine and its extension services helped to improve agriculture, which had moved far from the subsistence stage to family-run commercial operations including dairying, potatoes, and poultry, along with vegetables for canning. The gasoline motor and electricity transformed life, along with radio and telephone connecting once isolated homesteads with the world.

By World War I, industry—especially in Biddeford—was employing many immigrants, largely from eastern and southern Europe. Greeks, Albanians (Maine's first Muslims), and others worked in the mills, not always accepted by those earlier employed. In the factories of Biddeford, the postwar recession led to a drop in prices, an end to construction, and a long strike that led to a bitter replacement at Saco-Lowell. In the mid-1920s profits grew, only to be lost in the Great Depression.

172   Maine: The Wilder Half of New England

The making of shoes had become a representative industry in Maine. The shift was on from work shoes to sports, leisure, and casual models. In Freeport, L. L. Bean enjoyed extraordinary success with his rubber and leather hunting shoe, and provided footwear for Admiral Donald B. MacMillan's arctic expeditions. Wilton's G. H. Bass & Co. did similar work for MacMillan and for Admiral Byrd, produced flying shoes during and after the war, and, like Yarmouth's Abbott Company, manufactured golf shoes. By 1930 Bass had also entered the ski-boot market.

Pulp and paper remained the dominant industry in the woodlands, and big hydro plants for electrical power began to appear. Central Maine Power's Walter S. Wyman Dam was built at Moscow in 1928 and began generating power two years later.

❖

The most sweeping and visionary dream of the era belonged to the engineer Dexter P. Cooper, whom historians have likened to John A. Poor of an earlier day. While vacationing at Campobello in 1919, Cooper conceived the Passamaquoddy Tidal Power (Quoddy) Project, which he discussed with his neighbor, Franklin D. Roosevelt. In Eastport, while running for the vice presidency in 1920, Roosevelt first broached the plan to harness Quoddy's 18.1-foot tides. Gaining charters in Canada and in Maine, Cooper's company set up in the 1920s, and hopes were raised of bringing great industries into the depressed St. Croix region. By 1929 the initial effort collapsed in the face of Canadian opposition and the depression, in which Cooper lost $85,000 of his own money.

The Great Depression, triggered by the crash of 1929, had far-reaching effects on Maine and the nation. The Republicans held the White House under President Herbert Hoover and the Blaine House under the aristocratic William Tudor Gardiner of Gardiner. Efforts were made to correct the economic situation. In 1929 the state had created a *Commission to Pass on Applications for Relief*, which was to deal with dependents of servicemen from the Great War. In 1931 it was abolished, along with the Public Health Council, the Board of Mothers' Aid, the Board of Charities and Corrections, the Board of Health, and the position of commissioner of health. A new set of agencies was established under a commissioner of Health and Welfare, which was to cooperate with the federal government. In 1930 Hoover requested between $100 and $150 million for construction of public works to employ America's millions of jobless. Also begun were the Reconstruction Finance Corporation, the Federal Home Loan Bank Act, and the Relief and Construction Act, but no direct federal aid. Democrat Roosevelt offered a New Deal and swept to victory in 1932. Only six states, including Maine, voted Republican.

In fact, Mainers had reelected Gardiner in 1930, but his plurality declined from 82,000 votes to 15,000, largely because fewer Republicans

Opposite, top: Illegal whiskey is removed from a vessel at Portland under the watchful eyes of the police. During the era of Prohibition (1919–1933), Mainers built both rumrunning boats and fast boats for the Coast Guard. One successful smuggling run to the French islands of St. Pierre and Miquelon could easily pay for a new boat, and large vessels like *Good Luck*, *Ocean Maid*, *Mary L*, and *Kathleen Conrad* achieved fame beyond the twelve-mile limit. COLLECTION OF THE MAINE HISTORICAL SOCIETY

Opposite, bottom: Hard times, fast cars, and desperate men combined as gangs of bank robbers sped through the land. Maine's most celebrated brush with this violence occurred on the morning of October 12, 1937, when Al Brady, Public Enemy Number One, arrived to buy guns at a Bangor sporting-goods store. Recognized on an earlier visit, when Brady and his gang returned they were surrounded by FBI agents and state and local police. In a one-minute exchange of gunfire, windows were shattered, a storefront destroyed, one G-Man wounded, and Brady and a pal slain. COURTESY OF THE *BANGOR DAILY NEWS*, BANGOR, MAINE

voted. In 1932 the Democrats were better organized and were able to elect the popular Lewiston attorney Louis J. Brann as governor. The energetic, fiscally responsible Brann was not a New Dealer. He asked state employees to take a pay cut, cut expenses, and sought new sources of revenue.

Brann's personal popularity brought him re-election, but he failed to capitalize on Republican weakness and build Democratic strength. He lost in his bid for the Senate in 1936, and Maine was one of two states voting against Roosevelt. The president's campaign manager was to quip, "As Maine goes, so goes Vermont." Thus the state finished the thirties with Governor Lewis O. Barrows

The Walter S. Wyman Hydro Station at Moscow, on the Kennebec River, was started in 1928 and named for Central Maine Power's founder (1874–1942). The 3,200-foot-long earth and concrete dam creates a 14-mile-long lake that reaches to Caratunk. Generators went into operation in 1930 and 1931. Such projects provided electrical power that forever changed the way Mainers carried on their daily life. As the decades progressed, power became available to even the most isolated villages. COLLECTION OF THE MAINE HISTORICAL SOCIETY

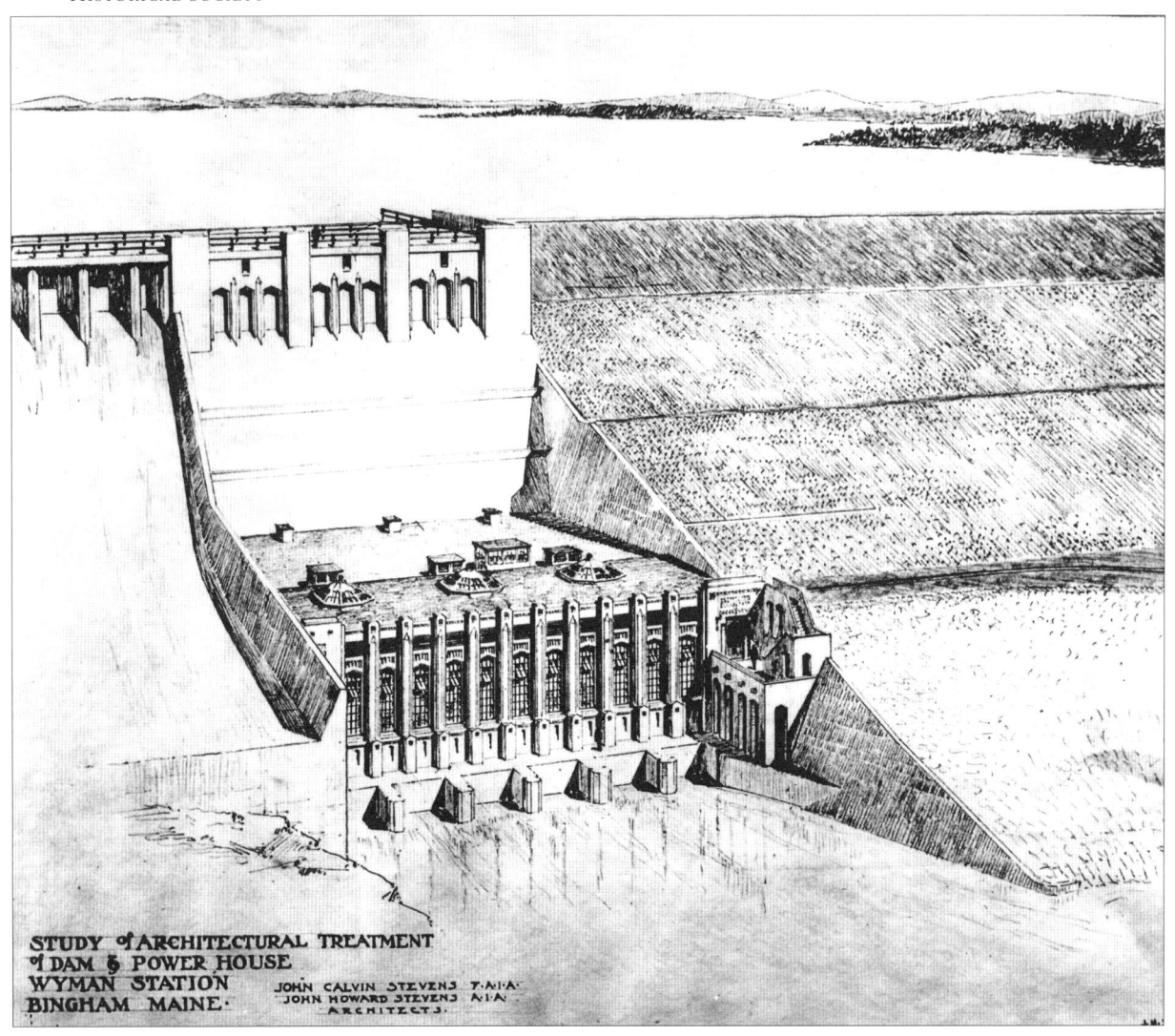

174 MAINE: THE WILDER HALF OF NEW ENGLAND

of Newport, and voters remained loyal to the GOP well into the 1950s.

The thirties, however difficult, were to prove remarkably productive. Among the most celebrated changes were the repeal of the Eighteenth Amendment in 1933 and the opening of state liquor stores the following year. Women began to win election to town and state offices. In 1929 attorney Gail Laughlin won a seat in the legislature and later served in the state senate. There, she helped pass legislation to prevent husbands from committing wives to mental hospitals solely on their testimony, and further legislation raising the marriage age of girls from thirteen to sixteen. By far the most radical change was the movement of federal and state governments into everyday life, an area previously reserved for town and city authorities. Old-line charities, pretty well self-sustaining before, now came under a variety of oversight agencies and mandates. Many felt these charities would fade away as the so-called welfare state grew. In fact, those old institutions that remained became professional, and the welfare state idea never fully materialized. People like Miss

Religion continued to play a vital role in the lives of most Maine people. When Mrs. Max B. Epstein presented a torah to Congregation Beth Israel in memory of her husband, it was a memorable occasion. In October of 1938, the *Bangor Daily News* reported: "This was in the traditional manner, the sacred book being borne beneath a canopy while various members of the congregation took turns in carrying it—a high honor. There was singing as the procession moved through the streets." Here the congregation passes Beth Abraham Synagogue. COURTESY OF THE BANGOR HISTORICAL SOCIETY, BANGOR, MAINE

Margaret Payson of Portland, with her emphasis on child protection and assistance, successfully bridged the gap between the new professionally trained social worker and the volunteers who had sustained the patchwork welfare net in the past.

Percival P. Baxter needs to be mentioned as a patron of the people. For years his interest in conservation had led him to urge the legislature to purchase woodlands around Maine's highest mountain. When his peers failed to act, Baxter bought Katahdin in 1931 and later added land around it to the amount of 200,000 acres. It was to be kept "forever wild" and "maintained as a wilderness recreation area for the people of Maine." Baxter State Park remains the jewel of nearly thirty state parks. In 1935 the Appalachian Trail was completed by the Civilian Conservation Corps. This wilderness footpath, with shelters, extends over 2,000 miles from Katahdin to Springer Mountain in Georgia. Mainers, thanks to public and private projects, were able to appreciate and claim their own land for the future.

This appreciation coincided with the younger generation's desire to get out more. High school and college sports expanded. Lewiston became the center of snowshoeing in the United States, hosting the first International Snowshoe Convention in 1925. Skiing also took off in these years and set the stage for Maine as a multiseasonal recreation area. By 1939 Maine claimed fifteen ski trails including Sanford, Caribou, and Bethel.

Fred Tootell of Bowdoin took a gold medal in the hammer-throw at the 1924 Olympics. Lewiston's Bob LaGendre was a winner of the world and national pentathlons in 1919 and an Olympic medal winner in 1920 and 1924. Edmund "Rip" Black of Bailey Island took third place in the hammer-throw at the 1928 Olympics.

In baseball Del Bissonette of Winthrop hit 25 home runs and batted .320 in his first season with the Dodgers. Boxing's golden years peaked in the 1930s with such class fighters as Lewiston's Paul Junior and Portland's Coley Welch a few years later. Harness racing at Old Orchard and elsewhere attracted fast horses, especially after 1932, when parimutuel betting was made legal. Boating and camping became far more widespread as automobiles extended people's range, making trips and vacations easier. Government, aware of the growing interest, expanded highways and facilities as part of the public works programs.

The "great alphabet soup" of New Deal agencies, including the WPA (Works Progress Administration; later Works Projects Administration), the CCC (Civilian Conservation Corps), NYA (National Youth Administration), AAA (Agricultural Adjustment Administration), and the FWP (Federal Writers Project), had a tremendous impact on Maine. Historian Elizabeth Ring, who served as state research editor of the Historical Records Survey wrote: ". . . WPA took care of some ten thousand unemployed, exclusive of Quoddy, when the total number of Maine families without a means of livelihood was estimated at twenty-two thousand. In other phases of the New Deal, government credit was extended to home owners in various federal programs, while benefits came to Maine from the Farm Credit Administration and the Agricultural Adjustment Act."

Much needed to be done. An estimated 35,000 Mainers had borrowed money to buy stocks that were now mostly worthless. Laborers could be hired for ten dollars a week. In Portland, two banks, including Fidelity Trust, went broke and the place was said to be "more nearly paralyzed than any other of the large cities in the country." The countryside was just as hard hit, as closings had an impact on other businesses and individuals. Some new businesses, however, did succeed, including Bar Harbor's Jackson Laboratory, founded in 1929. The government's economic jumpstart commenced. WPA alone is said to have spent $36 million in Maine on projects ranging from bridges to airport facilities to sewage works and a puppet

Members of the National Youth Administration at work in Quoddy Village, Eastport, in 1937. The buildings were constructed by the Army Corps of Engineers in preparation for the federally funded phase of Dexter Cooper's plans to harness the exceptionally high tides in Passamaquoddy Bay. Hopes to revive the project persisted into the 1960s. COLLECTION OF THE MAINE HISTORICAL SOCIETY

theater. After a poor start, the WPA in Maine was headed by Bowdoin's Albert Abrahamson, who proved an able and even-handed administrator.

Frances Perkins (1880–1965), who had Newcastle, Maine, roots, was the first woman to serve in a cabinet position when she accepted FDR's invitation to become secretary of labor in 1933. Among her many accomplishments was the passage of the Social Security Act in 1935.

In 1934 Governor Brann ran on a platform to revive the Quoddy project, and a committee headed by President Kenneth C. M. Sills of Bowdoin College recommended construction as a federal project. The Public Works Administration and Army Corps of Engineers became involved. The engineers erected what observers saw as "swank" Quoddy Village at a cost of over $2 million. Once again, the great hydro project came under attack from a variety of directions and work ended. In 1936 the National Youth Administration took over Quoddy Village as part of the New Deal in Maine.

In the forests the Civilian Conservation Corps was particularly successful employing 18,298 young men in building 468 bridges, 389 miles of truck trail, and 818 miles of horse and foot trails, as well as participating in firefighting, pest control, and other forestry projects. Perhaps the most famous participant was Maine author Bill Clark.

The government continued to run the Portsmouth Naval Shipyard, but only eleven submarines were constructed from 1930 to 1939, though things began to pick up after 1935. The most famous launch was USS *Squalus,* which sank off the Isles of Shoals during sea trials in 1939. The nation listened to the radio as thirty-three survivors were rescued by using a diving chamber,

THE EARLY TWENTIETH CENTURY

On May 23, 1939, the submarine USS *Squalus* sank off the Isles of Shoals in 240 feet of water during trials. She was located on the bottom, and Americans became glued to their radios as a rescue attempt using a diving chamber began. Thirty-three men were saved and twenty-six lost. In September the ship was raised and towed back to the Portsmouth Naval Shipyard, and is shown here in dry dock. She was rebuilt and recommissioned as USS *Sailfish*. COURTESY PORTSMOUTH NAVAL SHIPYARD, U.S. NAVY PHOTOGRAPH

although twenty-six men died. Eventually the submarine was refloated and recommissioned.

At the Bath Iron Works, "Pete" Newell and his talented crew struggled to keep things going, and in 1937 built the *America*'s Cup defender *Ranger* for Harold S. Vanderbilt, a deal sealed by a handshake. Newell also rebuilt BIW's relationship with the navy and began to modernize the facility. By the late 1930s, destroyers appeared alongside BIW trawlers and yachts. World War II later brought a shot of adrenalin to the economy, as Newell utilized the South Portland shore for a shipbuilding contract with the British as the Todd-Bath Iron Shipbuilding Corporation.

The WPA also entered the arts in a big way. Except for bands and some municipal organists, the arts were generally a private affair. Now came studies and inventories of town records and the publication of histories of places including Eustis, Avon, Brownville, and Coplin. The important *Portland City Guide* (1940) and *Maine: A Guide Down-East* (1937) also appeared. Post offices from Dexter to Norway to Millinocket to Westbrook got murals for their lobbies. At Kennebunk, however, writers Booth Tarkington and Kenneth Roberts led the campaign to remove Elizabeth Tracy's *Bathers*, which they termed "bumpy" and "very, very ugly." Aside from the mural projects, the Federal Art Project was directed by a young Smith College graduate, Dorothy Hay (Jensen) of Cape Elizabeth. From 1935 to 1942, she supervised thirty-four artists who produced entries for the *Index of American Design*, scenery for Portland Players and Children's Theater, posters and signs for fish hatcheries, and school murals. Maine had never witnessed a project of this scope.

178   MAINE: THE WILDER HALF OF NEW ENGLAND

Though little noticed in his native Maine, Marsden Hartley (1877–1943) was a major force in the modern movement in American painting. Shown here on the banks of the Androscoggin River, Hartley traveled the world and was linked to such artistic Mainers-by-choice as John Marin, Peggy Bacon, Gaston Lachaise, and the Zorachs. Some of his finest work includes Katahdin oils and poems about Maine, such as "Robin Hood" and "As the Buck Lay Dead." In recent decades, thanks to such scholars as Barbara Haskell and Gail R. Scott, and Bates College, Hartley's connection to the place has become more appreciated. MARSDEN HARTLEY MEMORIAL COLLECTION, MUSEUM OF ART, OLIN ART CENTER, BATES COLLEGE, LEWISTON, MAINE

Below: Young Marsden Hartley was on his own and working in an Auburn shoe factory when he had Cyrus W. Curtis of Lewiston take his portrait around 1892. COURTESY OF WILLIAM AND DEBRA BARRY

Dorothy Hay's appointment had come largely through the urging of Alexander Bower, longtime director of the Portland School of Art and the Portland Museum of Art. Successful students from that school were to include Claude Montgomery, Bernice Breck, and Norman Thomas.

Local practitioners were, throughout the period, obscured by a growing tide of well-known painters who continued to find Maine a beautiful and inexpensive place to work. There were no commercial galleries in the true sense, so one had to have an outlet beyond Maine. Lewiston's Marsden Hartley, who made frequent working visits back to Maine and died there, spent much of his brilliant career abroad or in New York. Bidde-

THE EARLY TWENTIETH CENTURY

Town meeting is one of the purest forms of democracy in which any interested citizen can voice an opinion. From earliest times, the meeting constituted Mainers' most direct link to politics. With sharp insight and gentle humor, artist Peggy Bacon (1895–1987) looks within such a local gathering. Her drypoint *Maine Problems*, 1941, was done soon after she settled at Ogunquit. One of America's foremost satirists, Bacon was one of the few artists able to support herself during the Great Depression. COURTESY OF THE PORTLAND MUSEUM OF ART (GIFT OF HAROLD SHAW), PORTLAND, MAINE

ford's John G. Lyman became a key figure in Canada's art scene during the 1930s and was a founder of the Contemporary Art Society. Waldo Peirce of Bangor is probably the best-known native-born artist to flourish in state. Western illustrator W. Herbert Dunton of Augusta also achieved national popularity that has endured.

The indelible Maine-related images from this period are largely the works of visitors or transplants. This was the heyday of the Ogunquit art scene. While Charles Woodbury continued his classes on the shore, younger "moderns" aligned with the ideas of Hamilton Easter Field began to appear. Some, such as Georgia O'Keeffe, stayed for short durations producing important work, while others, including Yasuo Kuniyoshi, Henry Strater, Robert Laurent, Bernard Karfoil, Rudolf Dirks, Isabella Howland, and Walt Kuhn (at nearby Cape Neddick), had a more lasting impact. Edward Hopper painted in Portland and along the coast, while Marguerite and William Zorach settled at Robinhood. On the stark shore of Cape Split, the painter John Marin put down roots. Ivan Albright worked at Corea, and photographer Paul Strand made several working trips down east. At the age of twenty-one, Georgetown's Dahlov Ipcar had a one-person show at the Museum of Modern Art in New York. Sculptor Gaston Lachaise also made Georgetown his home. Kennebunk was enlivened by the strong personalities and paintings of Mil-

Rudy Vallee (1901–1986) grew up in the industrial town of Westbrook and attended the University of Maine and Yale before appearing as an enormously popular radio performer. In 1930 he made the UMO "Stein Song," (written by his friend, the Searsport novelist Lincoln Colcord) the nation's number one hit. Vallee retained close connections to Maine, summering at Lovell. COURTESY OF DEBRA AND WILLIAM BARRY

dred Burrage and Edith Cleaves Barry. The latter founded the Brick Store Museum at Kennebunk in 1936. Though it would be some years before she achieved success as one of America's greatest sculptors, Louise Nevelson grew up in Rockland. Disliking the provincial strictures, she left in 1920 but retained close ties through her family.

In the field of music, lyric soprano Evelyn Jeanne Shah-Nazaroff also left her home in Rockland to pursue a career that took her to the Metropolitan Opera Company. Maine's best-known composer, Walter Piston, was born in the same town, and by the 1920s had begun his teaching career at Harvard. In 1923–1924, Portland followed Bangor in organizing a symphony orchestra. The Maine Music Festival continued until 1926. On a more popular level, Old Orchard Pier attracted the big bands, among them Count Basie, Duke Ellington, Tommy Dorsey, and Glenn Miller. Among the headliners were Rudy Vallee and the Connecticut Yankees. Vallee, who grew up in Westbrook and attended the University of Maine at Orono, became a national sensation on the radio. Indeed, his version of the UMO "Stein Song" became the nation's number one hit.

Movies and newsreels further wove Maine into the fabric of the nation. Though actually filmed in New Hampshire, *Way Down East* (1920) began to portray Maine to the nation in a new form. Locally, Holman Day was producing successful films such as *The Rider of the King Log* (1921) and would eventually gravitate to Hollywood. In California, Portland's Hiram Abrams became president of Paramount in 1914 and later headed United Artists until his death in 1926. William and Dustin Farnum of Bucksport became film actors, as did Indian Island's Molly Spotted Elk and Portland's Jean Arthur and Francis Feeney. The latter's younger brother, John, would change his name to Ford and become one of the industry's most respected directors. John Ford made 125 feature movies, including *The Informer* (1935), *Stagecoach* (1939), *The Grapes of Wrath* (1940), and *The Searchers* (1956), and won six Academy Awards.

In literature it was Edna St. Vincent Millay who captured the essence of the defiant young generation with the famous line, "My candle burns at both ends" (1920). Born at Rockland, Millay grew up in Camden and graduated from Vassar in 1917, the year she published *Renascence and Other Poems*. She won the Pulitzer Prize for Poetry (1923) and summered on Ragged Island in

At the turn of the century, sports offered a first stage for ambitious youngsters such as John "Bull" Feeney (1894–1973), one of the Portland High football team. Born to Irish parents who lived in Cape Elizabeth and later Portland, he graduated in 1914, went to Hollywood and changed his name to John Ford. In a long, distinguished career, he won six Academy Awards and directed such films as *The Informer*, *The Grapes of Wrath*, *Stagecoach*, and *The Searchers*, as well as important war documentaries. He followed the path to films taken by William and Dustin Farnum of Bucksport, his own brother Francis, and Portland's Hiram Abrams who would head Paramount Pictures and United Artists. COURTESY PRIVATE COLLECTION

Edwin Arlington Robinson (1869–1935) had just established himself, after years of struggle, when Lilla Cabot Perry (1848–1933) painted this likeness in 1916. Born at Head Tide (Alna), the poet grew up in Gardiner, which he later immortalized as "Tilbury Town" and peopled with characters such as Miniver Cheevy and Richard Cory. The popularity of Robinson's verse was matched by critical acclaim. He was given the first Pulitzer Prize for Poetry (1921), and won again in 1925 and 1928. The Edwin Arlington Robinson Memorial Room at Colby College contains the largest collection of his work, including 1,000 letters. COURTESY OF SPECIAL COLLECTIONS, MILLER LIBRARY, COLBY COLLEGE, WATERVILLE, MAINE

Casco Bay. Indeed, Mainers of this period had an almost magnetic hold on the Pulitzers. Laura E. Richards and Maude Howe Elliott, assisted by Florence Howe Hall, won the Pulitzer for the biography of Julia Ward Howe in 1917. Booth Tarkington, who came to Maine following his mentor William Deane Howells, spent summers at Kennebunkport and was probably America's highest-paid novelist. His *The Magnificent Ambersons* and *Alice Adams* won Pulitzers in 1919 and 1922. After years of struggle, Edwin Arlington Robinson came into his own with *The Man Against the Sky* (1916). His *Collected Poems* (1921) won the Pulitzer for 1922, and he was given the award again in 1925 and 1928. His narrative poems and wonderful psychological portraits were often set in, or influenced by, Maine, where he was born and raised. Robinson's closeness to the place is as palpable as any Maine poet's work. Rounding out the Pulitzer winners of the era is Brunswick poet Robert Peter Tristram Coffin, a prolific hard worker, who was selected in 1936.

Livermore Falls was the birthplace of Louise Bogan, one of America's truly first-rate poets and the longtime poetry review editor and essayist for the *New Yorker*. In 1932 author-naturalist Henry Beston and his wife, the writer Elizabeth Coatsworth, settled into long careers at Nobleboro, while writer Mary Ellen Chase of Blue Hill served as a distinguished professor of English at Smith College from 1926 to 1955. In 1933 the superb E. B. White and his wife Katherine bought a farmhouse in Brooklin with a view of Blue Hill Bay.

This curious mix of writers proceeds with Erskine Caldwell's arrival at Portland in 1926. Having lost his job as a book reviewer, Caldwell gathered up his review copies, left Georgia, and opened a bookstore using the volumes to fill his shelves. He wrote his first fiction in Maine, including *The Bastard* (1929), which was censored by local authorities. Gladys Hasty Carroll, who grew up in South Berwick and graduated from Bates College, produced her best-known book, *As the Earth Turns* (1933), which in part treated the arrival and settlement of a Polish family in rural Maine. Interest in folk literature came in the form of Roland Gray's collection, *Songs and Ballads of the Maine Lumberjacks* (1925), and Fannie Hardy Eckstorm and Mary Winslow Smyth's excellent *Minstrelsy of Maine: Folk Songs and Ballads of the Woods and Coast* (1927). The expansive list of worthy authors would also have to include Virginia Chase, Marsden Hartley, Wilbert Snow, and Lincoln Colcord.

Around this time, a number of poorly researched popular histories were also produced. Such glib and ultimately troublesome volumes need not be listed, for they were more than matched by such enduring works of nonfiction as Louis Clinton Hatch's *Maine: A History* (1919) and Robert G. Albion's *Forest and Sea Power* (1926). Dr. Albion, who lived in South Portland, went on to become Gardiner Professor of Oceanic History at Harvard University. Another noted maritime historian, Dr. Samuel Eliot Morison, was a summer resident of Northeast Harbor. Literary historian F. O. Matthiessen also worked in Maine, and his first project concerned Sarah Orne Jewett.

The University of Maine at Orono made important contributions to Maine history and literature in a period when the prestigious *New England Quarterly* was published on campus. Under the direction of Dr. Milton Ellis and Dean George Davis Chase, the crucial but often forgotten Maine Studies–Second Series began to be published. Included were such valuable works as Richard G. Wood's history of lumbering and Ava Chadbourne's history of education in Maine, along with biographies and monographs that greatly extended the shared knowledge of local culture. In 1938 and 1941 Elizabeth Ring's *Reference List of Manuscripts Relating to the State of Maine*, a landmark in bibliography, was published.

The archetypal Maine author of the thirties and forties was Kennebunk native Kenneth Roberts. Though often dismissed as a regionalist, Roberts has a just claim on the title "inventor of the modern historical novel." His sweep of vision and careful, scholarly attention to detail led to such popular and still underrated books as *Arundel* (1930), *Rabble in Arms* (1933), and the peerless *Oliver Wiswell* (1940). There is a timeless quality to Roberts's style, and in the unique way he asks questions about the nature of the individual and his or her relation to great causes. Roberts's focus on the Tory side of the Revolution brought outrage from the political right, just as his opinions on immigration brought attacks from the

Left to right: Novelist Kenneth Roberts (1885–1957), radio manufacturer A. Atwater Kent (1873–1949), and author-playwright Booth Tarkington (1869–1946) walk the Kent estate in Kennebunkport. A protégé of William Dean Howells, Tarkington settled in Maine in 1916, won two Pulitzer Prizes, and became the highest-paid writer in America. He also became the mentor of Roberts, who was the author of such books as *Arundel* (1930), *Oliver Wiswell* (1940), and *Boon Island* (1956). Credited with developing the modern historical novel, Roberts was given a special Pulitzer in 1957. COURTESY OF ROBERTS CENTENNIAL COMMISSION, BRICK STORE MUSEUM, KENNEBUNK, MAINE

left. His hatred of the "Vacationland" syndrome and its byproducts led to his call, in 1930, for citizens to "go forth with rope and grappling irons and tear the offending billboards down." Once again, a Maine original was holding forth, and by the end of the 1930s, Mainers in general were feeling more confident. As it became clear that America would soon enter another world war, citizens were in a mood to tackle anything.

President Franklin D. Roosevelt (1882–1945) arrived in Rockland fresh from his dramatic shipboard conference with British prime minister Winston Churchill in August, 1941. Before leaving the presidential yacht, he announced his "Atlantic Charter," which left America neutral but socially and economically closer to the Allies. Within the year the nation would be at war. Here FDR, a summer resident of Campobello and enthusiastic sailor of the Maine coast, waves to Rocklanders. COURTESY OF THE FRANKLIN D. ROOSEVELT LIBRARY, HYDE PARK, NEW YORK

9

WORLD WAR II IN MAINE (1941–1945)

On August 16, 1941, the presidential yacht *Potomac*, girded with machine guns and antiaircraft weaponry, entered the harbor at Rockland, Maine. In a dockside press conference, President Franklin Delano Roosevelt revealed his dramatic meeting at sea with embattled British prime minister Winston Churchill and their agreement to the "Atlantic Charter." Though the United States remained neutral, the charter firmly supported the Allied goals and began to consider the postwar world. Coupled with the earlier Lend-Lease Act, Bundles for Britain committees, and a rising American fear of Axis victory, the charter edged the United States toward war. Roosevelt's decision to announce the agreement in Maine was largely a geographic consideration, since it was the closest state to the meeting off Newfoundland. The location, however, underscored the nation's physical nearness to Canada, whose forces were already engaged, and the necessity of military hardware on a neutral pleasure craft told of the presence of German U-boats. Maine was also closer to Europe than any other state, not a small consideration in the days to come.

Within a year, the United States was fighting for its life against the Axis powers, though unexpectedly the spark was ignited in the distant Pacific, rather than the Atlantic. For Maine, along with the other forty-seven states, the conflict proved a watershed on the order of the Revolutionary and Civil Wars. After the first reaction, which saw the strengthening of coastal fortifications, the whole nation went on the offensive, and the economic, social, and attitudinal make-up of Maine underwent a virtual revolution. As young men went into the armed services, their jobs were often filled by women, who proved more than able in doing nontraditional tasks. In all, some 93,000 Maine women and men joined the armed services. People from rural towns moved to larger communities where war industries paid high wages, and others moved out of state to work. Young men and women from such diverse places as Skowhegan and Harpswell, Houlton and Portland met and married. Finally, the G.I. Bill encouraged and made possible the dream of a college education for people from every background. The much-discussed melting pot was at full boil by V-J Day.

After years of economic depression and isolationist feelings fostered by some of Maine's leading figures, attitudes began to shift. When the reality of the Nazi vision became somewhat apparent, volunteers began assistance programs . The plight of Jewish refugees helped form the Portland Zionist Council in 1940, under the direction of Saul G. Chason. A New Year's editorial in 1941 looked out of Portland and around the globe to predict, "Trouble and misery plainly lie ahead."

Earlier, in the autumn of 1939, as German armies overran Poland, the 5th Infantry Regiment, which had been garrisoned in the Casco Bay forts

The coves and islands of coastal Maine continued to support generations of families engaged in lobstering and other aspects of the shore fisheries. Fish houses, wharves, dories, and lobster pots marked the working waterfronts down east. This photograph, taken at the outset of the war, shows Monhegan Island. There was little the government could do to guard such isolated places, and happily no raids were made. Many fishing boats, though, were given ship-to-shore radios. COLLECTION OF THE MAINE HISTORICAL SOCIETY

since the 1920s, was sent to guard the Panama Canal. It was replaced by the 68th Coast Artillery Regiment, a newly created antiaircraft group. In September of 1940, it was given a new assignment when the 240th Coast Artillery Regiment of the Maine National Guard replaced it. The new regiment, brought up to strength by the first peacetime draft, began training at Fort Williams in Cape Elizabeth and necessitated construction of extensive wooden barracks.

Other signals of impending conflict were evident. In 1940 the president had personally inspected the Portsmouth Naval Shipyard, and in the next year, under the terms of Lend-Lease, the Kittery facility repaired three British and one French submarine while continuing its own production schedule. What had been a fishing village at South Portland was turned into a vast, modern shipyard. Pete Newell of BIW created the Todd-Bath Iron Shipbuilding Corporation in 1940 after signing a $50 million contract with the British Merchant Shipbuilding mission. The agreement called for the construction of thirty Ocean-class cargo vessels to be delivered to the British in 1942. By the time Roosevelt met Churchill, the first keels were being laid in state-of-the-art basins in the East Yard. In 1941 the West Yard was opened, and an extraordinary, all-too-brief period of building commenced.

Aircraft were, in similar fashion, finding their way to the Allies. On September 15, 1941, the trailers of the 94th Air Base Group were set up at

188 MAINE: THE WILDER HALF OF NEW ENGLAND

Some 93,000 Mainers entered the armed services during the conflict. As war raged in Europe, Asia, and Africa, the United States prepared for action. Here a young serviceman in the 103rd Infantry Regiment, Maine National Guard, gets an animated send-off at Portland's Union Station in March 1941. More than 2,500 Mainers would give their lives during the cruel war. COLLECTION OF THE MAINE HISTORICAL SOCIETY

William Stark "Pete" Newell (1878–1954) worked at the Bath Iron Works beginning in 1902, and in 1928 he and a partner revived the company after its collapse. During the Second World War, Newell ran the Bath yard as well as the two new Todd-Bath yards in South Portland. It was largely Newell's energy and foresight that kept Maine in the shipbuilding business in the twentieth century, a strength that endures into the present. COURTESY OF THE MAINE MARITIME MUSEUM, BATH, MAINE

Presque Isle. As historian Guy F. Dubay writes: ". . . Aroostook County being set in the extreme northeast is by aeronautical definition at the most proximate point to many places in Europe. As a result the flat, open, farm country just east of QuaKajo [Quaggy Jo] Mountain in Presque Isle lay, as set in globular perspective, is within the staging area of international flights to Europe." By the attack on Pearl Harbor, 1,200 Army Air Corps men were servicing aircraft for transatlantic flights. Billy Mitchell's 1923 visit to Maine took on, in retrospect, more serious implications than simple goodwill.

The shortage of oil tankers had brought the transfer of twenty-five such ships to Britain, and in May of 1941, it was decided to build a 236-mile pipeline from South Portland to Montreal; by November oil was flowing into Canada. Not only were tanker voyages shortened, but Montreal now had a steady winter source of oil when the St. Lawrence was frozen in. The "first national defense pipeline" not only survived the war but was to transform sleepy South Portland into a major oil terminal during the postwar decades.

Even before the hostilities began, there was a great deal of anxiety about spies and saboteurs. Numerous amateur intelligence operatives, usually rated 4-F, were apparently employed by the FBI and military. A Portland bookseller recalled that one of these "spooks" frequented his store because he was certain that radicals and agents would be drawn to such a place. The bookseller kidded this spy-in-residence unmercifully.

In the months before America joined the war, artist Alice Harmon Shaw Kirkpatrick continued to paint the sea and shore as usual. One day, near Portland Head Light, a jeep-load of soldiers pulled up and escorted her off to the guardhouse. Questioned by the commandant, she soon found herself required to get and carry a Coast Guard pass while working on the coast. Such regulations were unheard of before but would grow in the war years. Few citizens complained. An Italian-American family in Portland, one of many visited by the FBI, had its radio confiscated because it had (like most models of the day) a shortwave receiver.

Colonel Harold W. Coffin's book *Assignment in Military Intelligence* (1972) seems to be unique in covering the time and place. As early as 1940, Coffin recalled investigating strange doings in a quarry at Bickford's Point in South Addison. At this near-perfect isolated cove, he claims to have confronted a registered German agent and discovered a cargo of dynamite aboard the auxiliary schooner *Ann Sophia*. Coffin's report went unheeded and the schooner sailed on a mission he felt was directly related to the war. Like the rum-running incidents, the real stories behind this and other occurrences will probably never be known.

Life in Maine during the forties was moving apace. The Great Depression had begun to recede in fact and memory, and, as the economy improved, voters returned to the GOP and the victorious days of Governor Brann faded. The Blaine House was occupied by Lewis O. Barrows until 1941, when Sumner Sewall, a fellow Republican from Bath, took up residence. The wartime chief executive had been an army flyer in World War I and his wife, Helen Ellena, was a member of a noted Polish diplomatic family. During the war, the Sewalls used the governor's mansion for social fundraisers and entertainment for servicemen. There were blackout drills at the Blaine House, and in 1943, with gas rationing in force, the traditional Governor's Ball was cancelled. Governor Sewall gave up his car for a bicycle and became a familiar sight in the streets of Augusta and vicinity.

Lewis J. Brann's attempts to win a seat in Congress failed, and once more the Democrats seemed doomed. Filling Maine's senate seats in Washington were Republicans Wallace H. White, Jr., and the former governor, Ralph Owen Brewster. By far the most interesting Maine political figure, and one who would go on to an unmatched career, was Margaret Chase Smith of Skowhegan. In 1940 she won election to her late husband's seat in Congress and quickly became an integral component of the national decision-making process.

Though working outside her birth state, Congresswoman Edith Nourse Rogers was in the midst of her distinguished thirty-five year career as a representative of Massachusetts. The daughter of a Saco mill agent, Rogers was a fierce supporter of veterans' rights beginning in the 1920s, a lonely

Scrap drives, blackouts, meatless days, victory gardens, and rationing were all part of a tightly controlled lifestyle that saw the expansion of federal and state governments. Even school kids were involved, as this 1942 air-raid poster suggests. COLLECTION OF THE MAINE HISTORICAL SOCIETY

voice protesting Hitler's treatment of the Jews beginning in 1933, and later a major force behind the G.I. Bill of Rights. Rogers also sponsored legislation to create the Women's Army Auxiliary Corps in 1942 and the Women's Army Corps (WAC) in 1943.

❖

On December 7, 1941, the forces of Imperial Japan appeared over Pearl Harbor in the Territory of Hawaii and inflicted the worst naval defeat in American history. On December 8 the United States Congress declared war on Japan, and three days later Germany and Italy took up the cause of their Asian partner. As one of the states, Maine

Private First Class Leonard Parks, U.S. Army, foreground, and Privates Arthur Williams and Richard Sullivan stand guard at the Grand Trunk Railway bridge over the Royal River in North Yarmouth in 1942. Housed in a specially equipped railroad car, members of this African-American unit were held back from combat roles in the still-segregated military. They were apparently well received by the local white community, and a number of photographs of the soldiers were given to the Maine Historical Society by Beverly Atkins Varney. COLLECTION OF THE MAINE HISTORICAL SOCIETY

took her role seriously and, as ever, her extreme geographic position nearest Europe made her contribution important.

Initially, there was fear of an attack along the unevenly defended shore. As the Prohibition Era had proved, the thousands of inlets, bays, and islands were well adapted to smuggling. Criehaven, for instance, was virtually abandoned, losing its school, post office, and much of its population for the duration of the war. With this in mind, the possibility of infiltration by U-boat crews was taken seriously. The second light tower at Two Lights (Cape Elizabeth) was quickly armored and used as a directional tower for the new position, Battery Steele, on Peaks Island. Considerable property, including Little Chebeague Island in Casco Bay with its summer cottages, was taken by the government. That particular island was the site of a navy firefighting school, and a great steel form, used in practice, still dominates one beach. Property was also taken on Peaks Island, Jewell Island in Portland, and in Cape Elizabeth. Civilian coast watchers were organized and armed patrols sent out along beaches. Early in the war, the sound of cracking ice led to a bloodless shootout by a group of these soldiers.

In 1942 the state director of civilian defense announced that German spies were believed to have landed in Maine, but evidence remains sketchy. The one recorded case of Nazi spies landing by U-boat took place on Hancock Point near Ellsworth on November 29, 1944. Armed with revolvers, a shortwave radio, forged papers, and $60,000 in cash, Enrich Gimpel and William Colepaugh came ashore in a snowstorm. Oddly dressed and carrying luggage, the two were spotted by high school student Harvard Hodgkins, who was driving home from a dance. He drove on and reported the sighting. Though the spies made it to New York, the FBI was able to track their movements and arrest them a few weeks later. The episode was suppressed by the FBI until after the war, but in the meantime both were found guilty and sentenced to death. Later, President Roosevelt commuted their sentences. Six other spies who landed in Florida and New York were executed.

Very quickly, civilians throughout the state had become attuned to the potential for such trouble. By the spring of 1942, the Aircraft Warning Service proudly claimed some 12,000 civilian volunteers. Portland's waterfront was patrolled by the Coast Guard, while the army watched potential aircraft landing sites. With a shortage of regular troops available for guard duty, the still racially segregated army turned to black troops who had volunteered in great number. A posting in a boxcar alongside North Yarmouth's Grand Trunk bridge had certainly not been on the minds of these young, mostly southern, troops when they enlisted. The specially designed cars were adapted for winter use, but the bridge was rather bleak duty. However, the locals apparently appreciated their presence, got on well with the troops, and a selection of photographs documenting their stay is in the collection of the Maine Historical Society.

Casco Bay suddenly became a place of great military significance. In the first month of 1941 the navy designated it a fleet anchorage with a Navy Section Base in Portland (later a U.S. Naval Station for training destroyer and destroyer escorts). It was also a recreation port, fueling station, and safe anchorage. In November the USS *Denebola*, flagship of the commander of Destroyers Atlantic, steamed into the harbor and made it headquarters of the command. On Long Island in Casco Bay, a huge naval fuel depot was constructed, along with a seaplane facility for patrol bombers. The latter was in conjunction with the substantial naval air station at Brunswick, which also apparently serviced patrol blimps.

The forts themselves were impressive. In 1942 the last great series of coastal defenses began with the erection of massive batteries. In *The Forts of Maine, 1607–1945* Robert L. Bradley notes:

WORLD WAR II IN MAINE   193

Life on Maine's college and university campuses changed radically as a result of the conflict. Here a group of UMO men march to class. These students went to school year-round for three to seven semesters, but the mounting need for troops weakened the program. Professor David C. Smith's *The First Century: A History of the University of Maine, 1865–1965* (1979) amply covers these exciting years. COURTESY OF THE UNIVERSITY OF MAINE AT ORONO

At this time and in the following years, batteries in Portland Harbor were built or refitted with rifled guns of 6-, 12-, and 16-inch caliber, supported by dozens of smaller caliber anti-torpedo boat, anti-submarine, and anti-aircraft guns, weapons designed to parry the attacks of the last great vessels of conventional warfare, capital ships and aircraft carriers. A battery of two 16-inch guns was located on Peaks Island. Three batteries, each carrying two 6-inch long-range guns were established at Cape Elizabeth, Peaks Island, and Jewell Island. Extensive networks of searchlights, submarine nets, and electrically detonated mines supported these guns, designed to close all of the channels into Portland Harbor.

Thus, the last and, by some measures, most impressive forts were put in place. Battery Steele on Peaks is an extensive concrete structure buried under earth. Two 16-inch guns could fire a 2,340-pound shell some 26 miles, or a range extending from Boothbay to Kennebunk. During the war, fire-control towers were constructed to direct the great guns. These concrete giants pierced the shore from Popham Beach to Two Lights to Cape Porpoise.

According to USM Professor Joel Eastman, in April 1942 "[a daily] average of 63 vessels passed in and out of Casco Bay. . . ." More astonishing were the arrivals and departures around the time of the Normandy invasion in 1944. Eastman notes: "During the week ending August 12, 1944, a record 539 ships entered and 558 departed the anchorage. During the war Mainers saw everything from patrol boats to battleships and aircraft carriers."

Because of frequent patrols, the implementation of magnetic loop detection, and intense fleet activity, the great losses sustained by the allied merchant marine occurred mostly outside the Gulf of Maine. Similarly, attacks on German submarines were few, though the records are scattered and somewhat contradictory. Mt. Desert Rock, ten miles off the coast, marked the most dangerous area. Professor Eastman notes the torpedoing of a Norwegian freighter SS *Skottland* on May 17, 1942. Eighty-six persons were lost, including four Soviet officers who "bravely remained aboard and went down with the ship to permit others to escape."

On June 13, 1944, a fishing schooner, *Lark*, was attacked by a U-boat off the Rock but escaped. Not so lucky was the navy blimp *K-14*, which crashed on July 2 of the same year. There were four survivors, but what had occurred was not clear. A court of inquiry pronounced the disaster due to pilot error, but Captain Alexander W. Moffat, who salvaged the craft, states that the blimp was riddled with bullet holes. He believed the court wanted no evidence of U-boat activity so close to shore.

On December 13, 1944, the Canadian National Railway vessel *Cornwallis* was torpedoed off Mt. Desert Rock with the loss of forty-four. Six of its crew were picked up by local fishermen. One of the advantages of the war was that most fishing vessels were given ship-to-shore radios. Finally, on April 23, 1945, an Eagle patrol boat *PE-56*, out of the Brunswick Naval Air Station, blew up off Cape Elizabeth. Forty-nine of the sixty-two-man complement were killed.

The loss of USS *Eagle 56* was long attributed to "the explosion of its boilers." Through the efforts of Paul M. Lawson, it was proved to have been sunk by *U-853*. In 2001 the forty-nine crewmen killed and thirteen survivors were finally deemed eligible for Purple Hearts. USS *Eagle* was the last American warship sunk by a U-boat.

There were many rumors of U-boats and a number of stories persist. At least one incident apparently occurred in Casco Bay, though sources differ on the time and particulars. According to Nelson H. Lawry's article, "The Kennebec Defended Through a Dozen Wars," *Journal of the Council on America's Military Past* (May 13, 1985), a German submarine surfaced in eastern Casco Bay on June 22, 1942. A battery of 155mm mobile guns at Fort Baldwin was ordered to fire on the craft, but the order was reversed as American destroyer escorts hove into action around the target.

Other accounts provide a similar story with a different date, and a letter from the Naval Historical Center states that four destroyer escorts actually sank *U-866* near the mouth of the Kennebec on March 18, 1945. At present this report is contested, though it fits Colonel Harold Coffin's undated report in *Assignment in Military Intelligence*. Clearly much needs to be done in researching this aspect of the war on both physical and documentary levels.

Violent action in Maine waters was the exception, although a number of locals did come face to face with German soldiers on Maine soil. In 1944 German prisoners of war started arriving in Maine via Portland's Union Station. They headed north to prison camps and to work in lumber camps and on farms.

Camp Houlton held as many as 2,000 men between June 1944 and May 1946. The camp contained a library, recreation field, and facility for showing movies. The POWs also published a newspaper *Der Wacher*, copies of which are preserved in the Library of Congress. Correspondence courses were offered by the University of Maine.

Smaller camps holding between 250 and 430 prisoners were opened at Camp Keyes in Augusta, at Dow Field in Bangor, and in Princeton, Spencer Lake, and Seboomook. Prisoners were obliged to work on local farms such as that of H. Fenton

On May 5, 1945, Admiral Karl Doenitz, supreme commander of the German navy, ordered the surrender of all vessels, and within a few days, four U-boats surfaced off the coast of Maine. After surrendering, they were taken to Kittery. Here, a sullen group of German submariners lands at the Portsmouth Naval Shipyard. The prisoners were required to explain the workings of their vessels before being transferred from the naval prison to First Army Command. The surrender came as the blackout on newspapers was lifted, and was the real end to the war along the coast. COURTESY OF THE NATIONAL ARCHIVES, NEW ENGLAND REGION

Shaw in Easton, an episode recalled in the *Maine Sunday Telegram* of August 12, 1984.

The services of others were purchased by lumber operators. At Seboomook, on the edge of Moosehead Lake, the Great Northern Paper Company ran a sizeable POW operation. The farmer or company paid wages to the government, which issued canteen scrip to the workers. Most prisoners met their quota but properly refused to do extra work without extra pay. Since there were few hard-core Nazis in the Maine contingents, there was little trouble, and would-be escapees had virtually no place to run to. As the scope of the Nazi atrocities became evident toward the completion of the war, certain camp officials responded by cutting food and increasing work requirements. For many, though, the worst part of incarceration proved to be boredom coupled with the abundance of mosquitoes and blackflies.

❖

Maine's one known contribution to the German war effort was Portland native Mildred E. Gillars—better known to American servicemen as "Axis Sally." Born Mildred Sisk, she took her stepfather's name and later went to college in Ohio. In the 1930s she fell in love with a politically powerful German professor, traveled to Germany, and began to work for its national radio in 1940. As the war progressed, she secured a high-paying radio show, which she claimed was pro-American but anti-Roosevelt and anti-Jewish. Arrested in 1946, she was returned to America and tried for treason in a much-publicized case. Found guilty, she was given a thirty-year sentence and $10,000

Maine's only notable contribution to the Nazi cause was the notorious broadcaster known as "Axis Sally." Her real name was Mildred E. Gillars (1900–1988) of Portland, Maine. In the 1930s she fell in love with a party official. During the war, her "Midge at the Mike" propaganda show reached thousands of G.I.s, who gave her their own nickname. In this photograph, she attends her 1949 treason trial, which resulted in a conviction and twelve years in prison. COURTESY OF COLIN AND NANCY SARGENT

fine but was paroled after twelve years.

While Axis Sally was broadcasting her propaganda laced with hit tunes, air power was making itself known in Aroostook and the Penobscot Valley. Northern Maine airfields included bases at Presque Isle, Houlton, and Dow Field in Bangor. As ships came and went through Casco Bay in preparation for D-Day, Operation Snowball firmed up over Presque Isle. In April of 1944, 1,713,261 pounds of vital supplies were said to

Pulling together to win extended to all levels of society, including corporate culture. From July 1941 to September 1945, the workers in the South Portland shipyards read and contributed to the *Shipyard News*, which included national news as well as local contributions. A popular column was penned by Dave Glovsky, later a noted personality in Portland and Old Orchard. A complete run of the *News* is available at the Maine Historical Society. COLLECTION OF THE MAINE HISTORICAL SOCIETY

have been flown to Europe from Presque Isle. There were also radar installations such as U.S. Naval Section Base, Bar Harbor, with a station atop Mount Cadillac and transmitters in Winter Harbor, and elsewhere described in Captain Alexander W. Moffat's excellent memoir *A Navy*

The Todd-Bath shipyards at South Portland changed a sleepy little village into a huge industrial area that produced a total of 274 cargo vessels for Britain and the United States. At its height of production, the operation employed some 30,000 individuals. The Liberty Ship *Hannibal Hamlin* was launched at the West Yard on March 5, 1943; the *Jeremiah O'Brien*, finished in the same yard and year, is preserved at San Francisco as a memorial to merchant seamen and Liberty Ships. COURTESY OF DEBRA AND WILLIAM BARRY, IN MEMORY OF ELIZABETH RING

Maverick Comes of Age, 1939–1945 (1977). Planes from the Brunswick Naval Station made long reconnaissance flights, a pattern that continued until its closure began in 2010.

Maine industry and agriculture pushed itself to the limits in spite of a labor shortage. As never before, women stepped in to fill the gap in any number of jobs, and young people and retired people readily accepted volunteer roles. At the Todd-Bath shipyards, some 3,700 women worked in jobs ranging from welders to crane operators to firefighters and clerks. As a projection of corporate culture, a yard newspaper flourished. Maine artist and cultural activist Mildred Burrage worked in the yards as a counselor. With some 30,000 employed at Todd-Bath, housing became tight in spite of good wages. "Hot bed" apartments, rented to members of three shifts who duti-

The lack of manpower on the home front led to women filling a number of nontraditional jobs such as welders, crane operators, and bus drivers. Here a group of female volunteer firefighters and workers are assembled at the Todd-Bath Iron Works Shipbuilding Corporation in South Portland. COLLECTION OF THE MAINE HISTORICAL SOCIETY

fully took turns sleeping, were as much a part of the time as air-raid drills, blackouts, and sky watching. Rationing, victory gardens, and scrap-metal drives, along with war bonds, colored the atmosphere. As headquarters for the destroyer fleet and visiting ships of all kinds, Portland became a roaring town again. On the waterfront, prostitution flourished along with a black market. Even in small places like Belfast, the staff at the Children's Aid Society, which ran an orphanage, noted: "The importance of safeguarding the girls was discussed because of the presence of so many service men on the streets." Because of this situation curfews and regulations were instituted.

The housing shortage led to a wartime construction boom, though at first, places including Scarborough's Danish Village motor court were used by the government to house workers. One hundred trailers were also set up, but larger permanent projects were soon taken on. In July of 1943, the first 247 of 500 housing units in Redbank Village, South Portland, were dedicated.

The Federal Housing Administration, on its own or in partnership with private investors, built other housing projects in South Portland, Portland, and Cape Elizabeth. In 1942 two hundred fifty workers were finishing four houses a day at Stanwood Park in the latter town. This assembly-line approach created livable, uniform-looking dwellings adequate for the time but, in some places, in need of repair within a decade. Projects of similar scope took place in and around military bases, setting the style for postwar suburbia.

❖

America's Emergency Shipbuilding Program animated the Todd-Bath yards, which launched 274 Liberty (Ocean-class) ships, or 10 percent of all such ships produced. As historian Ralph Linwood Snow would later observe, this was "more than a good-sized commercial shipyard could expect to produce in three decades of operation." Some confusion over the records persists, the final list being Ralph Linwood Snow's *Bath Iron Works: The First Hundred Years* (1987). Each vessel bore the name of a great American, and they included the *Sarah Orne Jewett, Winslow Homer, Elijah Kellogg, Lillian Nordica,* and *James G. Blaine*. Many lasted into the 1960s, and one, the *Jeremiah O'Brien,* named for Machias's Revolutionary War hero, is preserved at San Francisco as a floating monument to the war's merchant marine.

Up on the Kennebec, BIW launched eighty-three destroyers and four cargo vessels (along with a yacht) between 1939 and the end of 1945. At the height of the conflict, the yard was completing one destroyer every seventeen days. Together with earlier vessels from the yard, many of these warships engaged in heavy action, and eleven BIW ships were lost. Among those built there were the USS *O'Brien,* eventually the veteran of three wars; the USS *Laffey,* which survived five kamikaze hits off Okinawa; and the all-Bath Destroyer Squadron 21. The latter, made up of the destroyers *Nicholas, Taylor, Chevalier,* and *O'Bannon,* began the drive to victory in the Solomon Islands.

The Portsmouth Naval Shipyard also began an enormous building program focused on the construction of submarines. At its peak, the installation employed more than 20,000 workers, and between 1939 and August 1945 produced 98 vessels. Among these were 85 submarines, which aided the war effort in both the Atlantic and the Pacific. By war's end, Portsmouth was the largest submarine navy yard on the East Coast, and would continue its role in the immediate postwar era. Production of vessels also flourished in other coastal locations. The Mount Desert Island District produced 724 small vessels; Rockland-Camden, 131; and Boothbay-Bristol, 92. Many of these were wooden craft. In all, Maine shipbuilders made a disproportionately large contribution to the national effort.

❖

Just a month before Pearl Harbor, *Life* magazine did an impressive story about L.L. Bean, Inc., of Freeport, which was selling a million dollars' worth of sporting equipment annually and was becoming part of the national folklore. Rather than capitalizing on the story, Bean, like other businesses, was soon producing defense supplies, in this case cold-weather army footwear. Likewise, G. H. Bass in Wilton was involved in similar cold-weather footwear. From 1942 to 1945 the Saco-Lowell shops received $44.5 million in defense contracts, and such industries as York Manufacturing and Pepperell Fabrics shifted to army and navy contracts. Women took new jobs in the factories as men went into combat. Shoes, paper products, lumber mills, foundries, and metal shops went into overdrive. Between 1939 and 1949, harvested cropland and pasture expanded by 23 percent.

In the report *Maine: Fifty Years of Change* (1983), the authors observed: "During World War II, production, wages, and consumption were tightly controlled. Rationing of food and gasoline was established. Social Security, public and private pension systems, income maintenance, and health programs removed much of the insecurity about being old in America." Indeed, it is difficult to find a time in American history with more of a consensus focused on

The involvement of businesses in the winning of the Second World War was pervasive, as judged by the advertisements of the time. This ad rounded out the equation by recalling Pepperell Mills' contribution in a postwar publication, *The Port of Portland: State of Maine* (1946). On all levels Maine was entering a new era. COURTESY OF PORTLAND PUBLIC LIBRARY SPECIAL COLLECTIONS & ARCHIVES

While a resident of the Pownal School for the Feebleminded, Lewiston's Richard Turcotte (1914–2001) was an enthusiastic member of the Army Air Force, Aircraft Warning Services Reserves, during the Second World War. Together with nearly all American citizens, he worked to achieve victory. He left his armband (shown here), reserve certificate, spotter book, and other items to the Maine Historical Society. COLLECTION OF THE MAINE HISTORICAL SOCIETY

what was perceived as a common goal.

The literary and entertainment front was vital. Writer Ben Ames Williams, a native of Mississippi, produced two of Maine's best historical novels, *Come Spring* (1940) and the uncompromisingly dark study, *The Strange Woman* (1941). Massachusetts native Louise Dickinson Rich wrote *We Took to the Woods* (1942), an unadorned account of contemporary life in the Big Woods. Walter van Tilburg Clark, a son of East Orland, published the excellent western *The Ox-Bow Incident* (1940). Seen by some at the time as a warning against the Nazi menace, it is in fact a classic study of human nature that rises above genre. It was followed by a popular film, directed by William Wellman, but not written by Clark. Portland's Francis Ford was a member of the cast. Another player with Maine connections, Kay Aldridge, appeared in *The Perils of Nyoka* (1942), a cliffhanger serial with a strong female character. *Thirty Seconds over Tokyo* (1944) served as the debut for Portland-born leading lady Phyllis Thaxter. Few in Hollywood took the war more seriously than director John Ford, who won Academy Awards in 1940 and 1941 for *The Grapes of Wrath* and *How Green Was My Valley*. He learned of the latter aboard the cruiser *Salt Lake City* while witnessing the takeoff of the Tokyo raid. He went on to film the battle of Midway, during which he was wounded, and the documentary won him another Oscar along with his Purple Heart. Ford also codirected the documentary *December 7th*, another Academy winner. Two historians with strong Maine connections, Admiral Samuel Eliot Morison and Dr. Robert G. Albion, were placed in charge of the operational and administrative histories of the United States Navy during the war.

The visual arts also continued productively. Mildred Burrage produced notable images of the South Portland shipyards, and William Muir did a splendid series of works focused on life at the Brunswick Naval Air Station. At the Portland Museum of Art, the shortage of men led to the choice of Bernice Breck to hang installations.

❖

Most of the 93,000 Mainers in the services had less fulfilling, though often more harrowing tasks.

WORLD WAR II IN MAINE 201

After the Japanese surrender on September 2, 1945, the men and women in America's armed services slowly returned home to parades and celebrations. Here, sailor James F. Keeley of Portland is greeted by his mom. Indeed, most of the "Greatest Generation," as they came to be called, flourished. For a more nuanced view from Temple, Maine, readers should consult John. E. Hodgkins's extraordinary book, *A Soldier's Son: An American Boyhood During World War II* (Camden: 2006). COLLECTION OF THE MAINE HISTORICAL SOCIETY

Indeed, they entered all the services, on land, on sea, and in the air. Some worked behind desks; others found themselves in foxholes from Guadalcanal to North Africa. In *Modern Maine* (1950), Richard A. Herbert cites such outstanding Maine units as the 43rd Infantry Division, the 103rd Infantry Regiment, the 152nd Field Artillery Battalion and Headquarters Company, and the 86th Infantry Brigade. A number of the state's young men were already adept at skiing and joined the famous 10th Mountain Division of alpine troops. Herbert lists 1,265 Mainers killed in action in the army and 399 killed in navy actions. His grand total of casualties (killed in action, died of wounds and injuries, missing, etc.) comes to 2,563. The list gives wounded for the navy, but does not seem to include the army. Almost certainly, a number of Maine-born participants served elsewhere and did not make the list. Not all died on foreign soil, for on July 25, 1944, a B-25 crashed into South Portland's Redbank Trailer Park, killing nineteen people including the young flying instructor. It was Maine's worst aviation disaster.

Throughout the war, Maine colleges participated in the effort. Beginning in May of 1941, ROTC officers were activated, and in January of 1942, University of Maine president Arthur A. Hauck announced a University Defense Council and stated: "No words of mine are needed to remind you that this is a war for national survival." Programs in drafting, ordnance inspection, and pre-radar were taught, and most students belonged to the Army Specialized Training Programs (ASTP).

In 1941 the Maine Maritime Academy was established at the Pentagoet Inn but soon moved to the abandoned Eastern State Normal School in Castine. Operated by the state and federal governments, it became one of five merchant marine schools in the country. Not only did it survive the war, it became one of the most respected and successful schools in Maine, harkening back to the oldest traditions of the coast. All the colleges of Maine contributed to the war, but as time passed, more and more students, now with tuitions paid by the G.I. Bill of Rights, began to fill the campuses. Never before had so many students, from so many ethnic and social backgrounds, sought education on this level. The American dream of a good education, good job, home, and family now became possible for a greater number of individuals. Wartime housing projects did not discriminate and promoted ethnic diversity. One of the signs of this attitudinal shift was the breakup of ethnic neighborhoods in Portland, as young men and women joined the move to more heterogeneous suburbs where the ideas of progress and success beckoned.

Mainers finished the war like most Americans, mourning the death of Roosevelt, cheering the surrender of Germany, and standing amazed before the power of the atomic bombs that broke the resistance of the Empire of Japan. Maine, however, experienced a unique and fitting incident that concluded the war along the coast. On May 5, 1945, Admiral Karl Doenitz, supreme commander of the German navy, ordered all vessels to surrender. In spectacular fashion, four surfaced off Maine. Captain Alexander W. Moffat, as officer in tactical command of the surrender unit, was aboard the cutter *Argo*. Each day, he met a U-boat and brought her into the Portsmouth Naval Shipyard. Included were *U-805*, *U-873*, *U-1223*, and *U-234*, several of the largest subs then operational. Aboard the latter were a rocket scientist and a Luftwaffe general, along with several Japanese officials en route to the Empire. Apparently the Japanese chose to kill themselves rather than surrender. Now that the wartime news blackout was over, the local press had a field day. The United States was about to enter the new era as one of two world powers.

On April 4, 1968, a stunned nation learned of the assassination of civil rights leader Dr. Martin Luther King, Jr. (1929–1968), and tributes like this one in Portland were quickly organized. In 1964 Dr. King had spoken at St. Francis College (University of New England) and at Bowdoin. In the same year, the Portland branch of the NAACP was founded. Among the marchers in this photograph (foreground, far right) was Gerald E. Talbot (born 1931), who became Maine's first black state representative in 1972. In 1986 Maine set aside the third Monday in January as Martin Luther King, Jr., Day. PHOTOGRAPH COURTESY OF GUY GANNETT PUBLICATIONS

10

CHANGING VISIONS FROM "DIGNIFIED WORK FOR ALL" TO UNKIND CUTS AND WHOOPIE PIES (1945–2012)

Between the Second World War and 2012, Maine underwent vast changes as the population grew from 847,000 in 1940 to 1,328,361 in 2010. Even though this rise was slower than in other states, Mainers retained a goodly measure of political clout by electing powerful, independently minded figures to represent them in Washington. Individually, down-easters continued to excel in fields from science to sports to business to arts and religion. Two brutal distant wars punctuated the long Cold War, along with a series of bloody conflicts after the unexpected collapse of the Soviet Union set the stage. The 9/11 attacks on American soil set off wars in Afghanistan and Iraq and political deadlock between the Democrats and Republicans.

Being immersed in events, it is difficult to write about them as history, so this chapter has more speculation than the previous ones. In Maine and the rest of the nation, a society that seemingly started with shared ideals and tremendous optimism appeared to fragment into groups based on more narrowly defined goals. There were hard times and flush times, often dependent on national trends and what part of Maine one lived in. Government and the service industry grew, while traditional blue-collar industry and agriculture faltered. Environmental issues came to the fore with a new alliance of citizens, politicians, and journalists. The fishing industry had good and bad years, with declining stocks, increased regulation, and the closing of processing plants. The Indian Settlement Act seemed to bring the discussion full circle as people of increasingly varied backgrounds and cultures began to debate their roles in society as well as the use, abuse, and ownership of the land itself. Finally, indifferent or inattentive stewardship by politicians and bureaucrats contributed in part to a long national recession and forced a rethinking of how things were done in both Washington and Augusta. In spite of this, state politicians found time to sponsor a bill to vote the "whoopie pie" the "official Maine treat" in 2011.

The first issue of the Maine Publicity Bureau's magazine, *The Pine Cone* (Spring 1945), sent out to all Maine men and women in the armed forces, outlined the objectives of Governor Horace Hildreth for the postwar era. Hildreth, who would soon pioneer the local television industry and serve as America's first ambassador to Pakistan, called for the "type of economy operating so that there is greatest opportunity, for dignified work for all with adequate wages." He concluded: "Maine is a state of opportunities, not withstanding the perennial cry of the pessimists who claim our youth must go elsewhere if they are in search of opportunities."

The Republican governor was preaching to members of a rising generation animated by a spirit of confidence achieved working side by side with their peers during World War II. Ethnic background seemed less a barrier, more a point of pride, as individuals began to imagine themselves

Standing to the right, Governor Horace A. Hildreth (1902–1988) welcomes old Harvard Law classmate L. Welch Pogue, chairman of the Federal Aeronautics Commission, on March 28, 1945. Pogue spoke to a joint session of the Maine legislature. Hildreth was a visionary Republican leader, a businessman who brought TV to Maine and was America's first ambassador to Pakistan. This administration embodied the "American era," which pictured a glorious future. COLLECTION OF THE MAINE HISTORICAL SOCIETY

as integral parts of the larger American Dream.

The G.I. Bill of Rights and widely available home and business loans opened things up. Professors at the University of Maine at Orono were astonished at the tidal wave of postwar students that surged through their modest facility. House trailers from Dow Air Base served as temporary dorms and, for a time, the navy base at Brunswick served as a second campus. Soon the university transformed its teachers colleges into branches, founded a school of law, and in 1967 established the University of Maine System. By 2011 Latin was no longer a major at UMO, and the University of Southern Maine in Portland and Gorham became the largest school in the system.

Private colleges experienced similar growth, mirroring American trends. Bates, Bowdoin, and Colby continued to rank high nationally. Led by President J. Seelye Bixler in the 1950s, the entire Colby College complex was moved from downtown Waterville to its picturesque new home on Mayflower Hill. By 1980 the state had seventeen institutes of higher learning, but Ricker, Nasson, and others would close when Baby Boomers failed to have as many offspring as their parents. The Maine Maritime Academy continued to provide unique high seas training, and by the twenty-first century, vocational-technical schools found success in shifting to community colleges.

Armed with college degrees, the new generation set to work. Those of many backgrounds began an exodus from family farms in Aroostook County to high-paying jobs in Connecticut. Portland's "Little Italy" drained to the nearby suburbs. In 1945 St. Peter's Catholic Church in the Italian neighborhood had 3,000 parishioners; in 1980 it had dwindled to 600. For a time, inner cities including Portland, Lewiston, Bangor, Belfast, and Waterville still boasted department stores, five & dimes, movie houses, and grocery stores but were constantly challenged by suburban shopping centers, drive-in theaters, fast-food restaurants, malls, and by century's turn, "big box" operations.

In the '60s urban renewal, the euphemism for slum clearance, made its appearance, though by the '70s Greater Portland Landmarks, Inc., and other preservation groups began to appear as citizens looked with horror at holes appearing in the manmade environment. Dying downtowns were in many cases seen as opportunities by under-funded entrepreneurs who turned Portland's Old Port from abandoned brick warehouses into a tourist destination with outstanding restaurants and small specialty shops. By the twenty-first century large tourist cruise ships made this city, and towns further down east, lucrative ports of call.

❖

In the transportation sector, Maine became almost totally dependent on the internal combustion engine, and government funds were targeted largely on building and maintaining roads. Trolleys were seen only in museums or on film, traditional rail passenger service made its last run from Vanceboro to Portland in 1960, and the latter's landmark Union Station was demolished in 1961. The Bangor & Aroostook stopped passenger runs in 1960, and the next year the Canadian National route from Portland to Montreal was discontinued. Though freight handling continued, so did competition from trucking and heavy regulation. Subsequently a variety of lines were abandoned, often becoming hiking trails. Late in the twentieth century, Amtrak, government-supported passenger service from Portland to Boston, was successfully restored.

Trucking companies including Cole's Express and Merrill Transportation diversified and flourished, although high fuel prices and other pressures were changing the situation by 2000. In 1990 there were 22,240 miles of public road. The most notable highway remains the Maine Turnpike, a toll road authorized by the legislature in 1941 from York to Portland and extended to Augusta in 1955. More than 60 million vehicles used the pike in 2011. Federal funds created Interstate 95, which connected Augusta and Houlton, but there has never been an east–west highway. At this writing only one thoroughfare, Route 201, extends from Maine into the Province of Quebec. Thus, for the general public, the Big Woods continue to serve as a barrier. By the late twentieth century, the U.S. Geologic Survey of Maine was only 90.2 percent complete, making it the least-mapped state on the east coast. Still, more than ever, Maine was commercially and transportation-wise linked to Canada and New Hampshire.

Air traffic grew in importance, and in 2011 there were sixty-eight airports. Bangor International (formerly Dow Air Base) became the largest, logging in hundreds of thousands of passengers and servicing the celebrated supersonic Concorde before that classic was retired in 2003. Portland International Jetport now boards the most passengers. New uses for the Brunswick Naval Air Station were explored when its famous field closed early in the twenty-first century. The base had been a major sub-spotting operation during the Cold War, with big transatlantic Orions frequently coming and going. Proximity between Maine and Europe, long the rallying cry of shipping, rail, and defense interests, was once again demonstrated when *Double Eagle II* lifted off from Houlton in 1974 and became the first manned balloon to cross the Atlantic. Ten years later, Colonel Joe Kittinger made the first solo flight in the *Rosie O'Grady Balloon of Peace*. On a more practical level, remote Maine places, including Matinicus Island and Big Woods camps, rely utterly on small airstrips and private flights.

Working vessels vied with pleasure craft in the growing thousands, and the waning decades saw relatively skilled local enthusiasts in 30-foot-plus boats sailing to Europe for fun. Those voyages were not commonplace, nor were they really deemed newsworthy. Coastal barges, container ships, and, especially in Casco Bay, portly tankers were constant visitors. With the completion of the wartime Montreal pipeline, Portland had become the largest oil port on the American east coast.

❖

Rural electrification, begun with New Deal funding, was extended to nearly everyone by the '60s. Electricity was cheap and most citizens took it for granted. The power crisis first loomed in the '70s during the Middle East oil embargo. In 1972, the Maine Yankee nuclear plant in Wiscasset went on line. Several citizen attempts to shut the facility down were defeated at the polls, but in 1997 the plant was shut down for economic reasons, and decommissioned in 2005. At the same time, a growing number of inhabitants came out against hydro projects, a fact that had already defeated the

At the finish of World War II, Limestone, Maine, was a sleepy agricultural town, but as the cars lining the street in this 1947 photograph show, things had begun to change. In 1950 Limestone Air Force Base (renamed Loring in 1959) opened as a front line in the Cold War. Its bombers were the closest of all SAC forces in North America to Moscow and the Russian heartland. The base itself was surrounded with Nike missiles. Loring greatly stimulated the local economy, plush new facilities were built, and the area's population grew. COLLECTION OF THE MAINE HISTORICAL SOCIETY

Aircraft capable of landing and taking off on lakes became an important and effective arm of the Department of Inland Fisheries and Wildlife beginning in the late 1930s, and they remain the principal form of transportation into the backcountry. Warden pilots (with the same powers as sheriffs) use planes for the enforcement of laws, data collection, and search-and-rescue operations in Maine's 15 million acres of forest. Here, the Division of Fisheries and Hatcheries is stocking fish. COURTESY DIVISION OF PUBLIC INFORMATION AND EDUCATION, DEPARTMENT OF INLAND FISHERIES AND WILDLIFE, AUGUSTA, MAINE, PHOTOGRAPH BY BILL CROSS

208   MAINE: THE WILDER HALF OF NEW ENGLAND

ambitious Dickey-Lincoln project on the St. John River. Similarly, oil terminals or refineries at Eastport, Machiasport, Searsport, and Casco Bay's Long Island were quashed by public opinion. Solar and wind power, once seen as clean alternatives, soon posed problems or attracted critics.

The revolution and continued perfection of communication techniques grew apace. Radio, popular for decades, had already launched a number of excellent country music performers and would continue to inform and entertain. Telephones, in use since the nineteenth century, became mobile, and in the 1980s, computers began to join major appliances in home and office. It is astonishing to reflect that even major corporations such as Bath Iron Works and Maine Medical Center functioned largely without computers until the '70s. By the twenty-first century, nearly every business was part of the Web, using e-mail or boasting its own website. Still, one suspects we are only on the doorstep.

In 1949 a scattering of southern Maine families could discern fuzzy images from Boston televisions stations. Then, on January 19, 1953, Station WABI in Bangor went on the air and Maine entered the TV age. The station was partly owned by former Governor Hildreth, a business visionary who helped start WMTW the following year. Soon the Rines and Gannett families entered the field with WCSH (1953) and WGAN (1954), and local

In 1961 little Andover, Maine, was chosen as the site for the first worldwide satellite ground station. Built by AT&T, Earth Station Andover began as the communication terminus for *Telstar* (renamed *Comsat*), and the Space Age commenced. The 1,000-acre site included the huge spherical radome, which measured 161 feet high and 210 feet across and was the largest earthbound, inflated structure ever built. The town's small population and isolation led to its selection. In 1990 the Air Force displayed its new Over the Horizon (OTH) radar, which could see 2,000 miles from Bangor, utilizing antennas in Columbia Falls and Moscow, Maine. COLLECTION OF THE MAINE HISTORICAL SOCIETY

advertisers including Day's Jewelry were suddenly famous throughout northern New England. Private and public stations grew, and in the early days local personalities such as Dave Astor, Eddie Driscoll, Agnes Gibbs, and Captain Lloyd Knight colored the local scene. By the 1970s, personalities were largely confined to reporting news and weather, and soon after, cable became almost a necessity, while otherworldly satellite dishes stippled rural areas.

For some, newspapers continued to be an important part of daily routine; for others, they augmented TV news and subscriptions fell. Five communities continued to support weekly or near-weekly papers, while Portland, Lewiston, and Bangor continued with dailies and the Sunday paper with feature articles and comics, for workers on the day of rest. That, too, went over the rail in 1990 when the State of Maine dropped its Sabbath Day law and allowed businesses to remain open on Sunday. For better or worse, this legislation destroyed long-held attitudes and ways of doing things, in all sectors of Maine life.

Smaller communities had always supported weekly papers, including the *Ellsworth American*, long under the editorship of the near-legendary James Russell Wiggins. Following the divisive '60s, alternative papers found fertile ground in Portland and other cities, beginning with *North Country* and today's *Portland Daily Sun*, the *Phoenix*, and the *Falmouth Forecaster*. The subscription weekly with the most lasting punch was the *Maine Times* (1968–2002), founded by Peter Cox and John Cole. During its yeasty life it attracted writers such as Phyllis Austin and Edgar Allen Beem and was a huge influence on regional business, environmental, political, cultural, and religious interests.

An abundance of magazines appeared after the *Pine Cone*, by far the most popular and long-lived of which is *Down East* out of Camden-Rockport. Launched in 1954, its iconic presentations of Maine living and history have played a large part in shaping an image of our state throughout the world. *Echoes* (founded 1988) extols the grandeur (and often difficulty) of living in northern Maine, while city periodicals such as *Portland* magazine unveiled the attractions, distractions, and occasional problems of what would seem to outsiders an oxymoron: "urban life down east."

In 1958 Down East Publications introduced the popular *Bert and I* recorded routines of Marshall Dodge and the Reverend Robert Bryan. These humorous stories were in the tradition of Seba Smith, but told by people "from away." Some Yankee hackles went up, but Maine-born humorists including Kendall Morse, the "Wicked Good Band," Tim Sample, and Bob Marley follow in the tradition with native wit not fearing to deal with social reality. Preserving local heritage is the mission of the Northeast Folklife Society at UMO, and studying ordinary life is that of the Salt Institute, whose students have recorded the daily lives of citizens from truck drivers to booksellers.

❖

The arts have thrived with Portland Players, Mad Horse Theater, and Lyric Theater being enriched each summer by Berwick's Hackmatack Playhouse, the Theater at Monmouth, Ogunquit Playhouse, and fabled Lakewood, to name a few. The Maine State Music Theater in Brunswick, begun in 1959 by Victoria Crandall and others, remains vibrant.

Though the 1973 *Maine Catalogue* proclaimed "dance and Maine don't appear especially attracted to each other," this flies in the face of history. Dance was central to Abenaki life as well as to nearly every new culture that has since arrived. Dancers of the era, including Grace De Carleton Ross and Anthony "Chan" Spotten, certainly suggest the opposite, as does the celebrated Ram Island Dance Company, founded by Millicent Monks in 1967, and since 1982 the Bates Dance Festival.

In the '50s movie stars Bette Davis and Gary Merrill lived in Cape Elizabeth, sometimes lending their spice to the area scene. Other homegrown actors included Linda Lavin, star of the TV series *Alice* (1976–84); Judd Nelson, featured in movies including *The Breakfast Club* (1985); and Liv Tyler, in popular films including *Lord of the Rings* (2001). Maine was the location for such memorable movies as *Lost Boundaries* (1949), *Carousel* (1956), *Peyton Place* (1957), and *The Whales of August* (1987). Several were made in other states based on works by Maine writers, including *The Strange Woman* (1946) by Ben Ames Williams, *Deep Waters* (1948) from Ruth Moore's novel *Spoonhandle*, *The Deep Six* (1958) by Martin Dibner, and Richard Hooker's *M*A*S*H* (1970). The latter became a long-running TV series and antiwar commentary.

Music, always a strong element, continued on every level. Rockland-born Walter Piston became Harvard's first Walter W. Naumberg Professor of Music and won Pulitzer Prizes in 1948 and 1961. He retained close working ties with local groups. Since 1962, when Arthur Bennett Lipkin became conductor, the Portland Symphony Orchestra has continued to grow in professional stature. The Bangor Symphony has also risen in esteem. Important composers include William Matthews of Bates College, Elliot Schwartz of Bowdoin, and Peter Re of Colby.

The state boasts a small but active jazz community that has included Brad Terry, Del Stratton, and former big-band trombonist Don Doane. Country and western music has been particularly popular and has featured such performers as Betty Cody, Dick Curless, Al Hawkes, and Ken MacKenzie. Perhaps the greatest rock composer from Maine was Claude Demetrius of Bath, who wrote "Mean Woman Blues" (1957) and "Hard Headed Woman" (1958). In folk, one can turn to such talents as Gordon Bok, Annie Clark, Noel Paul Stookey (of Peter, Paul, and Mary fame), and groups such as Schooner Fare and Devonsquare. Major rock, heavy metal—you name it—groups of national renown have appeared in the civic centers and fields of Maine. Tickets were already sold for Elvis's Portland concert when he left the building in 1977. In the years that followed, local groups played beer halls and events, a few rising to prominence. By the end of the twentieth century, Portland offered a national recording studio and local and regional groups were making their own CDs and beginning to flourish in nontraditional ways.

If young Mainers were attuned to louder sounds, writers generally continued to seek Maine's quiet, beautiful, low-pressure, low-cost environment. Belgian-born author Marguerite Yourcenar, whose unique prose won her election to the previously all-male L'Académie Française, settled at Mount Desert in 1950. Among her works are *Memoirs of Hadrian* (1951) and *Two Lives and a Dream* (1987). Listing the first-rate authors in this seventy-year period is too long for this book but would need to include E. B. White for *Charlotte's Web* (1952) and his essay on Maine speech; Henry Beston and Elizabeth Coatsworth, who spent decades working from a farmhouse in Nobleboro, and there is nothing that approaches her fable of the woods, *The Enchanted: An Incredible Tale* (1951); poet Philip Booth, one of the most tangible poets from Maine's postwar era, who captured the automobile culture to perfection in *Maine* (1960); while Robert Lowell provided a different slant with the poem *Fourth of July in Maine* (1967). The list continues with such stalwarts as Barbara Cooney, Jean Stafford, Kendall Merriam, Steve Lutrell, Richard Grant, Robert Chute, Betsy Sholl, Fred Bonnie, Colin Sargent, Ken Rosen, Sanford Phippen, Leo Connellan, and Jan Willem de Wetering to form a rich array.

Nativity may or may not be relevant when it is remembered that ultra-Maine writers, including John Gould and Bill Clark, were born outside the Pine State Curtain. Still, the superb Maine-born poet Patricia Smith Ranzoni makes a telling argument for special insight by local writers versus the

In the 1970s Stephen King (born 1947) became the best-known writer of horror since Edgar Allen Poe and the most widely read Maine author since Longfellow. Beginning with *Carrie* (1973), the Portland-born King created such memorable books as *Salem's Lot* (1975), *The Shining* (1977), and *Cujo* (1981) and produced seven of the decade's top twenty-five bestsellers. Here the writer is commemorated in his hometown by graffiti artists as the King of Horror. PHOTO COURTESY OF AUBIN THOMAS

Mainer by choice. (The author of this book, though a lifelong New Englander, was born in Vermont and takes no side.)

Carolyn Chute's startling, unrelenting exploration of the bleak bottom of post-agricultural family life in the *Beans of Egypt, Maine* (1985) brought high praise from the critics and outcries from locals who were repulsed by her characterization of Maine poverty as dysfunction. The long literary shelf life of the poor-but-noble and self-reliant down-easter came to an abrupt and ignoble end with the Beans. The serious reader, however, might justly compare the novel with Margaret Dickson's book the same year, *Maddy's Song*. Though focused on rural poverty and family abuse, few contemporary books rival this in terms of clear style, compassionate human insight, and storytelling ability. As the division between the bottom and the top of the socioeconomic order grew more pronounced, these fictional volumes provided insight and potential talking points.

Maine, which provided first-novelist Madame Wood with a delightfully stark gothic backdrop, continued to provide perfect country for a revived horror genre. First came the campy national TV series *Dark Shadows*, set in fictional Collinsport, Maine, then came the peerless horror novels and short stories of Portland-born Stephen King. The author and his writer wife, Tabitha, struggled until the publication of *Carrie* (1971). The book's success and King's unmatched ability to scare through artful tales led to one of the most astonishing success stories in publishing. By 2000 the "King of Horror" had produced more than thirty tomes,

212   MAINE: THE WILDER HALF OF NEW ENGLAND

many of them filmed, and joined the ranks of Edgar Allan Poe and H. P. Lovecraft. Our very region now became synonymous with the supernatural and unexplained.

Nonfiction, especially in the field of history, started slowly with classics including John J. Pullen's *The Twentieth Maine* (1957), Charles E. Clark's *The Eastern Frontier* (1970), and Gordon S. Kershaw's *The Kennebeck Proprietors* (1975), and then exploded into a field of its own. Mention should be made of Geraldine Tidd Scott's *Ties of Common Blood* (1992), a work much used by Canadian researchers of the northeast boundary, and W. H. Bunting's two-volume tour de force, *A Day's Work: A Sampler of Historic Maine Photographs, 1860-1920* (1977 and 2000), in a class of its own and a model for future works. Laurel Thatcher Ulrich's prize-winning *A Midwife's Tale* (1990), Alan Taylor's *Liberty Men and the Great Proprietors* (1990), and Joshua M. Smith's *Borderland Smuggling* (2006) are basic lenses, what some called the "new social history." In the late twentieth century, a change was in the air. Maine was no longer seen in isolation. Events here were seen as influencing or were influenced by national trends.

❖

In the 1940s the thought of historic architecture in Maine was reserved for a handful of structures connected to famous people or events. Beginning in the 1960s with the obliteration of major buildings (such as Portland's elegant Union Station) and their replacement by nondescript, utilitarian structures, a public outcry was heard. A new appreciation of the tangled past led to the creation of Greater Portland Landmarks, Inc., the Maine Historic Preservation Commission, and numerous grassroots organizations. Scholars including Deborah Thompson, editor of *Maine Forms of American Architecture* (1976), were followed by a regiment of writer-researchers including Patricia McGraw Anderson, Arthur Gerrier, Roger G. Reed, James F. O'Gorman, and Annie Robinson to name a few. Earle G. Shettleworth, Jr., director of the Maine Historic Preservation Commission and state historian, author of scores of books and monographs and articles, was the presiding eminence that made architecture perhaps the liveliest and most studied field in local history.

His predecessor at the commission, James H. Mundy, was a pioneer in the new ethnic history with *hard times, hard men* (1990), a no-nonsense study of the nineteenth-century Irish in Maine. Soon a fine selection of ethnic histories appeared including *Twelve Thousand Years: American Indians in Maine* (2001) by Bruce J. Bourque; *They Change Their Sky: The Irish in Maine* (2004) edited by Michael C. Connolly; *Maine's Visible Black History* (2006) by H. H. Price and Gerald E. Talbot (2000); *Voyages: A Franco-American Reader* edited by Nelson Madore and Barry Rodrigue; and *A History of the Italians in the State of Maine* (2010) by Vincent A. Lapomarda. Other books were more specially focused on the contributions of Jewish, Armenian, Latino, and other Mainers by choice. At last other groups were finding voices and the historic record was becoming richer and far more accurate.

A tidal wave of author-researchers ranging from scholars to journalists to genealogists to corporate historians and self-publishing amateurs makes any overview impossible. But works on social welfare, economics, foodways, women, and fields never considered previously joined those traditional pursuits of maritime, agriculture, fishing, biography, and politics. Maine writers were legion and getting stronger in all areas.

The growth of historical organizations in Maine towns has been impressive, and this book has availed itself of them. Public libraries from Fort Kent to Lewiston to Kittery have made themselves indispensable to their regions for students looking in and out. The New England Studies Program at USM and the Canadian Studies Program at UMO have proved substantive and exciting. The venerable Maine Historical Society (1822), third oldest such organization in the United States, has modernized with an expanded and restored library, a nationally recognized online network, and a statewide outreach program. Though privately funded, MHS has been actively reinforced in cultural and conservation activities by the Maine State Library (1836), the Maine State Museum (1971), the Maine State Archives (1965), the Maine Historic Preservation Commission (1971), and the Maine Humanities Council (1976).

❖

In terms of the visual arts, the Pine Tree State underwent a veritable renaissance, providing inspiration for a bewildering number of artists and actual sustenance for others. Though a number of young talents left for New York and other art centers, many natives were able to make a go of it in-state for the first time since the nineteenth century. New collecting institutions arose, old museums expanded, and by the 1970s year-round commercial galleries appeared, only to dwindle somewhat by late in the twentieth century.

In 1948 Rockland's William A. Farnsworth Library and Art Museum opened and soon became a mecca for Wyeth family paintings. In that same year, Andrew Wyeth painted "Christina's World" (Museum of Modern Art), an iconic image that made its sitter, Christina Olson, of Cushing, Maine, and its weathered coastal buildings world-renowned. As the century wore on the organization became the much-respected Farnsworth Art Museum with holdings that helped put Wyeth's strong American figurative works in context.

Revolutionary art ideas were reaching the state as well. In 1946, Willard Cummings and others founded the Skowhegan School of Painting and Sculpture. Governed by and for artists, it has influenced some of the country's most promising young men and women. The Museum of Art at Ogunquit, built by painter-adventurer Henry Strater in 1951, was the first Maine collecting organization dedicated to modern and contemporary art. The Barn Gallery, also in trendy Ogunquit, opened in 1958 to showcase area talents and the distinguished Hamilton Easter Field Collection on a seasonal basis. The collection was later placed at the Portland Museum of Art. In the early postwar decades, summer galleries and traditional themes remained the bread and butter of the local art scene. Of course established artists, including the Zorachs, John Marin, Waldo Peirce, Robert Laurent, and Peggy Bacon, were joined by the likes of Bernard Langlais, John Laurant, Fairfield Porter, Alex Katz, and William Thon. Most paintings remained representational or gently abstract.

Rockland's great sculptor Louise Nevelson produced her outstanding nonobjective work at this time, but it was made mostly in New York. Mildred Burrage, now in Wiscasset, continued to experiment with abstract painting and promote the Maine Art Gallery; she enjoyed a major retrospective before her death in 1983. Visionary changes began to penetrate the art scene with important works by American contemporary artists at Portland's Temple Beth El in the 1960s. The catalogues from these wonderful shows were well designed and make fascinating reading.

The appearance of Lewiston-born William Manning and his pure, elegant, nonrepresentational canvases brought controversy to the placid Portland School of Art. In 1969 Manning and Polly K. Brown founded the short-lived but influential Concept School. Soon after, the PSA underwent a revolution of its own, becoming the Maine College of Art with a home on Congress Street. By the '70s Portland was experiencing a cultural and economic boom, commercial galleries and local artists having the choice of actually making some sort of living at home or trying their hand elsewhere. For the first time since the 1820s, arts coverage in the local press became frequent and, in the reviews of writers such as Philip Isaacson, Bob

Keyes, and Edgar Allen Beem, serious and engaging. In 1990 the latter's best essays were compiled as *Maine Art Now*. The first true survey of the whole scene came in 1963 with Colby College's *Maine and Its Role in American Art, 1740–1963*, which brought in such outside art writers as Nina Fletcher Little, John I. H. Baur, James T. Flexner, and others. Now books on Hartley, Langlais, and Ipcar, or the art colonies at Ogunquit, Monhegan, and Seguinland began to proliferate.

Fresh museum facilities appeared at Colby (1973), Bowdoin (1976), Westbrook College (1977), the Portland Museum of Art (1983), Bates (1986), and the University of Maine (1986). Portland's impressive facility was the shared dream of Director John Holverson and patron Charles S. Payson, made manifest by visionary architect Henry Nichols Cobb of I. M. Pei and Partners. A remarkable architectural statement, it has helped transformed formerly drab Congress Square.

No list could begin to cover the worthy artists connected with the state in recent years, but it would need to include Berenice Abbott and Eliot Porter; sculptors Celeste Roberge and John Ventimiglia; and painters Neil Welliver, David Driskell, Robert Indiana, Abby Shahn, George DeLyra, and Wendy Kindred. The tough urban realism of a Michael Waterman cityscape or the line drawings of Michael Ricci are unmatched. In 1984 the comic book art of Buxton's Kevin Eastman and Peter Laird made *Teenage Mutant Ninja Turtles* an international favorite. In season, the late twentieth century was home to nationally known art critics Lucy Lippard and Hilton Kramer, as well as art historians Richard McLanathan and Elizabeth Gilmore Holt. If the scene tended to work on two levels—established artists from away and locals—there was more equality in the twenty-first century. Changing economics, though, had clearly damaged artists, galleries, and collectors on a financial level. Still, in a time of uncertainty, good things were being done personally and institutionally.

❖

Mainers of all ages were involved in sports and leisure more than ever before as participants and observers, amateurs and professionals. Traditional pursuits of hunting, fishing, and camping—once rather simple, inexpensive elements of life for most folk—took on the hardware and expenses once reserved for the wealthy sportsman. The serious joined the Sportsman's Alliance of Maine or the National Rifle Association. The sale of sporting equipment became big business and fishing in the ocean now required a license.

There is hardly a sport that is not played or watched in Maine, ranging from baseball to hockey to soccer to skiing to bowling to boxing to track and field, football, baseball, basketball, rugby, and boating. Thoroughbred racing ended in the '60s, but harness racing continued at Scarborough Downs, Lewiston, and the Bangor Raceway, as well as at county fairs. Oxford Plains Speedway (1949) and the Beach Ridge Speedway in Scarborough became two of the region's premier tracks.

Baseball has long held a special place in the hearts of down-easters. Professional minor league ball was brought to Portland in the '40s and Old Orchard Beach in the '80s but failed to pay for itself. In 1994, however, Hadlock Field was built in Portland and became home to the popular Sea Dogs, farm team for the Florida Marlins and then the Boston Red Sox. This allowed local fans to see potential major league stars of the future, including players Dustin Pedroia and Daisuke Matsuzaka. The University of Southern Maine won two division-three titles in the sport.

Individually, talented locals including Carlton Willey, Danny Coombs, Bob Stanley, and Bill Swift became big leaguers, and Stump Merrill managed the New York Yankees and David Littlefield served as general manager of the Pittsburgh Pirates.

Hockey, brought to universal popularity by Franco-American citizens, flourished in the colleges and high schools. In 1973 the Maine

CHANGING VISIONS   215

Winter Sports

IN MAINE...WINTER'S FAVORITE SNOW AREA

The snowfall starts early on Maine's ski slopes and a white Christmas means perfect skiing extending through Easter. One of the most dependable snow areas in the East, Maine is a favorite with all skiers. Modern lifts carry you to beginners' slopes or expert trails. Standing in line for a ride is the exception rather than the rule. The slopes are easy to reach, too, from a 70 mph 125-mile super highway.

Maine's famed summer resorts in the ski areas provide the finest of winter accommodations . . . tobogganning, skating, sleigh rides, ice fishing and snowshoeing . . . crackling log fires and delicious Down East cooking. And unsurpassed scenery makes an ideal setting for an exciting winter vacation. For complete area listings and accommodations, write: Maine Winter Vacations, 900 Gateway Circle, Portland, Maine.

Maine's pine trees dressed in snow, the snow that is so perfect for skiing.

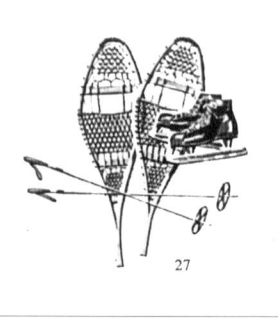

Finest lifts bring you up mountains overlooking ice-covered lakes and pine forests.

Beautiful days, a wonderful lodge, and time out for a bite to eat.

27

This period saw a new push to make Maine a winter as well as a summer vacationland, and by the 1980s, the health and wellness movement expanded interest in outdoor activities. Ski areas such as Shawnee Peak, Saddleback, Lost Valley, and Sugarloaf USA flourished during good winters. Interest in cross-country skiing, snowmobiling, and other sports continued to grow, along with summer activities including sailing, camping, hunting, and hiking. COLLECTION OF THE MAINE HISTORICAL SOCIETY

Opposite, top: In 1946 the Dibner brothers—Ed, Paul, and Martin—purchased a campground on Pleasant Lake in Casco and started Camp Tall Timbers. For the next twenty years, boys from New York, Ohio, Maine, and other states gained summer experience with the Maine outdoors in this non-sectarian operation. By the early 1960s the state claimed about 200 camps and 15,000 campers. Many returned to vacation with their own children or chose to live in Maine. One Tall Timbers counselor, Samuel Shapiro, not only moved to the state but later on became state treasurer. COURTESY OF MARTIN DIBNER, CASCO, MAINE

Opposite, bottom: Elizabeth and Randolph Dominic, Sr., at a camp built by her grandfather on Souadabscook Stream, Hermon, Maine, in the 1890s. The year is 1947 and none of the fish were wasted, ending up fried, in chowder, or as fish hash. The current generation of the family continues the tradition of fishing and hunting. COLLECTION OF THE MAINE HISTORICAL SOCIETY

CHANGING VISIONS   217

The outstanding Maine athlete of the postwar era is undoubtedly Joan Benoit Samuelson (born 1957), a native Mainer who grew up in Cape Elizabeth, graduated from Bowdoin College, and resides at Freeport with her husband, Dr. Scott Samuelson. Few people will forget her winning the Boston Marathon in 1979 and 1983 and her sensational Gold Medal run in the first Olympic women's marathon at Los Angeles in 1984. The town of Cape Elizabeth put up this monument by sculptor Edward Materson in front of the Thomas Memorial Library in 1984. PHOTO COURTESY STEPHEN G. BOOTH

Nordiques, a professional minor league, settled in Lewiston and lasted until 1977. In that year the Maine Mariners came to Portland, winning the American Hockey League Calder Cup in their first two seasons. In 1993 they were replaced at the Civic Center by the AHL's Portland Pirates, who again won the Calder Cup. At this date they remain popular. The Lewiston MAINEiacs hockey team played from 2003 to 2011, while other minor league teams in Bangor have been less successful.

Basketball, always popular in school sports, came late in the form of professional teams with the Portland Mountain Cats/The Wave in 1996–1997. In 2009 the Maine Red Claws, a NBA Development League associated with the Boston Celtics, caught on. Earlier, the amazing Cindy Blodgett of Clinton, Maine, led the nation in scoring at UMO (1994–1998), went on to play professionally, and from 2007 to 2011 served as head coach for women's basketball at her alma mater.

As in the past, boxing has had its standout fighters such as Peter Riccitelli, "Hurricane" Herrick, and Leo "the Lion" Difiore, and promoters or enthusiasts including Sam Silverman and Eddie Griffin. Lewiston's Joey Gamache won the WBA Super Featherweight title in 1991 and the WBA Lightweight title in 1992.

Finally, a number of Mainers or Maine-trained people competed in the Olympics, including Seth Westcott, the snowboarding Gold Medalist out of Carrabassett. By far the most outstanding sports figure of the era is Joan Benoit Samuelson, the first native Mainer to win an Olympic Gold Medal. Joan Benoit grew up in Cape Elizabeth and went on to Bowdoin College. In 1979 she came to prominence by winning the Boston Marathon, a victory repeated in 1983. Thanks to television, few Mainers missed her thrilling victory run in the first Olympic marathon, at Los Angeles in 1984; it was an effort that set a new standard of excellence.

❖

Maine proved rich ground for unorthodox but influential notions in the immediate postwar period. In 1952 Scott and Helen Nearing pulled up stakes in Vermont and began to homestead in Harborside, Maine. Their experiments in an alternative lifestyle and organic gardening prefigure hippies and the back-to-the-land movement of the late '60s and '70s. The Nearings' books, especially *Living the Good Life* (1954) and *Continuing the Good Life* (1979), remain popular. Locals were not immune to antiestablishment ideas. Kenneth Roberts, who earned a special Pulitzer in 1957, spent much of that decade studying and espousing the art of dowsing.

While Maine folks respected newcomers' rights to privacy, the federal government did not

Sailing for pleasure is one of the oldest pastimes—or obsessions—down east, having become affordable around 1815. Locals and vacationers found the waters and islands irresistible, and as boats became more sophisticated, longer adventures were possible. Steve Booth grew up in Falmouth exploring the coast and spent his career working in Maine. In the summer of 2005, Booth navigated his 32-foot cutter-rigged *Gandalf* out of Casco Bay to the Azores. He continued on to Portugal and Spain, realizing a lifelong dream.
PHOTO COURTESY DAVID CHENEY, WINDHAM, MAINE

Married partners Jen Joy (in the stern) and Dani Fazio (in the bow) navigate whitewater river rapids in their canoe, *Gladys*, during the 2011 Souadabscook Stream Race in Hampden. In the spring, when the rivers are at their highest, paddlers from across the globe come to compete in these whitewater races, the most notable being the 16.5-mile Kenduskeag Stream Race in Bangor. Joy, an eleventh-generation Mainer, and Fazio, a first-generation Mainer, find their home away from home in the great Maine woods—be it camping in Baxter State Park, hiking in Acadia, cross-country skiing in Rangeley, or paddling on rivers and lakes in all the sixteen counties. PHOTOGRAPH © MICHAEL ALDEN

always follow suit. Fear of communism, later replaced by terrorism, waxed and waned. Dr. Wilhelm Reich, the controversial psychoanalyst and philosopher, constructed his laboratory-home, "Orgonon" (now the Wilhelm Reich Museum) in Rangeley during the '40s. His experiments ran afoul of the Federal Food and Drug Administration, led to the burning of his books, his trial in Portland, and his death in federal prison in 1957.

Though the authorities dealt less harshly with Rachel Carson's sweeping environmental pronouncements, many businesses and scientists were alarmed. Carson's first trip to Maine came in 1946, and she soon became a fixture at Southport, where she wrote such influential volumes as *The Edge of the Sea* (1956) and *Silent Spring* (1961). These eloquent early warnings of global pollution and the growing interdependence of industry, science, and government were widely debated. Carson left money to begin the purchase of coastal land now called the Rachel Carson National Wildlife Preserve under the U.S. Fish and Wildlife Service. Many of her ideas achieved wide acceptance among Maine politicians including Senator Edmund Muskie, who went on to lead the nation in environmental matters. They also drew lightning from the unbelieving opposition that felt she was overstating the problem.

Religion, once integral to local life, seemingly shifted in relative importance. In 1940 the WPA *Dictionary of Churches & Religious Organizations in Maine* noted a growing inclination among Protestants to coordinate interfaith programs, the expansion of non-mainstream Protestant denominations in rural areas, and a tendency to still view Maine as a mission field. Summer residents tended

In the last months of 1982, Samantha Smith (1972–1985), a fifth grader from Manchester, Maine, wrote to Soviet leader Yuri Andropov. In her letter she noted: "I have been worrying about the Soviet Union and the United States getting into a nuclear war. Are you going to vote to have a war or not? If you aren't please tell me how you are going to help not have a war." In the spring of 1983 her letter was answered, and Samantha and her parents were invited to the USSR. Thus began a celebrated tour and one of the first indications of the Cold War's end. Samantha and her father, Arthur Smith, died in a tragic plane crash. This monument by Glen Hines of Houlton was placed near the State Cultural Building in 1986. Photo courtesy Stephen G. Booth

to play a large role in financing some organizations, and by 1989 the Commission on Maine's Future concluded that only half the population regularly attended a place of worship. Such statistics would certainly have shocked some earlier generations, but not that of Cotton Mather. Divorce, once an exception, was now 50 percent.

In 1989 Shoshana Hoose began a powerful series on religion in the *Maine Sunday Telegram*, which was reprinted for the Maine Council of Churches. In spite of living in the information age, religious feelings are still very difficult to measure except in numbers, and most reporting has focused on social events or scandals.

In 2000 the largest denomination was the Roman Catholic Church with 283,034 members, followed by the United Methodists with 31,689, the United Church of Christ (Congregational) with 29,122, the American Baptists with 26,259, and smaller groups of Protestants including the Episcopal Church, Unitarian-Universalists, Lutherans, Conservative Baptists, Presbyterians, and Seventh Day Adventists. Jews numbered 8,290. To this must be added smaller groups including Buddhists, Hindus, Baha'i, and Mormons. During the 1970s and 1980s the Pentecostal Christian churches gained a new vitality. While the arrival of immigrants from Somalia and the Middle East put the Muslim community at about 5,000 in 2012, Maine's first Islamic community began around 1910 in the Biddeford mills when families of skilled dyers arrived from Albania. Now the establishment of refugees from Iraq, Afghanistan, Sudan, and Somalia presented a major cultural change. Mosques now stand with meetinghouses, temples, and churches.

❖

Two major wars were fought in distant Asia, punctuated by the Cold War. The first began on June 25, 1950, when the army of North Korea swept into South Korea. Officially described as a United Nations "Police Action," the struggle between the communist East and American West lasted until 1953. Little attention was paid to the conflict in which 233 Mainers lost their lives, and most Americans wanted to forget it was happening or ever took place. Unlike service people returning from World War II, those returning from Korea got little credit, and even today have few monuments. One veteran from Maine, writing under the name of Richard Hooker (Dr. H. Richard Hornberger), produced *M*A*S*H*, perhaps the best-known novel about the war. The irreverent look at life in a forward hospital unit became the basis for a film (1970) and television series (1972–1983). *M*A*S*H* Comes to Maine* was published in 1972.

In fact, *M*A*S*H* had a strong influence on attitudes toward the Vietnam War (1964–1975), which lasted longer than the Revolutionary War and was the least popular engagement since the disastrous War of 1812. Many young Americans enlisted enthusiastically, particularly at the outset, but the persistent inability of the U.S. Government to define goals or win the minds of growing numbers of citizens led to questions and growing opposition at home. Governments came and went in Saigon, the cost in lives and materiel grew, and even the heavy bombing of North Vietnam, Cambodia, and Laos had seemingly no effect. In Maine many began to question the morality and necessity of the war, and protests flared in towns, cities, and campuses. Some draft-age men left for Canada and families divided along generational lines. On Moratorium Day 1969, some 4,000 people gathered at Portland's City Hall to decry President Nixon's painfully slow wind-down of the war. In the end, 336 Mainers died in Southeast Asia and 18 remain missing in action. Other impacts of the war would take longer to comprehend.

Subsequently the United States armed forces were engaged in global military actions ranging from President Gerald Ford's recovery of the SS *Mayaguez* in 1975 and the 1989 invasion of Panama to President George H. W. Bush's 1990 Persian Gulf War, which drove Iraq out of Kuwait, and President Bill Clinton's 1999 "relief intervention" in Kosovo. All had their impact on Maine.

On September 11, 2001, the nation was stunned as nineteen al-Qaeda terrorists, some beginning their mission through Portland International Jetport, seized commercial airliners and toppled the World Trade Center's Twin Towers in New York, killing over 3,000 people. A third flight damaged the Pentagon and a fourth was destroyed as passengers fought the pirates to the death. The date 9/11 marked a bloody turning point in history.

President George W. Bush then invaded Afghanistan and Iraq, eventually deposing both governments. The Maine National Guard (and the National Guard in other states) was deployed not as back-up or disaster-relief units, but as frontline troops. What made this different was that young men and now women just starting life were spending their first working years at low-paying jobs defending their country. Often they were called back several times. Upon their return, civilian jobs were at a premium and, in many cases, this made family life very difficult. The age of "the weekend warrior" had vanished.

❖

The turmoil of the '60s and '70s produced important social legislation, and with increased awareness of ethnic heritage, the role of old Yankees vs. "people from away" in building the state was debated. To some degree, assimilation, which had gone largely unquestioned in the can-do postwar years of the 1940s, came to be judged with distaste by some groups and individuals.

This was particularly true of Native American tribes and people in Maine, who were able to use the legal system to gain official federal recognition and win back a portion of Maine land along with an emerging prominence for individuals including Donna M. Loring, Donald Soctomah, Allen J.

U.S. Army Veteran William Lawrence Frost (Vietnam 1968–1969) visits the Maine Vietnam Veterans Memorial in Augusta. Designed by Roger Richmond of Peaks Island, it was dedicated in 1985. Three hundred thirty-six Mainers were killed and eighteen are listed as missing in action. Then America's longest war, it began with U.S. advisors in 1960 and continued until the fall of Saigon in 1975. The war generated widespread, bitter disagreement and ended with seeming ambivalence toward those who fought it. "We were, in fact, a lost generation of servicemen," said Phil Vampatella, director of the Vietnam Veterans Leadership Program of Maine. PHOTO COURTESY STEPHEN G. BOOTH

Above: In the 1830s Nathaniel Hawthorne was surprised to hear the sounds of French and Gaelic spoken along the Kennebec River, or as he put it, "on the borders of Yankee-land." As time went on, an increasingly diverse society evolved to include Jews, Italians, Finns, Swedes, Somalis, Armenians, and many more. Among the most recent arrivals have been several thousand refugees from Asia, anxious to become part of the American fabric while preserving what is best in their cultures—including family, religion, and the arts. Here the Cambodian dance troupe, organized in Portland by director Sakhann Duong, rehearses a traditional dance. STAFF PHOTO BY DAVID MACDONALD, COURTESY OF GUY GANNETT PUBLICATIONS

Opposite: The first cases of HIV/AIDS appeared to Maine health care officials in 1982. Soon blood recipients, drug users, and sexually active people with multiple partners were at risk. The gay community was hit the hardest and was first to respond through volunteers, educational pamphlets, and organizations including the AIDS Project. Fair-minded citizens, STD care workers, and the general community rallied. Many editions of *Our Paper* focused on the epidemic, which, though now better understood and somewhat controlled, still rages. COURTESY PRIVATE COLLECTION

224   MAINE: THE WILDER HALF OF NEW ENGLAND

Our Paper

free

A VOICE FOR LESBIANS AND GAY MEN IN MAINE

Vol. 3, No. 4   December, 1985

Cyclist Places in Spenco 500
by Elze

South Portland cyclist and artist Toni Wolf, who was featured in *Our Paper*, June 1985, recently placed third in the Women's Division of the Spenco 500, the world's longest and largest single-stage international bicycling classic. Starting and finishing in Waco, Texas, the Spenco 500 hosted top cyclists from Canada, England, Belgium, Denmark, Ireland and the United States.

Wolf, finishing after 42 hours of nearly-straight cycling, surprised even herself. "This was my first race ever," she stated. "I went into it wondering if I'd finish. There were a lot of big names who dropped out because of the weather conditions. It rained for the first 24-hours."

And finish she did! Placing 41st overall out of approximately 350 men and women, Wolf credited her success to "plugging along". "I didn't give up," she told *Our Paper*.

The course was, apparently, grueling. The top woman finisher, Betsy King, was quoted in the *Waco Tribune-Herald* (November 4, 1985); "This is the hardest thing in the world. It's even harder than the Ironman, and on the Tour de France you at least get to get off and go to bed every night." King continued, "I've ridden with the men over in Europe and it's child's play compared to this."

Wolf's competition was stiff. Susan Notorangelo, who finished second in the Women's Division, was the first place woman finisher in the Race Across America, a ten-day event covering over 3,300 miles. Even more amazing than the fact she'd never raced before, Wolf began the race after everyone else. "We got stuck behind a train on our way to the race," she remembered with exasperation. "I cycled the first 75-miles alone."

Wolf was assisted by her support team — Della Parker, her agent and public relations specialist, and Christopher Igleheart, owner of the Portland Bicycle Exchange. "They were terrific," Toni beamed. "Sleep was not a part of the race and they really kept me going."

Among Wolf's area sponsors were Nappi Distributors, Amaryllis, Alberta's, The Good Egg Cafe, Dock Fore, Portland Bicycle Exchange, Portland Clutch, Deering Memorial Post VFW 6859, Carr Brothers, and Union Station Cafe.

Her future plans? "It would be neat to get a women's team together and do some kind of ride across the country," she states. "But, for right now, I'd like to better the physical level I'm at right now in preparation for future events."

Maine Health Foundation Press Conference
by Skip Brushaber

On Thursday November 14, 1985 the Maine Health Foundation held a press conference at the Sonesta Hotel in Portland. The Maine Health Foundation, founded in 1983, is a non profit fund raising organization. The Foundation was founded to fund activities statewide. Since its inception, the M.H.F. has funded periodical reprintings, pamphlets on AIDS, the Maine AIDS-Line, and educational support to members of the state legislature.

Speaking for the Foundation were board members John Preston, Albert Nickerson, Bert LeClair, and John Holverson. Preston gave the introductory statements. He gave a brief, but moving statement concerning the occurrence of AIDS in Maine.

Nickerson outlined the Maine Health Foundation's long range goals, which are:
1) To provide for the mental and emotional well being of the gay and lesbian community.
2) Elimination of AIDS as a medical threat to the gay and lesbian communities.
3) Elimination of venereal diseases in the gay and lesbian community.
4) Elimination of substance abuse in the gay and lesbian communities.

Nickerson spoke of donations from lesbian and gay owned businesses. Also mentioned were memorial gifts from friends and relatives of AIDS victims. Writers Stephen King, Tabitha King, and May Sarton are among the state celebrities who have given generously.

LeClair outlined some of the needs of the gay and lesbian communities. As a substance abuse counselor, LeClair spoke of his work with gays and lesbians in developing positive self images and support systems. The need exists for counseling of people with AIDS for their friends, relatives, and lovers, he said. The Foundation also hopes to influence the medical community to produce humanistic health treatment.

Holverson concluded by giving information about AIDS as an epidemic, comparing it to the plagues of the Middle Ages and the influenza outbreaks early in this century. He pointed out that it is not a gay disease. Gay men were only the first to be exposed to the virus in this country, he said. Holverson went on to say that the Foundation's purpose is to stop AIDS, provide financial support for the Maine AIDS Line, and to educate the people of Maine about the disease.

The press conference concluded with board members fielding questions from those in attendance.

Photo: P.S. Sutherland

Dr. Michael Bach

AIDS Conference Enlightens Health Professionals
by Fred Berger

On October 23 a very well-organized, highly informative conference on AIDS was held at the Sonesta Hotel in Portland. Sponsored by Metro Medicare and Community Health Services, the event attracted a predominately female audience of nearly two hundred health care and social service workers.

The day-long program opened with a medical overview presented by Dr. Michael Bach, a Maine Medical Center physician who has attended several AIDS patients. Dr. Bach's stated purpose in addressing the conference was to educate health professionals so that they can deal with AIDS in a "sophisticated, rational fashion." He expressed the hope that Maine will be able to avoid the hysteria which has infected other places resulting, for example, in children being denied schooling.

As part of his clinical presentation Dr. Bach described ARC (AIDS Related Complex) as follows: periodic fever lasting more than 3 months; lymphadenopathy (swollen lymph nodes) for longer than 3 months; diarrhea, heavy night sweats, and profound fatigue over a prolonged period of time; weight loss of greater than 10% of body weight; and abnormal results on several specific blood tests. Although it is currently believed that 10% to 20% of people with ARC will develop AIDS, Dr. Bach hypothesized that the number will be closer to 50%.

Dr. Bach presented slides which showed the lesions caused by Kaposi's Sarcoma, as well as slides of thrush, a fungus which can appear on the tongue and mouth of people with AIDS. When thrush appears in the esophagus, he said, it diagnoses AIDS. Comments made by Dr. Bach lead some of us to understand that some of the slides we were viewing were of a recently deceased friend.

The morning session's second speaker was Kristen Kreamer, an Oncology Clinical Nurse Specialist with Community Health Services. Kreamer entitled her speech "Barriers to Health Care in the Community." She discussed the precautions that people working with an AIDS patient must take to protect themselves and also to protect the patient from infections which the health care provider might spread. Among her suggestions was the nurses need to wear rubber gloves when handling blood or other body secretions but not for routine care.

Kreamer also described the care of a person with AIDS in a home setting. She said that a person with AIDS need not have a separate bedroom and can use the same toilet, bathtub and sink as the rest of the household. He or she should have unrestricted contact with household members and unrestricted movement outside the home to restaurants, shops, etc. Kreamer said that a person with AIDS does not require separate tableware unless oral lesions are present. She said a household should maintain routine daily cleaning, using a solution of one part bleach to ten parts water to clean toilets and bathtubs.

Kreamer addressed some of the psychological barriers to proper care of people with AIDS, and suggested that it is the responsibility of supervisory personnel to allow care providers the opportunity to deal openly with their feelings about AIDS. This

continued on page 8

Sockabasin, and Barry Dana. Maine's small black community entered vigorous days with the reformation of the Portland branch of the NAACP in 1964 and the push that included Maine's first black legislator, Gerald Talbot. With H. H. Price, he co-authored *Maine's Visible Black History* (2006). By the new century, a stream of Africans were arriving from that war-torn continent and adding to Maine's black population in larger numbers.

Franco-Americans, the region's largest minority, still remained the "most ethnic" of all groups, in their own eyes and the eyes of their neighbors. So-called French jokes, often quite barbed, were common through the mid-twentieth century and, true or not, the community was thought to lag. In fact, as French-language newspapers failed, more and more children went to public rather than parochial schools and French was spoken less frequently at home and in public. By the 1970s Franco-American college students, some of whom had lost their language, began to rediscover the richness of their heritage. In 2011 Waterville's mayor, Paul LePage, became the first Franco-American elected governor. By then, centers for the study of the culture had appeared and festivals had begun in Lewiston and Biddeford as touchstones to a heritage and a way of sharing with others.

In Van Buren the Acadian Village opened the door on a whole way of life; Portland's Irish Heritage Center in the Old St. Dominic's Church and the Italian Heritage Center did the same. County fairs, such as Fryeburg, Cumberland, and others, brought seasonal crowds, a forum for agriculture, crafts, 4-H, and entertainment. Secular events such as the Yarmouth Clam Festival, Rockland Lobster Festival, Fort Fairfield Potato Blossom Festival, and Common Ground Fair were joined by the upscale Maine Festival, which drew artists and performers. A growing sense of neighborhood, often shaped by deteriorating conditions or crime, expressed itself through events and organizations.

Clashes of values and dreams in the '60s and '70s had a corrosive effect on many citizens, more of whom no longer trusted their government. Indeed, the postwar confidence and belief in a bright future seemed to evaporate as individuals tended to separate into groups with special agendas focused on age, social and economic position, sex, ethnicity, or special needs. At its most raw, the political left increasingly portrayed the right as "fascists," and the right increasingly termed the left "socialist," an adversarial situation that apparently offered little room for civility, discussion, or compromise.

Volunteerism tended to decline in the face of a harsher economy, though that which persisted achieved extraordinary things. In 1988 *Newsweek* picked one remarkable activist from each state. In Maine, energetic eighty-five-year-old Frances W. Peabody was selected for her pioneering work with the AIDS Project but could as well have been chosen for her achievements in historic preservation or with at-risk children at Sweetser-Children's Home. The following year, the magazine chose Herb Adams, a legislator and historian who used his volunteer skills to clean up his Portland neighborhood. In a time of sharply etched differences between the haves and have-nots, and disappearing traditional jobs and housing possibilities, private individuals could still make a difference.

❖

Since World War II, Maine courts have undergone more changes than in any other period with new Rules of Civil Procedure (1959), the creation of District Courts (1961), new rules of Criminal Procedure (1965), new Rules of Evidence (1976), and the placing of the administrative court within the Judicial Department (1978). In 1975 the Criminal Code was substantially revised, as were new rules for Probate Procedure (1981). The supreme court became noted for the quality of its decisions and many thought the judiciary more professional and responsive. Others were skeptical or outright critical, as funding remained parsimonious, caseloads are large, and by the twenty-first century cases were backed up. The now-famous Dennis Dechaine murder conviction may seem right and just to professionals within the system, but to wide numbers of the public there seems to be a lot of explaining necessary, just on a commonsense level. It seems clear that more funding and greater understanding of the system are needed.

Politically, postwar Maine produced a series of leaders who, in terms of stature, intellect, and national clout, rivaled the era of Hamlin, Fessenden, Blaine, and Reed. This came at a time when the state's relative size in the Union was shrinking. In 1820 it was ranked twelfth among twenty-four states and growing, sending seven representatives to the House. In 2011 Maine was rated fortieth out of fifty and sent two representatives to Washington.

The Republican ascendency continued for a decade after the war, with governors Horace Hildreth, Frederick G. Payne, and Burton M. Cross, and all three Congressional districts filled by the GOP. In the Senate the thorny career of former governor Ralph Owen Brewster rolled on from 1940 to 1952. During Senate hearings, industrialist Howard Hughes claimed that Brewster offered to sidetrack the proceedings if Hughes would merge Trans-World Airlines with Pan American. Denying all charges, Brewster dropped his right as a senator to appear as a witness and ended up looking foolish. In 1952 he was beaten in the primary by Frederick G. Payne.

Surer winds carried Lewiston's Wallace H. White, Jr., to the height of power. A grandson of Senator William P. Frye, White served in Congress from 1917 to 1930 and in the Upper Chamber until 1949. From 1944 to 1947 he was minority leader and then majority leader from 1947 to retirement.

Of course White's seat was hotly contested, and Margaret Chase Smith of Skowhegan quickly

On June 1, 1950, Senator Margaret Chase Smith (1897–1995) delivered her courageous "Declaration of Conscience," a statement prepared with six other Republicans decrying the excesses of Senator Joseph McCarthy's communist witch-hunt. Pulling no punches, the Skowhegan native began the process of restoring the nation to sanity. In 1940 she had succeeded her husband, Clyde H. Smith, in the U.S. House of Representatives, where she served four terms. In 1948 she defeated two former governors and began her distinguished career in the Senate. Margaret Smith's name was placed in nomination for the presidency during the 1964 GOP Convention. This portrait by Willard Cummings (1915–1975) graces Maine's State House. COURTESY OF THE MAINE STATE MUSEUM

CHANGING VISIONS 227

demonstrated her political acumen by trouncing three formidable GOP challengers, including former governors Hildreth and Sewall and her Democratic opponent. Senator Smith went on to become one of the most important figures in national decision making. In 1950 she delivered her famous "Declaration of Conscience" speech. Backed by six Republican senators, the declaration boldly confronted the anticommunist witch-hunting tactics of Senator Joseph McCarthy. Smith insisted on the rights of all to criticize, to hold unpopular beliefs, to protest, and to think independently. Returned to office in 1954, 1960, and 1966, Smith became in 1964 the first woman to have her name placed in nomination as president by a major party at a national convention. After her defeat in 1972, primarily because she supported the Vietnam War, she continued to play an active role. The Margaret Chase Smith Library Center in Skowhegan preserves her papers and memorabilia.

Nineteen fifty-four marked the rebirth of the Democratic Party in Maine when Edmund S. Muskie won election to the Blaine House over the incumbent. The alpha figure in the Democratic revival, Muskie was born in Rumford, the proud son of Polish Catholics. After graduation from Bates College and Cornell Law School, he saw service aboard a destroyer during World War II, and soon entered local politics. His common sense and liberal ideas attracted others to the Democrats, who were successful in building a twentieth-century infrastructure in a poor and what may be viewed as a "third world state." Elected to the Senate in 1958, Muskie chaired committees ranging from Legislative Review, Budget, and Foreign Relations, to the subcommittee on Air and Water Pollution.

Seen as the quintessential Yankee, he was chosen majority whip and in 1968 was the party's vice presidential candidate. During the 1972 campaign, his own bid for the presidency failed in the wind and tears of Manchester, New Hampshire.

Senator Edmund S. Muskie (1914–1996), the ideal postwar leader of the Maine Democratic Party revival, was born in Rumford, and after service in World War II entered politics. Elected governor in 1954 and senator in 1958, Muskie led the national environmental movement in Washington, and was his party's vice-presidential candidate and secretary of state under President Jimmy Carter. PHOTO COURTESY STEVE MUSKIE

In 1980 Muskie left the Senate to serve as secretary of state in the harried Carter administration. Few individuals have left such a positive legacy in Maine; his archives at Bates were established in 1985.

Since 1954 there have been five Republicans, five Democrats, and two Independents who have served as governor. Kenneth Curtis, who served from 1966 to 1975, was something of the model Democrat. His administration probably represents the height of his party's effectiveness. Independent James Longley was notable for spending as little as possible, looking good, and after one term letting

228   MAINE: THE WILDER HALF OF NEW ENGLAND

Nelson A. Rockefeller (1909–1979) was born in Bar Harbor and summered at his home in Seal Harbor, Maine. A complex man of many interests, he came to represent the once powerful liberal wing of the GOP, serving fifteen years as governor of New York and challenging Barry Goldwater for the Republican presidential nomination in 1964. This campaign pin is from that unsuccessful bid. Ten years later, "Rocky" was appointed vice president under Gerald Ford. COURTESY HENRY RANNEY, PRESQUE ISLE

the bills come due for Governor Joseph Brennan, who somehow got it done. Republican John McKernan served two terms in Congress before he became governor, and Independent Angus King, known at the time for trying to get laptops into schools, is presently remembered for the deregulation of the electric power industry, which puts the present decade of Mainers in a "not in my back yard" alternative energy conundrum. The two terms of Democrat John Baldacci are really too recent to assess thoroughly. The Republican Paul LePage administration claims that the cupboard is bare, government has been antibusiness, and that workers and citizens are asking too much. In the first sitting of the GOP majority legislature, more vetoes were cast than by any modern governor.

Election to national office continued the tradition of strong personalities who quickly found their way to power. Republican William S. Cohen of Bangor was an independent-minded law school graduate and poet elected to Congress in 1972, just in time to sit in judgment on the Watergate hearings. In 1978, this cool, fair-minded statesman toppled William Hathaway in a bid for the Senate. During the Democratic Clinton administration, Cohen resigned his Senate seat to serve as secretary of defense. Maine's then junior senator, George J. Mitchell of Waterville, son of a laborer and a Lebanese immigrant mother, served as a U.S. district judge and was appointed to fill Muskie's Senate seat in 1980. Elected on his own, the scholarly, well-spoken politician rose rapidly, being chosen majority leader in 1989; he was seen by many as the most respected man in the Senate. The two Maine senators wrote a book together on the Iran-Contra scandal. Mitchell, after retirement, served as the American special envoy for Northern Ireland in 1995–2000, helping to bring about the Belfast Peace Agreement (Good Friday 1998). Later he served the Obama administration in trying to bring about peace in the Middle East.

Olympia J. Snowe and Susan M. Collins, the elected senators from Maine, continue the tradition of strong personalities, independent thinking, and enormous power in Washington. In a time of political bloviation, rather than holding to the party line like commissars of old (and creating what many would argue is adversarial gridlock), the two senators have tended to vote by their own consciences and political calculations.

Olympia Snowe, née Bouchles, was born in Augusta, the daughter of a Greek immigrant father and orphaned at the age of ten. Succeeding her deceased husband Peter Snowe to the U.S. House of Representatives in 1979, she then won a seat in

Republican senator William Cohen (first left) and Democratic senator George Mitchell (second left) sign their book *Men of Zeal* (1988), the story of the Iran–Contra hearings. Both men were major players in national and world events and embodied an era in which political parties and individuals not only cooperated but enjoyed each other's company. COURTESY OF THE *BANGOR DAILY NEWS*

the Senate in 1995 (by this time, she was married to Governor John "Jock" McKernan" and was Maine's first lady) and has served on high-powered committees including Armed Services and Small Businesses and Entrepreneurship. In 2006 *Time Magazine* named her one of America's ten best senators, but in 2012 she decided not to seek reelection due to partisan politics in Congress.

Susan Collins, a native of Caribou, hails from a family that has been in the lumber business since 1844. Each of her parents served as mayor of her hometown. From 1975 to 1987 Collins was assistant to Senator Cohen and involved with the Senate Committee on Homelessness and the Small Business Administration. As a senator she has never missed a vote as of this writing. Collins sits on key committees and is chairwoman on Homeland Security and Governmental Affairs. Both Collins and Snowe tend to be somewhat bipartisan, and some term them RINOs (Republican In Name Only). Though they voted to confirm conservative U.S. Supreme Court candidates, Collins voted to acquit President Clinton during his impeachment trial. In 2005 their party labeled them part of "the Gang of Fourteen" for obstructionism, an ironic comparison based on conservative elements who failed to toe the Chinese Communist Party line in 1976.

Born in Augusta, Olympia Snowe succeeded her husband Peter to the House of Representatives in 1979 and has proudly served the State of Maine in the Senate since 1995. Snowe has been on powerful committees including Armed Services and Small Business and Entrepreneurship. Here, she visits with Maine soldiers Sergeant Eric Walker, Sergeant Seth Cote, Sergeant DeAngelo, and Private First Class Michael Stevens near Taji, Iraq, in 2007. COURTESY OF THE OFFICE OF SENATOR OLYMPIA SNOWE

Senator Susan Collins was born in Caribou and graduated from St. Lawrence University in New York. She worked on the staff of Senator William S. Cohen and held a number of government posts. In 1994 and 2002 Collins was elected to the U.S. Senate, where she became known for her outspokenness on behalf of the elderly, and worked on the Committee of Homeland Security and Governmental Affairs. COURTESY OF THE OFFICE OF SENATOR SUSAN COLLINS

CHANGING VISIONS   231

Government grew to dramatic proportions with tax-based operations reaching directly or indirectly into many aspects of life. In 1957 Harold B. Clifford included a chapter titled "Big Government" in his book, *Maine and Her People,* but what he describes seems meager in the early twenty-first century. During the 1960s and '70s the Great Society and the War on Poverty brought sweeping federal reforms to a local level, meeting some needs well and others badly. Professionalism permeated but volunteerism became more and more necessary. As traditional mental health institutions were examined and condemned, community health centers and halfway houses replaced them but never got adequate funding. Instead of the "Welfare Society" dreamed of or warned against after the war, an underfunded, badly managed patchwork resulted. The number of workers in the trenches could not keep up with caseloads, and much of the funding appeared to go to the top of the structure.

❖

As soon as the peace was won in 1945, the shipyards in South Portland laid off 30,000 workers, condemning the area to twenty years of hard economic times. The army forts were all abandoned soon after and, with the exception of Kittery, which launched nuclear submarines until 1971, and the Brunswick Naval Air Station, most of the navy departed. In 2011 the last navy presence at the Brunswick airbase left, including the commissary. Only the submarine repair base at Kittery and Coast Guard facilities remained. Saco Defense, Inc., claimed to be the "Free World's premier manufacturer of machine guns."

Shipbuilding experienced dark days in the '40s, but Bath Iron Works, Inc., dipped into its wartime cash reserve to keep a pool of skilled workers employed. The wisdom of this move became apparent in 1950 when the Korean War brought new government demands for ships and new contracts to BIW. Changes in naval policy, the move from local control to large corporations, and disagreements with unions have colored subsequent years. Still, as Ralph Linwood Snow states in *Bath Iron Works: The First Hundred Years* (1987), the company, its thousands of workers, and its reputation for on-time, under-budget vessels remains a bright spot in the state's sparse industrial economy. Similarly, the Portsmouth Naval Shipyard in Kittery was sparked by the Cold War. In 1955 the yard began to overhaul and build nuclear submarines. USS *Swordfish*, its first nuclear submarine, was launched in 1957. USS *Sea Dragon* first realized the dream of a northwest passage under the ice from the Atlantic to the Pacific Ocean. In 1963 tragedy struck off the east coast when the USS *Thresher* sank during sea trials carrying 122 men to their death.

Young women, with fewer opportunities at home, joined all branches of the military, particularly after 9/11. In 2011 it was reported that Maine, of all the states, suffered the largest percentage of casualties in Afghanistan.

The fishing industry has remained viable but with strange fluctuations. Equipment has improved since the '40s, both in methods of catching fish and in safety. Still, this is a remarkably hazardous business dependent on international and local markets. Issues include over-fishing and arguments over territory—between the United States and Canada, earlier with international fishing vessels, and inshore between different claimants. Along the shore, traditional working fishermen at the turn of the twenty-first century found fewer places to tie up as condo owners and well-to-do newcomers looked for attractive shore property. Regulations including limits and set times had pitted the industry against government in the opinion of many. In 2010, for the first time in recorded history, Maine citizens were required to purchase recreational fishing licenses for saltwater fishing.

Traditional industries in small towns began to

Even with modern navigational equipment and the presence of the Coast Guard, Maine fishermen and mariners still found themselves at the mercy of nature. On December 5, 1972, the fishing vessel *Alton A* grounded on the rocks at Cape Elizabeth. A 44-foot Coast Guard motor lifeboat rushed to assist, but it was also trapped as the weather worsened. The crews of both boats were assisted from shore and escaped hand-over-hand along a hawser, but efforts to save the vessels failed. COLLECTION OF THE MAINE HISTORICAL SOCIETY

Ray Verrier (1928-2011) of Biddeford operates a Morgan Nailer at the Biddeford Box Company in 1948–49. The machine was used to assemble crates for textile machinery shipped overseas. Skilled blue-collar jobs were a mainstay of the economy, but as the decades wore on a growing number of machine shops and woodworking operations went out of business. Verrier worked at Biddeford Box for a quarter of a century only to find the doors locked one day. COURTESY JANET CYR VERRIER COLLECTION

CHANGING VISIONS

Painters continue to find Maine a source of inspiration and power. Daniel James Barry's oil *Merrill's Wharf from Union Wharf* (2009) seems a timeless waterfront vision, with lobster boats, traps, and gear, and old warehouses. However, covertly parked vehicles likely suggest tension between traditional and hardscrabble fishermen and real estate interests bent on rehabbing empty or underutilized buildings for retirees seeking the amenities or businesses looking for a pretty view. Barry began his career in Maine as an architect. COURTESY KAY L. WILSON

Textile mills of all sizes, which had utilized Maine's streams since the nineteenth century, began to disappear after World War II. The Hughes Woolen Mill, built on the site of an old gunpowder mill, was one of five operations clustered along Camden's Megunticook River. It ceased production in 1952 and the building was turned into the Penobscot Poultry Company's chicken hatchery. The structure burned in 1964 and is now the site of a trailer park. COLLECTION OF JOHN J., PAULA, AND PATRICK MCAULIFFE

unravel in 1945 as cheap, unregulated labor and new state-of-the-art factories in other places made competition difficult if not impossible. First, most of the cotton and woolen mills folded or downsized, leaving magnificent brick complexes along the rivers of Lewiston, Biddeford, Brunswick, and elsewhere to be vandalized or condo-ized after cleanup. Smaller towns fared worse with the withdrawal of capital. Foreign competition later brutalized the once mighty Maine shoe industry, leaving the companies to sell out or go overseas. Even South Portland's General Electric moved on.

Hannaford Brothers supermarkets began as a farm stand in Cape Elizabeth, expanded, and absorbed the competition until it was taken over by Belgian Delhaize Group in 2000. Union Mutual

Insurance Company became UNUM, reporting 2.7 billion dollars in assets by the '80s, and L.L. Bean, Inc., which began in 1912 with its famous "Hunting Shoe," was, in its 100th year, a multi-billion-dollar international outdoor retail giant and one of Maine's largest employers. Bar Harbor's nonprofit Jackson Laboratories is world famous for its work in biomedical cancer research; Dr. George D. Snell of that organization shared a Nobel Prize in Medicine in 1980. Other re-imaged businesses such as Backyard Farms, with its hydroponically grown tomatoes, have captured important parts of the regional market share.

Old-style agriculture suffered. The potato, once a symbol of Aroostook County, if not Maine itself, sold well into the 1960s but has suffered from both competition and changes in American foodways. Harvested crop and pasture land declined by nearly 70 percent between 1950 and 1990. The poultry business boomed in the '50s and '60s, then vanished like drive-in movies and open dumps. Development, real estate, and financing expanded noticeably from the 1970s through the '90s and then got caught in the so-called Great Recession, during which each political party blamed the other for the thinning and possible destruction of the postwar middle class. A read through the local newspapers shows a focus on young overnight developers and investors who made fortunes. Indeed, they became as notable in their day as Brigadier Waldo or General Knox. This became intertwined with historic preservation, architectural literacy, an understanding of the environment, and sometimes a clash between the haves and the have-nots. Rents and wages failed to keep pace with the cost of living and land values. Given Maine's vast size and small population, the tax dollar had to stretch far to maintain roads, education, and social services, let alone "the amenities" demanded by new citizens.

In 1994 the *Maine Sunday Telegram* wrote of a man who bought a 150-acre saltwater farm in 1947 for $1,800. By 1990 it was appraised at $1.2 million, saddling his heirs with impossible taxes. In order to pass the land on, he granted a conservation easement to the Department of Fisheries and Wildlife. This protected the land forever and lowered the property value. For many on fixed incomes, rising property taxes made living in Maine difficult if not impossible in their later years. By taking property off the tax rolls, the environment was saved for the future, but the local or town coffers were reduced.

Forest covers some 90 percent of the state so it is no surprise that paper manufacturing, lumber and wood supplies, furniture manufacturing, and forestry services made up the largest export group during the late twentieth century. Work in the woods meant employment for local people with large companies or as jobbers. Chainsaws, skidders, mechanical loaders, and bulldozers continued to revolutionize this dangerous occupation. The public tended to see the industry as vital to the economy and relied on it to maintain roads and assist in prevention of fires. Only on rare occasions such as the Great Fires of 1947, when nine towns were burned and fifteen citizens were killed, did the forest intrude on civilians.

In the 1960s environmental awareness caused attitudinal changes, and in 1973 the Bureau of Public Lands was activated. In the next few years, journalist Bob Cummings wrote a series of excellent articles for the *Kennebec Journal* and *Maine Sunday Telegram*, while William C. Osborn, a member of the Ralph Nader Study Group, wrote *The Paper Plantation* (1974), a highly critical view of the industry. It was pointed out that much of the land used for cutting was on set-offs of 4,000 acres per township, leased decades earlier for timber and grass rights and treated as private property. "Corporate socialism," some claimed, and so began a series of land swaps and the return of land to the public. The last river drive occurred in 1975. The last decade of the twentieth century had six paper

In 1999 Maine union workers joined to protest the dramatic loss of local manufacturing jobs in Waterville, Milo, Lewiston, and elsewhere as a result of free-trade policies and a perceived attitudinal change by politicians in Augusta and Washington. COURTESY CHARLES SCONTRAS AND THE *MAINE LABOR NEWS*

companies owning 6,134 acres and large corporations buying up slightly smaller companies. The strike at the International Paper Mill in Jay (1997–1998) was bitter, and saw the smashing of the union and the hiring of a new workforce.

Early in this present century, foreign competition, decreased quality and demand, and the NAFTA treaty led to the closing of paper operations in Millinocket and elsewhere. The decline of the pulp and paper industry is a complex story involving international buyouts, bottom-line economics, re-tooling, competition, environmental advancements, and the gradual success of Maine labor laws protecting workers' health, safety, job security, and wages up to the Longley and McKernan administrations. By the last decade of the twentieth century, 11 percent of Maine was foreign owned, mostly by Canadians. This was the largest percentage of any state. A campaign was started to buy back land for the public, and as of this writing great tracts are also being purchased by wealthy entrepreneurs, some liberal and others conservative, whatever that means in 2012. Some wish to develop the North Woods, others hope to create a huge national park. Generally, this runs afoul of hunters, fishermen, loggers, all-terrain

CHANGING VISIONS

riders, and snowmobilers, who believe their rights are under assault.

❖

In the 1970s Native American tribes in Maine became involved in the Civil Rights movement that swept the continent. The famous Maine Indian Land Claims Settlement Act of 1980 captured the nation's attention and brought history full circle. Ignored since the end of the Revolution, those remaining on state reservations—Indian Township (Motahkomikuk) near Princeton, Pleasant Point (Sipayik) near Perry, and Indian Island near Old Town—tended to live a hard life in order to maintain their culture. Many existed on welfare with few educational or economic opportunities. A 1964 dispute over whites cutting timber on Indian land led to the courts and the finding that Maine and Massachusetts had violated federal law and had been illegally disposing of Indian land since the 1790s. The federal government took over the case and eventually provided $54.41 million to purchase 300,000 acres and set up a $27 million trust fund for the Passamaquoddy and Penobscots. Later, the Houlton Band of Maliseets was recognized, while other groups including the Aroostook Band of Micmacs sought recognition. For the first time in centuries, 5,000 Native Americans in Maine gained notice, some land, and a chance for the future. But at the dawn of the twenty-first century, the progress of this change and relationship with the state was not all sweetness.

❖

On the national stage, Maine came closer than ever to claiming a president when lifelong summer resident George Herbert Walker Bush of Walker's Point, Kennebunkport, was elected as a Republican to the Oval Office in 1989. (He was actually the second postwar vice president with down-east ties. In 1974 President Gerald Ford had appointed Nelson A. Rockefeller, born in Bar Harbor, his vice

On October 10, 1980, President Jimmy Carter signed the celebrated Maine Indian Land Claims Settlement Act. Achieved after a long legal campaign, the Native American tribes gave up claims to millions of acres in exchange for $54.41 million to buy land and a $27 million trust fund established for the Passamaquoddy and Penobscots. The federal government also recognized the Houlton Band of Maliseets and provided money to purchase land. Watching the signing are, left to right, Maine's Governor Joseph E. Brennan, U.S. Secretary of State Edmund S. Muskie, Secretary of the Interior Cecil Andrus, Maine Senator George Mitchell, and tribal representative Terrance Polchies. AP Photo/Barry Thumma

president.) Though Bush had been born in Massachusetts, he spent years on the seaside estate developed by his grandparents. During his presidency the compound became the focus of world attention with such guests as the president of France and the prime minister of Canada. His administration saw the collapse of the Communist Bloc and the success of Operation Desert Storm, which drove Iraqi armed forces out of Kuwait. His son, George W. Bush, also a Republican, won the first two presidential terms of the new century, but spent relatively little time in Kennebunkport. This was the era of 9/11, foreign terrorism, and long wars in Afghanistan and Iraq, conflicts that continue under his successor, President Barack Obama, a Democrat.

President Obama, the nation's first African-American president, reflected a growing change in the pattern of Maine people as well. Blacks, free and enslaved, in small numbers, have been integral to Maine's population since the 1600s. Shortly thereafter Azoreans, Irish, Scots, French, and Portuguese joined the mix. By the 1870s nearly every European nation was represented, and by the end of the twentieth century foreign conflicts and trade had brought newcomers from Vietnam,

Not all of the "First People" in Maine live on tribal land. John Wilson, born in Skowhegan, is a proud Passamaquoddy. In 1972, at the age of sixteen, he came to Maine's largest city, where he finished his education and, with the help of friends, found lodgings and has been employed in the city ever since. An avid reader, collector, and history buff, Mr. Wilson retains tribal affiliations and close family ties, but has made his life in the larger Portland community. PHOTO COURTESY STEPHEN G. BOOTH

On January 20, 1990, George Herbert Walker Bush (born 1924) was inaugurated as the forty-first president of the United States. A lifelong summer resident of Walker's Point in Kennebunkport, the new president and his wife Barbara continued to make frequent visits to Maine, where they received notable guests such as the president of France and the prime minister of Canada. Their son, George W. Bush (born 1946) served as president 2001–2009. PHOTO COURTESY OF THE WHITE HOUSE, DAVID VALDEZ, PHOTOGRAPHER

CHANGING VISIONS 239

Arleigh Burke destroyers, first commissioned as part of President Ronald Reagan's massive 600-ship navy, kept Bath Iron Works shipyards busy beyond the Cold War into the Gulf War, 9/11, and its aftermath. The workhorse of the surface fleet, the Burke-class vessels remain, in the words of Rear Admiral Michael K. Mahon, "the envy of the world." They have also drawn protest from local and national peace movements. PHOTOGRAPH COURTESY GENERAL DYNAMICS/BATH IRON WORKS

Bangor International Airport is a major point of arrival for overseas visitors, and witnessed the regular appearance of the supersonic Concorde (Franco-British) until that class was retired in 2003. After the 9/11 terrorist attacks, the airport became famous for enthusiastic greeters meeting returning service men and women at the gates. COURTESY BANGOR INTERNATIONAL AIRPORT, AIRPORT MANAGER'S OFFICE

Cambodia, Somalia, Central America, and Russia in some number. As in the last century, when Italian and French-Canadian food began to change foodways and ideas, Mainers, now the oldest population in the country, gradually altered their perceptions and expectations. Some, especially those looking for jobs and status, were threatened by the army of immigrants. Others saw a new secure tax base and a more progressive future for Maine.

❖

For the Maine community at large, the last decade has been characterized by asking hard questions and reexamining values and goals that seemed obvious in the postwar era and less so in the last of the twentieth century. The can-do, we-can-solve-every-economic-medical-military-and-social-problem-that-comes-up attitude seems naïve in 2012, yet so much has been accomplished that returning to a time before the two Roosevelt presidents—to the era of robber barons, company money, state troopers as union busters, and no social safety network—seems suicidal. The two major political parties seem deadlocked, unable or unwilling to seek reasonable compromise. The real fear can be measured by letters to the editor, blogs, and personal discussion. It is a time of obscurantism wrapped in too much so-called information.

It is important to be involved and concerned, and yet, in the long march of history, Maine has fostered and abandoned slavery, we have overthrown monarchy with our fellow inhabitants and replaced it with an increasingly representative republic which came to include non-landowners, people of color, women, and, while some may

Probably the most remarkable change to the religious pattern of Maine has been the growth of the Muslim population. At the start of the twentieth century a handful of skilled Albanian textile dyers practiced Islam in Biddeford. According to human rights activist Reza Jalali, there are now some 5,000 Muslims in Maine, hailing from the Sudan, Somalia, Iran, Afghanistan, Iraq, India, Bangladesh, Turkey, Morocco, the Balkans, Indonesia—indeed, from all over the world. Here, the self-described "foot soldier" for immigrant youth, Pious Ali, a native of Ghana who grew up in Nigeria, speaks to a class of Maine schoolchildren.
PHOTOGRAPH COURTESY OF PIOUS ALI

protest, prisoners. Awkwardly, Maine Today Media, publisher of a number of local newspapers, argued that readers and businesses should support local publications, yet outsourced its circulation customer services to Honduras.

Deregulation and the not-in-my-backyard syndrome, not to mention the very real dangers of nuclear power, have been clearly demonstrated in the U.S. and Japan. We have a governor telling the Maine branch of the National Association for the Advancement for Colored People to "Kiss my butt" and our best-known writer calling the governor a "Stone Brain." But we do not have massive fistfights the floor of the Maine Senate, or General Chamberlain and a Gatling gun on the steps of the State House. The state is not occupied by British troops as it was in 1815. Without a federal government we might never have gotten the territory beyond the Penobscot back.

In this state on the extreme borders of New England and New France, a pluralistic society has developed. The term Yankee itself, once applied in derision to English immigrants, has come to be proudly worn by a variety of individuals from innumerable backgrounds. That in itself is a triumph. Maine is the largest in territory, the first settled, the least settled, and in many ways the most independent-minded of the New England states. Its citizens of all races have never ceased to speak what they believe is the truth.

BIBLIOGRAPHY

A

Adams, John. *Diary and Autobiography of John Adams*. Edited by L. H. Butterfield. 4 vols. Cambridge, MA: Belknap Press of Harvard University Press, 1961.

Agger, Lee. *Women of Maine*. Portland, ME: Guy Gannett Publishing Co., 1982.

Ahlin, John Howard. *Maine Rubicon: Downeast Settlers During the American Revolution*. Calais, ME: Calais Advertiser Press, 1966.

Albion, Robert Greenhalgh. *Forest and Sea Power, 1652–1862: The Timber Problem of the Royal Navy*. Cambridge, MA: Harvard University Press, 1926.

Albion, Robert G., William A. Baker, and Benjamin W. Labaree. *New England and the Sea*. Middletown, CT: Wesleyan University Press for the Marine Historical Association, Inc., Mystic Seaport, 1972.

Anderson, Hayden L. V. *Canals and Inland Waterways of Maine*. Portland, ME: Maine Historical Society, 1982.

Anderson, Patricia McGraw, and William D. Barry. *Deering: A Social and Architectural History*. Edited by Susan L. Ransom and Margaret W. Soule. Portland, ME: Greater Portland Landmarks, 2010.

Anderson, Patricia McGraw, and Josephine H. Detmer. *Portland*. Edited by Martin Dibner. Portland, ME: Greater Portland Landmarks, 1986. Updated version of the 1972 classic.

Anderson, Will. *Good Old Maine: 101 Past & Present Pop Delights*. Portland, ME: Will Anderson, 1993.

———. *You Auto See Maine: When Cars Were Young and For Sale in Maine*. Bath, ME: Anderson & Sons, 1999.

Attwood, Stanley Bearce. *The Length and Breadth of Maine*. Augusta, ME: Kennebec Journal Print Shop, 1946.

Austin, Phyllis. *Wilderness Partners: Buzz Caverly and Baxter State Park*. Gardiner, ME: Tilbury House, Publishers, 2008.

B

Baker, Emerson W. *The Devil of Great Island: Witchcraft and Conflicts in Early New England*. New York: Palgrave MacMillan, 2007.

Baker, Emerson W., Edwin A. Churchill, Richard D'Abate, Kristina L. Jones, Victoria Konrad, and Harald E. L. Prins. *American Beginnings: Exploration, Culture, and Cartography in the Land of Norumbega*. Lincoln, NE: University of Nebraska Press, 1994.

Baker, Emerson W., and John G. Reid. *The New England Knight: Sir William Phips, 1651–1695*. Toronto: University of Toronto Press, 1998.

Baker, Madge. *Woven Together in York County, Maine: A History, 1865–1990*. Shapleigh, ME: Wilson's Printers, 1999.

Baker, William Avery. *Maine Shipbuilding: A Bibliographical Guide*. Portland, ME: Maine

Historical Society, 1972.

———. *A Maritime History of Bath, Maine, and the Kennebec River Region*. 2 vols. Bath, ME: Marine Research Society of Bath, 1973.

Bangor Public Library. *Bibliography of the State of Maine*. Boston: G. K. Hall & Co., 1962.

Banks, Charles Edward. *History of York, Maine*. Boston, MA: Calkins Press, vol. 1, 1931, vol. 2, 1935.

Banks, Ronald F., ed. *A History of Maine: A Collection of Readings on the History of Maine*. Dubuque, IA: Kendall/Hunt Publishing Co., 1969.

———. *Maine Becomes a State: The Movement to Separate Maine from Massachusetts, 1785–1820*. Somersworth, NH: New Hampshire Publishing Co. (for the Maine Historical Society), 1973.

———, comp. *Maine During the Federal and Jeffersonian Period: A Bibliographical Guide*. Portland, ME: Maine Historical Society, 1974.

Barringer, Richard, ed. *Changing Maine: 1960–2010*. Gardiner, ME: Tilbury House, Publishers, with the Muskie School of Public Service, University of Southern Maine, 2004.

Barrows, John Stuart. *Fryeburg, Maine: An Historical Sketch*. Fryeburg. ME: Pequawket Press, 1938.

Barry, William David. *AIDS Project: A History*. Edited by Susan Cummings-Lawrence. Portland: The AIDS Project, 1997.

———. *The History of Sweetser-Children's Home: A Century and a Half of Service to Maine Children*. Portland, ME: Anthoensen Press, 1988.

———. *A Vignetted History of Portland Business, 1632–1982*. Princeton, NJ: The Newcomen Society, 1982.

Barry, William David, and Patricia McGraw Anderson. *Deering: A Social and Architectural History*. Portland, ME: Greater Portland Landmarks, 2010.

Barry, William David, and Gael May McKibben. *Women Pioneers in Maine Art*. Portland, ME: Joan Whitney Payson Gallery of Art, Westbrook College, vol. 1, 1981, vol. 2, 1985.

Barry, William David, with Frances W. Peabody. *Tate House: Crown of the Maine Mast Trade*. Portland, ME: National Society of Colonial Dames of American in the State of Maine, 1982.

Beard, Frank A. *Two Hundred Years of Maine Housing: A Guide for the House Watcher*. Augusta, ME: Maine Historic Preservation Commission, 1981.

Beard, Frank A., Bette A. Smith, et al. *Maine's Historic Places*, Camden, ME: Down East Books, 1982.

Beedy, Helen Coffin. *Mothers of Maine*. Portland, ME: Thurston Print, 1985.

Beem, Edgar Allen. *Backyard Maine: Local Essays*. Gardiner, ME: Tilbury House, Publishers, 2009.

———. *Maine Art Now*. Preface by Arthur Danto. Gardiner, ME: Dog Ear Press, 1980.

Bibber, Joyce K. *A Home for Everyman: The Greek Revival and Maine Domestic Architecture*. Portland, ME: American Association for State and Local History Library and Greater Portland Landmarks, 1989.

Boardman, Samuel Lane, comp. *Agricultural Bibliography of Maine*. Augusta, ME: Samuel Boardman, 1893.

———, ed. *Peter Edes: Pioneer Printer in Maine*. Bangor, ME: printed for the DeBurians, 1901.

Bourque, Bruce J. *Twelve Thousand Years: American Indians in Maine*, with contributions by Steve L. Cox and Ruth H. Whitehead. Lincoln NE: University of Nebraska Press, 2001.

Bradley, Robert L. *The Forts of Maine, 1607–1945: An Archaeological and Historical Survey*. Augusta, ME: Maine Historic Preservation Commission, 1981.

Branin, M. Lelyn. *The Early Potters and Potteries*

of Maine. Augusta, ME: Maine State Museum, 1978.

Bridge, Horatio. *Personal Recollections of Nathaniel Hawthorne.* New York: Harper & Brother, 1893.

Bryant H. W. *A Check List of Maine Town Histories for the Use of Librarians and Collectors.* Portland, ME: private printing, 1904.

Bunting, W. H. *A Day's Work: A Sample of Historic Maine Photographs, 1860–1920.* Gardiner, ME: Tilbury House, Publishers, vol. I, 1997, vol. II, 2000.

———. *Live Yankees: The Sewalls and Their Ships.* Gardiner and Bath, ME: Tilbury House, Publishers, and Maine Maritime Museum, 2009.

Burrage, Henry S. *The Beginnings of Colonial Maine, 1602–1658.* Portland, ME: Marks Printing House for the State, 1914.

———. *Maine in the Northeastern Boundary Controversy.* Portland, ME: Marks Printing House, 1919.

Burrage, Henry S., and George Folsom. *John A. Poor and a Century of Historical Research with Reference to Early Colonial Maine.* State of Maine, 1926.

Butcher, Sally K. *Creative Survival: A Narrative History of Azel Adams of The Forks, Maine.* Brunswick, ME; Old Bess Publishing Co., 1991.

Butler, Joyce. *Wildfire Loose: The Week Maine Burned.* Kennebunkport, ME: Durrell Publications, 1978.

Byrne, Frank Loyola. *Prophet of Prohibition: Neal Dow and His Crusade.* Madison, WI: State Historical Society of Wisconsin for the Department of History, University of Wisconsin, 1961.

C

Calloway, Colin G., ed. *Dawnland Encounters: Indians and Europeans in Northern New England.* Hanover, NH, and London: University Press of New England, 1991.

Careless, J. M. S. *Canada: A Story of Challenge.* Toronto: Macmillian of Canada, 1965.

Cassidy, Donna M. *Marsden Hartley: Race, Religion, and Nation.* Hanover, NH: University Press of New England, 2005.

Chadbourne, Ava H. *A History of Education in Maine.* Orono, ME: University of Maine Press, 1936.

Chadbourne, Walter W. *A History of Banking in Maine, 1799–1830.* Orono, ME: University of Maine Press, 1936.

Chamberlain, Joshua L. "*Maine: Her Place in History*" *Address Delivered at the Centennial Exhibition, Philadelphia, November, 4, 1876.* Augusta, ME: Sprague, Owen & Nash, Printers to the State, 1877.

Chappelle, Howard I. *The History of American Sailing Ships.* New York: W. W. Norton Co., 1935.

Chase, Dollie M. The girl problem: social conditions in Portland, Maine, during World War II. Thesis, University of Southern Maine, 1994.

Chase, Edward E. *Maine Railroads: A History of the Development of the Maine Railroad System.* Portland, ME: A. J. Huston, c. 1926.

Chase, George Davis. *Sea Terms Come Ashore.* Orono, ME: University of Maine Press, 1942.

Chase, Mary Ellen. *Jonathan Fisher: Maine Parson, 1768–1847.* New York: Macmillian Co., 1948.

Clark, Calvin Montague. *History of the Congregational Churches in Maine.* 2 vols. Portland, ME: Southworth Press, 1926.

Clark, Charles E. *The Eastern Frontier: The Settlement of Northern New England, 1610–1763.* New York: Alfred A. Knopf, 1970.

———. *Maine: A Bicentennial History.* New York: W. W. Norton & Co., Inc., for the American Association for State and Local History, 1977.

———. *Maine During the Colonial Period: A Bib-*

liographical Guide. Portland, ME: Maine Historical Society, 1974.

Clark, Charles E., James Leamon, and Karen Bowden. *Maine in the Early Republic from Revolution to Statehood*. Hanover, NH: University Press of New England for the Maine Historical Society and the Maine Humanities Council, 1988.

Clark, John G., ed. *The Frontier Challenge: Response to the Trans-Mississippi West*. Lawrence, KS: University of Kansas Press, 1971.

Cleveland, Nehemiah, and Alpheus Spring Packard, Sr. *History of Bowdoin College with Biographical Sketches of Its Graduates*. Boston: James Ripley Osgood & Co., 1882.

Clifford, Harold B. *Maine and Her People*. Freeport, ME: Bond Wheelwright Co., 1957.

Clifford, Philip G. *Nathan Clifford: Democrat*. New York: G. P. Putnam's Sons, 1922.

Coburn, Abner. *Message of Governor Coburn to the Legislature of the State of Maine, January 8, 1863*. Augusta, ME: Stevens & Sayward, Printers to the State, 1863.

Coburn, Louise Helen, et al. *Skowhegan on the Kennebec*. 2 vols. Skowhegan, ME: Independent-Reporter Press, 1941.

Cohen, Michael. Jerusalem of the north: an analysis of religious modernization in Portland Maine's Jewish community, 1860–1950. Thesis, Brown University, 2000.

Colcord, Joanna Carver. *Sea Language Comes Ashore*. New York: Cornell Maritime Press, 1945.

Cole, Franklin, ed. *Nathan A. Cushman, Rugged Individualist: Memoirs of His Sons, Richard, Harold, and Kenneth*. Portland, ME: Casco Printing, 1984.

Conforti, Joseph A. *Imagining New England: Explorations of Regional Identity from Pilgrims to the Mid-Twentieth Century*. Chapel Hill, NC: University of North Carolina Press. 2001.

———, ed. *Creating Portland: History and Place in Northern New England*. Durham, NH: University Press of New England for the University of New Hampshire Press, 2005.

Conner, Selden. *Address of Governor Connor to the Legislature of the State of Maine, January 6, 1876*, Augusta, ME: Sprague, Owen, & Nash, Printers to the State, 1876.

Connolly, Michael C. *Seated by the Sea: The Maritime History of Portland, Maine, and Its Irish Longshoremen*. Gainesville FL: University of Florida Press, 2010.

———, ed. *They Changed Their Sky: The Irish in Maine*. Orono, ME: University of Maine Press, 2004

Cony, Samuel. *Address of Governor Cony to the Legislature of the State of Maine, January 7, 1864*. Augusta, ME: Stevens & Sayward, Printers to the State, 1864.

Coolidge, Philip T. *History of the Maine Woods*. Bangor ME: Furbush–Roberts Printing Co., 1963.

Craig, Béatrice, and Maxime Dagenais, with the collaboration of Lisa Ornstein and Guy Dubay. *The Land In Between: The Upper St. John Valley from Prehistory to World War One*. Gardiner, Madawaska, and Bar Harbor, ME: Tilbury House, Publishers, Maine Acadian Heritage Council, Acadia National Park and St. Croix Island International Historic Site, 2009.

D

Davis, Harold A. *An International Community on the St. Croix, 1604–1930*. Orono, ME: University of Maine Press, 1950.

Davis, Walter Goodwin. *The Ancestry of Nicholas Davis, 1753–1832, of Limington, Maine*. Portland, ME: Anthoensen Press, 1956.

Day, Clarence Albert. *Ezekiel Holmes: Father of Maine Agriculture*. Orono, ME: University of Maine Press, 1968.

———. *Farming in Maine, 1860–1940*. Orono,

ME: University of Maine Press, 1968.

———. *A History of Maine Agriculture, 1604–1860*. Orono, ME: University of Maine Press, 1954.

Dean, Nicholas. *Snow Squall: The Last American Clipper Ship*. With an expedition account by David C. Switzer. Gardiner and Bath, ME: Tilbury House, Publishers, and Maine Maritime Museum, 2001.

de Champlain, Samuel. *Les Voyages du Sieur Champlain*. Paris: Chez Jean Berjon, 1613.

Dejardin, Thomas A. *Stand Firm Ye Boys from Maine: The 20th Maine and the Gettysburg Campaign*. Gettysburg, PA: Thomas Publications, 1995.

Demeritt, Dwight B. *Maine Made Guns and Their Makers*. Augusta, ME: Friends of the Maine State Museum, 1997.

de Paoli, Neill. Life on the edge: community and trade on the Anglo American periphery Pemaquid, Maine, 1610–1689. Thesis, University of New Hampshire, 2001.

de Tocqueville, Alexis. *Democracy in America*. 2 vols. Cambridge, MA: Sever & Francis, 1864.

DeWolfe, Elizabeth. *The Murder of Mary Bean and Other Stories*. Kent, OH: Kent State University Press, 2007.

Dicky, Dallas C. *Seargent S. Prentiss: Whig Orator of the Old South*. Baton Rouge: Louisiana State University Press, 1945.

Dictionary of American Biography, 20 vols. New York: Charles Scribner's Sons, 1928-1936.

Dillon, Merton L. *Elijah P. Lovejoy: Abolitionist Editor*. Urbana, IL: University of Illinois, 1961.

Dodge, Marshall, and Robert Bryan. *Bert and I and Other Stories from Down East*. Ipswich, MA: Bert and I Books, 1981.

Dominic, Randolph P. "Down from the Balcony: The Abyssinian Congregational Church of Portland, Maine." Durham, NH: University of New Hampshire, 1982. (Typescript, copy at Maine Historical Society.)

Donaldson, Scott. *Edwin Arlington Robinson: A Poet's Life*. New York: Columbia University Press, 2007.

Dow, Neal. *The Reminiscences of Neal Dow: Recollections of Eighty Years*. Portland, ME: Evening Express Publishing, 1898.

Drake, Samuel Adams. *Nooks and Corners of the New England Coasts*. New York: Harper and Brothers, 1875.

E

Eastman, Joel W. *Harbor Forts: A Look Behind the Wall, 1775–1945*. Portland, ME: Portland Harbor Museum, 2006.

Eaton, Cyrus. *Annals of the Town of Warren in Knox County, Maine*. Hallowell, ME: Masters & Livermore, 1877.

———. *History of Thomaston, Rockland, and South Thomaston*. Hallowell, ME: Masters Smith & Co., 1865.

Eckstorm, Fannie Hardy. *Indian Place Names of the Penobscot Valley and the Maine Coast*. Orono, ME: University of Maine Press, 1941.

———. *Old John Neptune and Other Maine Indian Shamans*. Portland, ME: Southworth–Anthoensen Press, 1945.

———. *The Penobscot Man*. Bangor, ME: printed for the author, 1924.

Edwards, George Thornton. *Music and Musicians of Maine*. Portland, ME: Southworth Press, 1928.

Elwell, Edward H. *Portland and Vicinity*. Portland, ME: W. S. Jones and Loring, Short & Harmon, 1876.

Ernst, George. *New England Miniature: A History of York, Maine*. Freeport, ME: Bond Wheelwright Co., 1961.

F

Fairfield, Roy P. *Sands, Spindles and Steeples*. Portland, ME: House of Falmouth, 1956.

Fassett, Frederick Gardiner, Jr. *A History of Newspapers in the District of Maine, 1785–1820*.

Orono, ME: University of Maine Press, 1932.

Fairchild, Byron. *Messrs. William Pepperrell: Merchants at Piscataqua*. Ithaca, NY: Cornell University Press for the American Historical Association, 1954.

Faulkner, Alaric, and Gretchen Faulkner. *The French at Pentagoet, 1635–1674*. Augusta, ME: Maine Historic Preservation Commission and the New Brunswick Museum, 1987.

Fox, William F. *Regimental Losses in the American Civil War, 1861–1865*. Albany, NY: Albany Publishing Co., 1889.

Frederick, Paul B. *Canning Gold: Northern New England's Sweet Corn Industry: A Historical Geography*. Latham, MD: University Press of America, 2002.

Freeman, Samuel. *The Town Officer*. Boston: Thomas & Andrews, 1805.

French, George. *New England: What It Is and What It Is to Be*. Boston: Chamber of Commerce, 1911.

G

Gadberry, Greg. A contagion of Quakerism: the Society of Friends in Falmouth and Portland, Maine, from settlement through the Revolution. Thesis, University of Southern Maine, 1997. (Copy at USM.)

Gerrish, Theodore. *The Blue and the Gray: A Graphic History of the Army of the Potomac and that of Northern Virginia*. Bangor, ME: Brady, Mace & Co., 1884.

Gilman, A. W., ed. *Maine Agricultural Statistics, Resources, and Opportunities*. Augusta, ME: Maine Department of Agriculture, 1910.

Goold, William. *Portland in the Past*. Portland, ME: B. Thurston & Co., 1886.

Gorman, Leon. *L. L. Bean: The Making of an American Icon*. Boston, MA: Harvard Business School Press, 2006.

Greenleaf, Jonathan. *Sketches of the Ecclesiastical History of the State of Maine*. Portsmouth, NH: H. Gray, 1821.

Greenleaf, Moses. *A Statistical View of the District of Maine*. Boston, MA: Cummings and Hilliard, 1816.

———. *A Survey of the State of Maine*. Portland, ME: Shirley & Hyde, 1829.

Griffin, Joseph, ed. *History of the Press in Maine*. Brunswick, ME: The Press, 1872.

Grindle, Roger L. *Quarry and Kiln: The Story of the Maine Lime Industry*. Rockland, ME: Courier-Gazette, 1971.

———. *Tombstones and Paving Blocks: The History of the Maine Granite Industry*. Rockland, ME: A Courier of Maine Book, 1977.

Grumet, Robert S. *Historic Contact: Indian People and Colonists in Today's Northeastern United States in the Sixteenth through Eighteenth Centuries*. Norman, OK: University of Oklahoma Press, 1995.

Guyton, Kathy. *U.S. State Names: The Stories of How Our States Were Named*. Nederland, CO: Mountain Storm Press, 2011.

H

Hamlin, Charles Eugene. *The Life and Times of Hannibal Hamlin*. Cambridge, MA: Riverside Press, 1899.

Harrison, James L., comp. *Biographical Dictionary of the American Congress, 1774–1949*. Washington, DC: United States Government Printing Office, 1950.

Harwell, Richard. *Hawthorne and Longfellow: A Guide to an Exhibition*. Brunswick, ME: Bowdoin College, 1966.

Hatch, Louis Clinton, ed. *Maine: A History*. 3 vols. Centennial Edition. New York: American Historical Society, 1919.

Hayward, John. *The New England Gazetteer*. Concord, NH, and Boston: Israel S. Boyd and William White and John Hayward, 1839.

Hill, George T. *History, Records, and Recollections of Gray, Maine*. Portland, ME: Seavey Printers, Inc., 1978.

Hodgkins, John. *A Soldier's Son: An American*

Boyhood During World War II. Camden, ME: Down East Books, 2006.

Holbrook, Stewart H. *The Yankee Exodus.* New York: Macmillan Company, 1950.

Holmes, Oliver W., and Peter T. Rohrbach. *Stagecoach East: Stagecoach Days in the East from the Colonial Period to the Civil War.* Washington, DC: Smithsonian Institution Press, 1983.

Holt, Jeff. *The Grand Trunk in New England.* Toronto: A Railfare Book, 1996.

Holtwijk, Theo H. B. M., and Earle G. Shettleworth, Jr., eds. *Bold Vision: The Development of the Parks of Portland, Maine.* West Kennebunk, ME: Published for Greater Portland Landmarks, Inc., by Phoenix Publishing, 1999.

Howe, Stanley Russell. *"A Fair Field and No Favor": A Concise History of the Maine State Grange.* Augusta, ME: Maine State Grange, 1994.

Hunt, Gaillard. *Israel, Elihu, and Cadwallader Washburn.* New York: Macmillan Company, 1925.

Hunt, H. Draper. *Brother Against Brother: Understanding the Civil War Era.* Portland, ME: J. Weston Walch, Publisher, 1977.

———. *Educating a President: Abraham Lincoln and Learning, 1809–1854.* Portland, ME: University of Southern Maine, 1983.

———. *Hannibal Hamlin of Maine: Lincoln's First Vice-President.* Syracuse, NY: Syracuse University Press, 1969.

———. *Lincoln the President: Learner and Mentor, 1854–1865.* Portland, ME: University of Southern Maine, 1984.

I

Ilsley, Charles P. *Forest and Shore: Legends of the Pine Tree State.* Revised and edited by Gudrun Cram-Drach and Neva Cram. Portland, ME: Afterlight Publishing, 2006. (150th-anniversary edition of the 1856 classic; excellent notes.)

Isaacson, Doris A., ed. *Maine: A Guide "Down East."* 2nd ed. Rockland, ME: Courier-Gazette, Inc., for the Maine League of Historical Societies and Museums, 1970.

J

Jackson, Charles F. *First Report on the Geology of the State of Maine: Atlas of Plates, Illustrating the Geology of the State of Maine, 1837.* Augusta, ME: Smith & Robinson, Printers to the State, 1837.

Jay–Livermore Falls Working Class History Project. *Pain on Their Faces: Testimonies on the Paper Mill Strike, Jay, Maine, 1987–1988.* Peter Kellerman, coordinator. New York: Apex Press, 1998.

Jellison, Charles A. *Fessenden of Maine: Civil War Senator.* Syracuse, NY: Syracuse University Press, 1960.

Jewett, Frederick E. *A Financial History of Maine.* New York: Columbia University, 1937.

Johnston, John. *A History of the Town of Bristol and Bremen.* Albany, NY: Joel Munsell, 1873.

Jordan, William B., Jr. *A History of Cape Elizabeth, Maine.* Portland, ME: House of Falmouth, 1965.

———, comp. *Maine in the Civil War: A Bibliographical Guide.* Portland, ME: Maine Historical Society, 1976.

———. *Red Diamond Regiment: The 17th Maine Infantry, 1862–1865.* Shippensburg, PA: White Mane Publishing Co. Inc., 1996.

Josselyn, John. *John Josselyn, Colonial Traveler: A Critical Edition of Two Voyages to New-England.* Edited and with an introduction by Paul J. Lindholdt. Hanover, NH: University Press of New England, 1988.

Judd, Richard W. *Aroostook: A Century of Logging in Northern Maine.* Orono, ME: University of Maine Press, 1988.

Judd, Richard W., Edwin A. Churchill, and Joel W. Eastman, eds. *Maine: The Pine Tree State from Prehistory to the Present.* Orono, ME: University of Maine Press, 1995.

K

King, Angus. *Angus King, Independent for Governor: Making a Difference.* Brunswick, ME: Angus King for Governor, 1994.

Kirkland, Edward C. *A History of American Economic Life.* New York: Appleton-Century-Crofts, Inc., 1951.

Knight, Ernest H. *A Guide to the Cumberland and Oxford Canal.* Bowdoin, ME: Will-Dale Press/Oxford Canal Association, 2006.

Krichels, Deborah Tracey. Reaction and reform: the political career of James Phinney Baxter, mayor of Portland, Maine, 1893–1897, 1904–1905. Thesis, University of Maine, 1986.

L

Lapham, William B., and Silas P. Maxim. *History of Paris, Maine.* Paris, ME: Printed for the author, 1884.

———. *History of Rumford.* Augusta, ME: Press of the Maine Farmer. 1890.

Leach, Douglas Edward. *The Northern Colonial Frontier, 1607–1763.* Albuquerque, NM: University of New Mexico Press, 1966.

Leamon, James S. *Revolution Downeast: The War for American Independence in Maine.* Amherst, MA: University of Massachusetts Press, 1993.

Lease, Benjamin. *That Wild Fellow John Neal and the American Literary Revolution.* Chicago: University of Chicago Press, 1972.

Levett, Christopher. *A Voyage into New England Begun in 1623 and Ended in 1624.* London: William Jones, 1628. (See Roger Howell, Jr., and Emerson W. Baker, *Maine in the Age of Discovery: Christopher Levett's Voyage 1623–1624,* and a guide to sources. Portland, ME: Maine Historical Society 1988.)

Libby, Charles Thornton, ed. *Genealogical Dictionary of Maine and New Hampshire.* 5 vols. Portland, ME: Southworth Press, 1928–1938.

Libby Gary W. "Chinese in Portland, Maine." Portland, ME: Typescript, 2002 (copy at Maine Historical Society).

Library of Congress. *Maine: The Sesquicentennial of Statehood.* Washington, D.C.: Library of Congress, 1970.

Lipman, Jean. *Rufus Porter: Yankee Pioneer.* New York: Clarkson N. Potter, Inc., 1968.

Little, George Thomas, ed. *Genealogical and Family History of the State of Maine.* 4 vols. New York: Lewis Historical Publishing Co., 1909.

Little, Jean (Sister). *Sisters of Mercy, Missioned in Maine.* Annual Report 2003. Portland, ME: Sisters of Mercy, 2003.

Longfellow, Samuel. *Life of Henry Wadsworth Longfellow.* 3 vols. New York: Ticknor & Co., 1886, 1887; and Boston: Houghton, Mifflin & Co., 1891.

Lovejoy, Myrtle Kittredge. *This Was Stroudwater, 1727–1860.* Portland, ME: National Society of Colonial Dames of America in the State of Maine, 1985.

Lucey, William Leo. *The Catholic Church in Maine.* Francestown, NH: Marshall Jones Company, 1957.

———. *Edward Kavanagh: Catholic, Statesman, Diplomat from Maine, 1795–1844.* Francestown, NH: Marshall Jones Company, 1946.

M

MacWilliams, Don. *Yours in Sports: A History.* Lewiston, ME: Monmouth Press, 1969.

Madore, Nelson, and Barry Rodrique, eds., with Corinna Miller and Chase Hebert. *Voyages: A Maine Franco-American Reader.* Gardiner and Lewiston, ME: Tilbury House, Publishers, and the Franco-American Collection of Maine, USM Lewiston-Auburn, 2007.

Marcigliano, John. *All Aboard for Union Station.* South Portland, ME: Pilot Press, 1991.

Marriner, Ernest Cummings. *The History of Colby College.* Waterville, ME: Colby College Press, 1963.

———. *Kennebec Yesterdays.* Waterville, ME:

Colby College Press, 1954.

May, Earl Chapin. *The Canning Clan: A Pageant of Pioneering Americans.* New York: Macmillan Co., 1937.

McBride, Bunny. *Molly Spotted Elk: A Penobscot in Paris.* Norman, OK: University of Oklahoma Press, 1990.

McCall, Samuel W. *The Life of Thomas B. Reed.* Boston: Houghton Mifflin Co., 1914.

McCrum, R. C. *Dear Mom: World War II Remembered in a Sailor's Letters.* Orono, ME: University of Maine Press, 1994.

McCulloch, Hugh. *Men and Measures of a Half a Century.* New York: Charles Scribner's Sons, 1888.

McKee, Christopher. *Edward Preble: A Naval Biography, 1761–1807.* Annapolis: Naval Institute Press, 1972.

McKeon, Edward G. *In the Streets Half Heard: A Biographical Novel.* Bangor, ME: Penobscot Press, 2004.

McKibben, Gael May, and William David Barry, eds. *A Passionate Intensity: The Life and Work of Dorothy Healy.* Portland, ME: Baxter Society, 1994.

McLane, Charles B. *Islands of the Mid-Maine Coast: Penobscot and Blue Hill Bays.* Woolwich, ME: Kennebec River Press, 1982. (Revised edition, *Islands of the Mid-Maine Coast: Penobscot Bay*, Gardiner and Rockland, ME: Tilbury House and the Island Institute, 1997.)

McLellan, Hugh D. *History of Gorham, Maine.* Katherine B. Lewis, ed. Portland, ME: Smith & Sale, 1903.

Mellen, Gertrude A., and Elizabeth F. Wilder, eds. *Maine and Its Role in American Art, 1740–1963.* New York: Viking Press for Colby College, 1963.

Merriam, Paul G., Thomas J. Molloy, and Theodore W. Sylvester, Jr. *Home Front on Penobscot Bay: Rockland During the War Years.* Rockland ME: Rockland Co., 1991

Merrill, Paul E. *50 Years a Truckman.* Portland, ME: Casco Printing, 1979.

Miller, E. Spencer. *Maine Central Railroad, 1940–1978.* New York: Newcomen Society, 1979.

Mitchell, Wilmot Brookings, ed. *Elijah Kellogg: The Man and His Work.* Boston: Lee and Shepard, 1904.

Mohney, Kirk F., ed., *Along the Rails: A Survey of Maine's Historic Railroad Buildings.* Portland, ME: Maine Historic Preservation Commission, 2000.

Mooney, James E. *Maps, Globes, Atlases, and Geographies through the Year 1800: The Eleanor Huston and Lawrence M. C. Smith Cartographic Collection at the Smith Cartographic Center, University of Southern Maine.* Freeport, ME: privately printed, 1988.

Morison, Samuel Eliot. *Maritime History of Massachusetts.* Boston: Houghton Mifflin Co., 1921.

———. *The Oxford History of the American People.* New York: Oxford University Press, 1965.

Morris, Gerald E., ed. *The Maine Bicentennial Atlas.* Portland, ME: Maine Historical Society, 1976.

Morris, Richard B., ed. *Encyclopedia of American History.* New York: Harper & Row, 1965.

Mundy, James H. *hard times, hard men: Maine and the Irish.* Scarborough, ME: Harp Publications, 1990.

———. *No Rich Men's Sons: The Sixth Maine Volunteer Infantry.* Cape Elizabeth, ME: Harp Publications, 1994.

———. *Second to None: The Story of the 2nd Maine Volunteers, "The Bangor Regiment."* Scarborough, ME: Harp Publications, 1992.

Mundy, James H., and Earle G. Shettleworth, Jr. *The Flight of the Grand Eagle: Charles G. Bryant, Maine Architect and Adventurer.* Augusta, ME: Maine Historic Preservation Commission, 1977.

Murphy, Kevin D. *Jonathan Fisher of Blue Hill, Maine: Commerce, Culture, and Community on the Eastern Frontier.* Amherst, MA: University of Massachusetts Press, 2010.

Murray, Eva. *Well Out to Sea: Year-Round on Matinicus Island.* Gardiner, ME: Tilbury House, Publishers, 2010.

Myers, Denys Peter. *Maine Catalogue: Historic American Buildings Survey.* Augusta, ME: Maine State Museum, 1974.

N

Nash, Charles Elventon. *The History of Augusta.* Augusta, ME: Charles E. Nash & Son, 1904.

Nasson, Emma Huntington. *Old Hallowell on the Kennebeck.* Augusta, ME: Press of Burleigh & Flint, 1909.

Neal, John. *Wandering Recollections of a Somewhat Busy Life: An Autobiography.* Boston: Roberts Brothers, 1869.

Nearing, Helen, and Scott Nearing. *Continuing the Good Life: Half a Century of Homesteading.* New York: Schoren Books 1979.

Nicolar, Joseph. *The Life and Traditions of the Redman.* Bangor: C. H. Glass & Co. 1893. Paperback edition, Frederickton, NB: Saint Annes Point Press, 1979.

O

O'Brien, Francis M. *A Backward Look: 50 Years of Maine Books and Bookmen.* Portland, ME: Anthoensen Press, 1986.

O'Gorman, James F., and Earle G. Shettleworth, Jr. *The Maine Perspective: Architectural Drawings, 1800–1980.* Portland, ME: Portland Museum of Art, c. 2006.

O'Leary, Wayne M. *Maine Sea Fisheries: The Rise and Fall of a Native Industry, 1830–1890.* Boston: Northeastern University, 1996.

Osborn, William C. *The Paper Plantation. Ralph Nader's Study Group Report on the Pulp and Paper Industry in Maine.* New York: Gross Publishers, a division of Viking Press, 1974.

P

Pancoast, Patricia, and Josephine H. Detmer. *Portland.* Martin Dibner, ed. Portland, ME: Greater Portland Landmarks, Inc., 1972.

Parker, Everett L. *Beyond Moosehead: A History of the Great North Woods of Maine.* Greenville ME: Moosehead Communications, Inc., 1996.

Parkinson-Tucker, Janice. *Hermann Kotzschmar: An Appreciation.* South Portland, ME: Casco House Publishing 2006.

Perley, Jeremiah, ed. *The Debates and Journal of the Constitutional Convention of the State of Maine, 1819–1820.* Augusta, ME: Maine Farmers' Almanac Press, 1894.

Pinkham, Steve. *Mountains of Maine: Intriguing Stories Behind Their Names*: Camden, ME: Down East Books, 2009.

Podmaniczky, Christine B., and Earle G. Shettleworth, Jr. *Through a Bird's Eye: Nineteenth-Century Views of Maine.* Rockland, ME: William A. Farnsworth Library and Art Museum, 1981.

Price, H. H., and Gerald E. Talbot. *Maine's Visible Black History: The First Chronicle of Its People.* Gardiner, ME: Tilbury House for Visible Black History, Portland, 2006.

Pullen, John J. *A Shower of Stars: The Medal of Honor and the 27th Maine.* Philadelphia: J. B. Lippincott Co., 1966.

———. *The Twentieth Maine: A Volunteer Regiment in the Civil War.* Philadelphia: J. B. Lippincott Co., 1957.

Putnam, Cora M. *The Story of Houlton.* Portland, ME: House of Falmouth, Inc., 1969.

R

Randall, Peter. *There Are No Victors Here: A Local Perspective on the Treaty of Portsmouth.* Portsmouth, NH: Portsmouth Marine Society, 1985.

Ray, Roger B., comp. *The Indians of Maine: A Bibliographical Guide.* Portland, ME: Maine

Historical Society, 1972.

Rice, Douglas Walthew. *The Life and Achievements of Sir John Popham, 1531–1607. Leading to the First English Colony in New England.* Madison, NJ: Fairleigh Dickinson University Press, 2005.

Richards, David L. *Poland Spring: A Tale of the Gilded Age, 1860–1900.* Dublin & Hanover, NH: University of New Hampshire Press, 2005.

Rickles, Milton, and Patricia Rickles. *Seba Smith.* Boston: Twayne Publishers, a division of G. K. Hall & Co., 1977.

Ridlon, Gideon Tibbetts. *Saco Valley Settlements and Families.* Portland, ME: private printing, 1895.

Ring, Elizabeth. *Maine in the Making of the Nation, 1783–1870.* Camden, ME: Picton Press, 1996.

———. *The McArthurs of Limington, Maine: The Family in America a Century Ago, 1783–1917.* Falmouth, ME: Kennebec River Press, 1992.

———. *The Myth of a One Party State.* Part 1. Political handbook, prepared and printed by the Maine Democratic Party, 1966.

———. *The Myth of a One Party State.* Part 2. Political handbook, prepared and printed by the Maine Democratic Party, 1968.

———, comp. *Maine Bibliographies: A Bibliographical Guide.* Portland, ME: Maine Historical Society, 1973.

———, ed. *A Reference List of Manuscripts Relating to the History of Maine.* Orono, ME: University of Maine Press, vol. 1, 1938, vol. 2, 1939, and vol. 3, 1940.

Rivard, Paul E. *Made in Maine: An Historical Overview.* Augusta, ME: Maine State Museum, 1985.

Rolde, Neil. *The Baxters of Maine: Downeast Visionaries.* Gardiner, ME: Tilbury House, Publishers, 1997.

———. *Continental Liar from the State of Maine: James G. Blaine.* Gardiner, ME: Tilbury House, Publishers, 2006.

———. *The Interrupted Forest: A History of Maine's Wildlands.* Gardiner, ME: Tilbury House, Publishers, 2001.

———. *Unsettled Past, Unsettled Future: The Story of Maine Indians.* Gardiner, ME: Tilbury House, Publishers, 2004.

Rosier, James. *The Voyage of Archangel: James Rosier's Account of the Waymouth Voyage of 1605, A True Relation.* Annotated by David C. Morey. Gardiner, ME: Tilbury House, Publishers, 2005.

Rowe, William Hutchison. *The Maritime History of Maine.* New York: W. W. Norton & Co., 1948.

Ryden, Kent C. *Landscape with Figures: Nature and Culture in New England.* Iowa City, IA: University of Iowa Press, 2001.

S

Sargent, Colin. "A John Calvin Stevens House for John Calvin Stevens." *Portland Monthly Magazine,* July/August 1997.

Schmidt, Patricia L. *Margaret Chase Smith: Beyond Convention.* Orono, ME: University of Maine Press, 1966.

Scontras, Charles A. *Collective Efforts Among Maine Workers: Beginnings and Foundations, 1820–1880.* Orono, ME: Bureau of Labor Education, 1994.

———. *Labor in Maine: Building the Arsenal of Democracy and Resisting Reaction at Home, 1938–1952.* Orono, ME: Bureau of Labor Education, 2006.

———. *Labor in Maine: War, Reaction, Depression and the Rise of the CIO, 1914–1943.* Orono, ME: Bureau of Labor Education, 2002.

———. *Time-Line of Organized Labor: Selected Highlights of Maine Labor History, 1632–2003.* Orono, ME: Bureau of Labor Education, 2003.

Scott, Geraldine Tidd. *Ties of Common Blood: A*

Sears, Donald A. *John Neal*. Boston: Twayne Publishers, a division of G. K. Hall & Co., 1978.

Sherman, Sarah Way. *Sarah Orne Jewett; An American Persephone*. Hanover, NH: University Press of New England for the University of New Hampshire, 1989.

Shettleworth, Earle G., Jr. *Norlands: The Architecture of the Washburn Estate*. Augusta, ME: Maine Historic Preservation Commission, 1980.

Shettleworth, Earle G., Jr., and William David Barry. *Mr. Goodhue Remembers Portland: Scenes from the Mid-19th Century*. Augusta, ME: Maine Historic Preservation Commission. 1981

Shettleworth, Earle G., Jr., and Frank A. Beard. *The Maine State House: A Brief History and Guide*. Augusta, ME: Maine Historic Preservation Commission, 1981.

Silsby, Herbert T., II. *Memorable Justices and Lawyers of Maine: An Historical Perspective*. Ellsworth, ME: private printing, 2006.

Smith, David C. *A History of Lumbering in Maine, 1860–1960*. Orono, ME: University of Maine Press, 1972.

———, comp. *Lumbering and the Maine Woods: A Bibliograpical Guide*. Portland, ME: Maine Historical Society, 1971.

Smith, Edgar Crosby, comp. *Maps of the State of Maine: A Bibliography of the Maps of Maine*. Bangor, ME: C. H. Glass Co., for the author, 1903.

———, ed. *Moses Greenleaf, Maine's First Map-Maker*. Bangor, ME. C. H. Glass Co., for the DeBurians, 1902.

Smith, Joshua M. *Borderland Smuggling: Patriots, Loyalists, and Illicit Trade in the Northeast, 1783–1820*. Gainesville, FL: University Press of Florida, 2006.

Smith, Marion Jacques. *General William King: Merchant, Shipbuilder, and Maine's First Governor*. Camden, ME: Down East Books, 1980.

Snow, Ralph Linwood. *Bath Iron Works: The First Hundred Years*. Bath, ME: Maine Maritime Museum, 1987.

Speck, Frank G. *Penobscot Man: The Life History of a Forest Tribe in Maine*. Philadelphia: University of Pennsylvania Press, 1940.

Sprague, John Francis. *The Northeast Boundary Controversy and the Aroostook War*. Dover, ME: Observer Press, 1910.

Sprague, Laura Fecych, ed., *Agreeable Situations: Society, Commerce, and Art in Southern Maine, 1780–1830*. Essays by Joyce Butler, Richard Candee, Laura F. Sprague, and Laurel Thatcher Olrich. Kennebunk, ME: Brick Store Museum, 1987.

———, ed. *The Mirror of Maine: One Hundred Distinguished Books that Reveal the History of the State and the Life of Its People*. Orono, ME: University of Maine Press, 2000.

Stanley, R. H., and George O. Hall. *Eastern Maine and the Rebellion*. Bangor, ME: R. H. Stanley & Co., 1887.

Starkey, Glenn Wendell. *Maine: Its History, Resources, and Governments*. New York: Silver, Burdett and Co., 1930.

Stephens, Ann Sophia, ed. *Portland Sketch Book*. Portland, ME: Colman and Chisholm, 1836.

Stevens, John Calvin, and Albert Winslow Cobb. *American Domestic Architecture: A Late Victorian Stylebook*. Introduction by Earle G. Shettleworth, Jr., and William David Barry. Watkins Glen, NY: Library of Victorian Culture, 1978.

Stevens, John Calvin, II, and Earle G. Shettleworth, Jr. *John Calvin Stevens, Domestic Architecture, 1890–1930*. Scarborough, ME: Harp Publications, 1990.

Stoddard, Roger E. *Abundant Bibliophiles: Hubbard Winslow Bryant on the Private Libraries* of Portland, 1863–1864. Portland, ME: Baxter Society, 2004.

Stoehr, Kevin L., and Michael C. Connolly, eds. *John Ford in Focus: Essays on the Filmmaker's Life and Work.* Jefferson, NC: McFarland, 2007.

Stover, Arthur Douglas. *Eminent Mainers: Succinct Biographies of Thousands of Amazing Mainers, Mostly Dead, and a Few People from Away Who Have Done Something Useful Within the State of Maine.* Gardiner, ME: Tilbury House, Publishers, 2006.

Sturtevant, Arnold H., ed. *Josiah Volunteered.* Farmington, ME: Knowlton and McLeary for the editor, 1977.

Sudlow, Lynda L. *A Vast Army of Women: Maine's Uncounted Forces in the American Civil War.* Gettysburg, PA: Thomas Publications, 2000.

Sullivan, James. *The History of the District of Maine.* Boston: L. Thomas and E. T. Andrews, 1795. Reprinted by the Maine State Museum, 1970.

T

Taylor, Alan. *Liberty Men and the Great Proprietors: The Revolutionary Settlement of the Maine Frontier, 1760–1820.* Chapel Hill, NC: University of North Carolina Press, 1990.

Taylor, Robert L. *History of Limington, Maine, 1668–1900.* Norway, ME: Oxford Hills Press, 1975.

Thompson, Deborah, ed. *Maine Forms of American Architecture.* Camden, ME: *Down East Magazine* for Colby College Museum of Art, 1976.

Thompson, Kenneth E. *Civil War Maine Hall of Fame: Political, Judicial, and Military Leaders, 1861–1865.* Portland, ME: Thompson Group, 2000.

———. *Deceive to Win: The Maine–New Hampshire Border Controversy.* Portland, ME: Thompson Group, 2003.

Thompson, Margaret Jefferds. *Captain Nathaniel Lord of Kennebunk, Maine, and the Ships He Built, 1811–1889.* Boston: Charles C. Lauriat Co., 1937.

Thoreau, Henry David. *The Maine Woods.* Boston: Ticknor and Fields, 1884.

Thurston, David. *A Brief History of Winthrop, from 1764 to October 1855.* Portland, ME: Brown Thurston, 1855.

Titone, Nora. *My Thoughts Be Bloody.* New York: Free Press, 2010.

U

Ulrich, Laura Thatcher. *Good Wives: Image and Reality in the Lives of Women in Northern New England, 1650–1750.* New York: Alfred A. Knopf, 1982.

———. *A Midwife's Tale: The Life of Martha Ballard, Based on Her Diary, 1785–1812.* New York: Alfred A. Knopf. 1990.

V

Vallier, Jane E. *Poet on Demand: The Life, Letters, and Works of Celia Thaxter.* Camden, ME: Peter Randall–Down East Books, 1982.

Varney, George J. *A Gazetteer of the State of Maine.* Boston: B. B. Russell, 1882.

Vickery, James Berry, III. *A History of the Town of Unity, Maine.* Manchester, ME: Falmouth Publishing House, 1954.

———. *Made in Bangor: Economic Emergence and Adaptation, 1834–1911.* Bangor, ME: Bangor Historical Society, 1984.

W

Walker, Mark. *Maine Roots: Growing Up Poor in the Kennebec Valley.* Camden, ME: Picton Press. 1999.

Warner, Ezra J. *Generals in Blue: Lives of the Union Commanders.* Baton Rouge: Louisiana State University Press, 1964.

———. *Generals in Gray: Lives of the Confederate Commanders.* Baton Rouge: Louisiana State University Press, 1959.

Washburn, Israel. *Address of Governor Washburn to the Legislature of the State of Maine, Janu-

ary 3, 1861. Augusta, ME: Stevens & Sayward, Printers to the State, 1861.

Washburn, Lillian. *My Seven Sons*. Portland, ME: Falmouth Publishing House, 1940.

Westcott, Richard R. *A History of Harpswell, Maine*. Nobleboro, ME: Blackberry Books in collaboration with the Harpswell Historical Society and Curtis Memorial Library, 2010.

———. *New Men, New Issues: The Formation of the Republican Party in Maine*. Portland, ME: Maine Historical Society, 1986.

Wheeler, George Augustus, and Henry Warren Wheeler. *History of Brunswick, Topsham, and Harpswell, Maine*. Boston: Alfred Mudge & Son, 1878.

Whitman, William E. S., and Charles H. True. *Maine in the War for the Union*. Lewiston, ME: N. Dingley, Jr. & Co. 1865.

Whitney, Edward Bonner. The Ku Klux Klan in Maine, 1922–1928: a study with particular emphasis on the city of Portland. Thesis, Harvard College, 1966. (Copy at Maine Historical Society.)

Whitten, Jeanne Patten. *Fannie Hardy Eckstrom: A Descriptive Bibliography of Her Writings Published and Unpublished*. Northeast Folklore Series, No. 14. Orono, ME: Northeast Folklore Society, 1975.

Whitten, Maurice M. *The Gunpowder Mills of Maine*. Gorham, ME: by the author, 1990.

Wiggin, Frances Turgeon, comp. *Maine Composers and Their Music: A Biographical Dictionary*. Rockland, ME: Bald Mountain Printing Co. for the Maine Federation of Music Clubs, 1959.

Wilder, Philip S. *General Catalogue of Bowdoin College and the Medical School of Maine: A Biographical Record of Alumni and Officers, 1794–1950*. Brunswick, ME: Bowdoin College, 1950.

Wilkins, Austin H. *The Forests of Maine: Their Extent, Character, Ownership, and Productivity*. Augusta, ME: Maine Forest Service, 1932.

———. *Ten Million Acres of Timber: The Remarkable Story of Forest Protection in the Maine Forestry District, 1909–1972*. Woolwich, ME: T. B. W. Books, 1978.

Williamson, Joseph, ed. *A Bibliography of the State of Maine*. 2 vols. Portland, ME: Thurston Print, 1896.

Williamson, William D. *The History of the State of Maine: From Its First Discovery A.D. 1602 to the Separation A.D. 1820, Inclusive, 1832*. 2 vols. Hallowell, ME: Glazier, Master & Co., 1832.

Willis, William. *A History of the Law, the Courts, and the Lawyers of Maine*. Portland, ME: Bailey and Noyes, 1863.

———. *The History of Portland*. Portland, ME: Bailey & Noyes, 1865.

———, ed. *Journals of the Rev. Thomas Smith and the Rev. Samuel Deane: Pastors of the First Church in Portland*. Portland, ME: Joseph S. Bailey, 1849.

Winchester, Alice. *Versatile Yankee: The Art of Jonathan Fisher, 1768–1847*. Princeton, NJ: Pyne Press, 1973.

Witherell, James L. *L. L. Bean: The Man and His Company—The Complete Story*. Gardiner, ME: Tilbury House, Publishers, 2011.

Wood, Henrietta Danforth. *Early Days in Norridgewock*. Skowhegan, ME: Skowhegan Press, 1941.

Wood, Richard G. *A History of Lumbering in Maine, 1820–1861*. Orono ME: University of Maine Press, 1935.

Woodard, Colin. *The Lobster Coast: Rebels, Rusticators, and the Struggle for a Forgotten Frontier*. New York: Viking, 2004.

Y

Yerxa, Donald A. *The Burning of Falmouth, 1775: A Case Study in British Imperial Pacification*. Portland, ME: Maine Historical Society, 1975.

INDEX

Illustrations are indicated with bold page numbers.

A

Abbott (shoes), 173
Abbott, Berenice, 215
Abbott, Jacob, viii, 104
Abbott, John S. C, viii, 98, 104, 113, 145; *History of Maine* (1975), viii, 145
Abenakis, 4, 23-26, 29, 30; dictionary (Râle), 26. *See also* Native Americans, Wabanakis.
Abolition (of slavery) movement, **99**, 102, 119, 123, 240
Abrahamson, Albert, 177
Abrahms, Hiram, 181-82
Absentee landowners, 10, 32, 33, 44, 58, 59, 60, 240, 241. *See also* landowners.
Academies, 67, 80, 90, 98. *See also* schools, education.
Academy Awards, 181-82
Acadia (Arcadia), 1-15, 16-20, 25-28, 36, 56-58, 61-62, 84-102
Acadian Civil War, 19-20, 36; Acadian removal by British (Grand Derangement, 1755), 20, 36
Acadian Village, Van Buren, **62**, 226
Acadia National Park, 168. *See also* parks.
Account of Two Voyages into New-England, An (1679, John Josselyn), 21
"Act of Separation" (Maine as state), 77
actors (lists), 67, 90, 105-06, 109, 113, 148, 181, 201, 211. *See also by name.*
Adams, USS (corvette), 74
Adams, Herb, 92-93, 114, 226
Adams, John (President), 38-40, 43, 45, 63
Admiral of New England, **13-14**, 17
Afghanistan, war in, 222, 232, 239
African Americans, 20-22, 42, 44, 53, 55, 90, 94, 98, **99**, 102, 119, 123, **126**, **146**, 165, 192, 204, 239-**41**
Agamenticus, USS (ironclad), 116
Agawam, USS (gunboat), 116
aggression: Acadians, 19; David Dunbar, 33; Dutch, 12; English, 10, 12, 55, 73-75, 241; Iroquois, 22; Micmac, 22; Plymouth, 19; Virginia, 12
Agrarian Democrat Party, 63
agriculture, 3, 9, 21-22, 33, 44, 58-63, 68, 70, **78**, 84, 93-94, **105**, **108**, 109, 127, 133, 135, **138**, 139, 155-56, 159, 171, 176, 196, 205, 207, 215, 236; agriculture vs. timber interest, 93
AIDS crisis, 224, **225**, 226. *See also* epidemics, gay and lesbian.
Aircraft Warning Service, 193, **202**
airplanes and airports: bush pilots, 170, **191**, 208, Concorde (supersonic jet), **169**, 207, 240. *See also by name.*
Air Raid Instructions, **191**, 193, 202
Akers, Benjamin Paul, 113
Alabama (CSA raider), 116
Albanians, 171, 241
Albion, Robert G. (Dr.), 183, 201; *Forests and Sea Power* (1926), 183
Albright, Ivan, 180
Alden, James (Adm.), **122**, 123
Alden, John, 19
Aldridge, Kay, 201
Aley, Robert G, 163
Alfred, Maine, 67
Ali, Pious, **241**
Allagash River, 92
All-Bath Destroyer Squadron 21, 200
Allan, John (Col.), 51

256

Allen, E. C., 153
Allen, Thomas (Lt.), 39
almanacs, 70
almshouse, Falmouth, 37. *See also* poverty.
Almochiquois. *See* Armouchiquois, Native Americans.
Alton A (fishing vessel), 233
American Colonization Society, 99
American Dream, 203-04, 240
American Federation of Labor (union), 133. *See also* labor.
American flag, 49, 84, 101
American Independence, 30-50, 51-55, 63, **64**
American Legion (1919), 164
American Revolution, 37-55, 57, 63-64, 183-84; bicentennial, 51; Continental Army, 46; Continental Congress, First, 44, Second, 46, 64; Continental Navy, 48; Declaration of Independence, 49, 50, 240; Grand Army of the Republic, 120; patriots, 37-55. *See also by name and action.*
American troops in London, 165
America's Cup, 147, 178
Amherst, Jeffrey (Gen.), 36
Ames, Adelbert (Gen.), 121
Amity, Maine, 84
amusement parks, **144**
Andover, Maine, 97, **209**
Androscoggin County, 83
Androscoggin River, 179
Anglicans (Episcopalians), 11-15, 17, 41, 42
Anglin, John, 121
Anna Sophia (schooner), 191
antique dealing, 158
anti-Catholic outbreaks, **iv**, 81, 100, 101, 165. *See also* mobs.
anti-German outbreaks, 161, 163. *See also* mobs.
anti-Semetic outbreaks, 165. *See also* Ku Klux Klan, mobs, Nazis.
Anunciada, La (caravel), 4
Appalachian Trail, 176
Appledore (Isles of Shoals), 152
apples (orchards), 94, 157
Appomattox (Lee's surrender), 124
Arcady (cottage at Blue Hill), 171
Archangell (ship), 9, 10

Archer (schooner), 119
architecture: buildings, 7, **9**, 11, 22, **29**, 31, 34-35, 40, 43, 59, 63, 66, 73, 74, **81**, 83, 101-03, **128**, 132, **137**, 138-39, 143, **147**, **149**, 150, 154, **155**, 163, 178-81, 193, 194, **202**, 207, 213, 236; as honored profession, 149; preservation movement, 207, 213; Shingle Style, **149**
Arctic, exploration, 153, 166
Argall, Samuel (Capt.), 12-13, 18
Arleigh Burke (destroyer), 240
Armenian Americans, 130, 145
Armouchiquois, 4, 9, 17. *See also* Native Americans.
Army Air Corps, 170, 188-89, 190
Arnold, Benedict (Gen.), **46**, 47; Letter Book, **46**, 47; march, **46**, 47, 59
Aroostook County (1839), 83, 84, 86, 87, 88, 91, 120, 127, 135-36, 159, 169, 190, 207, **208**
Aroostook Falls, 91
Aroostook War, 79, 84, 85, 86, 87, 88
Articles of Confederation, 57, 63, 64. *See also* Constitution, U.S.
Arthur, Chester A. (President), 155
Arthur, Jean, 181
art and artists, ii, xv, 5-9, 10, 11, 14, 20, 23, 27, 30, 33, 37, 38, 39, 40, 41, 42, 45, 47, 48, 49, 50, 51, 52, 54, 56, 59, 61, 63, 64, 65, 67, 72, 75, 76, 78, 79, 80, 81, 82, 85, 86, 87, 88, 90, 91, 92, 93, 94, 95, 96, 97, 98, 99, 101, 102, 103, 104, 105, 106, 108, 113-14, 115, 117, 118, 122, 123, 127, 145, 148, 149, 150, 151, 158, 161, 162, 163, 178, 179, 180, 181, 182, 190, 198, 201, 214-15, 218, 221, 223, 227, 234; art colonies, 149, 179-80; critics, 104, 148, 214-15; gallery (first commercial), 67; itinerants, 106, 148. *See also by name.*
Arundel (1930, Kenneth Roberts), 183
Arundell, Thomas, 10
"As Maine Goes, So Goes the Nation" (maxim), 155, 157
"As Maine Goes, So Goes Vermont" (maxim), 174
As the Earth Turns (1933, Gladys Hasty Carroll), 183
Assolant, Jean, 169, 170
Astor, Dave, 210
athletics and athletes, 3, 94, 104, **128**, 146-48, **182**, 215-16, 218. *See also by name.*

Atlantic Carrying Trade, 63, 66, 74; Bangor, 96, 97; Civil War, 164
Atlantic Charter, **186**-87
Atlantic & St. Lawrence Railroad, 89, 97. *See also* Grand Trunk Railway.
Atlantic Neptune (charts), **41**, **42**, 90
Attien, Joe, 90, 91
attorneys (lawyers), **ii**, viii, 10, 15-38, 39, 41, **43**, 44-45, **53**, 57, 60, **64**, 80, 98, 102, 104, 109, 110, 111, 112, 114, 154, 164, 175, 201, **225**, **228**, **230**, **238**. *See also by name*.
Auburn, Maine, 132, 179
Audubon, John James, **92**
Augusta, Maine (Cushnoc), 19, 35, 46, 80, 82, 112, 124, 153, 155, 156, **157**, **158**, **159**, 164, 191, 221, 222, 229, 230, 231
Augustine, Michael (Micmac chief), 51
Austin, Henry, 103
Austin, Phyllis, 210
automobiles, 142, 147, 158, 159, 160, 168, **173**, **186**, 191, 211, 215; racing, 147, 215; filling stations, 168. *See also* gasoline.
Avon, Maine, 102, 119
aviation, airplanes, and air travel, 160, 168, **169**, 170, 176, 188-89, 190, 195, 197, 198, 203, **206**, 207, **208**, 222, 227, **240**
Axis Sally. *See* Gillars, Mildred.
Azores and Azoreans, 2, 219, 239

B

baby boomers, 206-41
Backyard Farms Company, 236
back-to-the-land movement, 219
Bacon, Peggy, 179-80, 214
Bacon, William, 102
Badger, Thomas, 75
Badger's Island, Maine, 31, 48, **83**,
Bagaduce (Castine), 15, 22, 47, **52**
Bagnall, Walter, **19**
Baha'i (religion), 221
Bailey Island, Maine, 176
Baker, John (Aroostook settler), 84
Baker, S. B., 150
Baldacci, John (Gov.), 229
balloons, trans-Atlantic, 208; *Double Eagle II*, 208; *Rosie O'Grady Balloon of Peace*, 208

bands (municipal), 150. *See also* music.
Bangor, Maine, viii, ix, 4, 5, 14, 15, 74, 79, 88, 89, 90, 100, 105, 109-10, 111, **129**, 130, 131, **147**, 167, 170, **172**, 173, **175**, 195, 209, **240**; fire (1911), 132; lumber capital of the world, 79, 89-90, 131; ransom by British, 74. *See also* Queen City.
Bangor & Aroostook Railroad, 169
Bangor Democrat (newspaper), 111
Bangor House (hotel), 129
Bangor International Airport, 170, 195-97, 206, 207, **240**
Bangor Opera House, 156
Bangor Symphony, 150
Bangor Theological Seminary, 67, 123
bankruptcy (of Massachusetts), 52, 58
banks, 66, 96, 97, 173, 176. *See also by name*.
Banks, Charles E., 10
Bapst, John (Fr.), 101
Baptist Church, 41, 42, 61, 63, 67, 221; Freewill Baptists, 61
Bar Harbor, Maine, 12, 93, 143, **145**, 176, 197, 207, 229; estates, 143, 145
Bar Harbor Naval Section Base, 197
barbeque, 37
Barbary Wars (North Africa), 71, **72**; bombardment of Tripoli, 72
barges, coastal, 180
Baker, John, 84-85
baronet, first American, 32
Barring, House of, 60
Barrows, Lewis O. (Gov.), 174-75
Barry, Daniel James, 234
Barry, E. C., 181
baseball, **215**
Bashabes (Bessabez, Etchemin leader), 8, 14, 15
baske-shallop, 6
basketball, 219
Basques, 3, 6; fishery, 2
bateaux, 46, **140**
Bates College, Lewiston, 179, 183, 206, 228
Bates Mills, 95
Bath, Maine, iv, 45, 77, 96, 101, 125, 135, 141, 148, 151, **162**, 170, 188, 190, 200
Bath Iron Works, 96, 135, 164, 170, 188, **190**, 200,

258   MAINE: THE WILDER HALF OF NEW ENGLAND

209, 232, **240**
Bath Iron Works: The First Hundred Years (1987, Ralph Linwood Snow), 200, 237
Bath Military and Navy Orphan Asylum, 125
battles: Battle of Bagaduce (Penobscot), *see* Battle of the Penobscot; Battle of Concord, 45; Battle of *Enterprise* and *Boxer* (1813), 73; Battle of Gettysburg, 122, **123**; Battle of Machias, 45; Battle of Mobile Bay, 122; Battle of the Penobscot (Bagaduce/Castine) 51, 52, 55, painting, **51**; Battle of Saratoga, 50; Battle of Somes Sound, 12, **13**
Baxter, James Phinney (Mayor), 128, 129, 133, 152, 165, 166
Baxter, Percival P. (Gov.) 161, 165, **166**, 176. *See also* Baxter State Park.
Baxter State Park, 166, 176, 220. *See also* Baxter, Percival P.
Beach Ridge Speedway, Scarborough, 215
Beale, Walker Blaine (Lt), 164. *See also* Blaine House.
Bean, Leon Leonwood, 43, 161. *See also* L.L. Bean, Inc.
beans, 9, 133
Beans of Egypt, Maine, The (1985, Carolyn Chute), 212
Bear, Ambrose (Maliseet chief), 51
Beem, Edgar Allen, 210, 214
Beethoven Society, 67
Beckett, Charles E., **81**, **93**
Belcher, Supply, 67, 68
Belfast, Maine, 53, 61, 168, 207
Belfast (Ireland) Peace Agreement, 229
Berry, Hiram (Gen.), 113
Bert and I (records, Dodge and Bryan), 210
Berwick, Maine, ii, 32, 39, 44, 66. *See also* South Berwick.
Beston, Henry, 183
Bethel (Sudbury Canada), Maine, 32, 54, 61, 63, 176
Betterment Act, 60, 77
Bible, 21, 70, **99**
Biddeford, Maine, 15, 25, 132, 171. *See also* Winter Harbor (Biddeford Pool).
Biddeford Box Shop, 233
big box stores, 207

billboards, 165, 185
Bill of Rights, 64
Bingham, Maine, 174
Bingham, William (Sen.), 60
Bird, Thomas, 71
birds, 92
Bissonette, Del, 176
Bixler, J. Seelye, 206
Black, "Rip" Edmund, 176
Black, Persis Sibley Andrews, **106**
Blackpoint (Scarborough), 21, 23
Blaine, James G., 111, 112, 127, 143, 144, 153, **154**, 164, 200, 227
Blaine House (Augusta), 164, 191. *See also* Beale, Walter Blaine.
Blimp K-14, 195
blockhouses, **85**
Blodgett, Cindy, 219
Blossom (ship), 64, **65**
Blue Hill, Maine, 61, 68, 69, 102, 171, 183
Blythe, Benjamin, 38
Board of Corrections (1913, Maine), 159
Board of Health (1885, Maine), 158, 173
Bogan, Louise, 183
bomber crash, South Portland (1944), 203
books, 70-71, 129, 190, 220, 230; banned, 183. *See also by title.*
Boon Island (1956, Kenneth Roberts), 184
Booth, John Wilkes, 113, **114**, 124
Booth, Philip, 211
Booth, Steve, **219**
Boothbay, Maine, 18, 47, 48, 149, **166**, 194, 200
Boston, Massachusetts, 20, 22, 25, 27, 31, 34, 35, 36, 44, 45, 48, 57, 66, 89, **96**, 97, 104, 126, 127, 141, 170, 209
Boston Boat, **96**, 141, 170
Boston Maine Airways, 170
Boston Marathon, 218, 219
Boston Tea Party (1773), 44
Bowdoin (schooner), 166
Bowdoin College, 66, 79, 94, 98, 103, 122, 123, 149, 165, 166, 176, 177, 204, 206, 218, 219
Bowdoin Family, 44
Bowen, Ashley, 54
Bower, Alexander, 179

INDEX   259

Boxer (brig), 73
Boy and Girl Scouts, 143
Brackenridge, Hugh Henry, 46-47
Brackett, Edward Augustus, 104
Bradley, Emma Morse, 120
Bradley, Robert L., 193-94
Brady, Al, **172**, **173**
Brain, John Clibbon, 119
Brann, Louis J. (Gov.), 174, 177, 191
Breck, Bernice, 179, 201
Bremen, Maine, 73
Brennan, Joseph (Gov.), **229**, **238**
Brereton, John, 6, 7
Brewer, Maine, 122, 152, 166, **167**
Brewster, John, Jr., 61, 67
Brewster, Ralph Owen (Gov.), 165-66, 191, 227
bricks, 44, 60, 62, 95, **126**, 207, 235
Brick Store Museum, Kennebunk, 181
Bridgton, Maine, 149
Bristol, Maine, 48, 200
British: blockade of Maine, 73-75; officials, 44; opinion of Yankees, 37
Broadmayne, xi
Brooklin, Maine, 2. *See also* Norse coin.
Brown, Harrison, B., 103, 118, 148
Brown, J. B., 97, 130
Browne, Charles Farrar, **113**. *See also* Ward, Artemus.
Brunswick, Maine, 45, 64, 77, 103, 113, 122, 149, 163, 193, 206, 210, 232
Brunswick Convention, 77
Brunswick Naval Air Station, 193, 195, 198, 201, 206, 207, 232
Bryan, Robert (Rev.), 210; *Bert and I* (records, Dodge and Bryan), 210
Bryant, Charles (Capt.), 87
Buckley, John P. 147
Bucksport, Maine, 52
buffer zone (Maine as), 17-21, 27, 37, 51, 52, 57, 58, 74-77
buildings. *See* architecture.
Bulfinch, Charles, 83, **124**, 159
Bull, Dixie, 19
Bullard, Laura J. C., 164
bulldozers, 236

bully mates, 135
Buntline, Ned, 100
Bunyan, Paul (fictional), 143
Burlingame, Anson, 120
Burnham's Tavern (Machias), 41
Burnham & Morrill Company, 133
Burr, Aaron, 46
Burrage, Mildred, 180-81, 198, 201, 214
bush pilots, 170, **208**
Bush, Barbara, **239**
Bush, George H. W. (Pres.), 238-**39**
Bush, George W. (Pres.), 239
businesses and business persons, 34-36, 40, 47, 48, 54, 56, 58, 66, 88, 89, 96, **97**, 98, 111, 114, 127, **129**, 133, **134**, 135, **141**, 153, **158**, 162, **190**, 200, 201, **216**, 229, 230, 232, 233, 234, 235, 236, 238, 240, 241. *See also by name.*
Butler, Benjamin (Gen.), 122
Butler, Joyce, 158
Buzzelites, 61
C
Cabbot, John (Cabotto), 1, 2
Cadillac Mountain, 197
Calais, Maine, 119, 152; raid, 119
Caldwell, Erskine, 183
Caleb Cushing (revenue cutter), **118**, 119
Calef, John (Dr.), 51, 52, 55
Calvinists, 42
Cambodia, Cambodian Americans, 222, **224**
Camden, Maine, 210, **235**
Camp Houlton (POW), 195
Camp Keyes, Augusta, 195
Camp Tall Timbers, 216, **217**
Camp Wyonegonic (1902), 143
camping, 143, 168, 216, **217**
Canabis (Native Americans), 23
Campobello, New Brunswick, 144, 173
Canada: Canadian rebellions (1837), 86, 87; relations with, 232-37; winter railhead, 79, 97, 161, 169. *See also* New Brunswick, Northeast Boundary, Nova Scotia, Quebec. *See also* by event, place name, personal name.
"Canada" townships, Maine (1753), 32, 54
canals, 56, 96

Canceaux, HMS (sloop-of-war), 45, 48
canning industry, **133**, 145, **135**, **136**, 165
canoes, 3, 10, 17, **24**, **25**, 61, **91**, **142**, **220**
Cape Ann, Massachusetts, 47
Cape Elizabeth, Maine, 12-14, 21, 73, 93, 152, 178, 182, 195, **218**, 233, 235
Cape Henry, Virginia, 47
Cape Neddick, Maine, 6, 23
Cape Split, Maine, 180
Captain January (1890, Laura E. Richards), 152
captives, 23. *See also* kidnapping.
Caratunk, Maine, 174
Caribou, Maine, 230
Carrie (1971, Stephen King), 212
Carroll, Gladys Hasty, 183; *Country of the Pointed Firs, The*, **151**, 152
Carson, Rachel, 220; *Edge of the Sea, The* (1956), 220; *Silent Spring* (1961), 220
Carter, Jimmy (Pres.), 228, **238**
Cartier, Jacques, 5
Cary, Annie Louise, **150**, **151**, *See also* divas.
Cary, Austin F., 143
Casco, Maine: current, 216, 217; fall of ancient Casco, 22; later Portland, 23, 25. *See also* Falmouth.
Casco Bay, Maine, 1, 17, 21, 23, 25, 31, 39, 45, 46, 48, 72, 73, 118, 153, 182, 188, 193-95, **219**
Cassidy, Hopalong (fictional character), 152
Castin, Baron. *See* de Saint-Castin.
Castine, Maine (Bagaduce, Penobscot), 19, 22, 47, 51, 52, 54, 60, 74, 135, 203
Catholic Church, 3, 8-15, 22, **26**, 41, 42, 61, 62, 100, **101**, 145, 153, 161, 207, 221; Diocese of Portland, 101; fish days, 3; population, 100. *See also by name.*
cattle drives, 60, 94
Cavalli, François A., **122**
Central Maine Power, 141, 152, 166, 167, **174**
Chadbourne, Ava, 183
Chamberlain, Joshua L. (Gen./Gov.), 122-24, 127, 155, 156, 241; house, **122**
Champlain. *See* de Champlain.
Chandler's Band, 150
chainsaws, 236
Chaney, William, 101

chapel, Roman Catholic at Norridgwock, **26**
Chapman, William R, 150
Charles I (King), 13
Charles V (Emperor), 4
Charleston, South Carolina, 66
Charlotte's Web (1952, E. B. White), 211
charts. *See* maps and by name.
Chase, George Davis, 183
Chase, Mary Ellen, 152, 183
Chase, Solon, **155**, **156**-59
Chason, Saul G., 187
Chaudière River, Quebec, 4, 28, 47
Chelsea, Maine, 125
Chesapeake (steamer), **118**, 119; capture of, 119
Chesapeake (U.S. naval training ship), 135
children, 99, 125, 134, 135, 143, 147, 151, 152, 166, 175-76, 178; born at sea or ports, 150, 151; children's authors, 152. *See also* labor, children.
Children's Aid Society, Belfast, 147, 199
Chisholm, Hugh J., 139
Church, Benjamin (Maj.), 23
Church, Frederick E., 92
Churchill, Edwin A., ix
Churchill, Winston (prime minister), 186, 187, 188
Chute, Carolyn, 212; *Beans of Egypt, Maine, The* (1985), 212
Cilley, Jonathan, 79, 98
City of Rockland (steamer), 170
Civil War (American), 108-25, 132, 158; and money, 111, 125, 127, 128; birthrate, decline, 125; casualties, 121-25, 128; Confederate generals from Maine, 119; Confederate succession, 108-11; Confederate raid on Portland, 118; Confederate sympathizers (Copperheads), 111, 118, 120; debt, 125, 128; Maine generals, 121; Maine statistics, 121-25; Maine regiments, 106, **115**, 120, 121, 121-24, 125; nurses, 120; recruiting, 110; relief societies, 126; soldiers in field, **115**, **123**; troup numbers, 110, 121, 123-25. *See also* by event, individual name, place name.
Civilian Conservation Corps, 176, 177
Clapp, Asa (Capt.) **75**
Clarence (brig), 119
Clark, Bill, 177

Clark, Walter van Tilberg, 201; *Ox-Bow Incident, The* (1940), 201
Clarke, Sophia Rebecca, 152
Cleveland, Grover (Pres.), 153-54
Clifford, Harold B., 232; *Maine and Her People* (1957), 232
Clifford, Nathan, 79, 111
Clinton, William J. (President), 222, 229, 230
Coast Artillery, 188
coastal trade, 63, 66
Coatsworth, Elizabeth, 183
Cobb, Albert Winslow, 149
Coburn, Abner (Gov.), 111, 112
Cobb, Henry N., 215
Cochranites, 61
Co-cum-go-mus-sis Lake, iv, **86**, 87
Codd, Nicholas, 62
Codman, Charles, **78**, 82
Coffin, Harold W. (Col.), 190-91, 195
Coffin, Robert P. T., 183
Cohen, William S. (Sen.), 229, **230**; *Men of Zeal* (1988, Cohen and Mitchell), 230
Colby College, 67, 102, 111, 122, 182, 206
Colcord, Lincoln, 181, 183
Cold War, 205, 207, 220, 221, 227, 232, 239. *See also* Smith, Samantha, and Smith, Margaret Chase.
Cole, A. J. "Allie," 168; Cole's Land Transportation Museum, 169
Cole, C. O., **98**
Cole, John, 210; *Maine Times* (newspaper), 210
Cole, Thomas, 93
colleges: Maine, 66, 67, 98, 102, 159, 203, 204, 206, 207, 213, 215; out of state, 37, 32, 50, 64. *See also by name.*
Collier, George (Adm.), 47, 51, 52
Collins, Susan (Sen.), 229-**31**; family, 230
Collins, William (Lt.), 119
Come Spring (1940, Ben Ames Williams), 201
Columbia Falls, Maine, 209
Comfort Magazine, 153
committees: American Revolution, 44, 49; World War I, 164
Common Ground Fair, 139, 226
Common Sense (pamphlet), 47

communication, 71, 141, 205, 209, 210. *See also* newspapers, television.
commutation (draft), 120, 125
Concept School (art), 214
computers, 209, 240-41
Concord (bark), 6
Concorde (supersonic jet), 207, **240**
condominiums, 234-35
Confederates. *See* Civil War.
Congregation Ahawas Achim, 147
Congregation Beth Israel, Bangor, **147**, 175
Congregational Church, 22, 25, 31, 32, 37, 40, 41, 42, 66, 67; ministers, 27, 28. *See also* Standing Order
Congress. *See* United States Congress, United States House of Representatives, United States Senate, and senators and representatives by name.
Congress, USS (frigate), 83
Conners, Larry, 90
conscription. *See* draft.
Constitution, USS (frigate), 72
Constitution, U.S., 63, 64. *See also* Articles of Confederation.
Continental Army, 46
Continental Congress: First, 44; Second, 46, 64
Continental Navy, 48
Continuing the Good Life (1979, Scott and Helen Nearing), 219
Coombs, John W., 148
Cooper, Dexter P. 173, 176, 177
Copley, John Singleton, 37, 40
Copperheads. *See* Civil War.
Corea, Maine, 180
Corinna, Maine, 152
corn, 9, 132; packing, 132
Corn Husking (painting), 108
Corne, Michele Felice, 72
Cornwallis (CRN vessel), 195
Cornwallis, Charles (Lord), 54
Corsair (yacht), 170
cotton: shipped, 66, 102. *See also* textile mills.
Cote, Seth (Serg), 231
Cottrill, Matthew, 62
Coulson, Thomas, 45
Council for New England, 15, 17

counties, Maine. *See by name.*
Country of the Pointed Firs, The (1886, Sarah Orne Jewett), 151, 152
courthouses, 226-27. *See also by name.*
courts, early, 20, 22, 38, 39, 40, 43, 45, 226-27
Cox, Peter, 210; *Maine Times* (newspaper), 210
craftspersons. *See* mechanics.
Craig, Béatrice, 63; *Land in Between, The* (2004, Craig and Dagenais), 63
Crandall, Victoria, 210
credit (paper IOU), 63, **66.** *See also* paper money, specie, Taber notes.
Criehaven, Maine, 193
Crignon, Pierre, 1, 4; *Discourse of a Great French Sea Captain of Dieppe* (1547), 4
crime and disorder, 10-13, 18-19, 22, 39, 43-48, 50, 53, 60-61, 67, 71, 74, 77, 79, 84, 100, 101-02, 119, 120, 135, 143, 153, 169, 170, **172**, 173, 193, 196, 204, 226-27, 241. *See also* mobs, prisons.
Crosby, Thurza "Fly Rod," 142-43
Cross, Burton M. (Gov.), 227
Crouch, F. Nichols, 107
Crown (privateer), 74
Cumberland Center, Maine, 170
Cumberland County (1760), 40, 44, 56, 64, 80, 81; courthouse (first), 80
Cumberland & Oxford Canal, 56, 96
Cummings, Bob, 236
Cummings, Dr., 81
Cummings, Willard, 214, 227
Curless, Dick, 211
Curtis. Cyrus H. K., 153
Curtis, Cyrus W., 179
Curtis, Kenneth (Gov.), 228
Curtis, Oakley C. (Gov.), 157, 161
Cushing, Maine, 10, 19, 214
Cushing, William, 43
Cushnoc. *See* Augusta.
customhouses, 39, 44
Cyr, Joseph, 62
Cyr, Marguerite Thibodeau, 61, 63
Cyr Plantation, Maine 62, 125

D

Dagenais, Maxime, 63; *Land in Between, The* (2004, Craig and Dagenais), 63
dairy industry, 171
dam, **174**
Damariscove Island, Maine, 6, 15, 18
"Dam the Torpedoes," 122
dance and dancers, 3, 88, 210, **224.** *See also by name.*
Daniel Webster (vessel), 95
Danish Village (motor court), 168, 199
Dark Shadows (TV program), 212
Dash (privateer), 33
d'Aulnay, Charles de Menou, 19-20
Dauphine, La (vessel), 2
Davie, George (Capt.), 23
Davie, Mary M., 23
Davies, Charles S, 88
Davis, Bette, 210
Davis, W. G., 133
Dawnland (Native American name for Maine), 14
Day, Holman, 130, 140, 143, 153, 181
Dead River, 46
DeAngelo, Sergeant, 231
Deane, Samuel (Rev.), 47, 57, **61**, 68; *New England Farmer* (1790), 68
Death of General Montgomery (play), 47
debt, 45, 59, 60, 61, 66, 76
Dearborn, Henry (Col./Gen.), 46, 59, 77
December 7th (film), 201
Dechaine, Dennis, 227
de Champlain, Samuel, 7-9
"Declaration of Conscience," 227, 228. *See also* Smith, Margaret Chase.
Declaration of Independence, 49, 50, 240
Deer Isle, Maine, 54; raid, 54
Deering, James, 53
Deering Oaks Park (1879), 128
Defence (privateer), 51
de Guercheville, *See* de Pons-Ribérac.
d'Iberville, Sieur. *See* Le Moyne, Pierre.
de La Tour, Claude, 18, **19**, 20
Demetrius, Claude, 211
Democratic Party, 80, 81, 102, 106, 108-10, 111, 112, 152-59, 161, 173-74, 191-205, 226-28,

INDEX 263

232, 240-41
Democrat-Republican Party (Jeffersonian), 61, 75-77, 80, 81
deMonts, Sieur. *See* du Guast, Pierre.
Denebola (destroyer), 193
Denmark, Maine, 93-94, 143
Dennett, Lydia, 102
Denys, Nicholas, 6
Department of Agriculture, Maine, 135
Department of Extension, 139
Department of Health, Maine, 161, 173, 200
Department of Industry, Maine, 132
Department of Inland Fisheries, 143, **208**, 236
dependent care (state), 125
depression. *See* Great Depression.
de Pons-Ribérac, Antoinette, 12, **13**
de Razilly, Isaac, 19, 20
Dermer, Thomas (Capt.), 13
Der Wacher (newspaper), 195
de Saint-Castin, Jean Vincent d'Abbadie (Baron), 22, 26
Des Barres, H. F. W., charts, **41**, **42**
description of North America (1672), 6
Desert of Maine, 168
Desmond, G. Henri, 159
"Devil's Half Acre," 131
Diamond (Hog) Island, Maine, 37
Dibner, Martin, 211, 216, **217**; brothers, 216, **217**
Dickson, Margaret, 212; *Maddy's Song*, 1985
Diligence (HMS schooner/privateer), 46
Dingley, Nelson (Rep.), 154-55
"Dirigo" (state motto), 79
Discourse of a Great French Sea Captain of Dieppe (1547, Pierre Crignon), 4
diseases, 15, 61, 62. *See also* epidemics, medicine, nurses, physicians.
Discoverer (bark), 8
distillery, 47
divas (opera), 150-51. *See also* by name.
Division of Indian Affairs, Massachusetts, 58
Dix, Dorothea, 102, 120
Dixfield, Maine, 106, 138
Dochet Island. *See* St. Croix.
Dodge, Marshall, 210; *Bert and I* (records, Dodge and Bryan), 210

dogs, 15, 165, 184, **239**
Dole, Sanford, 153
Dominic, Randolph and Elizabeth, 216, **217**
Dominion of New England (1685-88), 23
Dorr, G. B., 168
Double Eagle II (balloon), 208
Dover (ship), 64, **65**
Dover-Foxcroft, Maine, 167
Dow, Neal, 102, **121**, 157-58, 164; house, 121. *See also* prohibition.
Dow Air Force Base, Bangor, 195, 197, 206, 207
down east, down-easter (terms), ix, 57, 78, 88, 102
Down East (painting), **78**
Down East magazine, 210
Downeast and Different (2006, Neil Rolde), ix
Down Easter (vessel type), 134
Down-East Quickstep (music), **88**
Downeasters, The (novel, John Neal), 104
Downing, Jack (fictional character), 107, 113
draft (military), 120, 188, 222; draft dodgers, 120; draft riot, 120
dreams, 59, 60, 79
Dresden, Maine, 40, 43. *See also* Pownalborough.
drinking habits, 18, 22, 33, 35, 38, 41, 42, 61, 153, 157-58, 164-65, 170, **172**. *See also* prohibition, taverns, WCTU.
dugouts, 25
du Guast, Pierre, 7-9
Dummer's War (Lovewell's, 1725), 33
Dunbar Grant, 34
Dunbar, David, 33, 34
Dunlap, William, 105
Dunn Family, 152
Dunton, Ebenezer, 59
Dunton, W. Herbert, 180
Duong, Sakhann, **224**
du Thet, Gilbert, 12
Dutch Americans, 12, 22, **165**
Dwight, Timothy (Rev.), 61
Dwinel, Rufus, 89
E
Eagle 56, USS (patrol boat), 195
Eagle Island, Maine, 153
Eagle II, 208
Eames, Emma, 150

East Andover, Maine, 97
Eastern Steamship Company, 141
East Harrington, 163
Eastman, Joel W., ix, 194-95
Eastman, Seth, 117
Easton, Maine, 196
East Oxford, Maine, 138-39
Eastport, Maine, 57, 60, 74, **137**, 137, 149, 209
Eaton, Elisha, 34
Eaton, Harvey, 141
Echoes magazine, 210
Eckstorm, Fannie Hardy, 152, 183
economy: center or gravity, 33, 57, 60, 63, 66, 89-90, 96, 104, **126-27**, 155, 161, 175, 190-91, 194, 205-04, 233-36; competition from away, 130, 161, 177, 233-35; panics, 90, 96, 127, 133, 146
Eddy, Jonathan (Col.), 51
Edge of the Sea, The (1956, Rachel Carson), 220
education, 21, 22, 27, 28, **29**, 31, 43, 67, 68, 80, 98, 103, 109, 120, 136, 137-39, 147, 152, 161, 183, **194**, 203, 206-07, 213, 226, 224, **241**. *See also* colleges, schools, universities, by name.
Eighteenth Amendment, 164, 175; repeal, 175
elderly, 23, 231
elections: 1860, 108-110; 1879 crisis (Augusta), 156, **157**
electric power, 41, 174, 208, 209, 235. *See also* Central Maine Power, Fernald Law, and Insull, Samuel.
elephant (Old Bet), 67
Elliot, Maine, 55
Eliot, Charles, 168
Elizabeth I (Queen of England), 5, 10
Elliot, Robert, 119-20
Ellis, Milton (Dr.), 183
Ellsworth, Maine, 66, 101, 210
Elm Hotel (Portland), **82**
Elwell, Edward H., vx
Ely, Samuel (Rev.), 60
Emancipation Proclamation, 124. *See also* slavery.
Embargo of 1807, 66, 72-75
Embden, Maine, 5. *See also* petroglyphs.
Emerson, Ralph Waldo, 90, 119
Emery, Marcellus, 111

Emory, Noah, 38
Enfield, Maine, 169
English: civil war, 18, 21; early settlers, 18; overseas empire begins, 5
environmental movement, 207, 220, 236-38. *See also* Carson, Rachel.
Episcopal Church. *See* Anglican.
Enterprise (brig), 73
entertainment. *See by type*.
epidemics, 15, 26, 163, 224. *See also* diseases, hospitals, medicine, nurses, physicians.
Epstein, Mrs. Max B., 175
Etchemin (Penobscot), 4, 12, 14, 15, 23. *See also* Native American.
ethnic changes, postwar, 204, 205
eugenics, 146-47. *See also* Malaga Island.
European & North American Railroad, **129-31**
evictions, 44, 60, **146**. *See also* squatters.
Experiment Station, 137, 139

F

Fagundes, Joao Alvares, 3
Fairfield, John (Gov.), 87
fairs (agricultural), 136-37, **138**, 139, 147, 215, 226
Falmouth (becomes Portland after 1786), 22, 25, 27, 28, 31, 33, 36, 38, 39, 40, 41, 45, 47, **48**, 57; burning and bombardment (1775), 47, **48**; proprietors, 32; view of, **48**. *See also* Casco.
Falmouth (Foreside), Maine, 219
Falmouth Gazetteer, 5, 68, **69**
family: basic unit of labor, 321; settlement, 67, 125
famine, 61, 62
Fern, Fanny (Sarah Payson Willis Parton), 104
farms, 21, 22, 33, 44, 59, 60, 61, 64, **70**, **78**, **81**, 94, 105, **108**, 125, 133, 135-36, 138, 139, 171, 176, 196, 207, 236; assistance, 176, 196; buildings, **105**, **108**
Farmer's Almanack, 70. *See also* almanacs.
Farmington, Maine, 67, 68, 150-51
Farnsworth, Eugene "Doc," 166
Farnsworth Museum, Rockland, 214
Farnum Brothers, 148, 181, 182
Farragut, David (Adm.), 122
Fassett, Francis H., 128
Fazio, Dani, **220**
Federal Art Project, 178

Federal Bureau of Investigation, 173, 190
federal government, 100, 121, 122, 161, 173, 206-07, 235, 241; funding, 168, 170, 173, 178. *See also* by branch.
Federal Housing Authority, 199
Federalist Party, 61, 64, 76-77, 80, 81, 82
Feeney Family. *See* Ford.
Feke, Robert, 35
Female Charitable Society, 66
Fernald Law (hydro), 141, 165, 167. *See also* Central Maine Power, electric power.
Fernald's Point (Somes Sound), 12
Fessenden, William Pitt (Sen.), 79, 82, **112**, 153, 227
Field, Hamilton E., 149, 180, 214
filling stations, 168. *See also* automobiles.
films and film actors, 145, 152, 181, 195, 201, 207, 211. *See also* by name.
Furbish, Kate, 148; Furbish's lousewort, 148
fires, iv, **48**, 93, **101**, **126**, 128, 130, 143, 155, 177, 193, 194, **199**, 236; control towers, 194; firefighters, **199**; Fire of 1947, 236; underwriters, 126, 128
firearms, 17, 22, 23, 87, 100-01, 109, 125, 155
First Century: A History of the University of Maine, 1865–1965, The (1979, David C. Smith), 194
First Parish, Falmouth, 57, 80, **82**. *See also* Smith, Thomas, and Dean, Samuel.
First Radio Church of America, 167
Fisher, Jonathan (Rev.), 61, 68, 69, 102
fishing: bounty, 63, 118, 135; Canadian rights, 232; commercial, xv, 1, 2, 3, 4, 5, **6**, 13, 15, 18, 28, 36, 63, 94, 109, 135, 170-71, **188**, 205, 232, **233**, **234**; early fleet, 63; flakes and staging, **6**; French rights, 36; hatcheries, 178, **208**; salmon, 25, **91**; sport, 104, **142**, 168, 178, **208**, **216**, 232; vessels, 94, **137**, **233**
fish and game licenses, 143, 170, 208, 232
Flagg, Gershom, 35, 43
"Flaming Argument," 147-48
Flannagan, David, 152
floods, 61
Flucker, Lucy, 60. *See also* Knox, Lucy Flucker.
Fogg, John S. H., 50; autograph collection (MHS), 50
folklore, 5, 21, 89, 143, 183, 200, 210, 226. *See also* Maine Folklife Center.
food shortages, 57, 200. *See also* famine.
footwear. *See* shoes.
Ford, Francis (Feeney), 181, 201
Ford, Gerald (Pres.), 222, 238
Ford, John (Feeney), 148, 181, **182-84**, 201
Forest City (steamer), **118**, 119
forests and trees, 3, 5, 17, 22, 25, 36, 44, 45, 61, 78, 79, 81, 85, **86**, 90, 91, 92, **93**, 131, 139, **140**, 142-43, 170, 176, 177, 183, 190-95, 201, 207, 208, 220, 236; fear of, 22, 25, 28, 33, 36, 41; forest commissioner (1891), 143; management, 143; mystique, 143, 220; 'strip and waste," 44
Forest Life and Forest Trees (1851, John S. Springer), 92
Forests and Sea Power (1926, Robert G. Albion), 183
forts, 7, **9**, **10**, **11**, 12-17, 19, 25, 28, 35, 41, 46, 51, 71, 85, **116**, **117**, 155, 193-94, 195, 232; condition of, 116; First System, 71; Second System, 72; Third System, 100; WWII, 193, 194. *See also* by name.
Fort Baldwin, Maine, 195
Fort Cumberland, Nova Scotia, 51
Fort Fairfield, Maine, 85, 226
Fort Halifax, Maine, 36
Fort Kent, Maine, **85**, **168**; blockhouse, 85
Fort Knox, Maine, **117**
Fort McClarey, Maine, 116
Fort New Casco, Maine, 28
Fort Pentagoet (Castine), Maine, 19
Fort Popham, Maine, 116
Fort Pownal, Maine, 35
Fort Saco (Saco Fort), Maine, **25**
Fort St. George, Maine, 10-12, 50, 51
Fort Shirley, Maine, 35
Fort Sumner, Maine, 72
Fort Sumter, South Carolina, 109, 110, 114
Fort Ticonderoga, New York, 46
Fort Western, Maine, 35, 46
Fort William Henry, Maine, 25, 26
Fort Williams, Maine, 188
"Fortune's Temple," **56**
Foster, Stephen, 102
Fourth of July, 140

France and French. *See by name or activity.*
Francis I (King of France), 1, 2
Francis, Joe, **144**
Francis, William (Maj.), 56
Franco-Americans (French Canadians), 46, 61, 79, 117, 127, **131**, 132, 145-46, 213, 226, **233**, 236; *La Justice,* (newspaper), 146, 226; *La Messager,* (newspaper), 146, 226; population, 132, 240
Franklin County (1838), 83
Frederickton, New Brunswick, 86
Freedman's Bureau, 123
Freedom, Maine, 106
Freeman, Enoch, 37
Freeman, Frederick W., 162
Freeman, Nathaniel, 29
Freeman, Samuel, 49
Freemasons (Masonic Lodge), 64
Freeport, Maine, 143, **148**
Free Soil Party, 82
French and Indian War. *See* Seven Years' War.
French at Pentagoet, The (Christopher J. Turnbull), 19
French West Indies, 28
Frenchman's Bay, Maine, 48
Friendship (Meduncook), Maine, 36
frolics, 37, 40. *See also* leisure.
Frost Family, 27
Frost, Mary Pepperrell, **27**
Frost, William L., **223**
Frye, William (Sen.), 154, 227
Fryeburg, Maine, 54, 66, 67, **108**, 109, 134, 152, 226; Fair, 139, 226
Fuller, Melville W., 154
fur trade, 13
Fusion Party, 156, 157

G

Gamache, Joey, 219
gambling, **56**
game wardens, 143, 170; first pilot, 170, 208
Gandalf (sailboat), **219**
Gannett Family, Augusta, 153, 209
Gannett, Guy, 161, 166
Gannett, W. H., 153
Garcelon, Alonzo W. (Gov.), 155-56
Gardner, Obadiah (Gov.), 157

Gardiner Family, 44, 94
Gardiner, Robert H., 94
Gardiner, William Tudor (Gov.), 173
Garland, Maine, 120, 152
Garfield, James (Pres.), 153
gasoline: rationing, 191; tax, 168
Gaspe (HMS sloop), 39
Gastaldi, Giacomo, xv, 1, 5; *Terzo Volume della Navigation et Viaggi* (1556), xiv
Gatling gun, 157, 241
gay and lesbian, 220, 224, **225**
Gazetteer of Maine (1882), viii
General Court (Massachusetts), 23, 32, 49
Generall Historie of Virginia, New England.... (1624, John Smith), 12-15
George III (King of England), 37
General Henry Knox Museum, **59**. *See also* Knox, Henry; Knox Museum; and Montpelier.
Georges Bank, 3
Georgetown, Maine, 180
German Americans and Germany, 34, 42, 79, 94, 130, 161-**62**, 163-64, 186-87, **196**
Ghana, 241
G. H. Bass Company, 133, 161, 200
G. I. Bill of Rights, 187, 191, 203, 206
Gibson, Charles Dana, 144
Gift of God (ship), 12
Gilbert, Bartholomew (Capt.), 6
Gilbert, Humfrey (Sir), 5, 6
Gilbert, Raleigh, 11-12
Gilchrist, William Wallace, 163
glass manufacturing, 114
Gillars, Mildred E. "Axis Sally," 196, **197**
Gladys (canoe), **220**
Glovsky, David, 197, **198**
Gluskap, 3
Godfrey, Edward, 21
Godfrey, J. E., 131-32
gold rush (California, 1849), 96, 97
Goldwater, Barry (Sen.), 229
Gordon, Nathaniel (Capt.), 119
Gorgeana, 16, 20, 21. *See also* York, Maine.
Gorges, Ferdinando (Sir), 12-15, 17-21
Gorges, Robert (Gov.), 17, 20
Gorges, Thomas (Deputy Gov.), 20, 21

Gorham, Maine, 40, 44, 45, 53, 55, 57, 95, 123, 165
Gorham, William, 57
Gorman, Larry, 140
Gosnold, Bartholomew (Capt.), 6, 10
government. *See by name, branch, or activity.*
governors. *See by name.*
governor's mansion (Blaine House), 164, 191
graffiti, 10, 212
Grand Army of the Republic, 120
Grand Banks, **xv**, 1-3, **6**, 28, 118, 135
Grand Derangement (1755), 20, 36. *See also* Acadian Civil War.
Grand Trunk Railway, 97, 132, 161, 169, 192-93
Grand Turk (privateer), 73
Grange movement, 157
Granger, Charles Henry, **99**, 104
granite, 133. *See also* stone.
Grant, Ulysses S. (Pres.), **129**, 154
gravestones, **32**, **34**, 41, 66. *See also* stone.
Graves, Samuel (Adm.), 45, 47, 48
Gray, Roland, 183
Gray (New Boston), Maine, 44, 64
Great Black-Backed Gull (painting), **92**
Great Depression, 171-73, 185, 191
Great Northern Paper Company, 139, 196
Great Recession, 205, 236
Greater Portland Landmarks, 213. *See also* architecture, preservation.
Greek Americans, 145, 170, 229-30, **231**
Greenland (vessel), 64, **65**
Greenback Party, 111-12, 155-**56**, **157**, 158-59
greenbacks, 111, 112. *See also* money.
Greenleaf, Moses, 83, 84; *Map of the District of Maine,* (1815), 83
Greenville, Maine, 143
Greenwood, Isabel, 164
Greenwood, John, 33
Grover, Cuvier (Gen.), 121
Gruenining, Ernest (Dr.), 167
Guecheville, de Pons-Ribérac. *See* de Pons-Ribérac.
guides, Maine, 90, 91
Guignard, Michael, 131
Gulf War, 240
gunpowder mills, 95, 116
Gyles, John, 22, 23

gymnasiums, 94

H

Haines, William T. (Gov.), 157
Hakluyt, Richard, 5, 6
Hale, Eugene (Sen.), 155
Half Moon (vessel), 12
Halifax, Nova Scotia, 39, 49, 52, 169
Hampden, Maine, **74**, 102, 220
Hamlin, Cyrus, 153
Hamlin, Hannibal (Vice Pres.), 79, 82, 107, 108, 109, **110**, 111-25, 153, 198, 227
Hancock Barracks (Houlton), 85
Hancock County, Maine (1789), 60
Hancock Point, Maine, 193
Hancock, John (Gov.), 58
Handel Society, 67
Hannaford Brothers, 235
Hannibal Hamlin (Liberty Ship), **198**
Hanrahan, Cornelius, 120
harbors. *See by name.*
Harding, Chester, **63**
Hardy Family, 104
Hardy, Jeremiah P., **88**, 104
Harley, J. B., 13
Harmony of Maine, The (publication), 67, **68**
Harpswell, Maine, 34; meetinghouse, **34**
Harpswell Historical Society, 34
Harrison, Benjamin (Pres.), 153
Hartford Convention, 74
Harriet (brig), **95**
Harry, P., **cover**, iv, **86**, 87
Hartley, Marsden, 149, 161, **179**, 183
Harvard College, 27, 32, 50, 64, 66, 68, 103, 151, 152, 165, 181, 183, 211; Harvard professors from Maine, 68, **98**, 103, 151-52
Haskell, Barbara, 179
Hassam, Childe, 149
Hatch, Louis C., ix, 55, 183; *Maine: A History* (1918), ix
Hathaway, William (Sen.), 229
Hauck, Arthur A., 203
Hawaiian missions, 157
Hawthorne, Nathaniel, 90, 100, 224
hay, 42, 44, 143; salt hay, 42
Head Tide, Alna, 152

hemlock bark, 61, 133
Henry IV (King of France), 8
Henry VII (King of England), 1, 31
Henry VIII (King of England), 4
Herbert, Richard A., 203; *Modern Maine* (1950), 203
Hermon, Maine, 216
herring. *See* sardines.
Hersey, Samuel F., 90
Hildreth, Horace (Gov.), 205, **206**, 209, 227, 228
Hill, Lyman, 143
Hilling, John, **back cover**, iv, **101**
Hine, Lewis W., 150
Hines, Glen, 221
hippies, 219
Hiram, Maine, 50
Hirschmann, Johann Baptist, **64**
Hispanic Americans, 240
historians. *See by name.*
Historic New England, 41
historic preservation, 236. *See also* architcture, preservation.
History and Description of New England, A (1859, Coolidge and Mansfield), viii
History of Maine (1875, John S. C. Abbott), viii, 145
History of Portland (1865, William Willis), 114, 127
History of the District of Maine (1795, James Sullivan), **viii**
History of the State of Maine (1832, William D. Williamson), vii, 80
hockey, 215-19
Hodgkins, Harvard, 193
Hodgkins, John E., 202; *Soldier's Son, A* (2006), 202
Hog (Diamond) Island, Maine, 37
Hollywood (Maine in), 148, 181-83
Holmes, Ezekiel, 94
Holverson, John, 215
Homeland Security, 230
Homer, Winslow, **115**, 127, 148-49, 200
Honduras, 240
Hoose, Shoshana, 221
Hoover, Herbert (Pres.), 173
"Hopalong Cassidy." *See* Cassidy, Hopalong.
Hopper, Edward, 180
Hornberger, H. Richard (Dr.), 211, 222

horses, 38, 39, 60, **81**, 82, 83, **107**, **116**, 120, 121, 128, **138**, 139, 140, 147, **168**, 176, 215; racing, 94, 128, **130**, 147, 176, 215
hospitals, 100, 111, 120, **128**, 155, 158, *See also* diseases, epidemics, medicine, nurses, physicians.
hotels, **82**, 93, 114, 129, 143-45, 158, **160**. *See also* taverns and by name.
Hough, Howard O. (Rev.), 167
Houlton Band. *See also* Maliseets, Native Americans.
Houlton, Maine, 60, 85, **116**, 120, 164, 195, 207-08, 221
housing, 198-99, 203. *See also* architecture and shelter.
Howard, John Quay, 119
Howard, Oliver Otis (Gen.), 123
Howe, T. O., 155
Howells, William D., 152, 182, **184**
Hudson, Henry (Capt.), 12
Hughes, Howard, 227
Hughes Woolen Mill, **235**
Hugenots, 8, 42
Hull, John T., 148
Hume, Frank M. (Col.), 164
humor (Maine), 92, 104, **107**, 113, 152, 210, 226
Humphries, Joshua, 72
Hunt, John, 11, 12
Hunt, Thomas (Capt.), 13
Hunters Lodge Movement, 87
hunting: market, 143; sport, 91, 104, 108-09, **142**, 143, **168**, 173
Hurricane Island, Maine, 133
Hyde, Thomas W. (Gen.), 135
hydro power, 141, **174**, 177. *See also* Central Maine Power, electric power, Fernald Law, and Insull, Samuel.

I

Iberville, Pierre le Moyne. *See* Le Moyne, Pierre
ice industry, 94 134
Illustrated History of Maine, An (1995, Neil Rolde), ix
immigrants, 17-18, 55, 79, 96, 100, 101, 127, 130, 132, 133, **139**, 145, 146, 165, 171, 180-82, 183, 203, 213, 222, 239-40, **241**
I. M. Pei and Partners, 215
Impartial History of the War in America (1782,

INDEX 269

James Murray), **48**
impeachment, 112, 153
Index of American Design (Dorothy Hay Jensen), 178
Indians. *See Native Americans.*
Indian Island, Maine, 58, 181
Indian Rock Camps, 143
Indian Township, Maine, 238
industry. *See manufacturing.*
Industry (vessel), 64, **65**
influenza, **163**
Ingraham, David, 5
institutionalization, 146
Insull, Samuel, 164-65, 167. *See also* Central Maine Power, electric power, Fernald Law.
insurance companies, 66, 126, 128, 129, 235-36
intelligence network, 119
International Paper Mill, 237
Interstate 95, 207. *See also* roads, transportation.
Intrepid, USS (sloop), 71
inventors, 67, 80, 94, 100, 133, 140
Ipcar, Dahlov, 180, 215
Iran–Contra Scandal, 229, **230**
Iraq War, 222, **231**
Irish Americans, ii, 5, 10, 15, **62**, 79, 100, 101, 145, 146-47, 182, 213, 226, 229, **230**, **238**, 239, 240
Irish Heritage Center, 226
Isaacson, Philip, 214
Islam, 153, 171, 222, **241**
Isles of Shoals, 6, 15, 18, 25, 27, 53, 93, 149, 152, 177-78, 232
Islesboro, Maine, 144
Italian Americans, 1, 2, 3-4, 6, 133-34, **139**, 145, 171, 190, 191, 207, 213, 226, 229; stonecutters, 133
Italian Heritage Center, 226
Italian Villa Style, 102, 103

J
"Jack Downing." *See* Downing, Jack.
Jackson, Charles Thomas, 84
Jackson Laboratory, 176, 236
Jacobin Society (Radical Republicans), 64
Jacobsen, Antonio, **141**
jails, **28**, 60, 87, 120, 158
Jalali, Reza, **241**

James I (King of England), 11
Jamestown, Virginia, 11, 12
Japan, cultural ties, 153, 155, 191, 200, 203, 241
Jay, Maine, 237
Jefferson, Thomas (Pres.), 59, 72-76
Jeffersonians (Democrat-Republicans), 61, 75-77, 80-81
Jensen, Dorothy Hay, 178, 179; *Index of American Design*, 178
Jeremiah O'Brien (Liberty Ship), 200
Jersey (prison hulk), **49**
Jesuits (Society of Jesus), 12, 13, 22, 25. *See also* Catholic Church.
Jewett, Sarah Orne, 127, **151**, 152, 200; *Country of the Pointed Firs, The* (1886), **151**, 152
Jewish Americans, 130, 145, **147**, 167, **175**, 187, 191, 213-14, 220
John Taber & Son, **66**; Taber Notes, **66**
John Winslow Jones Company, 133
Johnson, Andrew (Pres.), 112, 153. *See also* impeachment.
Johnson, (Jonathan) Eastman, 105, **106**
Jonathan Fisher of Blue Hill, Maine (2010, Kevin D. Murphy), 61
Jones, Harry, 169, 170
Jones, Ichabod (Capt.), 45
Jones, Isaac, 133
Jones, John Paul (Capt.), 48
Jones, Lieutenant, **52**
Jonesport, Maine, **136**, 137
Jongeleen, Peter and Yvonne, **165**
Jordan Family, 23
Jordan, Robert, 21, 23
Josselyn, John, 21; *Account of Two Voyages into New-England, An* (1679), 21; *New-England Rarities Discovered* (1672), 21
Joy, Jen, **220**
Judd, Richard W., ix; *Maine: The Pine Tree State* (1995), ix
Junior, Paul, 176

K
Kaler, James Otis, 152; *Toby Tyler* (1880), 152
Katahdin, **front cover**, iv, 86-87, 90-91, 166, 176, 179
Katahdin (gunboat), 122

Kathleen Mavourneen (song), 107
Kavanagh, Edward (Gov.), 62
Kavanagh Family, **62**
Kavanagh, James, 62
Kearsarge, USS (steam sloop), 83, 116
Keeley, James F., 202
Kellogg, Elijah, Jr., 152, 200
Kelly, Norman, 150
Kennebec-Chaudière River Corridor, 36, 37, 46, 47, 85
Kennebec County (1799), 60
Kennebec Journal (newspaper), 236
Kennebec River, 4, 10, 11, 12, 17, 21, 22, 23, 25, 28, 35, 36, 37, 39, 82, 134, 170, **174**, 195, 200
Kennebeck Proprietors, 19, 33, 35, 41, 43, 44, 46, 47, 57, 60, 85, **134**
Kennebunk, Maine, 9, 12, 180, 181, 194
Kennebunkport, Maine, 58, **158**, 182, **184**, **239**
Kent, Atwater, 144-45, **184**
Kent, Edward (Gov.), 87
Keyes, Bob, 214-15
kidnappings, 10, 11, 12, 13, 50, 53
Kidney Pond Camps, 143
Kimball, Charles F. 148
King, Abraham, 10
King, Angus (Gov.), 229
King, Horatio, 79
King, Martin Luther King, Jr., 204; assassination, 204; Day, 204
King, Richard, 45, 63, 64, 76
King, Rufus, 63, **64**, 76
King, Stephen, **212** 241; *Carrie* (1971), 212
King, Tabitha, 241
King, William (Gov.), 64, 76-77, 80, 82
King Philip's War, 23, 32, 153
King William's War, **23**, 25
King Riot, 102
Kingfield, Maine 120, 142
Kingfield Draft Riot, 120, 148
Kirkpatrick, Alice Harmon Shaw, 190
Kittery, Maine, 18, 21, 22, 25, 27, 31, 41, 48, 58, 59, 72, 75, **83**, 152, 169, 188, 232
knighthood, first American, 26
Knights of Labor, 133, 146
Know Nothing Movement (Nativist), iv, 81, 100, 101. See also Malta War, Woodland Rebellion.
Knox County (1860), 83
Knox, Henry (Gen.) 59, 60, 236; Knox Mansion (Montpelier), **59**, 60. See also General Henry Knox Museum and Knox, Lucy Flucker.
Knox, Lucy Flucker, 60. See also Knox, Henry.
Korean War, 221-22, 232
Kosovo Intervention, 222
Kotzschmar, Hermann, 107, 150-51, 153; Kotzschmar Municipal Organ, 153
Ku Klux Klan, 161, 164, 165, 166, **167**. See also by individual names.

L

L-8 (submarine), 164
labor, 21, 33, 34, 95-96, 100, 108, 109, 117, 126, 130, **131**, 132, 133-35, **139**, 145-46, 158-59, 161, 172, 175-76, **177**, 183, 195-96, 197, 198, 199, 200, 205-06, 222, 229, 232-33, 234-36, **237**, 240-41; child, 21, 109, 133, 134, 135, **136**-37, 146, 158-59, 175, 176; Labor Day, 133; unions, 121, 133, 161, 236, **237**, 240-41. *See also* Knights of Labor.
Lachaise, Gaston, 180
Laconia Mills, 95
Laconia, New Hampshire, 17
La Dauphine (ship), 2
Ladd, William, 102
La Fanfare Painchaud, 150
Lafayette National Park. *See* Acadia National Park.
Laffey, USS (destroyer), 200
La Gendre, Bob, 176
La Justice, (newspaper), 146, 226
Lake Champlain, 46
Lake Sebago, 96, 128
Land in Between, The (2004, Craig and Dagenais), 63
Lakewood Theater, 152
La Messager, (newspaper), 146, 226
land: agents, 85, 87, 89, 142, 236; clearing, 60; divided between Maine and Massachusetts, 56, 82, 83-84, 238; grants to Loyalists, 54; grants to soldiers, 32, 58, 59; lottery, 56, 58; Maine sovereignty, ii, 15-21, 55, 56, 58, 60, 63, 84, 87, 236-37; Massachusetts policy, 59, 84, 236; ownership, ii, 5-15, 17-21, **32**, 33, 34, 36, 37,

43, 44, 55, 57, 59, 60, **78**, 87, 135-36, 142, 176, 205, 236-37, 240-41; public, 85, 87, 89, 142, 236; sold by Maine, 56, 58, 76, 77-78, 80, 87, 236-37; sold by Massachusetts, 56, 59, 82, 83, 84, 238; speculators, 59, 60, 83, 84, 87, **88**
"Land of Bad People," 1
Lane, Fitz Henry, **82**, 83
L'Anse aux Meadows, Newfoundland, 2
Laos and Laotian Americans, 222
Lark (fishing schooner), 195
La Saussaye, Capt. 12
Latter Day Saints (Mormons), 221
Laughlin, Gail, 164, 175
Lawry, Nelson H., 195
laws, ii, 19, 20, 22, 25, 37, 38, 39, 54, 60, 71, 77, 80, 90-91, 98, 102, 119, 141, 146, 157, 159, 163-64, 167, 170, 175, 176, 208, 210, 226, 236-38. *See also* by name.
Le Moyne, Pierre, 16, 26
Leadbetter, Danville (Gen.), 119
Leaflets of the Artists (1883 pamphlet), 149
League of Nations, 164
Lebanon and Lebanese Americans, 145, 229, **230**, 238
LeBlanc Family, 36
L. D. M. Sweat Museum. *See* Portland Museum of Art.
Lee, Robert E. (Gen.), 124
Leeds, Maine, 102, 119, 122, 123
leisure, 21, 22, 33, 35, 37, 40, 67, 71, 90-**93**, 94, 114, 127, 144, 147, **148**, 152, 160, 164-65, **166**, 170, 176, 208, 215-16, **217**, 218, **219**, 220, 226, 236, 238-40, 241. *See also* by name of activity.
Lend-Lease, 187, 188
Le Page, Paul (Gov.), 226, 229, 241
Letters of Marque, 48
Leavett, Christopher, 17, 18; *Voyage to New England, A* (1628), 17, 18
Levinge, Richard R. E. A. (Sir), 91
Lewiston, Maine, 95, 110, 114, 117, 174, 176, **179**, 226, 237
Libby Family, **105**
Libby Prison, 121
Liberia, Maryland County, 98-99, 119
Liberty (sloop), 46

Liberty Bonds, 163-64
Liberty Men and the Great Proprietors (1990, Alan Taylor), 213, 219
Liberty Ships (WWII), 188, 197, **198**, 199, 200
libraries, 47, 98, 102, 129, 132, 150, 152, 163, 166, 195, 213, **218**
lighthouses: during WWII, 193; first in Maine, 72, **73**; number in Maine, 72, **73**, 100
Life Saving Service, 71, 100.
lime industry, 60
Limestone Airforce Base, 208
Limestone, Maine, **208**
Lincoln, Abraham (Pres.), 108-25; cabinet, **113**, 132
Lincoln, Benjamin (Gen.), 59
Lincoln County (1760), 40, 43
Lincoln County Cultural and Historical Society, 43
Lindbergh, Charles, 170
Line of Settlement, 39
Lion (steam engine), 89
Lippard, Lucy, 215
literature in Maine, ii, 2, 4, 5, 6-10, 12, 14, 17-18, 21, **24**, **26**, 38, 39, **61**, 66, 68, 69, 70, 71, 79, 82, 92, 97, **98**, 102-03, **104**, 107, 109, **113**, **114**, 127-28, 137, 138, 145, **151**, **152**, 153, 158, 161, 178, **179**, 181, **182**, 183, **184**, 201, 209-11, **212**, 213-14, 222, **230**. *See also* by author's name and title.
Little Chebeague Island, Maine, 193
Livermore Falls, Maine, 183
Liverpool, Great Britain, 66
livestock, 44, 54, 60, 78, 94, **138**, 139, **156**
Livingston, Deborah K., 164
L.L. Bean, Inc., 143, 173, 200, 236. *See also* Bean, Leon Leonwood.
lobsters and lobstermen, **133**, 135, **171**, **188**, 226
Locke's Mills (Greenwood), Maine, 143
locomotive manufacturing, 97, **116**
log buildings, **29**, **62**
Lombard, Alvin, 140; Lombard Steam Log Hauler, 140
Long Carry, 46
Longcreek Youth Development Center, 99, **158**
Long Island (Casco Bay), Maine, 193, 209
Long Reach, Maine, 39
Long Robert (vessel), 13

272   MAINE: THE WILDER HALF OF NEW ENGLAND

Longfellow, Henry Wadsworth, 79, **98**, 102-03, 109, 113, 152, **158**, 212
Longfellow, Stephen, Jr., 57
Longley, James (Gov.), 228
London Company, 11
Loring, Donna M., 222
lotteries, **56**, 58; office, 56
Louis XIII (King of France), 13
Louisbourg, Nova Scotia, 32, 33, 34, 35, 36
Louisiana, 26, 36
Lovell, Maine, 105, **106**
Lovell, Solomon (Gen.), 52
Lovewell's War. *See* Dummer's War.
Lovejoy, Elijah P., 102
Lovewell, John (Capt.), 33
Loyalists (Tories), 37, 55, 57, 62, 183
Lubec, Maine, 57, 71
lumbering, 29, 33, 35, 44, 45, 59, 60, 78, 83, 84, 85, 89-90, 131, **140-43**, 153, 183, 195, 230, 236. *See also* Bangor, lumber capital, and timber.
Lumbermen's Museum, Patten, 140
Lutherans, 42
Lydia Bailey (1947, Kenneth Roberts), 40
Lygonia Grant, 19
Lyman, John G., 180
Lyon, James (Rev.), 43

M

MacMillan, Donald B. (Adm.), 173
Machias, Maine, **41**, **42**, 43, 45, 47, 48, 51, 54, 200; battle, 45
Machias River, **41-42**, 45
Machiasport, Maine, 5, 209
Madawaska, Maine, 61, 85
Madawaska Territory, 61, 62, 63, 84, 101
Maddy's Song (Margaret Dickson, 1985), 212
Magalloway, Maine, 83
Mahon, Michael K. (Adm.), 240
Maine: absorption by Massachusetts, 19, 21; achieves national identity, 107; as district, 35, 55, 57, 75-77; as military buffer zone, 17-21, 27, 37, 51, 52, 57; as small republic, 21; as twenty-third state, 77; British occupation of, 75; capital, 82, 83, 158; coast during WW II, 188, 193; considers Acadian rule, 21; description (1524), 3; geographic description, 3; identity, 35, 57, 174; importance in British Empire, 28, 31; Mainers by choice, 179; occupations, 1860, 105; origin of name, xi, 3, 15, 17-21; power of, 227; province of, 15, 17-21, 15; purchased by Massachusetts, 21; ranking among states, 79, 125; resettlement, 27; response to economic crisis, 127, 161, 206; secretaries of war, 59; seen as provincial, 181; teaching Maine history, 152; term "Mainer," 57. *See also* by place, name, or event.
Maine, USS (battleship), 155
Maine: A Guide Down East (1937), 178
Maine: A History (1918, Louis C. Hatch), ix
Maine Agricultural Society, 139
Maine and Her People (1957, Harold B. Clifford), 232
Maine and Its Role in American Art (1963, Colby College), 215
Maine Catalogue (1973), 210
Maine Central Railroad, 129
Maine Charitable Mechanic Association, 66, 100, 113
Maine College of Art, 119, 179, 214
Maine Festival, 226
Maine Fire and Marine Insurance Company, 66
Maine General Hospital, 111, **128**, 158. *See also* Maine Medical Center.
Maine Health and Welfare Agency, 58
Maine Historic Preservation Commission, 213
Maine Historical Society, 19, 46, 50, 98, **158**, 214
Maine Law Party (Temperance), 83, 100, 102, 175
Maine Maritime Academy, 203, 207
Maine Maritime Museum **134**, 135
Maine Medical Center, **128**. *See also* Maine General Hospital.
Maine Music Festival, 150
Maine Problems (painting), 180
Maine Province and Court Records, 21
Maine School for the Feeble-Minded (Pineland), 147
Maine State College of Agriculture. *See* University of Maine at Orono.
Maine State Legislature, 157, 176
Maine State Museum, 2, 89, **221**
Maine State Music Theater, 210
Maine State Pier, 169
Maine State Police (1925), 169

Maine Sunday Telegram (newspaper), 236
Maine in the Making of the Nation (1996, Elizabeth Ring), ix
Maine: The Pine Tree State (1995, Richard Judd, ed.), ix
Maine Times (newspaper), 210
Maine Today Media, 241
Maine Turnpike, 207
Maine Woods, The (1846-57, Henry David Thoreau), 92
Maine Woods magazine, 142
Maine Yankee Nuclear Power Plant, 208, 211
Maine's Visible Black History (2006, Price and Talbot), 226
Maison Roy (Roy House), 62
Majabigwaduce (Castine), 51, 52
Malaga Island, Maine, 146, 147; destruction, 147
Maliseets, 23, 24, 25, 36, 51, 61, 91, 238. *See also* Houlton Band.
Malta War, 60
Malvern, USS (warship), 119
Manchester, Maine, 221
Manning, William, 214
manufacturing, 89, 94, 97, 120, 132, 133, **134-36**, 137, 139, 146, 171, 200-01, 205, 229, 232-33, **235**, 237; WWII, 200-01
Man Against the Sky, The (1916, E. A. Robinson), 182
"Man from Maine" (James G. Blaine), 112
Map of the District of Maine, (1815, Moses Greenleaf), 83
maps, **xv**, 1, 2, 6, 7, 8, 9, 11-12, 13, 14, 15, 36, 37, 83, 84, 207
marble, quarrying, 74. *See also* stone.
Margaretta, HMS (schooner), 45
Marin, John, 179-80
Marine Hospital, 155
marine society, 66. *See also* Portland Marine Society.
mariners (master), 33, 35, 45, **64**, 66, **75**, 162
maritime museums, 96. *See also by name.*
marshes, 42
Mars Hill, Maine, 84
Marston, George W., 150
Marston, Levi (Capt.), **95**
martial law, 53

Martin Luther King Day, 204. *See also* King, Martin Luther, Jr.
Marx, Karl, ix
Mary and John (vessel), 12
*M*A*S*H**, 211, 221
Mason, John (Capt.), 15, 17-21
Mason, Moses, (Dr.), 61, **63**
Massachusetts: bankruptcy of, **51**, 52; charter restored, 23; defeat of navy, **51**. *See also by name or action.*
mast trade, 28, 33, 34, 40, 44, 45, 84; agent, 31, 32, 33, 34, 45; impounded, 45; monopoly, 31, 34, 44; port, 31, 40, 44, 45; ships, 34, 37, 45
Materson, Edward, **218**
Mather, Cotton (Rev.), 18, 221
Matinicus Island, Maine, 208
Mayaguez, SS (container ship), 222
Mayflower Hill, Colby College, 206
McAuliffe, Jack, 147
McCulloch, Hugh, 112, 155
McIntire Garrison House, York, **29**, 31
McIntire, Rufus, 87
McCarthy, Joseph (Sen.), 227
McKernan, John (Gov.), 229, 230
McLean, Francis (Gen.), 51
McLellan Family, 44, 63, **64**, **66**
McLellan, Alexander (Capt.), 53
McLellan, Arthur (Capt.), 96
McLellan, C. H. P., 133; *Workingman's Advocate* (1835), 133
McLellan, Hugh, 44, **66**
McLellan, Isaac, Jr., 104
McLellan, Joseph, Jr. (Capt.), **64**
McLellan, Joseph, Sr. (Capt.), 64
McLellan, Plato, 53
McLellan, Prince, 53
mechanics, 66, 67, 133. *See also* trade.
Medal of Honor, 121
medicine, 6, 21, 26, 41, 57, **63**, 95-96, 108, 111, 120, 124-25, **128**, 155, 158, **163**, 224, **225**. *See also* hospitals, individuals, institutions, and nurses by name.
Meduncook (Friendship), Maine, 36, 61
Megunicook River, **235**
Mell, Joe, 142

Men of Zeal (1988, Cohen and Mitchell), 230
merchants, 31, 32, 33, 34, 35, 39, 40, 50, 53, 54, 57, 61, 62, 63, **64, 66**, 71, 73-74, 75, **76**, 88, **95**, 96, 97, 108, 111, 114, 129-30, 134-35, 143, **158**, 161, **162**, 166, 173, 200, 207. *See also* business persons.
mercenaries, 20
merchant seamen, 66. *See also* seamen.
Merrick, John, 67
Merrill, Gary, 210
Merrill, Paul E., 170; Merrill Transportation, 170
Merriwell, Frank (fictional character), 157
Methodists, 61, 221
Metropolitan Opera, 150, 107, 181
Micmac (Souriquos), 3-15, 23, 24, 25, 36, 51, 238. *See also* Native Americans.
militia, 23, 31, 32, 45, 50-52, 53, 77, 84, 85-87, 88, 102, 110, 156, 164, 222; Fite [sic] at Falmouth, 23, 25
Millay, Edna St. Vincent, 161, 181-82
Milliken, Carl F. (Gov.), 161, 164
Millinocket, Maine, 139, 178, 237
mills (waterpower), 34, **41, 42**, 59, 60, 61, 117, 139, 140. *See also* hydro power
Milo, Maine, 237
Minerva (mast ship), 45
ministers, 41, 42, 43
Minot, Maine, 102
Minstrelsy of Maine (1927, Mary Winslow Smyth), 183
Miquelon Island (French), 36, 173
missiles, 208
Missouri Compromise, 77. *See also* slavery.
Mitchell, Billy (Gen.), 170, 190
Mitchell, George (Sen.), 229, **230**, 238; *Men of Zeal* (1988, Cohen and Mitchell), 230
mobs, 39, 44, 45, 100, 101, 102-03, 111, 120; "mobocracy," 45
Modern Maine (1950), Richard A. Herbert), 203
Moffat, Alexander W. (Capt.), 195, 197, 203; *Navy Maverick Comes of Age, A* (1977), 197-98
Moffat–Ladd House, 50
molasses, 28, 97
Molasses, Molly, 90
money. *See* specie.

Monhegan Island, Maine, 1, 6, 10, 12, 14, 15, 149, 188
Monks, Millicent, 210
Monks, Robert A. G., xi
Monmouth, Maine, 59, 149, 210
Monroe, James (Pres.), 64, 74-77
Montgomery, Richard (Gen.), 46, 47
"Montpelier" (Knox Mansion), 59, 60. *See also* Knox, Henry, and General Henry Knox Museum.
Montreal to South Portland pipeline, 190, 208
Moratorium Day, 222
Montresor, John (Lt.), 36, **37**, 46; survey, 36, 37
Moody, Samuel (Rev.), 27, 32, 35
Moore, James (Lt.), 46
Moosehead Lake, 92, 196
Morgan, Daniel (Capt.), 146
Morison, Samuel Eliot, 183, 201
Mormons (Latter Day Saints), 221
Morrill Land Grant, 137
Morrill, Anson P. (Gov.), 81, 100
Morrill, Lot M. (Gov.), 111, 155
Morris, Charles (Capt.), 74
Morse, Charles Wyman, 134, 140
Morse–Libby House. *See* Victoria Mansion.
Morse, Edward, 153
Morse, Ruggles Sylvester, **102**. *See also* Victoria Mansion.
Morse, Samuel, 80, 96
Moscow, Maine, 173, **174**, 209
Motahkomikuk (Indian Township, Maine), 238
Mother Goose Comes to Portland (1918, F. W. Freeman), **162**
motto. *See* "Dirigo."
motels and motor courts, 160, 168
Mount Desert, Maine, 1, 161, 168, 200; Mount Desert Rock, 195
Mount Katahdin. *See* Katahdin.
Mount Kineo Hotel, 143
Mowat, Henri (Lt.), 45, **47**, 48
Muir, William, 201
Mulford, Clarence S., 152
Munjoy Hill, 45, 102
Murphy, Kevin D., 61; *Jonathan Fisher of Blue Hill, Maine* (2010), 61

Murray, James, 48; *Impartial History of the War in America* (1782), **48**
Muscongus Patent (Waldo), 19, 34
museums, 67, 89, 90, 128, 129, 149, 158, 201, 214. See also by name.
music and musicians, 3, 43, 67, **68**, 87, 88, 90, 102, 107, 109, 111, **124**, 129, 150, 156, **175**, **181**, 183, 210, 211; attitudes toward, 67, 68, 102, 107, 111, 127, 150, 181, 210, 211, **224**; country, 211; folk, 211; jazz, 211; societies, 67, 107. See also by name.
Muskie, Edmund (Sen.), 220, **228**, **238**
Muslims. *See* Islam.

N
Nabobs, 66, 76
Nader, Raph, 236
NAFTA Treaty, 237
names: of Maine, xi, xv, 1-15; of New England, 13
Narragansett Townships, 32
Nasson, Samuel, 64
National Association for the Advancement of Colored People (NAACP), **204**, 276, 241
National Guard, 164, 188, **189**, 222. *See also* militia.
National Rifle Association, 215
National Youth Administration, **177**
Native Americans, ii, 1-2, 3, 4-8, 9, 10-15, **17**, 22–24, 25, 29, 30, 36, 51, 55, 57, 58, 90, **91**, 130, 132, 140, 143, **144**, 205, 210, 213, 222-23, **238**, **239**; excluded from voting, 90-91; Indian Exhibition, 91; Land Claims Settlement, **238**; last raid, 54 religion, 3, 41, 152; technology, 4, 17, 24, 25, **91**, 216, *See also by name*, Indian Land Claim, by tribal name, Wabanaki.
Navy Maverick Comes of Age, A (1977, Alexander W. Moffat), 197-98
Nazis, 191, 193, 196-97, 201, 203
Neal, John, 79, 82, 88, 94, 102-03, **104**, 127, 130, 164; *Downeasters, The* (novel), 104. *See also* art and artists, and art: critics.
Nearing, Scott and Helen, 219; *Continuing the Good Life* (1979), 219
Nelson, Molliedellis (Mary Alice), 181
Neptune, Francis Joseph, 51
Neptune, John (Lt. Gov.), 90
Neutral Profits Era, 66
neutrality, 54-73, 186, 187
Nevelson, Louise, 181, 214
Nevin, Anne Paul, **171**
Nevin, Ethelbert, 171
New Boston (Gray), Maine, 41; proprietors, 44. *See also* Gray, Maine.
New Brunswick, 36, 40, 51, 52, 55, 57, 62, 84, 87; entry into Aroostook, 84; set off from Nova Scotia, 55, 62
Newcastle, Maine, 62
New Deal, 173-85
Newell, William Stark "Pete," 170, 178, 188, **190**
New England, 13, **14**-15, 16-37, 42, 43, 55, 66, 79, 91, 101, 210, 213, 241; discussion of secession from Union, 75
New England Chronicle (newspaper), 48
New England Farmer (1790, Samuel Deane), 68
New England Observed (map), 13-14
New-England Rarities Discovered (1672, John Josselyn), 21
Newfoundland, xv, 1, 2-5, **6**, 8, 26, 36, 187-88
New France, xv, 1, 7, 16-37, 213, 241; end of, 36-37
New Hampshire, 15, 17-21, 32, 33, 34, 39, 47, 49, 50, 57, **83**
New Ireland, 51, 52, 55
New Orleans, Louisiana, 36, 102, 103
New Somersetshire, 20
newspapers, 31, 48, 57, 68, **69**, 99, 101, 107, 109, 114, 129, 146, 153, 163, 166, 167, 168, 195, **197**, 210, 224, **225**, 236, 240-41; newsprint, 140; publishers, first, 68-71. *See also by name*.
New Sweden, Maine, 127
New York, 26, 40, 49, 50, 52, 179, 205, 222
Nickles–Sortwell House, **74**
Niles, Charles, 143
9/11, 205, 222, 230, 232, 239
Nineteenth Amendment, 164
Nixon, Richard, (Pres.), 222
Nobleboro, Maine, 183
Nobel Prize, 236
Nobel, W. Clark, **159**
Nordica. *See* Norton, Lillian.
Norfolk, Virginia, 47
"Norlands" (Washburn Estate), **132**
Normandy Landing, 194

Norridgwock, Maine, 152; mission, 26, 28, 33
Norse: coin, 2; explorations, 2
North American Squadron, 45, 51
North Country (newspaper), 210
Northeast Boundary, **front cover**, 39, 51, 52, 55, 79, 84, 85, **86**, 87-88, 232
Northeast Folklife Society, 210
Northeast Harbor, Maine, 41, 51, 52
Northern Virginia. *See* Virginia.
North Jay, Maine, 133
North Yarmouth, Maine: ancient, 23, 34, 44; contemporary, 192-93
Northwest Passage, xv, 4, 6
Norton, Lillian "Nordica," 127, **150**; homestead, 150
Norumbega, xiii, 1, 2, 4, 5, 14, 90
Norway, Maine, 149, 152
Nova Scotia, 18, 19, 34, 36, 39, 51, 52, 55
novels: historical, modern, 183-89, 201. *See also by title.*
nuclear power plant, 208, 211, 241. *See also* Maine Yankee Nuclear Power Plant.
nurses, 120, 125, **163**. *See also* diseases, epidemics, hospitals, medicine, physicians.
Nye, Bill, 152

O

Oakland, Maine, 141
Obama, Barak (Pres.), 229
O'Brien, Jeremiah (Capt.), 46, 200
O'Brien, Morris, 42
O'Connell, William E., 147
Ocean Queen (hospital ship), 120
Ocean Park, 144
Odanak (St. Francis), 30, 36
O'Donnell, John (Fr.), 101
Ogunquit, Maine, 149, **180**, 210, 214
"Oh, Have You Heard How Old Maine Went," 81
oil, 190, 208, 209
O'Keeffe, Georgia, 180
Ocean Class vessels, 188-190
Old Curiosity Shop, Kennebunkport, **158**
Oldfield, Barney, 147
Old Gaol, York, **28**
Old Orchard Beach, Maine, 93, **144**-45, 147, **169**, 170, 197, 215; pier, 145

Old South Meeting House, 101
Old Town, Maine, 90-91, **144**
Old York Historical Society, 29
Olmsted, Frederick Law, 128
Olsen, Christina, 214
Olympic Games, 147, 176, 218, 219
Oneida (steamship), 122
opera, 127, 132, **150**
Operation Desert Storm, 239. *See also* war, in Iraq.
Operation Snowball, 197. *See also* World War II.
Opportunity Farm, New Gloucester, 147
Oranbega. *See* Norumbega.
Oreto, USS (cruiser), 122
Orgonon (Reich Museum), 220. *See also* Reich, Wilhelm.
Oriental Powder Company, 116
Orono (Native American leader), 51
Orono, Maine, 88, 135-36, 152
orphans, 99, 101-02, 125, 195, 161, 166
Osborn, William C., 236; *Paper Plantation, The* (1974), 236
Osborne, James, 105
Ottoman Empire, 4
Our Paper (newspaper), 224, **225**
Ox-Bow Incident, The (1940, Walter van Tilberg Clark), 201
oxen, **78**, 81, **85**, **93**, 140, 156
Oxford County (1805), 60, 94, 106
Oxford Plains Speedway, 215

P

Pakistan, 205, 206
Paderewski, Ignace Jan, 150
Paine, John K. 150-51
Paine, Robert Treat, 43
Palmer & Machiasport Railroad, 89
panoramas, 67
paper, 34, 70, 139, 236-37; mills, 34, 139, 236-37
paper money, 63, **66**, 111, 112. *See also* specie.
Paper Plantation, The (1974, William C. Osborn), 236
Paris Hill, Maine, 60, 110
Park, Maude M., 164
Parkhurst, Frederick (gov.), 165
Parkman, Francis, 103
parks, 126, 129, 161, 165, 166, 168, 176, 237-38.

See also by name.
Parks, Leonard (Private), **192**
Parton, Sarah P. Willis "Fannie Fern," 104
Passaconaway (ironclad), 116
Passamaquoddy, 36, 51, 58, 91, 177, 238, **239**. *See also* Native American.
Passamaquoddy Tidal Power Project, 173, 176-77. *See also* Central Maine Power and electric power.
patriotism, 111, 113, 187, 190
Pattangall, William Robinson, 152
Patten Family (shipbuilders), 96
Patten, Gilbert, 152-53
Patten, Maine, 140
Payne, Frederick C. (Gov.), 227
Payson, Charles S., 215
Payson, Margaret, 176
Peabody, Frances W., 226
peace: actions, 111, 120, 222, 240; societies, 102, 221
Peaks Island, Maine, 223
Pearl Harbor, attack, 52, 190-91
Peary, Robert E. (Adm.), 153
Peary-MacMillan Arctic Museum, 153
peaveys, 130
Peirce, Waldo, 180, 214
Pemaquid, Maine, 10, 15, 18, 19, 22, 23, 25, 26
Pembroke, Maine, 152
Penobscot (Castine), Maine, 19, 50, 51, 53
Penobscot Bay, 60
Penobscot County (1816), 60, 87
Penobscot (Bagaduce) Expedition, 50, 51, 52, 53, 57
Penobscot Indian Nation, 36, 51, 58, 59, 90, **144**, 147, 181, 238; treaty with, 59, 238. *See also* Etchimin, Native Americans.
Penobscot Marine Museum, 168
Penobscot Poultry Company, 235
Penobscot Purchase, 19, 20, 60
Penobscot River, 4, 5, 15, 19, 20, 36, 37, 50, 51, 52, 53, 57, 58, 60, 88, 89, **90**, 92, 117, 130, 170
Pentagoet, 19, 20
Peppermint Row, 90
Pepperrell-Frost, Limner, 27
Pepperrell Manufacturing, 95, **131**, 200, **201**
Pepperrell, William (Sir), 27, **32**, 34, 35, 40

Pepperrell, William, Sr., 27
Percy & Small (shipyard), **134**-35
Perkins, Frances, 177
Perry, Maine, 91, 238
Perry, Lilla C., **182**
Perry's Nut House, 168
petroglyphs, 5
pets, 17, 21, 40, **152**, 165, **239**, **184**
Phillips, H. O., **162**
Phips, William (Sir/Gov.), 25, **26**
photography, 105, 114, 148-49, 159
physicians, 6, 21, 26, 41, 63, 224, **225**. *See also* diseases, epidemics, hospitals, medicine, nurses, and by name.
Pierce, Anne Longfellow, 158
Pierce, Franklin (Pres.), 98
Pierce, Moses, 67
pine, 28, 31, 33, 44, 45, 78, 89, 130
Pine Cone, The (magazine), 205
Pineland Hospital, 147, 158, 201. *See also* Maine School for the Feeble-Minded.
pirates, 13, 19, 71, **72**, 119, 205, 222, 230, 232, 239
Piscataqua River, 15, 17, 18, 27, 31, 49, 50, 57, **83**
Piscataquis County (1838), 83
Piston, Walter, 181, 211
Plaisted, Harrison (Gov.), 157, 158
plays: banned, 67; first to mention Maine, 46-47, 66. *See also* actors and theaters.
Pleasant Lake, **216**
Pleasant Mountain, **93**; House, 93
Pleasant Point (Sipayik), Maine, 238. *See also* Passamaquoddy, Native American.
plow patent, 15
"Plumed Knight." *See* Blaine, James G.
Plymouth Colony, 15, 19, 20
Plymouth Company, 11, 19, 20, 33
Plymouth Grant, 19
poets, 98, 103-04, 161, 179, **181**-82, 183, 211, 229. *See also* literature and by name.
Pogue, L. Welch, **206**
Poland Spring Hotel, 74, 143, **160**
Polchies, Terrance, **238**
police, 102, **172**
Polish Americans, 145, 150, 183, 191, 228
politics: first primary, 161; parties, 61, 63, 75-77, 81-

82, 110-12, 153-59, 161, 226; political power of Maine, 154; politicians, 77, 127, 152-59. *See also by name.*
Pontoosuc (gunboat), 116, 121
Poor, John A., 89, **97**, 116, 127, **129**, 130-31, 170.
Popham Colony, 10, 11, 12
Popham, John (Sir), 10, 11, 12
Popham, George, 12
Popular Party, 44, 45
population: Acadia, 19, 36; eastern Maine, 42; ethnic, 42, Franco-American, 132; Lincoln County, 42; Maine, 15, 27, 31, 39, 55, 59, 79, 125, 127, 205, 240-41; New England, 19; religious, 42
Port of Portland: State of Maine, The (1946), 201
Porter, Rufus, 67
Portland, 57, 60, 63, 70, 71, 77, 78, 79, 80, 81, 82, 88, 97, 103-04, 105, 110, 111, 114, **116-17**, **126**, 128, 148, **149**, 155, **158**, 164, **165**, 167, 168, 169, 170, 171, **172**, 181-82, **191**, 197, 202, 204, 207, 210, 212-13, 214, 215, 222, 226, 207, **237**, **239**; first capital, 78, 82; Great Fire of 1866, **126**; harbor defense, 116-18; high school, 98; Naval Section Base, 193, 194-95; role as port in WWII, 193-95; separates from Falmouth, 57; schools, **191**; statehood convention, 77. *See also* Falmouth, and individuals, businesses, and events by name.
Portland (clipper ship), 96
Portland (magazine), 104, 210
Portland (steamer), 141
Portland Bank, 66
Portland Company, 97, **116**
Portland Evening News (newspaper), 167
Portland Glass Company, 114, 150
Portland International Jetport, 170, 207
Portland Marine Society, 66
Portland Museum of Art, 128, 143, 214, 215
Portland Packing Company, 133
Portland Press Herald (newspaper), 166
Portland, Saco & Portsmouth Railroad, 96
Portland School of Art. *See* Maine College of Art.
Portland Symphony Orchestra, 181, 211
Port Royal, Nova Scotia, 6, 12, 25
Portsmouth, New Hampshire, 47, 49, 50, 57, 83
Portsmouth Naval Shipyard, 72, 75, 83, 100, 116, 155, 164, 170, 178, **179**, 188, **196**, 200, 203, 232
Portuguese and Portugal, 2, 3, 4, 146, 239
postal service, 39, 79, 81, 100, 155
Postillion (ship), **54**
potatoes, 61, 94, 171, 226
Potomac (presidential yacht), 187
poultry, 171, 235, 236
poverty, 23, 36, 54, 60, 61, 66, 98, 99, 125, **126**, 128, 145, 158, 173, 226, 228, 230, 232
power: crisis, 208, alternatives, 209. *See also* Central Maine Power, electric power.
Pownal, Thomas (Gov.), 36
Pownalborough (Dresden), Maine, 35, 38, 39, 40, 42. *See also* Dresden.
Pownalborough Court House (1761), 35, 38, 39, 40, **42**
Preble, Edward (Commodore), 49, 63, 71
Preble, George H. (Adm.), 122
Preble, Jedediah (Brig. Gen.), 50
Presbyterians, 27, 41, 42, 221
Presque Isle, Maine: airbase, 169, 189-90, 197
Price, H. H. 226; *Maine's Visible Black History* (2006, Price and Talbot), 226
Primrose (sloop), 64, **65**
Primus, 53
Prinz Eitel Friedrich (raider), 162
prisoners of war (POWs), 195, **196**
prisons, 22, 27, 28, 49, 50, 53, 119, 120, 121, 158, 240; at Thomaston, 99, 119; hulk *Jersey*, **49**. *See also* crimes and disorder.
privateers. *See* by name or under vessels.
processions, **163**, **167**, **204**
Proclamation of 1763, 42
professions, 19, 27, 37, 38, 39, 40, 41, 60, 61, 62, 63, 67-68. *See also* labor and manufacturing, and occupations by name.
prohibition, 121, 157, 158, 170, 172, 173. *See also* Dow, Neal, and Maine Law.
Prospect, Maine, 117
Protestants: missions, 153, 220; radio, 167. *See also* Standing Order and by denomination.
prostitution, 102, 114, 131, 199
Province of Maine, 15, 17-21, 25
Proulx, E. Annie, 152

Public Utilities Commission (PUC), 161
Public Works Projects, 173-85
publishers, 104, 153, 166, 210, 240-41
Pulitzer, Joseph, 143, 145
Pulitzer Prizes, 181, 182, 183, 184, 211, 219. *See also* by individual's name.
Pullen, John J. 213
pulp and paper industry, 138, 140, 142, 174, 236. *See also* labor, mills, paper.
Puritans (Massachusetts), 15, 20, 102
Putnam, Black Hawk (Capt.), 120, 121

Q

Quakajo Mountain, 190
Quakers (Society of Friends), 41, 42, 55, 102
quarries. *See* stone.
Quebec City, 5, 17, 25, 28, 36, 37, 46, 54, 79, 207
Quebecois, 61, 79, 117, 146. *See also* French Canadian and by name.
Queen Anne's War, 28, 30
Queen City, 131. *See also* Bangor.
Quint, Ammi, 64
Quock Walker Case, 53
Quoddy Tides Project, 173, 176, **177**
Quoddy Village, **177**

R

radar, 197, 207, **209**. *See also* radome, World War II.
Radical Republican Society (Jacobin), 64
radio, 167-68, 171, 177, 181, 186, 190, 193, 195-97, 209; Bangor WAIB, 167; Dover-Foxcroft, 167; first broadcast, 167-68; Portland WCSH, 167; ship to shore, 188
radome, **209**
Ragged Lake, 142
railroads, 79, 82, **89**, 94, 96, 97, 98, 114, 116, 127, **129**, 131, 135, 137, 142, 144, 158, 160, 169, **189**, **192**, 195, 207, 213; bridge, **192**; gauges, 131; guide, 94. *See also by name.*
Raleigh, Walter (Sir), 5, 6
Râle, Sebastian (Fr.), **26**, 33
Ram Island Dance Company, 210
Ramusio, Giovanni Battista, iii, 1, 2
Rangeley Lakes, 143, 220
Ranger (racing yacht), 178
Ranger (sloop, Continental Navy), 48
Rapid (privateer), 73

Rebecca of Sunnybrook Farm (1903, Kate Douglas Wiggin), 152
Read, Charles W. (Lt.), 118
Reagan, Ronald (Pres.), 240
Red Bank, bomber crash, 203
Red Cross, 162, **163**, 164
Red Jacket (clipper ship), 96, 107
Red Record (publication), 135
Reed, Thomas Brackett, 127, 153-55, 227; *Reed's Rules of Order*, 155
reform school. *See* Longcreek.
refugees: Abenakis, 28, **29**, 30; Acadian, 36; English, 23, 25, 26, 28; Loyalist, 51, 52; modern, 221, 222, **224**, 239-40; villages, 28, **29**, 30, 36
Reich, Wilhelm (Dr.), 220
religion: 3, 7, 8, **11**, **13**, 17, 18, 22, **26**, 32, **34**, 37, 40, 41, 42, **48**, 61, 62, 80, 82, 100, 101, 102, **129**, 144, 145, **147**, 152, 167, 171, 175, 207, 210, 220 **241**, **back cover**; reformation, 4, 8; wars end, 37. *See also* by denomination.
Republican Party, 81, 102, 106-09, 111-12, 127, 132, 153-59, 161, 173-75, 191, 221, 206, 226-32, **238**, **239**, **241**; RINOS, 230. *See also* by party member name.
resorts. *See* hotels.
Revere, Paul, 52, 103
Revolutionary War. *See* American Revolution.
Richards, Laura, E., 152, 182; *Captain January* (1890), 152
Rich, Louise D., 201; *We Took to the Woods* (1942), 201
Richmond, Roger, 223
Richmond's Island, 18, 19
Ring Family, ix, 143, **152**
Ring, Edgar, 143
Ring, Elizabeth, ix, **152**, 164-65, 176, 183; *Maine in the Making of the Nation* (1996), ix
riots. *See* mobs.
Rittal, Francis, 53
river-drivers, 90, **130**, **140**, 236
roads, 25, 31, 38, 39, 40, 57, 58, 61, 168, 176, 207; federal funding, 168, 176, military, 85
Roaring Twenties, 164
Robbinston, Maine, 92
Roberts College, Turkey, 153

280   MAINE: THE WILDER HALF OF NEW ENGLAND

Roberts, Kenneth, 40, 46, 165, 183-84, 185, 219; *Arundel* (1930), 183; *Boon Island* (1956), 184; *Lydia Bailey* (1947), 40; *Why Europe Leaves Home* (1922), 166
Robinhood, Maine, 158, 179, 180
Robinson, Edwin Arlington, 152, 182-83
Rockefeller, Nelson A. (Vice Pres.), 143, **229**, 238, 239
Rockland, Maine, 95, 113, 114, 181, **186**, 187, 200, 226
Rogers, Edith N. (Rep.), 191
Rogers, Robert (Maj.), 36; Rangers, 36
Rolde, Neil, ix; *Downeast and Different* (2006), ix; *Illustrated History of Maine, An* (1995), ix
Roman Catholic. See Catholic.
Romer, Wolfgang (Col.), 25
Roosevelt, Franklin Delano (Pres.), 144, 173-85, 186-203, 240
Roosevelt, Theodore (Pres.), 143, 153, 155, 240
Rosenberg, Hilary, xi; *Traitor to His Class* (1999), xi
Rosier, James, 10
Rosie O'Grady Balloon of Peace, 208
Ross, Alexander, 40
Ross, Elizabeth, 40
Ross, Grace De Carleton, p. 210
Rothermel, Peter Frederick, 123
Route One, 168
Route 201, 85, 207
Rowse, James (Dr.), 120
Roy House (Maison Roy), Van Buren, **62**
Royal Navy, 28, 31, 34, 35, 44, **47**, **48**, 50, 51, 52-55, 84, 187-88
Royal River, Maine, **192-93**
rum, 44, 47, 101; riot, 101, 121; "Rum, Romanism and Rebellion," 153
Rumford, Maine, 104, 106, 139, 228
Rummery, Samuel, 133
Russia, 71, 155, 195, 208, 221, 240. *See also* Soviet Union.

S
Sabbath Day, 18; repeal, 210
Saco, Maine, 23, 25, 47, 48, **99**, 232; fort, 25
Saco Defense, Inc., 232
Saco-Lowell Mills, **131**, 171, 200, **201**
Saco River, **9**, 25, 131

Saddleback Peak, 216
Sagadahoc (Popham) Colony, 10-11
Sagadahoc County (1854), 83
Sailfish, USS (submarine), 178
St. Andrew, New Brunswick, 55
St. Croix, 7, 9, 8, 36, 57
St. Croix River, 7-9, 36, 52, 64, 55, 84
St. Francis (Odanak), 30, 36, 54
St. Francis College. *See* University of New England.
St. George River, 10, 59
Saint-Jean-Baptist Day, 140
St. John, New Brunswick, 87, 131, 170
St. John River, 20, 36, 57, 62, 84, 91, 131
St. Joseph's College, 161
St. Lawrence River, xv, **2**, 3, 5, 9, 22, 46, 47, 57, 84
St. Patrick's Church, **62**
St. Paul's Church, 47
St. Pierre Island (French), 36, 173
St. Stephen, New Brunswick, 117
Sally (ship), 64, **65**
SALT Institute, 210
Saltonstall, Dudley (Com.), 52
Samoset, 15
Samuelson, Joan Benoit, **218**
sardines, 135-37
sassafras, 6
Saunders & Son, 143
Savage, Arthur, 44
sawmills, 34, **41**, **42**, 45, 78, 88-89, 141
Sayward, Jonathan, 45
Scalping, 26, 33
Scandinavian Americans, 127, 130
Scarborough, Maine, 21, 42, 45, **105**, 148, 168, 215, 241
schools, 22, 28, 29, 31, 43, 66, 67, **68**, 96, 98, 181, 191, 194, 203, 207, 226; school cart, **168**. *See also by name.*
Scotland (neighborhood), York, Maine, 29
Scots and Scotland, 18, 19, 20, 29, 34, 40
Scots Irish, 41, 42, **64**
Scott, Gail R., 179
Scott, Geraldine Tidd, xi, 213; *Ties of Common Blood* (1992), xi
Scott, Winfield (Gen.), 87, 88
sculling, 147

S. D. Warren Company, 140, 146. *See also* pulp and paper, and Westbrook, Maine.
Seal Harbor, Maine, 144
seamen (ordinary), 100; impressments of, 73, 75. *See also* merchant seamen.
Sea Captains Carousing in Surinam (painting), 33
Sears, Richard D., 144
Searsport, Maine, 209
Seaside Inn, 58
Sea Dragon, USS (submarine), 237
Seboomook, Maine, 195-96
2nd Maine Regiment. *See* World War I.
segregation, in military, 192-93
Serres, Dominic, 51
servants, 109
service industry, 205. *See also* Vacationland.
Seven Years' War (French and Indian War), 36, 37, 39
Sewall Family, 96
Sewall, Arthur, 154
Sewall, Joseph Ellis (Capt.), 135
Sewall, Stephen (Dr.), 68
Sewall, Sumner (Gov.), 191
Sewall, William, 142
Seymour, Richard (Rev.), 12
Shah-Nazaroff, Evelyn Jeanne, 181
Shakers, 61, 67
Shapiro, Samuel, 216
Shattuck, Cato, 53
Shaw, H. Fenton, 196
Sheepscot, Maine, 33
shelter, 22, 29, **139**. *See also* architecture, poverty.
sheriff, 40, 44, 45, 49, 87, 69. 208
Shettleworth, Earle G., Jr. x-ix, 152, 213
Shingle Style, **149**, 150
shipbuilding, 11-12, 15, 27, 31, 34, 35, 40, 60, 62, 75, 79, **83**, 89, 96, 107, 109, 116, 162, 164, 170, 188-90, **197**, **198**, **199**, 200, 232; owners, 32, 40, **75**, 96, 134, 164, **190**, **197**, **198**-99, 203; ship house, **83**
ship crews, 135
Shipyard News (newspaper), **197**
shipwrecks and sinkings, **54**, 72, 73, **95**, 162, 195, **233**
shiretowns, 40, 43, 60

Shirley, Maine, 152
shoes, 43, 133, 161; manufacturing, 89, 95, 116, 133, 175, 179, 200, 235
Sieur de Monts National Monument. *See* Acadia National Park.
Silent Spring (1961, Rachel Carson), 220
Sills, Kenneth C. M., 177
Simancas, 11-12
Simmons, Franklin, 103-04, 113
Sipayik (Pleasant Point), Maine, 238. *See also* Native Americans. Passamaquoddy.
Skedaddler's Ridge, 120
skiing. 173, 176, 203, **216**, 219
Skottland, SS (freighter), 195
Skowhegan, Maine, 152, 191, 214, 227, 239
Skowhegan School of Art, 214
slate, 94. *See also* stone.
slavery, 12, 20, 27, 40, 44, 50, 53, 55, 77, 102, 119, 239; bill of sale, **53**; Emancipation Proclamation, 124; slave trader hanged, 119. *See also* abolition and enslaved people by name.
Smibert, John, 35
Smibert, Nathaniel, 23
Smith, Arthur, 221
Smith, Clyde H., 227
Smith, David C., 149; *The First Century: A History of the University of Maine, 1865–1965* (1979), 194
Smith, Elizabeth Oakes, 92, 104, 107
Smith, F. O. J. (Cong.), 79, 80
Smith, John (Sir), 13-14; *Generall Historie of Virginia, New England....* (1624), 12-15
Smith, Margaret Chase (Sen.), 191, **227**-29; "Declaration of Conscience," 227, 228
Smith, "Mysterious" Billy, 147
Smith, Samantha, **221**
Smith, Seba, 92, 104, **107**
Smith, Thomas (Rev.), 27, 32, 37, 57, 68
Smith-Fisher, Carol, xi
smuggling, 17, 25, 39, 71, 75, 76-77, 153, 169, 170, 173, 190-91, 193, 213
Smyth, Mary Winslow, 183; *Minstrelsy of Maine* (1927), 183
Snell, George D. (Dr.), 236
snow: removal, 169; snowshoes, 16, 25, 91, 146, 176, **216**

282   Maine: The Wilder Half of New England

Snow, Ralph Linwood, 200, 232; *Bath Iron Works: The First Hundred Years* (1987), 200, 237
Snow, Wilbert, 183
Snow Squall (clipper ship), 96
Snowe, Olympia J. (Sen.), 229-31
Snowe, Peter (Cong.), 229, 231
social causes, 79, 89-101, 147, 166, 173, 175, 176, **204**, **222**, **225**, 232-38, 240-41. *See also by name.*
social hierarchy, 21, 27, 40, 41, 67, 98-100, 198-99, 107, 147, 232-38, 240-41
Social Security Act, 177, 200
Sockabasin, Allen J., 222, 226
Sockalexis, Andrew, 147
Sockalexis, Louis Francis, 147
Soctomah, Donald, 222
soldiers, **16**, 20, 22, 23, 25, 32, 34, 35, 46, **49**, **50**, 109-25, 164, 187, **189**, **192**, 221-22, 223, 240-41; bonus, 164; disabled, 125. *See also* battles, G. I. Bill of Rights, and military engagements by name.
Soldier's Son, A (2006, John E. Hodgkins), 202
Somali Americans, 221, 240
Someset County (1809), 60
Sons of Liberty, 29
Sorrento, Maine, 54
Souadabscook Stream, 216, 220
Souriquois, 3-4, 15, 24. *See also* Micmac, Native Americans.
South Addison, Maine, 190
South Berwick, Maine, 23, 42, 150-51. *See also* Berwick.
South Carolina, 66, 109-10
Southport, Maine, 220
South Portland, Maine, 152, 153, 164, 178, 232, 235; shipyards, 164, 188-90, **197**, **198**, 203
Soviet Union, 205, 211. *See also* Russia.
Spain and Spaniards, 1, 4, 5, 11-12, 154, 156
Spanish–American War, 154, 155, 156
specie (money), **19**, 21, 61, 63, 73-75, 111
Spencer Mountain, ix, 86, 87
spies, 11-12, 118-19, 120, 190-191, 193
Spofford, Harriet Prescott, 152
sports. *See* athletics and athletes, leisure, fishing, hunting.

Sportsman's Alliance of Maine, 215
Spotted Elk, Molly. *See* Nelson, Molliedellis.
Spotten, Anthony, 210
Springer, John, S., 92; *Forest Life and Forest Trees* (1851), 92
spruce, 130
Squalus, USS (submarine), 177
Squanto, 13, 15
squatters, 33, 44, 57, 59, 60, 77, 93, **146**. *See also* evictions.
Squirrel (vessel), 5
stagecoaches, 39, 57, **82**
Stamp Act, 39, 45
Standing Order Church, 22, 25, 31, **32**, **34**, 40-41, 42, 45, **61**, 71, 77. *See also* Congregational Church.
Stanley, Francis E. and Freelan O., 142
Stanwood, Harriet, 112
Strater, Henry, 214
starch: factories, 94; towns, 94
Starkey, Glen W., 164
State of Maine, SS (steamer), 141
State House: Portland, 78, 80, 82; Augusta, 83, 98, **128**, **159**, 226, 241
statehood, movement, 50, 56-78, 61, 68, **69**, **76**, 77, 80
Strand, Paul, 180
"Stein Song," **181**. *See also* Vallee, Rudy.
Stephens, Ann S., 104
Stephens, Charles A., 152
Stevens, John Calvin, **149**, **150**, **174**; house, **149**
Stevens, Lillian M. 157-78
Stevens, Michael (Pvt.), **231**
Stevens, Minnie Plummer, 151
Stobie, George, 170
stock company, 33, 48
Stockton Springs Harbor, Maine, 51
Stoppel, Franz Xavier, 94
stone, cutting and quarries, **32**, **34**, 41, 60, 94, 133
Stowe, Harriet Beecher, 113; *Uncle Tom's Cabin* (1852), 113
Strange Woman, The (1941, Ben Ames Williams), 201, 211
street railway, 114, 142, 161, 207
Strickland, Hastings, 87

INDEX 283

Stroudwater Village, Portland, 3, 33, 34, 68
Stuart, Gilbert, ii, **76**
Student Army Training Corps, 163
suburbs, 199-200, 203, 207
Sudbury Canada (Bethel), Maine, 54
sugar trade, 28, 47, 138; refinery, 97
Sugarloaf, 216
Sullivan, James (Gov.), ii, 49, 71, 76; *History of the District of Maine* (1795), viii
Sullivan Richard (Pvt.), **192**
Sully, Thomas, 105
summer: camps, 143, 216, **217**; notable summer residents, 144
Surinam, 33
Survey of the State of Maine, A (1839, Moses Greenleaf), 84
surveying, **front cover**, 37, 59, 60, 78, 79, 83, 84, 85, **86**, 87, 88, 207; surveyors-general, 31, 33, 44
swamps, 39, 46, 47
Sweat, L. D. M. (Col.) 102, 111, 128
Sweat, Margaret Jane Mussey, 128-29, 149
Sweden and Swedes, 127
Sweetser-Children's Home, 99-101, 147, 166
Swordfish, USS (submarine), 232

T

Taber, John 66; Taber Notes, **66**, 72, 73
Tacony (bark), 119
Talbot, Gerald E., 204, 226; *Maine's Visible Black History* (2006, Price and Talbot), 226
Talcott, Andrew (Capt.), **front cover**, **86**, 87; Talcott Survey, iv, 86, 87
Tales of the Night (1827, Sarah Barrell Keating Wood), 70
tanning, tanneries, 35, 61, 116, 133
"Tante Blanche," 61, 63. *See also* Thibodeau, Marguerite Blanche.
Tarkington, Booth, 178, 182, **184**
Tate, George, Sr. (Capt.), 31; Tate House, Portland, 31, 168
Tate, George II (Adm.), 71
tattoos, 154, **165**
taverns, 18, 22, **33**, 40, 41, 43, 58, 67, 82, **99**, 102, **129**, **158**. *See also* hotels.
taxes, 19, 43, 58, 60, 98, 125, 127, 236, 240
Taylor, Alan, 213; *Liberty Men and the Great Proprietors* (1990), 213
telegraph, 80, 96
telephones, 41, 167, 171, 209
television, 205, 209, 210, 212; personalities, 210
Telstar, **209**
Temiscouata Portage, 84
Temperance Movement, 81. *See also* Dow, Neal; prohibition; taverns.
Tempel Beth El, Portland, 214. *See also* Jewish Americans.
Temple, Maine, 202
Tenney, Ulysses Dow, 50
tents, **88**, 114
Terzo Volume della Navigation et Viaggi (1556, Giacomo Gastaldi), xiv
Tewksbury, Samuel H. (Dr.), 128
Texas, 96, 141
textile mills, 94-95, 114-15, **117**, **131**, 133, 140, 171, 200-01, **235**, 241
Thaxter, Celia, 152
Thaxter, Phyllis, 201
theaters, 67, 90, 91, 113, **114**, 152, 178, 171, 207, 210, 211, 236
Thibodeau, Marguerite Blanche "Tante Blanche," 61, 63
Thirty Seconds Over Tokyo (film), 201
Thomaston, Maine, 50, 53, 54, 58, 59
Thompson, Samuel (Col.), 45, 64
Thompson's War, 45. *See also* mobs.
Thomas, Elizabeth Widgery, 102
Thomas, William W., 127
Thomaston, Maine, 59, 60, 99, 119, 120, 158
Thoreau, Henry David, 90, 92-93, 96; *Maine Woods, The* (1846-57), 92
Thresher, USS (submarine), 232
tidal power, 173
Ties of Common Blood (1992, Geraldine Tidd Scott), xi, 213
"Tilbury Town," 152. *See also* Robinson, Edwin Arlington.
Tilson, David (Gen.), 134
timber trade, 35, 44, 45, 59, 60, 61, **78**, 79, 84, 86, 87, 88, 89-93, 130-33, **140**, 207, 236. *See also* Bangor, mast trade, sawmills.
Titcomb, Benjamin, Jr., 68-69

tobacco, 16, **33**, 38, **182**
Toby Tyler (1880, James Otis Kaler), 151, 152
Todd-Bath Iron Shipbuilding Corporation, 178, **188**, **198**-99, 200, 232. *See also* shipbuilding, World War II.
Togus (National Home for Disabled Soldiers), 125
Toleration Act, 77
tourism, modern, 142. *See also* vacations, Vacationland.
towns: government, 22, 25, 31, 32, 33, 43, 45, 57, 61, 98; loyalty, 57; meeting, 180; records, 178
Towns, Thomas, 53
Tracy, Elizabth, 178
trade: colonial, 19, 20, 27, 33, 39, 58; early federal, 58, 61, 66, 68; fur trade, 13; laws, early, 39, 44, 63, 73; restricted, 63; unrestricted, 17, 25, 39, 44, 54, 77. *See also* mechanics, smuggling.
trans-Atlantic flight, 168, 169, 170, 190, 193, 197, 207-08. *See also* balloons.
transportation, 89, 168, 169, 207. *See also* by type.
Traitor to His Class (1999, Hilary Rosenberg), xi
treason: charges, 74; trials, 53, **196-97**
treasures, **19**, 26
treaties: Treaty of Paris, 55, 59, 63, 84; Treaty of Washington, 87
trees. *See* forests and trees.
truck houses, 19, 22, 23, 51, 58
trucking, 168, 169, 170
Tripoli, 61, **72**
trolley. *See* street railway.
Trumbull, John, **49**
Tuck, Fred, 158
Tucker, Daniel, 49
Tucker, Samuel (Com.), 74
Turcotte, Richard, 201
Turgeon, Bill, 170
Turnbull, Christopher J., 19; *French at Pentagoet, The*, 19
Turner, Maine, 155, 156
Twilight in the Wilderness (painting), 92
Twitchell, Moses, 44
Tyng, Edward, 35
Tyng, Elizabeth Ross, **40**.
Tyng, William, 40, 44, 45, 49; schooner, 44

U
Ulrich, Laurel T., 213
Ulster, Northern Ireland, 41
Uncle Tom's Cabin (1852, Harriet Beecher Stowe), 113
Unicorn (ship), **95**
Union Mutual Insurance Company (UNUM), 129, **235-36**
Union Station, Potland, **189**, 195, 213
Union Wharf, Portland, 66
United Hebrew Charities, 145
United Society of Believers. *See* Shakers.
United States Air Force (Army Air Service, Air Corps), 170, 209
United States Coast Guard (Revenue Cutter Service), 71, 170, 190, 232, **233**
United States Congress, 50, **63**, **64**, 79, 153-54, **155**, 227-232. *See also* congressmen/women by name, United States House of Representatives, and United States Senate.
United States Constitution, 63, **64**, 76-77
United States House of Representatives: Speakers of the House, 153-55. *See also* United States Congress, and representatives by name.
United States postmaster general, 79, 155
United States presidents, 46-49, 59, 64, 73-77, 79, 81, 99, 107, 108, 125, **129**, 228, 229, **238-39**. *See also* by name.
United States Revenue Service, **118**. *See also* United States Coast Guard.
United States Sanitary Commission, 20
United States secretary of defense, 229, **230**
United States secretary of state, 153, **154**, 228
United States secretary of the treasury, 112, 154, 155
United States Senate, 49, 64, 79, 110, 112, 132, 153-59, **227**, **228**, 230, 231. *See also* senators by name.
United States Supreme Court, 79, 111
Unity, Maine, 104
Universalists, 61, 132
University of Maine: law school, 163, 206; Orono, 135, 59, 171, **181**, 183, **194**, 203, 206, 210, 214; Southern Maine, 206; system, 206
University of New England, 204, 215
Urania (1761, music), 42

urban renewal, 207

V

Vacationers, Vacationland, 90-92, **93**, 114, 127, **138**, 141, **142-45**, 160, 166, 170, 176, 185, 188, 205, 208, **216**, 217, **219**-20, **238**-39. *See also* hotels, leisure, summer.

Vallee, Rudy, **181**. *See also* "Stein Song."

Valley Forge, 55

Vampatella, Phil, 223

Van Buren, Maine, **62**, 226. *See also* Madawaska Territory.

Vanceboro, Maine, 83

Vanderbilt, Harold S., 178

Varney, George J., viii; *Young People's History of Maine, The* (1873), viii

Vassalboro, Maine, 104, 153

Veazie, Maine, 88

Veazie, Samuel (Gen.), 88, 89, 111

Vedder, Elihu, 58

Vermont, 42, 57, 60

Verrazzano, Giovanni, **xv**, 1, **2**, 3-4, 6

Verrazzano, Girolamo, **xv**, 1, **2**, 3-4, 5

Verrier, Ray, 233

vessels, 1, 2, 4, 5, 6, 8, 11, 12, 13, 54, 64, 65, 94, 104, 105, 208; Confederate war vessels (list), 118, 119; privateers, 19, 22, 45, 48, 49, 51, 52, 118, 119; reach boat, **136**-37, rumrunners, 170, 173; sailing types, 64, **65**; shares, 40; sharpshooters, 121; steamboats, 89, 96, **141**, **145**, 170; steel-hulled, 135; submarines, 162, 164, 170, 177, **178**, 187, 193-95, **196**, 203, 232; U-Boats, 162, 187, 193-95, **196**, 203. *See also* by name.

Victoria Mansion (Morse Libby House), 102, **103**

Vietnam and Vietnamese Americans, 222, 239-40

Vietnam War, 222, **223**, 228; Vietnam Veterans Memorial, **223**

Vines, Richard, 15

Virginia (Maine part of), 5-6, 11-15

Virginia (pinnace), 11-12

Voyage to New England, A (1628, Christopher Levett), 17, **18**

W

Wabanaki Alliance, 23, 28, 29, 30, 58. *See also* Abenakis, Native Americans, and by tribal name.

WABI (Bangor TV), 209

Wadsworth, Peleg (Gen.), 50, 51, 52, 53, 54, 57, **158**

Wadsworth–Longfellow House, Portland, 50, **158**

Wait, John B, 68-69, 71

Waldo, Francis, 44

Waldo, Samuel (Brig. Gen.), 34, 35, 40, 60

Waldo (or Muscongus) Grant, 19, 34, 35, 36, 60

Walker Art Gallery, 149

Walker, Eric, **231**

Walter S. Wyman Dam, 173-74

war: in Afghanistan, 205, 232; in Iraq, 205, **231**; of the Austrian Succession, 34; of 1812, 73-75, 84, 241; methods, 16, 22, 23, 46, 162-64. *See also by name of action.*

"War on Poverty," 232

Ward, Artimus, 113

Wardwell Family, 105

Wardwell, Caroline, **106**

warp room, **131**

Warren, S. D., 140, 146. *See also* S. D. Warren.

Washburn Family, 110, 112, 116, **132**, 154. Washburn-Norlands Foundation, **132**. *See also* Norlands.

Washburn, Israel (Gov.), 110, 116, 132

Washburne, Elihu B., 154

Washington, George (Pres.), 46, 48

Washington County (1789), 58, 60, 92, 94, 149, 177, 209

water: drinking water, 126, 128; hydropower, 95, 133, 173, **174**, 177; transportation, 25, 39, 46, 47, 61, 91, **141**, 142, **145**, 219

Waterford, Maine, 113

Watergate hearings, 229

Waterman, Michael, 215

Waterville, Maine, 140-41, 206, 226, 229, 237

Waterville Sentinel (newspaper), 166

Way Down East (film), 181

Waymouth, George (Capt.), 10

Wayne, Maine, 50

WCSH (Portland TV), 209

We Took to the Woods (1942, Louise Dickinson Rich), 201

weather, 54, 95

Webster–Ashburton Treaty, 85

Welch, Coley, 176
"Welfare Society," 232
well sweeps, **58**, 107
Welliver, Neil, 215
Wells, Maine, 21, 23, 25, 28, 54; Wells Beach, 54
West Indies Trade, 27, 28, 33, 35, 40, 55, 63, 64, 95, 96
West Paris, Maine, 151
Westbrook, Maine, 140, 181
Westbrook, Thomas (Col.), 31, 32
Weston, Edward, Payson, 147
WGAN (Portland TV), 209
Whig Party, 81, 112
Whipple, James (Gen.), 49, 50
White Mountains, 21, 55
White, E. B. and Katherine, 183, 211; *Charlotte's Web* (1952, E. B. White), 211
White, Wallace H., Jr. (Sen.), 191, 227
Whoopie Pies, 205
Why Europe Leaves Home (1922, Kenneth Roberts), 166
Wicked Good Band, 210
Widgery, William, 64
Wiggin, Kate Douglas, 152; *Rebecca of Sunnybrook Farm* (1903), 153
Wiggins, James Russell, 210
Wild English, 18
Wilde, Oscar, 132
Willey, Carlton, 215
William P. Frye (bark), **162**
Williams, Arthur (Pvt.), **192**
Williams, Ben Ames, 201; *Come Spring* (1940), 201; *Strange Woman, The* (1941), 201, 211
Williams, Seth (Gen.), 121
Williamson, William D., viii, 80-81; *History of the State of Maine* (1832), vii, 80
Willis, N. P., 104
Willis, William, 100, 103, 114, 127; *History of Portland* (1865), 114, 127
Wilson, John, **239**. See also Passamaquoddy.
Wilton, Maine, 200
Wilson, Woodrow (Pres.), 161
windpower, 47, 209
Windham, Maine, 36
Windsor, Maine, 60

Wingate, Joshua P. (Gen.), 59
Wingate, Julia Dearborn, 59
Winslow, Maine, 36
winter: activities, 16, 81, 94, 97, 146, **168**, 173, **216**, 237-38; scene, 81. See also school cart, skiing, snowshoes.
Winter Harbor (Biddeford Pool), Maine, 15
Winterport, Maine, 152
Wiscasset, Maine, 23, 43, 60, 66, 70, **74**, 208
Wisdom (sculpture), 159
WMTW (Bangor TV), 209
Wolfe, James (Gen.), 36
women: education, 67, 97, 98, 102, 106, 120, 147, 164, 187, 191; laborers, 23, 95, 106, 108, 109, 111, 131, 135, **136**, 150, 151, 191, 198, **199**, 200; reformers, 12, 13, 99-100, 102, 157-58, 164, **227**, 228-230, **231**, 239-41; rights, 104, 157, 164, 175, **180**, 187. See also by name.
Women's Army Corps, 191
Women's Christian Temperance Union (WCTU), 121, 157-58, 170
Wood, Sarah Barrell Keating, 70, 71, 102; *Tales of the Night* (1827), 70
Woodbury, Charles, 149, 180
Woodbury, Marcia Oakes, 151
Woodland Rebellion, 44, 45, 60
woodlots, 60, 61, 236. See also timber, forests and trees.
woolen mills. See textile mills.
Woolwich, Maine, 26
Workingman's Advocate (1835, C. H. P. McLellan), 133
Works Projects Administration (WPA), 176, 177, 190, 220; murals, 178
World War I, 160-61, **162**, 163, 164-65, 169, 170, 173, 189: 2nd Maine Regiment, 164; Student Army Training Corps, 163. See also by name.
World War II, 178, 185, 186-200, 201, 202, 203, 205, 228, 235: prisoners, 195, **196**; radar installations, 197, 207; segregation, in military, 192-93. See also by name.
writers. See by name.
Wyeth Family, 149, 214
Wyman, Walter S., 141, 173, **174**
Wyoming (schooner), **134**

INDEX 287

Y

Yankee (term), 17, 28, 32, 36, 37, 42, 58, **72**, 73, **86**, 87, 100, 103, **104**, 130, 134, 146, 162, 210, 222, 224, **228**, 240, 241; opinion of British, 37
Yankee, The (periodical), 103, **104**
Yarmouth, Maine, 173
Yeaton, Hopley (Capt.), 71
York, Maine, **16**, 20, 21, 22, 25, **28**, **29**, 32, 42, 48, 58, 60. *See* also Gorgeana and Old Gaol.
York, Zebulon (Gen.), 102, 119
York County, Maine (1636), 40, 60; attack on, 16, 25
York Manufacturing Company, 95
Yorktown, 54, 55
Young Men's Christian Association (YMCA), 147
Young Men's Hebrew Association (YMHA), 147
Young People's History of Maine, The (1873, George J. Varney), viii
Yourcenar, Marguerite, 211
Youth's Companion (magazine), 152, 156-57

Z

Zionist Council, 187. *See also* Jewish Americans.

Bill and Deb Barry at Sebago Lake State Park, Naples, Maine, c. 1985.
PHOTOGRAPH BY JANET CYR VERRIER

William David Barry, historian, writer, exhibition curator, and native New Englander, has lived or worked in five of the region's states. Awarded the first of two Webb Fellowships at the University of Vermont/Shelburne Museum, he earned an MA (1974) in American Cultural History. At the outset of the 1970s, he became a Mainer—by choice—and joined the staff of the Portland Museum of Art as curator of research. Along with John Holverson he co-curated "The Revolutionary McLellans" (1977), an effort termed "The most beautifully installed [exhibition] and best organized in museum history" by critic Philip Isaacson.

In 1978 Barry resigned from his position at the Portland Museum of Art, becoming a cultural mercenary to write or co-author books with a local focus ranging in topic from the colonial mast trade to the care of orphans in Maine institutions, L.L. Bean, Inc., the early HIV/AIDS crisis in Maine, and the "lost" city of Deering, Maine. In 1983 he collaborated with lifelong friend Randolph Dominic on the historical novel *Pyrrhus Venture* (Atlantic Monthly–Little Brown). He has written essays and reviews for *Down East Magazine*, *Portland* magazine, *Magazine Antiques*, *Art New England*, and the *Maine Sunday Telegram*, and guest-curated over a dozen exhibitions for organizations including the University of Southern Maine, the New Hampshire Historical Society, Barridoff Galleries, and the Brick Store Museum. In his spare time, he co-authored monographs of architectural interest for the Maine Historic Preservation Commission and of business successes for the Newcomen Society. In 2005 the Trustees of the Maine Historical Society awarded Barry the prestigious Neal Allen, Jr., Award "for outstanding contributions to the field of Maine history."

In tandem with his freelance career, Barry has worked as a reference librarian at the Portland Public Library and since 1994 at the Maine Historical Society's Brown Library. He lives in Portland with his wife and amanuensis, Debra, and an elderly cat, Keegan.